# PEN FOR A PARTY

# PEN FOR A PARTY

DRYDEN'S TORY PROPAGANDA
IN ITS CONTEXTS

*PHILLIP HARTH*

PRINCETON UNIVERSITY PRESS

PRINCETON, NEW JERSEY

Copyright © 1993 by Princeton University Press
Published by Princeton University Press, 41 William Street,
Princeton, New Jersey 08540
In the United Kingdom: Princeton University Press,
Chichester, West Sussex

*Library of Congress Cataloging-in-Publication Data*

Harth, Phillip, 1926–
Pen for a party: Dryden's Tory propaganda in its contexts /
Phillip Harth.
   p.  cm.
Includes bibliographical references and index.
ISBN 0-691-06972-7 (acid-free paper)
1. Dryden, John, 1631–1700—Political and social views.
2. Politics and literature—England—History—17th century.
3. Great Britain—Politics and government—1660–1688.
4. Conservatism—England—History—17th century.
5. Conservative Party (Great Britain)
6. Dryden, John, 1631–1700—Prose.
7. Propaganda, English.  I. Title.

PR3427.P6H37  1993  821′.4—dc20  92-27140  CIP

This book has been composed in Adobe Sabon

Princeton University Press books are printed
on acid-free paper and meet the guidelines for
permanence and durability of the Committee on
Production Guidelines for Book Longevity
of the Council on Library Resources

Printed in the United States of America

10  9  8  7  6  5  4  3  2  1

The Design, I am sure, is honest: but he who draws his Pen for one Party, must expect to make Enemies of the other. For, *Wit* and *Fool*, are Consequents of *Whig* and *Tory*: And every man is a Knave or an Ass to the contrary side.

"To the Reader," *Absalom and Achitophel*

# CONTENTS

## PREFACE

THIS BOOK BRINGS a new perspective to bear on Dryden's literary activity on behalf of Charles II and his policies during the closing years of that monarch's reign. Dryden's great public poems of this period—*Absalom and Achitophel* and *The Medall*—along with his dramatic works of the same era—*The Duke of Guise* and *Albion and Albanius*—have commonly been considered against a broad historical background of public events—the Popish Plot, the Exclusion Crisis, the "Tory Reaction"—that may serve well enough to identify Dryden's topical allusions, but can throw very little light on the noticeable differences among these works or on the specific purposes for which they were written. It is understandable, therefore, that such differences are most often attributed to changes in Dryden's attitudes rather than in his strategies, while the specific purposes differentiating these individual works remain for the most part unexamined.

It is my thesis in this book that the immediate contexts of these works are not the well-known historical events themselves but a constantly developing series of propaganda offensives, both Tory and Whig, designed to influence public opinion toward fluctuating conditions and to attract popular support for the immediate policies adopted by either side in response to each new development. Since it is the public's perception of events that is at issue in these contests between the makers of opinion on either side, the issues that party propagandists choose to emphasize and the relative importance they attribute to events will often differ considerably from those familiar in modern historical accounts. In relating political developments from the perspective of party propaganda, therefore, I have had to isolate and bring forward certain historical episodes, now little noticed, that nevertheless acquired considerable importance at the time.

Accustomed to relying on the clergy of the Established Church to develop habits of obedience in the faithful that should prove adequate to any emergency, the government of Charles II was slow to respond to the Exclusion Crisis by developing new organs of public opinion specifically adapted to this unprecedented challenge to its authority. Instead, it allowed the Whigs to seize the initiative and, by choosing issues most advantageous to themselves, to dictate the terms of public debate between government and opposition. It was only in 1681, a few months before Dryden tardily joined the ranks of Tory propagandists, that the government's publicists began developing the machinery by which, in spite of occasional setbacks, they would eventually win public acquiescence in the extraordinary measures adopted to defeat the Whig opposition. This process could not begin, however, until the Tories had learned to exploit the enormous advantages for molding public opinion available to the party in power, to take the offensive against their opponents so that they rather than the Whigs could now select the issues for public debate, and, perhaps most important, to capitalize on new and unexpected developments amid the rapidly fluctuating events between 1681 and the end of Charles's reign. Consequently the Tory propaganda of this period is by no means a single entity. It consists of three successive campaigns, in each of which Dryden participated fully. These three campaigns have not previously been identified in this way, yet each was initiated by separate events, characterized by distinct issues, and aimed at influencing public opinion in support of different, though complementary, policies.

Since new turns of events, and the appearance of new propaganda campaigns to exploit them, occur in a matter of weeks, not years, their identification depends on being able to date publications, which are the stuff of propaganda, more precisely than is normally possible when dealing with seventeenth-century texts. Luckily, the period of political crisis with which I am concerned affords a degree of chronological precision rare for that century. The emergence of newspapers, beginning in mid-1679, with which to present the case for either party, makes possible the close dating of an enormous amount of Whig and Tory propaganda—not only these partisan journals themselves, but also the numerous publications advertised for sale in them. But these, and every other source of information of this kind, are overshadowed in importance by the vast collection of poems, pamphlets, broadsides, and other publications formed by Narcissus Luttrell and now preserved in some half-dozen research libraries in England, the United States, and Australia. Beginning 1 January 1680, a fortunate time for my subject, Luttrell recorded the price, and also a date, on the title page of every publication he acquired. It is still widely assumed that these precise dates (day, month, and year) record the time of Luttrell's purchase of the respective works. But in an article some years ago in *The Book Collector* (6 [1957]: 15–27) that deserves to be better known, James M. Osborn, whose knowledge of the Luttrell collection was probably unparalleled, proved beyond any reasonable doubt that what Luttrell had recorded in each case was the date of publication, a conclusion I have adopted in putting these works to use in my own study.

It is a pleasure to record obligations I have incurred to a number of institutions and individuals in the course of writing this book. My research was supported at various stages by an American Council of Learned Societies Fellowship, by a Senior Research Fellowship at the William Andrews Clark Memorial Library, by various grants from the Graduate School of the University of Wisconsin, and by a continuing senior membership in the Institute for Research in the Humanities of the University of Wisconsin, Madison. I wish to thank the staffs of the Bodleian Library, the British Library, the Huntington Library, the Newberry Library, the University of Wisconsin Library, the William Andrews Clark Memorial Library, and Yale University Library for their help on many occasions. I am grateful to friends and colleagues who have made my task easier in various ways, among them W. J. Cameron, Judith Milhous, Gerard Reedy, Alan Roper, John Wallace, and Howard Weinbrot; I am indebted to James Winn for several valuable suggestions that I was able to put to good use; and I welcome the opportunity of acknowledging Robert Hume's characteristic generosity in sharing his unequaled knowledge of Restoration drama on more occasions than I can now remember. Loretta Freiling and my colleagues at the Institute for Research in the Humanities have made my work easier and pleasanter. But my warmest thanks are due as always to my wife Sydney, who has never tired in her encouragement and support.

I gratefully acknowledge permission from the University of Wisconsin Press, the William Andrews Clark Memorial Library, and the University of California Press to include excerpts from several of my earlier essays:

"Legends No Histories: The Case of *Absalom and Achitophel*," in *Studies in Eighteenth-Century Culture*, ed. Harold E. Pagliaro (Madison: University of Wisconsin Press, 1975), 4:13–29. Copyright (c) 1975 by The American Society for Eighteenth-Century Studies.

"Dryden's Public Voices," in *New Homage to John Dryden* (Los Angeles: William Andrews Clark Memorial Library, 1983), pp. 1–28. Copyright (c) 1983 by The William Andrews Clark Memorial Library, University of California, Los Angeles.

"Dryden in 1678–1681: The Literary and Historical Perspectives," in *The Golden and the Brazen World: Papers in Literature and History, 1650–1800*, ed. John M. Wallace (Berkeley: University of California Press, 1985), pp. 55–77. Copyright (c) 1985 by The Regents of the University of California.

# PEN FOR A PARTY

## Chapter 1

## THE PULPIT

THE SERIES of political crises that began in 1678 and came to monopolize the attention of Dryden and most other literary figures during the closing years of Charles II's reign may strike the observer as the very antithesis of the outward harmony with which the reign had begun in 1660.[1] Yet those who spoke and wrote for the government during the Exclusion Crisis and its aftermath were in many cases exploiting a legacy of political rhetoric inherited from the framers of the Restoration Settlement and its apologists. It is with the Restoration, therefore, that we must begin.

．　．　．　．　．

On the day of Charles II's triumphant entry into his capital, 29 May 1660, John Evelyn witnessed the procession, which he recorded in his diary:

> I stood in the strand, & beheld it, & blessed God: And all this without one drop of bloud, & by that very army, which rebell'd against him: but it was the Lords doing, *et mirabile in oculis nostris*: for such a Restauration was never seene in the mention of any history, antient or modern, since the returne of the *Babylonian* Captivity, nor so joyfull a day, & so bright, ever seene in this nation: this hapning when to expect or effect it, was past all humane policy.[2]

The procession ended at Whitehall where, in the Banqueting House, the speaker of the House of Commons, Sir Harbottle Grimston, addressed the king in the presence of all the members: "The restitution of your Majesty to the exercise of Your just and most indubitable Native Right of Soveraignty, and the deliverance of your people from Bondage and Slavery hath been wrought out and brought to pass, by a miraculous way of Divine Providence beyond and above the reach and comprehension of our understandings, and therefore to be admired, impossible to be expressed."[3]

By the time the day of solemn thanksgiving for Charles's restoration was observed a month later, on 28 June, its miraculous character had become fixed in the national consciousness. Preaching before the king at Whitehall on that occasion, Gilbert Sheldon, the future archbishop of Canterbury, alluded to General Monck as "a *Deliverer*, never to be mentioned without Honour, nor to be forgotten in the *Prayers* of all good people," but immediately cautioned his congregation that "whoever were the Instruments of our *deliverance*, we must still remember to raise up our thoughts to him by whose power they wrought it, and give him the glory of all; since nothing is more certain that none did it, none could do it but he."[4]

In making Divine Providence responsible for the Restoration, these civil and religious leaders were moved by the same consideration that had led Evelyn to conclude that it was "the Lords doing" since it had happened "when to expect or effect it, was past all humane policy." It was the improbability of the Restoration on natural grounds—the inadequacy of any human causes to account for so unlikely an event—that led most Englishmen to accept a supernatural cause as the only reasonable explanation. As Sheldon reminded his congregation,

> All we did or could do toward a Settlement proved nothing worth, all attempts vain, no *Treaties*, no *Armies*, no *Endeavors* by our selves or others that wished well to our Peace did us good, though never so probable, never so hopeful; they were all lost and frustrate, all vanished into nothing. How visible was Gods hand in it, when all rash and unreasonable *attempts* prospered with some, while others failed in the best and most probable? And either the *worst Counsels* were followed (as it usually happens when God determines to judge and afflict a sinful Nation) or the *best* never prospered, but when brought to ripeness miscarried in the birth. Thus it constantly was, and thus it would have been till we had been utterly consumed, had not he had mercy on us.[5]

Two months later, on 29 August, Parliament set its official seal on the miraculous nature of the Restoration when it secured the royal assent to "An Act for a Perpetual Anniversary Thanksgiving on the Nine and Twentieth Day of May," which began by declaring that "Almighty God, the King of Kings and sole Disposer of all earthly crowns and kingdoms, hath by his all-swaying providence and power miraculously demonstrated in the view of all the world his transcendent mercy, love and graciousness towards his most excellent Majesty Charles the Second . . . by his Majesty's late most wonderful, glorious, peaceable and joyful restoration . . . and that without the least opposition or effusion of blood." In grateful acknowledgment of this singular miracle, it was ordered that its anniversary be observed "in every church, chapel and other usual place of divine service and public prayer" throughout the kingdom "in all succeeding ages," and that "all and every person and persons inhabiting within this kingdom" attend the thanksgiving service each year.[6]

Finally, as one of its concluding acts before being dissolved on 29 December, the Convention Parliament enacted similar provisions for a second perpetual anniversary, that of the execution of Charles I on 30 January, which, as a day of national humiliation and mourning, would serve as a counterpart to the day of joyful thanksgiving to mark the double anniversary of the king's birth and restoration. Together these two annual solemnities would continue to remind all Englishmen of the depth of abasement from which Providence had miraculously delivered them.

In establishing the anniversary sermons, Parliament was acting from more complex motives than simple piety and gratitude. It was endorsing and taking measures to perpetuate the belief that the recent political settlement was an act of God commanding the assent of all Englishmen, whatever their religious differences. The providential character of this settlement legitimated the new regime, and the government, by insuring that subjects would be continuously reminded of this fact, was publishing its own credentials. What one recent historian has called "the incredible tangle of cabals, allegations, rumors, insurrections, and abortive attempts to revolt in the 1660s," each breeding fears of more conspiracies still concealed, served as periodic reminders to the government that the Restoration Settlement could come undone as quickly as it had been made.[7] In propagating their own no doubt sincere belief in a miraculous Restoration whose agents were no more than instruments of Providence, divines and statesmen were employing a tactic that would be repeated a generation later, in 1689, to legitimate another bloodless revolution benefiting the Church of England. On that occasion also the Anglican clergy would assure troubled Englishmen that the change in government had taken place through the intervention of Providence, while Parliament would once more follow suit by declaring, in its proclamation of William and Mary as king and queen, that "it has pleas'd Almighty God, in his great Mercy to this Kingdom, to vouchsafe us a *Miraculous Deliverance* from *Popery* and *Arbitrary Power*," in which the Prince of Orange had acted simply as God's chosen instrument.[8] Indeed, what Dryden wrote of the vicissitudes of government during the Interregnum could be applied to every new regime from one end of the century to the other: "Observe them all along, and Providence is still the prevailing Argument: They who happen to be in power, will ever urge it against those who are undermost; as they who are depress'd, will never fail to call it Persecution."[9]

As a means of claiming divine sanction for the political, ecclesiastical, and social changes that accompanied and followed the Restoration, both martyrdom and thanksgiving sermons assumed particular importance.[10] When Providence miraculously intervenes in the affairs of a nation, Thomas Sprat, the future bishop of Rochester, pointed out, "it is with a peculiar design of punishing, or rewarding, or forewarning mankind."[11] The martyrdom sermons were intended to remind Englishmen that the execution of Charles I had been permitted as a providential judgment upon a people who had departed from righteousness, just as the thanksgiving sermons proclaimed the restoration of Charles II as a providential deliverance of that people from their sufferings. Thus Sheldon declared in his sermon celebrating Charles's return that "as 'tis He, and He only that brings us into danger, that layes afflictions on us for our sins (. . . . Just our case, we served him so, he served us so; our great sins brought his great judgments upon us. And) so again 'tis He, and He only that must remove those afflictions, that must deliver out of those dangers."[12]

But while the anniversary sermons originated with the Restoration and served as a means of commemorating that event as well as the earlier tragedy that had made it necessary, they took their place as part of a much older homiletic tradition in the Established Church. The notion that sermons were an indispensable means of buttressing the civil order was already a century old at the time of the Restoration, and accepted as a matter of course by the Anglican clergy.

.   .   .   .   .

"The great Business of government," Robert South reminded the members of Lincoln's Inn in 1660, "is to procure obedience, & keep off disobedience: & the great springs upon which those two move are Rewards and Punishments answering the two ruling affections of mans mind, Hope and Fear." Hence the crucial importance to the state of sermons that will instill these dispositions into the minds of the populace.

> Were not these frequently thundred into the understandings of men, the Magistrate might enact, order and proclaime, Proclamations might be hung upon Walls and Posts, and there they might hang, seen and despised, more like Malefactors, then Lawes: But when Religion binds them upon the Conscience, Conscience will either perswade or terrify men into their practice. . . . If there was not a Minister in every Parish, you would quickly find cause to encrease the number of Constables: And if the Churches were not imployed to be places to hear Gods Law, there would be need of them, to be Prisons for the breakers of the Lawes of men.[13]

Somewhat less bluntly, John Tillotson, later to become archbishop of Canterbury, explained to the members of the same society why religion offers the most dependable means of instilling those hopes and fears that encourage obedience:

> And that *not only for Wrath*, and out of fear of the Magistrates Power, which is but a weak and loose Principle of Obedience, and will cease when ever men can Rebel with safety, and to advantage; but out *of Conscience*, which is a firm and constant, and lasting Principle, and will hold a man fast, when all other

Obligations will break. He that hath inbibed the true Principles of Christianity, is not to be tempted from his Obedience and Subjection, by any worldly Considerations; because he believes that *whosoever resisteth Authority, resisteth the Ordinance of God*; and that *they who resist, shall receive to themselves damnation.*[14]

Apart from biblical texts such as Rom. 13:2, which Tillotson is quoting from memory here, the most important pronouncement on the religious duty of obeying kings and magistrates was the "Homily against Disobedience and Wilful Rebellion" in the second of the two Books of Homilies, whose special authority as a repository of "godly and wholesome doctrine" is set forth in the thirty-fifth of the Thirty-nine Articles. Occasioned by the Northern Rebellion of 1569, this homily, which consists of six parts, was separately published in 1570 and made a permanent part of the Homilies the following year in hopes of discouraging all future attempts on the crown by presenting civil obedience as one of the most serious religious obligations commanded by God. It is the argument of all six parts "that Kings and Princes, as well the evil as the good, do raign by Gods Ordinance and that Subjects are bounden to obey them"; that "such Subjects, as are disobedient or rebellious against their Princes, disobey God, and procure their own damnation"; and that rebellion is "the greatest of all mischiefs" as well as "the worst of all vices." But the third part of the "Homily against Disobedience and Wilful Rebellion" in particular is devoted to showing "what an abominable sin against God and man Rebellion is, and how dreadfully the wrath of God is kindled and inflamed against all Rebels, and what horrible plagues, punishments, and deaths, and finally eternal damnation doth hang over their heads." So terrible is this crime, in fact, "that all sins possible to be committed against God or man, be contained in Rebellion."[15]

Convinced that obedience to princes was one of the central principles of Christianity and that imparting this principle to the faithful was one of their chief duties, Anglican clergymen after the Restoration performed this obligation in their pulpits on any number of occasions. The numerous sermons on this subject that Evelyn recorded testify that they might be preached at any opportunity, not simply at anniversary services.[16] But because the sermons commemorating the royal martyrdom and the Restoration (along with the 5 November sermons instituted under James I to memorialize the providential discovery of the Gunpowder Plot) enjoyed official sanction as a principal means of reminding Englishmen of their civic duties, they are particularly valuable for tracing this subject.

It was never, of course, the purpose of the anniversary sermons solely to attest the providential character of the events they commemorated. Once that point had been sufficiently established, their enduring importance would be not historical but precautionary. As Robert Twisse pointed out in a martyrdom sermon in 1665, it was hoped that by their annual observance of this solemnity Englishmen "will not onely lament what is past, but likewise dread the thoughts of attempting the like Villany for the future."[17] It was as analogues available to fit any new political crisis that the royal martyrdom and the miraculous Restoration would prove their lasting worth, for what these cases of providential judgment and deliverance chiefly testified was that God continues to punish rebellion and reward loyalty wherever they occur. In the interest of proving that useful thesis, preachers did not have to rely on these instances alone.

All "remarkable occurrences of Providence," Isaac Barrow declared in his 5 November sermon of 1673,

> are set before our eyes to cast us into a very serious and solemn frame; to abash, and deter us from offending, by observing the danger of incurring punishments like to those which we behold inflicted upon presumptuous transgressors. . . . They do plainly demonstrate, that there is no presuming to escape, being detected in our close Machinations by God's All-seeing Eye; being defeated in our bold Attempts by God's All-mighty Hand; being sorely chastised for our Iniquity by God's impartial Judgment. Extreamly blind and stupid therefore must we be, or monstrously sturdy and profane, if such experiments of Divine Power and Justice do not awe us, and fright us from sin.[18]

Cases where particular or special Providence was acknowledged to have intervened miraculously in affairs of state to change the course of events were comparatively rare in seventeenth-century England. General or common Providence continually oversaw human affairs, of course, through the normal operation of the laws of nature, but the needless multiplication of latter-day miracles, associated with Roman Catholic errors, was discouraged among the Anglican faithful. "It is a dangerous mistake, into which many Good men fall," Sprat warned,

> that we neglect the *Dominion of God over the World*, if we do not discover in every Turn of human Actions many supernatural *Providences*, and miraculous *Events*. Whereas it is enough for the honor of his *Government*, that he guids the whole Creation, in its wonted cours of *Causes*, and *Effects*: as it makes as much for the reputation of a Prince's wisdom, that he can rule his subjects peaceably, by his known, and standing Laws, as that he is often forc'd to make use of extraordinary justice to punish, or reward.[19]

Sacred and profane history, however, offered an abundance of providential judgments against evildoers that could supplement the dwindling list of recent interventions commemorated in the anniversary sermons. The greatest single repository of divine retributions, of course, was to be found in the historical books of the Old Testament. Citing the words of St. Paul, "now all these things happened unto them for ensamples" (1 Cor. 10:11), William Whitaker, the prominent Elizabethan divine, had observed:

The meaning of the place is, that we should accommodate the events of the ancient Jewish people to our instruction, so as that, admonished by their example, we may learn to please God, and avoid idolatry and other sins. . . . The Jews were punished when they sinned: therefore, if we sin in like manner, we shall bear and pay to God similar penalties. He hath set before us the punishment of the Jews pourtrayed as it were in a picture, that we may constantly have it before our eyes.[20]

The fourth part of the "Homily against Disobedience and Wilful Rebellion" is devoted to singling out some of the most notable "examples set out in Scriptures, written for our eternal erudition," from which we can learn God's abhorrence of rebellion and the terrible punishments he has meted out in the past. Drawing a distinction between sedition and treason, the homily chooses as its chief example of sedition the behavior of Corah and his associates, who challenged the authority of Moses and Aaron.

Some of the Captains with their band of murmurers not dying by any usual or natural death of men, but the earth opening, they with their wives, children, and families, were swallowed quick down into Hell. Which horrible destructions of such *Israelites* as were murmurers against *Moses*, appointed by God, to be their Head and chief Magistrate, are recorded in the Book of Numbers, and other places, of the Scriptures, for perpetual memory and warning to all Subjects, how highly God is displeased with the murmuring and evil speaking of Subjects against their Princes.

Turning to treason, the homily continues:

Now concerning actual Rebellion, amongst many examples thereof set forth in the holy Scriptures, the example of *Absalom* is notable: who entring into conspiracy against King *David* his father, . . . a great tree stretching out his arm, as it were for that purpose, caught him by the great and long bush of his goodly hair, lapping about it as he fled hastily bare-headed under the said tree, and so hanged him up by the hair of his head in the air. . . . A fearful example of Gods punishment (good people) to consider. Now *Achitophel*, though otherwise an exceeding wise man, yet the mischievous Counsellor of *Absalom*, in this wicked Rebellion, for lack of an Hangman, a convenient Servitor for such a Traitor, went and hanged up himself. A worthy end of all false Rebels, who rather then they should lack due execution, will by Gods just judgment, become Hangmen unto themselves.[21]

Thus, since the early years of Elizabeth's reign, these notable examples of traitors and seditionists from sacred history had been appearing in the numerous editions of the Homilies—some two dozen of the second book by the time of the Restoration—which provided the Anglican clergy with models they could use for their own sermons. It is not surprising then to find Sheldon, in his Restoration sermon discussed earlier, following an account of David's troubles at the time of Absalom's rebellion with a reminder of Moses's difficulties from Corah's sedition.[22]

But if the Homilies helped popularize Absalom, Achitophel, and Corah as the most important biblical traitors and seditionists, the Old Testament itself offered a far richer fund of examples, since, as George Stradling pointed out in his martyrdom sermon of 1675, "there will be Rebels while there be Kings, and never greater store of such than among the Jews, whom the Prophets frequently style *A Rebellious Nation*."[23] A host of these disobedient subjects peopled the anniversary sermons, among whom the traitor Zimri and the seditionist Shimei were two of the most popular. Such examples of rebellion could be discussed at some length and their sensational punishments recounted in detail, but, as their repeated appearance in the pulpit converted them into homiletic commonplaces, a simple allusion would often serve the preacher's purpose, or a brief catalogue of Old Testament rebels that coupled the same familiar examples again and again. "None of all those persons guilty of rebellion in Scripture, went to their Graves in peace," warns the preacher at a Cambridge Restoration service in 1660, "*Achitophel, Absalom, Sheba, Abner, Abiathar, Joab, Athaliah, Zimri, Adoniah*."[24] "Now if not the highest, if not *Dathan*, nor *Corah* . . . may open their lips against *Moses*; how much lesse the son of *Shelomith*, one of the meanest of the people?" asks a preacher in 1662. "If neither *Nabal*, nor *Achitophel*, nor *Absalom* may speak evil of *David*; how much lesse *Shimei* a *Benjamite*, or *Sheba* the son of *Bichri*?"[25] "In sacred Story," declares a 30 January preacher in 1674, "you find *Moses*, though the meekest and mildest man the World then had, yet is mutinied against, and like to be deposed by *Corah* and his Complices. *David* is a man after Gods own heart, yet fowl-mouthed *Shimei* bespattereth him, and fair-tongued *Absalon* stealeth away the peoples hearts from him."[26]

In their role as examples, these biblical rebels, seditionists, and usurpers function in the sermons as brief and forceful analogues. When used as cautionary examples, their deterrent effect for a Restoration congregation depends on the assumption that like causes produce like effects, or, in Whitaker's words above, "if we sin in like manner, we shall bear and pay to God similar penalties." When used in martyrdom sermons as examples of "how dreadfully the wrath of God is kindled and inflamed against all Rebels," in the words of the "Homily against Disobedience," it is their likeness to the English regicides that confirms the enormity of that recent crime. Their modern counterparts need not resemble them in other respects, however, nor replicate the terrifying manner in which biblical rebels met their ends. William Sancroft, the archbishop of Canterbury, preaching a sermon before the House of Lords in 1678, noted that "the season is chang'd" since Old Testament times, indeed, when the Sea divided, and suddenly turn'd green Meadow; and when an Angel went forth, and dispatcht so many Thousands in a Night. . . .

. . . The Glory of God descends not visibly now adayes upon our Palaces, as of old upon the Tabernacle of the Congregation, to rescue our *Moses* and *Aaron* from being massacred by a desperate Knot of Mutineers: Nor doth the Earth open her Mouth any longer, to swallow up our Rebels and Traitors alive. 'Tis a Scepter of ordinary Justice, not a Rod of Wonders, that fills the Hand of our Governours.[27]

It is enough that such biblical examples prove how heinous in God's sight are all cases of disobedience to princes. If he no longer chastises malefactors in as direct and spectacular a manner as before, he now punishes them through second causes, or where, like Cromwell, Bradshaw, and Ireton, they escape punishment in this life, he will surely exact a terrible retribution in the next.

By repeatedly associating these Old Testament examples with the execration of treason and sedition, the anniversary sermons fostered a mental habit that would figure prominently in the propaganda of the Exclusion Crisis and its aftermath. But a far more important contribution to the popularity of historical analogy in that propaganda can be traced to another feature of many anniversary sermons: the use of extended and often elaborate parallels between past and present.

.   .   .   .   .   .

Parallels, unlike examples, consist of more than a simple analogy. They involve comparison of two persons or events at some length, and in considerable detail. In the anniversary sermons they figure as a method of accommodation in which the preacher "runs a parallel" between his scriptural text and the Gunpowder Plot, the royal martyrdom, or the miraculous Restoration.

The earliest person to draw a biblical parallel with the royal martyrdom was the victim himself. On the scaffold, Bishop Juxon read the king the lesson appointed for 30 January in the Book of Common Prayer. By coincidence it was Matthew, chapter 27, on Christ's passion and death. Charles remarked on the appropriateness of the lesson, and in doing so inspired a custom that would flourish after the Restoration, when many preachers drew elaborate parallels between Christ's sufferings and those of the Royal Martyr, exploiting the *Imitatio Christi* theme in the interest of sanctifying the memory of Charles I.[28] But just as often, martyrdom preachers drew extensive parallels between Charles's sufferings and those of such biblical victims as Abel in Genesis, Zedekiah in 2 Kings, and Stephen in the Acts of the Apostles.[29]

The model for these homiletic parallels, as for their secular counter-parts, was of course Plutarch's *Lives*. Of his twenty-two surviving pairs of Greek and Roman lives, eighteen still retain the separate "compari-sons" in which Plutarch draws an explicit and detailed parallel between the individuals whose lives and characters are related in the preceding narratives. The invariable feature of these parallels is that the most re-markable actions of the two individuals are both compared and con-trasted, their differences being as indispensable to Plutarch's conception of a parallel as their similarities.[30] "The Comparison of Numa with Lycurgus," for example, begins in typical fashion:

> Having thus finished the Lives of *Lycurgus* and *Numa*; we shall now (though the work be difficult) compare their Actions in that manner together, so as easily to discern wherein they differed, and wherein they agreed. It is apparent that they were very agreeable in the actions of their lives, their Moderation, their Religion, their civil Arts and political Government were alike; and both insinuated a belief in the people, that they derived their Laws and Constitutions from the Gods: yet in their peculiar manner of managing these excellencies, there were many circumstances which made a diversity.[31]

Whereupon Plutarch proceeds to examine these circumstances in detail. In every case he weighs and balances the behavior and motivation of the pair under scrutiny, praising one individual and censuring the other in those respects wherein they differ, although in summary each will prove to have excelled his opposite number in certain instances and to have fallen short in others.

In adapting Plutarch's method of parallel lives to their sermons, the anniversary preachers substituted for biography an episode of biblical history found in their scriptural text, which they first expounded to their congregations in the usual manner before applying it to the present occa-sion by running a parallel between past and present. They modified Plu-tarch's practice, of course, by introducing a wide variety of individuals—rebels and loyal subjects as well as their aggrieved rulers—and, since the episodes turned on the intervention of Providence, by considering them *sub specie aeternitatis*. But they consistently adhered to Plutarch's indis-pensable procedure of bringing out differences as well as similarities in the parallel. On the whole, preachers tended to favor the likenesses be-tween the English regicides and notorious biblical rebels, an effective means of denigrating the enemies of Charles I and his heir. In the case of the rulers, however, they dwelt on differences between the English mon-archs and their biblical counterparts as well as similarities, the propor-tions varying from one sermon to another, in order to enhance the impor-tance of the Royal Martyr or his son.[32]

This procedure is aptly expressed by the title of Simon Ford's martyr-dom sermon of 1661: *Parallēla dusparallēla*. In the case of Charles I the paradox of the unparalleled parallel is used to magnify his tragedy (and consequently his stature as a martyr) by insisting that, in spite of the many similarities between his circumstances and those of earlier victims, his sufferings inevitably exceeded theirs. Essentially, these sermons offer an a fortiori argument that first treats the royal tribulations on a scale of biblical importance and then further raises them to a status unique in human history. In these accounts, the infamous murders of Abel and Zedekiah, the protomartyrdom of Stephen, and (digressing from the scriptural text to supply further analogues from profane history) the fatal depositions of Edward II, Richard II, and Conradin, king of Naples, pale in comparison with the supreme tragedy in Whitehall. "If I had the Liberty of choosing a *Text* this day, not onely out of the *Sacred Bible*, but out of any other *History* in the world," a martyrdom preacher declared in 1664, "I suppose it would be impossible to find a *Parallel* for that *Tragedy* which *England* this day saw acted; there never having been such a *piece of Villany* acted in the World before."[33]

In sermons commemorating the Restoration, the paradox of the unparalleled parallel is used to portray God's mercies on this occasion as similar in kind to earlier instances of Providence but unprecedented in degree, since the plight from which Charles was rescued (as well as his own importance) was greater than that of his biblical predecessors. Peter Heylyn, for example, preaching the 29 May sermon at Westminster Abbey in 1661, first expounds his text, one of David's psalms of thanksgiving relating "to his deliverance from the house of *Saul*" while still a youth, before turning to the "parallel betwixt the Persons" of David and Charles II, where, explicitly citing Plutarch's authority, he emphasizes the differences between the two monarchs over their similarities.

> A parallel, right worthy of the pen of *Plutarch*, if any such were found amongst us; but, such as seems to have been done in part already, by laying before you *David*'s troubles and his great deliverance. And therefore passing by those things which apply themselves, and those in which the Story of both Princes seems to make but one; we will observe the method which is used by *Plutarch*, in laying down the points in which they differ, or, those wherein one party seems to have preheminence above the other.[34]

Heylyn then proceeds to discuss seven major differences between Charles's circumstances and David's, all of which give the English king "preeminence" above his illustrious predecessor because Charles's trials were greater than David's or his person and behavior superior. Thus, Charles II "was born a Prince. . . . Which cannot be affirmed of *David*, nor of *David*'s Ancestors. . . . And as his Birth was higher, so his Fall was lower, and his afflictions so much greater." Or again, "we do not find that *David* ever hazarded his own person in the day of Battail. . . . Which gave him means and opportunity to provide for himself, though all his Forces had been routed, and their General taken. But our great Master put himself into the head of his Army [at Worcester], . . . charged and recharged through the thickest of his enemies, the first that came into the field, and the last that left it."[35]

Nothing was more responsible for indelibly imprinting in the public mind certain specific biblical parallels with the two Stuart kings than the lessons in the Book of Common Prayer ordered for the anniversary services. Preachers might adopt any number of scriptural texts for their sermons on these occasions, but the same lessons were read year after year, and heard by everyone attending the service.

In the new anniversary service for the martyrdom of Charles I, separately published in 1661 and incorporated in the revised Book of Common Prayer the following year, Matthew, chapter 27, now consecrated by the comfort it had offered Charles on the scaffold, was retained as the second lesson of the day. But the scriptural passage chosen for the first lesson was the opening chapter of 2 Samuel, in which David mourns the death of Saul and orders that the Amalekite claiming responsibility for his death be put to the sword, declaring: "Thy blood be upon thy head; for thy mouth hath testified against thee, saying, I have slain the Lord's anointed. . . . Ye daughters of Israel, weep over Saul."[36]

The choice of Saul, David's unjust persecutor yet the Lord's anointed whom no one dared touch with impunity, was useful for emphasizing that no circumstances, however egregious, can ever justify regicide, since subjects are bound to obey all kings and princes, "the evil as well as the good." But at the same time it suggested a parallel with the sainted Charles in which the dissimilarities far outweighed the resemblances. Ford nearly despaired of showing how Saul's death could "be *accommodated* by way of *Parallel* to the sad *occasion of this daies Solemnity*," observing that "there is little to be seen, but *Concordia discors*, an *agreement* in nothing but *this*, that there is *scarce any Circumstance wherein they agree*," and comparing himself to the "*Painter*, who to set off the vast bigness of an *Elephant*, draws a *Mouse* by his side."[37] Nevertheless, preachers proved equal to the challenge. The formal symmetry of some of these exercises is suggested by Gilbert Burnet's martyrdom sermon of 1675, the first part expounding three respects where "the Parallel of *Saul* and our *Martyred King* hath held good," the second part balancing these with three other respects in which they widely differed to Charles's advantage.[38]

The obvious reason for making David's lamentation over Saul in 2 Samuel the first lesson of the martyrdom service was the implied parallel between Israel and England led in national mourning by the successors to their slain kings: David and Charles II. In this way the lesson for 30 January was deliberately meshed with those for the other two anniversaries.

The first lesson for the older anniversary service, that of 5 November in thanksgiving for the discovery of the Gunpowder Plot, was 2 Samuel, chapter 22, David's song of deliverance from his enemies (a version of the Eighteenth Psalm). In the new anniversary service for the restoration of Charles II, also separately published in 1661 and incorporated in the revised Book of Common Prayer the following year, the scriptural text chosen as the first lesson of the day was 2 Samuel, chapter 19, in which David returns to Jerusalem from exile following the defeat of Absalom's rebellion. "And Absalom, whom we anointed over us, is dead in battle. . . . So the king returned, and came to Jordan. And Judah came to Gilgal, to go to meet the king, to conduct the king over Jordan."[39] The implicit parallel with Charles's return from an exile also originating in rebellion and his triumphant entry into his capital made the choice of this lesson practically inevitable.

Ford, preaching on the day of solemn thanksgiving a month after the Restoration took place, had anticipated those who would later design the thanksgiving service by choosing 2 Samuel, chapter 19, as his text. "It is a matter of greatest wonder to me," he tells his congregation, "to observe how exactly the *two Histories* run *parallel*. Insomuch that it were no hard matter for an *ingenious phancy*, by altering the Names of *David, Absalom, Joab, Abishai, Zadock, Abiathar, Shimei, Ziba, Mephibosheth, Jordan*, &c. into others proper to our late affairs, to insert *verbatim* the *greatest part of the Chapter* into a *Chronicle* of *these Times*."[40]

But Ford is even more interested in the disparities between the two histories, and, like Heylyn preaching on David's earlier exile under Saul, he singles out seven major differences between David's circumstances at the time of Absalom's rebellion and Charles's recent plight, concluding, as we might expect by now, that we "may easily perceive, that, in point of *mercy*, and *miracle*, King *Davids* restitution came short of King *Charles*'s." Thus, David was only restored after a great battle, whereas "*our Soveraign* is recalled by *Parliament*, and resetled in the *royall Throne* without a *blow-striking*, or a *bloody-nose*." Or again, "*Davids* banishment (in all probability) was not as many *weeks*, as our Soveraigns was *years*, (for if it had, *Mephibosheth* had been in a *nasty pickle* at his return, seeing the *Holy Ghost* tells us, *he had not so much as washed his cloathes, from the day the King departed to that day*,) and by consequence this mercy *to our Soveraign* after *twelve years* banishment, vastly exceeds *Davids*."[41] John Parker, bishop of Elphinstone, on the other hand, preaching on the same text the next year at the first of the anniversary services for the Restoration, chooses to dwell mostly on the likenesses between Charles's recent exile and that of David at the time of Absalom's rebellion.[42]

Thus all three of the anniversary services conferred central importance on 2 Samuel and the implied parallel between David and the English king. In ordering that these lessons be read at the anniversary services, the authorities indirectly insured that the same texts would often be chosen for the sermons as well. At the anniversary service for 29 May that Pepys attended in 1661, the text chosen by the vicar of Walthamstowe for his sermon was, like Bishop Parker's, 2 Samuel, chapter 19, and it is reasonable to assume that many preachers followed the same convenient practice in numerous sermons that were never published.[43]

Not all, of course, or even most anniversary preachers ran elaborate parallels between their scriptural texts and the event being commemorated. But when they did so, their choice of text was governed by its special appropriateness to the occasion. It is important to remember that while disparities are as essential to Plutarch's conception of a parallel as are likenesses, the differences would be of no significance if they were not grounded on meaningful similarities. More than one episode from the Old Testament is capable of suggesting significant parallels with the royal martyrdom or the Restoration, but no two will offer quite the same advantages. It becomes the preacher's responsibility, therefore, in accommodating his text to the occasion, to stress those features of the biblical story that can be appropriately compared and contrasted with the event commemorated, while ignoring or minimizing those that cannot.

Thus when the preacher of a 29 May sermon chose 2 Samuel, chapter 19, he would relate the entire story of Absalom's rebellion—its rise, progress, and defeat in chapters 15–18 as well as David's triumphant return to Jerusalem in chapter 19—in the course of expounding his text. But when he proceeded next to apply his text to the occasion by comparing David and Charles, he would usually ignore Absalom's rebellion and David's flight from his capital, circumstances more analogous to those of the king's father, and commence his parallel with 2 Sam. 19:9–14 (the actual beginning of the lesson for the anniversary service), where, following the death of Absalom, "all the people were at strife throughout all the tribes of Israel" until "they sent this word unto the king, Return thou, and all thy servants." So when Bishop Parker finishes relating the story of Absalom's rebellion and is ready to apply his text to the circumstances of the Restoration, he declines to "lead your attention into the parallel and application, as I did into the story of the Text, through the many contrivances and managements of the Rebellion, and shew you how our Sovereign became an exile from these Kingdomes, as *David* from *Hierusalem*; this were to rake in the dunghill, or to open *Pandora*'s box, and so infection might flie abroad." Instead, he announces that he will "begin my application of the storie, with the Text" for the day, concerning David's return to Jerusalem at the invitation of his people.[44] As long as the anniversary preachers continued to accommodate the Absalom story to the restoration of Charles II, David would completely overshadow Absalom and Achitophel as the protagonist of a drama in which the pivotal event was his triumphant return from exile, not the rebellion that preceded it.

In the propaganda of the Exclusion Crisis and its aftermath, parallels drawn from both sacred and profane history would figure prominently, yet even when the same biblical stories as before were used, they would have to be accommodated to very different circumstances from those made familiar in the anniversary sermons. These homilies alone cannot account for the frequent use of parallels as a means of praise or blame during the last years of Charles's reign, but they played a significant role in familiarizing the public with this ancient rhetorical strategy, and in popularizing the choice of certain episodes of sacred history for that purpose.

But parallelism was not the only legacy of Anglican homiletics to the defenders of government policy in the years of crisis after 1678. The miraculous intervention of Providence commemorated in the thanksgiving sermons year after year served as a perpetual reminder that the Restoration settlement had been divinely sanctioned; in a time of national emergency, as we shall see in the final chapter, that same theme would be refurbished, and Anglican preachers would celebrate yet another providential intervention as confirming the government's earlier charter. Most important, by using the pulpit to persuade the faithful to regard obedience to kings and magistrates as one of their most serious religious obligations, and rebellion as the most heinous of sins, the clergy of the Established Church would continue to exploit an invaluable opportunity for supporting the restored monarchy.

## Chapter 2

## PARLIAMENT AND THE PRESS

THE PROPAGANDA on behalf of the government in which Dryden was to play so active a role in the last years of Charles II's reign was designed to justify a series of maneuvers that the court had been constrained to adopt, under pressure from Parliament and the public, since the autumn of 1678. Until early 1681 those maneuvers were carried out in a series of intermittent contests between the king and Parliament in which many of the Crown's prerogatives were at stake. But beyond Westminster lay an aroused public with whose temper the king must contend, and on the outcome of this wider contest might depend his continued possession of the throne. In June 1677, his lord treasurer, the earl of Danby, had warned him in a private memorandum that "till hee can fall into the humour of the people hee can never bee great nor rich, and while differences continue prerogative must suffer, unless hee can live without Parliament."[1] A year later the Popish Plot hysteria began and the king was to feel the force of Danby's warning. While the suspicions of his people grew and festered, the king found his prerogatives being eroded as he struggled with four successive parliaments. When he dissolved the last of them in March 1681, he had found a way to live without Parliament and to begin recovering his prerogatives. But he still must deal with the humor of his people if he hoped to insure the stability of his throne. Against Parliament his weapons had been a series of cautious thrusts and tactical retreats by which he had gained the time he needed. In dealing with the public he came increasingly to rely on propaganda as a means of allaying popular fears and winning some measure of acceptance for his policies.

.   .   .   .   .

It was of course the widespread belief in the existence of a Popish Plot that first aroused public hysteria. Its disclosure by Titus Oates and Israel Tonge in the late summer of 1678 created terrors in the public mind that were confirmed by the discovery of Sir Edmund Berry Godfrey's body in October, and increased as William Bedloe, Miles Prance, Stephen Dugdale, and other informers came forward in the following months to add further details to the story and implicate more parties in the plot. But it is easy to exaggerate the role of the Popish Plot in the ensuing political crisis. The period during which public hysteria over the supposed conspiracy was at its height—the era of sensational revelations and trials of the victims in open court—lasted only a year: from the discovery of Godfrey's body in October 1678 until the early autumn of 1679. The trials and convictions of the five Jesuits and of their lawyer Richard Langhorn— what John Kenyon calls "the last of the great Plot trials"—took place in June 1679, and the circuit trials up and down the land—"the great holocaust of the Plot," in Kenyon's words—followed in July and August.[2] But the event that heralded the turning of the tide also took place in July 1679: the trial and acquittal of Sir George Wakeman, the queen's physician, along with three Benedictine monks in the face of testimony from the same four Plot witnesses—Oates, Bedloe, Prance, and Dugdale— whose credibility had until then borne all before it.[3] In a few more months the emotions engendered by the Popish Plot had become a smoldering brand that could ignite the fires of public unrest only as new fuel was added. Its lasting importance was that by magnifying the public's apprehensions of English Catholics at home and French Catholics abroad it gave the parliamentary opposition an opportunity to use those fears to win increasing majorities in the House of Commons, to focus them gradually on the prospect of a Popish Successor, and to create from them popular support for a confrontation with the Crown. Once this situation had been achieved, the Exclusion Crisis came to usurp public attention and the Popish Plot became a part of this larger issue. In this new state of affairs, the king, whose life had been the subject of popular fears at the time of the Plot, was to become a principal target of suspicion himself. But this could not occur until the popular imagination had been sated on daggers, poisons, and night riders, and could be diverted to less spectacular dangers.

It was while public panic over the Plot prevailed that the first two of the four parliaments of 1678–81 took place. From this popular agitation they would acquire a character that differed noticeably from that of the two later parliaments, held at the height of the Exclusion Crisis. But already we can find developing those opposing views of the king's actions as "just prerogatives" or "arbitrary power" that were to divide the nation by 1681.

"There are two Reasons for calling Parliaments," Henry Powle reminded the House of Commons in November 1680, "one for raising of Money, the other for making Laws, as the Legislative Power, upon any new emergencies."[4] For the king the first of these two reasons was often the more compelling. His ordinary revenue might suffice for domestic management, but wars or preparations for war—the stuff of foreign policy in the seventeenth century—entailed extraordinary expenses that could only be met from supplies voted by Parliament. In the autumn of

1678 the king was badly in need of money. He had persuaded Parliament to finance an expeditionary force the previous spring as a prelude to aiding the Dutch against the French. But these preparations for war had been overtaken by peace negotiations, and Parliament had voted supplies in June for disbanding these unnecessary forces which were arousing the usual suspicions of a standing army in time of peace. Instead, the king had used the money to maintain the army as a means of coercing France into coming to an agreement. Now the French had signed a peace treaty with the Dutch, the army's pay was seriously in arrears, and fresh supplies must be voted to pay off and disband the forces. The king had no choice but to summon Parliament again, only three months after it had last been prorogued.

To Parliament, coming together on 21 October 1678, four days after the discovery of Godfrey's body, the second reason for calling parliaments was far more important at this moment than the first. The members were intent upon investigating the Popish Plot and making laws to deal with this new emergency. Within six weeks the House of Commons had examined Titus Oates and ordered the arrest of five Catholic peers on his testimony; they had quickly passed a Test Bill to exclude Catholics from sitting in either house of Parliament; they had passed a resolution, with which the Lords concurred, "That this House is of Opinion, that there hath been, and still is, a damnable and hellish Plot contrived and carried on by the Popish Recusants, for the assassinating and murdering the King; and for subverting the Government; and rooting out and destroying the Protestant Religion"; they had listened to the treasonable correspondence between Edward Coleman, the duke of York's former secretary, and Père La Chaise, confessor to Louis XIV; and they had impeached the five Catholic peers, now lodged in the Tower, of high treason.[5]

But Danby was still lord treasurer, and with his support the position of the duke of York, the king's brother and heir in default of any legitimate royal offspring, remained unshaken despite his open avowal of the Catholic faith. Neither the Plot witnesses nor Coleman's correspondence had directly implicated him; a debate in the Commons on a motion that in view of his recusancy the duke "withdraw himself from the King's person and councils" had been adjourned without coming to a vote; and when the Lords amended the Test Bill with a proviso exempting the duke from its stipulations, Danby managed to muster enough strength for the amendment to pass the Commons by two votes.

The House of Commons now was at leisure to turn to the problem of the infamous standing army and the necessity of voting supplies a second time to disband it. Lest the nation be deprived of armed security when a Popish Plot was supposed to be afoot, the Commons began by passing a bill to put part of the militia on a war footing. This moved through the Lords without comment, but the king, perceiving that it would deprive him of his prerogative of controlling the militia, had recourse to another prerogative he had not exercised since 1662 and vetoed the bill. Surprised and irritated, the Commons now voted supplies for disbanding the army but, to insure that this time the money would be put to the use for which it was intended, they specified that it should be paid into the Chamber of the City of London rather than the Exchequer. The Lords, alerted by now to threats to the royal prerogative, insisted on amending a bill that "would have invaded the King's declared Power and Authority." The Commons angrily rejected the amended bill amid cries of "Let it fall!"[6] Their temper was due to an event that had occurred two days earlier, haunting them for the rest of the session.

On 19 December Ralph Montagu, the former English ambassador at Paris, disclosed to the Commons the unsuccessful negotiations Danby had carried on with the French the previous spring for a subsidy to allow the king to dispense with parliaments for two or three years. These had taken place at the very time Parliament was voting money for the army, so that, as Sir Thomas Clarges pointed out to the members, "Here was Money given for a War with *France*, and here is a Peace made, and six millions of livres yearly to be given for it, to prevent the meeting of the Parliament."[7] Aroused to a frenzy by this news, the Commons voted to impeach Danby of high treason, heedless of Serjeant Maynard's prophecy that the next parliament would make good: "The business of the Impeachments of the Lords in the *Tower* is now impending. . . . And whilst you hunt this one hare, you will lose five."[8] The Lords, among whom Danby numbered many friends and supporters, declined to commit him to custody, and a deadlock developed between the two houses that brought all business to a halt. In the midst of this impasse, the king prorogued Parliament on 30 December to the following February.

The king had suffered a serious setback. He had raised no money, had seen several of his prerogatives threatened, and had been compelled in the face of hysteria over the Popish Plot to give his consent to a Test Act that infringed another of his prerogatives. For as William Williams reminded the Commons, "Cannot the King call what Lords he pleases into the House of Peers? And yet he passed that Act, to exclude his own power, that they cannot sit without the Oaths and Test."[9]

With his lord treasurer in disgrace and his former majority a shambles, the king decided to dissolve Parliament on 24 January 1679 and to order elections for a new parliament, summoned to meet in March. His decision was greeted with general rejoicing. The Cavalier Parliament had lasted some eighteen years, fewer than half its present members were veterans of the last general election held in 1661, and the opposition had been calling for its dissolution since 1674. The elections that now ensued greatly increased the number of opposition members in the new Commons and sorely disappointed the king. Yet these elections were not, in fact, fought on party lines.[10] Apart from local interests, the issue of greatest importance in the winter of 1678–79 was the continued investigation of the Popish Plot and the prosecution of the conspirators. This was not a party issue, since everyone professed abhorrence of the Plot, but it ensured the return of candidates who were eager to pursue their quarry all the way to Whitehall if necessary. Nevertheless, the king was now desperate for money and the newly elected members must be called together without delay.

·   ·   ·   ·   ·

The new parliament that assembled on 6 March 1679 has come to be known as the first Exclusion Parliament, because it was during its meeting that a bill was first introduced to exclude the duke of York from the throne. But in its character and concerns it was related much more closely to the final session of the previous parliament, which it followed by only two months, than to the other two Exclusion Parliaments, which were to take place a year and a half or two years later. It took its popular mandate from the hysteria still in full cry over the Popish Plot rather than from the emotions later generated by the high tide of the Exclusion Crisis. Coming after so short an interval, it naturally found its chief concerns in the unfinished business left over from the preceding parliament—the investigation of the Plot and the prosecution of Danby and the five Catholic peers—just as the king's own concern was with raising the same money he had failed to obtain on the earlier occasion. The first act of the Commons, in fact, after losing a week in a quarrel over the choice of a speaker, was to resolve that a committee inspect the Journal of the House so that, as one member declared, "we may know how we left affairs the last Parliament, and that we may the better know what we have to do."[11] They then sent the Lords a message requesting that Danby be committed to custody, and settled back to hear the Plot witnesses retell and embroider their story for the benefit of the new members.

On 22 March the king came down to Westminster and announced to Parliament that he had granted Danby a pardon under the Great Seal. This was a hazardous step that was to prove futile as well. By attempting to pardon Danby before he came to trial in the House of Lords, the king was laying himself open to charges of interfering with justice and encroaching on the privilege of Parliament. He was also inviting a challenge to one of his most important prerogatives. But the king was intent on saving Danby not only because the lord treasurer had been carrying out the king's instructions in the negotiations for which he now stood in peril of his life, but because Charles was anxious to prevent any further revelations that would almost certainly come to light at Danby's trial. The Commons were aroused to fury. Two days later they voted the king an address of expostulation against "the Irregularity and Illegality of the Pardon" and "the dangerous Consequence of granting Pardons to any Persons that lie under an Impeachment of the Commons of *England*."[12] Next day a message from the Lords informed them that the upper house had at last agreed to commit Danby to custody, only to find that he had flown. When, in an effort to forestall more severe measures, the Lords sent them a bill of banishment against Danby, the Commons threw it out unceremoniously and answered by sending the Lords a bill of attainder to go into effect if Danby did not surrender by 21 April. The Lords amended the bill to convert it into a bill of banishment, the Commons stubbornly rejected the amendments, and a struggle ensued between the two houses in which at last, on 14 April, the Commons prevailed. In the face of this abject surrender by the Lords, the king was too intimidated to veto the bill of attainder, yet he shrank from incurring the odium his father had borne for assenting to a similar bill against Strafford in 1641. He therefore yielded, giving Danby permission to surrender to Black Rod the next day, which rendered the bill moot.

In the midst of this furor the Commons had taken up the Disbandment Bill again, moved not by generosity toward the king but by hatred of a standing army. What had been a sore point to the previous parliament, asked to pay a second time for disbanding an army that had been illegally kept in existence since the previous summer, had become a festering wound now that it was known the preparations for war with France had been a sham. There was considerable sentiment among the opposition members for simply disbanding the forces without voting money to pay them off. As William Garroway suggested, "I would have you declare them disbanded, and they are disbanded, and then see who dares head them."[13] But their fear of the army mingled with a sense of justice persuaded them to heed the arguments of such as Sir William Coventry who cautioned, "I would not give an alarm to those who have arms in their hands," and reminded them that "the soldiers could not help their being together; the blame must be in some other place."[14] With some reluctance, therefore, they agreed on a bill to pay off as well as disband the army. This time, mollified somewhat by the Lords' recent acquiescence in the bill of attainder, they specified that the money should be paid into the Exchequer. The bill made its way through the Lords in due course and at last, on 9 May, the king had his money. But by this date the Commons were becoming embroiled with the Lords once more.

Since 16 April, when Danby was sent off to join the five Catholic peers in confinement, there had been six lords in the Tower. All had been impeached of high treason by the Commons, who now eagerly awaited their trials. In cases of impeachment, as Richard Hampden reminded the Commons, "You are as a Grand Jury; and the Lords are in the nature of a Jury and Judges," the articles of impeachment serving as the indictment and the Commons acting as prosecutors at the trial in place of the attorney general.[15] In mid-April four of the Catholic peers were arraigned at the bar of the House of Lords, the fifth, Lord Belasyse, being too ill to put in an appearance.[16] On 25 April Danby was brought to his arraignment and, at the king's insistence, pleaded his pardon under the Great Seal.

During the month that remained to the session, the Commons were to spend the greatest part of their time and energy debating the pardon, considering alternative ways of proceeding against Danby and the five Catholic peers, and expostulating with the Lords. They quickly agreed that this abuse of the king's prerogative must be checked at all costs, for if it were once allowed, the consequences would not be limited to saving Danby. As Serjeant Maynard declared, "The five Lords in the *Tower* may have such Pardons, by the same reason, and what then becomes of all your Liberties?"[17] The upshot was a series of messages from the Commons over the next few weeks demanding that the House of Lords, as court of last resort, hand down a decision that this pardon in bar of an impeachment was illegal and void. Once this matter was settled, the Lords were to proceed to immediate judgment on Danby, who by pleading a pardon had confessed his guilt and forfeited his right to trial, and to put the five Catholic peers on trial. Finally, the bishops, who by custom withdrew from capital cases, were to abstain from voting on Danby's pardon.

In the midst of all these legal maneuvers, the Commons at last, some two months after the session had begun, gave some of their divided attention to the prospect of a Popish Successor. The subject was first seriously broached on 27 April when they debated and passed a resolution "That the Duke of *Yorke*'s being a Papist, and the Hopes of his coming such to the Crown, has given the greatest Countenance and Encouragement to the present Conspiracies and Designs of the Papists against the King, and the Protestant Religion."[18] The king, sensing the direction in which they were moving, came down to Westminster on 30 April and offered Parliament assurances, which he was to repeat frequently over the next two years, that he would agree to any expedients for protecting the Protestant religion in the next reign, "so as the same extend not to alter the Descent of the Crown in the right Line, nor to defeat the Succession."[19] The Commons were not impressed. It was not until 11 May that they could divert their attention from the business of the pardon and the lords in the Tower long enough to return to the problem of the Succession, but when they did so they debated and passed a motion to bring in a bill "to disable the Duke of *Yorke* to inherit the Imperial Crown of this Realm."[20] On 15

May, after spending most of the morning in recriminations against the House of Lords over the bishops' participation in the impeachment proceedings, the Commons found time to pass the first reading of the Exclusion Bill without a division. On 21 May they broke off their quarrel with the Lords long enough to pass the bill on its second reading by a lopsided vote of 207 to 128. The Commons then turned their attention once again to the lords in the Tower.

There has been considerable speculation as to why the Commons delayed taking up a third reading of the Exclusion Bill, and historians have attempted to explain the delay as a tactic of the opposition leaders who may have been doubtful of its final passage. But the size of the majority on the second reading coupled with the fact that the opposition had been carrying everything before it in the Commons throughout the session suggests a different conclusion: that the opposition was confident of its passage and wished to settle the business of the pardon and the impeachments before sending up a new bill that would almost certainly precipitate a fresh struggle with the Lords. Unmistakable evidence of where the opposition's priorities lay right up to the end of the session is provided by a debate in the Commons over a new request for supplies from the king. Encouraged by his success over the Disbandment Bill, the king on 14 May asked for supplies for the fleet so that the nation could honor its alliances. In refusing to entertain any such request at this time, the members were swayed by the consideration that once the king obtained his supplies he would be free to prorogue Parliament before it had finished its most important business. In the next parliament this argument was to be offered again and again in urging that no supplies be voted until an Exclusion Bill was passed. On this occasion, however, it was not the Exclusion Bill, scheduled for its first reading the following day, that riveted the attention of the members who rose one by one to argue, in the words of William Sacheverell, "Once give your Money, and fairly part, and the Lords in the *Tower* will not be tryed, and nothing done."[21] While this parliament lasted, the six lords in the Tower were to preempt all other considerations.

By this time the Lords and Commons were at loggerheads. The Lords were not to be intimidated again over Danby as had happened with the bill of attainder. Ignoring both his pardon and his impeachment, they prepared to put the five Catholic peers on trial. The Commons responded by insisting that the pardon be settled before these trials could begin. Bearing out Serjeant Maynard's prophecy that while they hunted one hare they would lose five, most members agreed with William Garroway when he declared, "I had rather the five Lords should escape, than that *Danby*'s Pardon should stand good."[22] Once again, as at the end of the previous parliament, matters were at an impasse over Danby, and on 27

May, the day on which the trials of the five Catholic peers were scheduled to begin before the Lords, the king seized the excuse of a deadlock between the two houses to come down to Westminster and prorogue Parliament until the following August. But on 12 July, deciding he had had enough of this obstreperous Commons, he dissolved Parliament, and shortly afterwards ordered elections for a new parliament summoned to meet on 17 October.

.    .    .    .    .

It was this dissolution, coming just when the tide of the Popish Plot was starting to turn, that marks the real beginning of the Exclusion Crisis.[23] The public was taken by surprise, the opposition furious, and the ground laid for a long and increasingly acrimonious struggle between the court and its antagonists along different lines. Within three months the king had dismissed the earl of Shaftesbury from the Privy Council and the rupture between the two was complete. In the hostilities that followed, Shaftesbury, now openly heading the opposition soon to be known as Whigs, was to find himself in direct confrontation not with Danby, who was in the Tower, nor with the duke of York, who was in exile most of this time in Brussels and later in Edinburgh, but with the king, who now assumed direction of the government forces that would come to be styled Tories.

From the two recent sessions of Parliament both sides carried away valuable ammunition as well as lessons for the future. At the height of the Exclusion Crisis the Whigs would be able to draw freely on the events of 1678–79 to lengthen the train of abuses they would lay at the door of Whitehall: an illegal standing army in time of peace, a flagrant abuse of the prerogative to pardon a traitor in bar of an impeachment, attempts to hinder the prosecution of the Plot and its perpetrators, a prorogation and dissolution of Parliament in the midst of its essential business. The Tories would be able to cull from the same events a different arsenal to use against Shaftesbury and his allies: delays and refusals in granting the king the money he needed to pursue a vigorous foreign policy, repeated encroachments on the king's just prerogative, an attempt to alienate the Succession.

From their recent experience Shaftesbury and his supporters were to derive three valuable lessons that their future conduct would show they had taken to heart. First of all, Danby was a hare they had pursued far too long, diverting them from more important business. Once he surrendered the treasurer's white staff and was committed by the Lords, his power had vanished. True, he continued to advise the king from the Tower, but neither this irritation nor the wish to see him punished was worth the price his opponents had been paying to have the head of a fallen minister. In the next parliament they would wisely ignore him, seldom even mentioning his name. Second, the perpetual quarrels the Commons had raised with the Lords in the last two sessions had been a disastrous policy, hindering their progress and offering the king a welcome excuse for proroguing them on both occasions. In the next parliament they would show unaccustomed restraint in the face of many provocations from the upper house, heeding the advice of Colonel Titus: "Consider the matter, and if it be possible, avoid all difference with the Lords."[24] Last and most important, the opposition had been pursuing too many simultaneous aims in the last two sessions, veering from one to another and yet another, insisting on all and achieving none. In the next parliament they would be more single-minded, following a course on which again Colonel Titus offered the best counsel: "Pray observe one Rule from me: If you will do nothing till you can do every thing, we shall do nothing."[25] For by this time the Whigs were a party with an overriding objective: Exclusion.

By dissolving Parliament in the summer of 1679 and providing a long interval before the meeting of the next, the king, without intending them any such favor, allowed the opposition to rid themselves of their recent obsessions and to reexamine their priorities. For too long their attention had been caught and held by the recent past. In dividing so much of their time between Danby's malfeasance and the Popish Plot, they had been riveted to two events belonging to the spring and summer of 1678. They insisted, of course, that the Plot still continued, but public excitement was beginning to wane. With Parliament no longer in session, Oates and the other witnesses had lost their most important public platform at the same time that Lord Chief Justice Scroggs was beginning to challenge their credibility in the courtroom. Freed from these distractions, Exclusion could at last acquire the priority that its inherent importance had dictated all along. To opposition thinking, the prospect of a Popish Successor promised the same threats of subverting the government and destroying the Protestant religion as the Popish Plot, but in a more dangerous form: not in secret consults by a few conspirators during the lifetime of the present king, but openly and with all the powers of the executive during the reign of his successor.

By the time of the general elections in the late summer of 1679, therefore, the opposition candidates were soliciting the electors as members of an exclusionist party, and were winning more seats than before in the new House of Commons. Over the next year and a half the issue would increase steadily in importance, catching the public imagination, providing the Whig politicians with the popular support they desperately needed, and yet assuming a different dimension in the public mind from that of their leaders. To the Whig magnates, Exclusion was all along exactly the negative position that its name implies. They were intent on keeping the present heir from succeeding to the throne, but they studiously avoided any attempt at naming a substitute heir, which could only lead to divisions in their ranks among rival candidacies. To the public, however, it was not simply Exclusion but the Succession that captured their attention. If the Popish Duke was to be contemned and then excluded, he must have a replacement, and who better than the Protestant Duke: Charles's natural son, the popular duke of Monmouth? After so many revelations and so much disillusionment, the public needed an icon; for them, Exclusion was seen as a contest between two rivals, each of whom had his supporters attesting their loyalty at public dinners and mass meetings and in the press, where toasts, bonfires and broadside poems pitted Old Jemmy against Young Jemmy. The king, attempting to dispel the idea of a contest between the two, unwittingly encouraged it. In March 1679, shortly before the first Exclusion Parliament was to meet, he had packed his brother off to Brussels to divert attention from him. The duke had returned in early September when the king fell ill. Once Charles recovered, he decided that matters had reached a critical stage where both his brother and his son must be taken from the public eye. In late September, and within twenty-four hours of each other, Monmouth set off for Holland and the duke of York for Flanders, encouraging the view of them as two rival candidates for the throne sent off to await the outcome of the contest.

This was a heady experience for Monmouth, but for Shaftesbury and his allies it was an opportunity for keeping up excitement over Exclusion without committing themselves to the duke's support. Yet his absence from the country would make this more difficult. In October the duke of York was permitted by the king to change his place of exile, and he stopped off in London for two weeks en route to Edinburgh. The opportunity this gave his supporters to express their loyalty suggested to the Whigs that Monmouth must return. Shaftesbury urged him to do so, and in November he was back in London against his father's orders. When the king stripped him of his offices, he defied him and stayed on, courting popularity from the public and encouraged by Shaftesbury and the other Whig leaders with infinite good will but no promises. Uneasy at his son's advantage in having the stage to himself, the king ordered his brother to return to London, where he arrived in February 1680. But Monmouth continued to capture public attention. In April began the excitement over the mysterious black box supposed to contain proof of the king's marriage to Monmouth's mother, Lucy Walter, and the more gullible were convinced of his legitimacy, establishing his prior claim as heir to that of his uncle. As a result, Monmouth captured even greater attention, which at last forced the king to issue a humiliating declaration in June 1680

denying that he had ever been married to Monmouth's mother, or indeed
to anyone but Queen Catherine. Charles also pointed out that he had
already made two similar declarations in January and March 1679; but
the reminder itself implied that these had been widely disbelieved, since he
was forced to repeat his disavowal yet again.[26] In August and September
1680 Monmouth made his famous progress through the west of England,
acclaimed by mass meetings at every stop.[27]

If Exclusion was the overriding objective of the Whigs in late 1679 and
throughout 1680, the question of how it would ever be achieved created
a second issue of equal importance. To the king in the summer of 1679,
the experience of the two recent parliaments had offered different lessons
from those it held for the opposition. First of all, the House of Lords,
despite the presence of Shaftesbury, Monmouth, Essex, and other antagonists, could be a useful ally in which the king's supporters constituted a
permanent majority unaffected by elections. But the Lords were not simply a tool that the king could manipulate at will. They had certainly supported Danby and it was a safe assumption that they would oppose altering the Succession as long as the king remained firm. They had jealously
guarded the king's prerogative on occasion, and time and again they had
served as a stumbling block to the more precipitate Commons. But they
were not immune to determined pressure from the lower house, as had
been shown in the case of Danby's bill of attainder, and where they felt,
and indeed shared, the public's emotions over the Popish Plot, they had
been willing to pass such a measure as the Test Act. They were a source
of potential aid that was not always dependable.

The second lesson for the king was that his prerogatives were under
fire, that some of these could prove more incendiary than others, and that
his survival might depend on his choosing to make use of some in place of
others. Several prerogatives—his direct control over the militia or parliamentary revenues and his right to summon peers to the House of Lords—
had recently been threatened or limited by Parliament, but in his exercise
of certain other prerogatives the king had been finding himself increasingly constrained by the heated emotional state of the nation. It was his
unquestioned prerogative to veto bills, but, as his dilemma over Danby's
bill of attainder had revealed, this was not a privilege that he could safely
invoke in times like these. His firmly reiterated warning over the next two
years that he would never assent to an Exclusion Bill gave public notice
that if driven to it he would veto such a bill, but the probable cost would
be rioting if not armed rebellion. Before matters were brought to that
pass, however, an Exclusion Bill would have to pass the House of Lords,
and before that unlikely event could take place Parliament would have to
be once more in session. Small wonder that in this emergency he should
fall back upon his prerogative of summoning parliaments at a time and

place of his own choosing, subject only to the limitations set by the Triennial Act of 1664 that he should do so "once in three years at the least," and to the practical requirements determined by his need for money.

Another royal prerogative increasingly limited by popular passions was that of granting pardons. The king's pardon of Danby in bar of an impeachment had created a storm, but this was in fact an abuse of his prerogative that would be outlawed after the Revolution by the Act of Settlement. More important, his unquestioned prerogative of pardoning traitors after verdict in arrest of judgment could not, in simple prudence, be extended to the five Catholic peers, in spite of his scruples about their innocence, in the face of public hysteria over the Popish Plot. Once again, his prerogative of summoning, proroguing, and dissolving parliaments offered a solution to his dilemma. By impeaching Danby and the five Catholic peers, the Commons had unintentionally provided the king with a remedy, since impeachments could be tried by the House of Lords only while Parliament was in session. The trials of Danby and the five Catholic peers, therefore, like the passage of an Exclusion Bill, could be postponed and possibly prevented by delaying the sitting of Parliament, or curtailing it once it had begun.

For all these reasons, once the elections of the late summer of 1679 had returned a larger number of opposition members than ever to the Commons, the king determined to prevent their coming together as long as possible. When 17 October arrived, the date on which its opening session was to begin, he immediately prorogued Parliament until 26 January 1680; when that date arrived he immediately prorogued it again; and he continued to repeat the process a total of seven times until the autumn of 1680. By that time, there had not been a session of Parliament for seventeen months. This long an interval was not unprecedented, nor even unusual. There had been an earlier seventeen-month recess in 1668–69, and a much longer one of twenty-two months duration between 1671 and 1673. In more recent years, the recesses of 1674–75 and of 1675–77 had fallen short of this latest interval by only two or three months. But in the present emergency the king's continued refusal to allow the newly elected Parliament to meet and "redress the nation's grievances," in the popular phrase of the time, created a furor as great as, and closely related to, the emotions over Exclusion.

Whenever a barrier is erected in the way of an overwhelming mandate for change, the means by which the national will is being frustrated will capture at least as much attention as the original objective. In this way any issue can be transformed into a constitutional crisis. To the Whigs' way of thinking, Exclusion was an objective that enjoyed just such a popular mandate, as was proved by the recent elections. Yet its achievement was being frustrated by the king, who instead of allowing Parliament to meet was employing his prerogative as an obstructive tactic to prevent the legislators from carrying out the nation's wishes. As long as he continued to use his lawful powers to defy the electorate, his behavior was bound to form part and parcel of the Succession issue, transforming a parliamentary and public debate over what was already a serious constitutional issue—Exclusion—into an even graver constitutional crisis in which the royal prerogative, severely threatened or seriously abused in the eyes of the respective parties, would eventually take precedence over every other issue. In the face of intransigence by the supreme magistrate, the Whigs were without any legal redress. Short of some desperate remedy, they could only try to bring popular pressure to bear on the king. From the Tory point of view, before the Whigs were ready for treason, they would see what sedition could do.

. . . . .

Their earliest effort in this direction was the Petitioning Movement in the winter of 1679–80. The first petition calling on the king to allow Parliament to meet, bearing the signatures of Shaftesbury and sixteen of his fellow peers, was presented to Charles on 7 December 1679.[28] Five days later the government attempted to discourage others from following their example by issuing a royal proclamation forbidding tumultuous petitions, but without success.[29] By the first week in January the newspapers were reporting that "the chief discourse at present is about Petitions, some for them, some against them; some that mean well refuse to subscribe, being deterred by the late Proclamation, but it is thought the number of the Subscribers exceed all the rest; and it is reported, that Tables, Pen, Ink, and Petitions have been placed upon the *Royal Exchange* in Change time, and people invited to subscribe them: It is also reported, that some Petitions will be presented this week."[30] The first of these mass petitions, bearing fifty or sixty thousand signatures, was presented to the king on 13 January, and came from the residents of Westminster and Southwark. Before the end of the month the king received the first of the county petitions, bearing the signatures of thirty thousand residents of Wiltshire.

Casting about for some means of responding to the petitions they were unable to prevent, the Tories attempted to launch a countermovement in which various small bodies of citizens loyal to the Crown, for the most part grand juries and justices of the peace assembled at the quarter sessions, would draw up "abhorrences": addresses to the king condemning tumultuous petitions. These abhorrences, like the unwelcome petitions themselves, would be presented to the king, from whom a markedly different reception could be expected, however, and the ceremony would be reported in the *London Gazette,* which would also print the texts of the abhorrences themselves. Such, at any rate, must have been the wishful thinking of government officials who could have made no effort to test beforehand the extent to which their ill-conceived hopes offered any prospect of success. As they could have learned from the small band of government supporters in the Commons who, during the first Exclusion Parliament, wisely refused on many occasions to challenge a division of the House, weakness should be concealed, not publicized. In the event, the Abhorrence Movement, if the straggling response can be called a movement at all, was the greatest public-relations disaster the government would suffer in a year filled with political setbacks. Not only was the number of abhorrences printed in the *London Gazette* pitifully small in absolute terms, but the long intervals between their infrequent appearances emphasized their paucity even further.

But it was not only the logistics of the Abhorrence Movement that was poorly conceived and badly implemented. The substance of the abhorrences was quite as weak as their numbers, for they had nothing to say except that the signers, few in numbers like the abhorrences themselves, deplored the appearance of petitions that were expressing the wishes of a vast number of dissatisfied subjects. As the brevity of their texts made clear, the abhorrences were never more than a poll whose outcome a wiser government would have suppressed.

In spite of their overwhelming victory in this contest with their opponents, the Whigs did not rely on petitions alone to keep up popular pressure on the government. They launched a massive propaganda campaign in the press that was favored by the fact that the Licensing Act, the principal means by which the government controlled the press, had expired on 10 June 1679, Parliament having refused to renew it before being prorogued in May. "Now were there Papers, Speeches, Libels, publiquely cried in the streetes against the *Duke* of *York,* & Lauderdail &c obnoxious to the Parliament, with too much, & indeede too shamefull a liberty," Evelyn wrote in his diary under 6 July, "but the People & Parliament had gotten head, by reason of the vices of the greate ones."[31] Faced with a flood of Whig pamphlets and broadsides, the government resorted to prosecutions under the Treason Act, or for libel. But the king's "major problem caused by the want of a Printing Act," Timothy Crist has pointed out, "was regulation at the source, the printing house. Only after publications reached the streets could the government act to punish the offending stationers, both printers and booksellers. But by then the propaganda value had probably been achieved through various means of distribution and the damage done."[32]

Within a month of the expiration of the Licensing Act, the Whigs had begun issuing newspapers on a regular basis. The first and most important of these was Benjamin Harris's *Domestick Intelligence,* as it was called at first, which began twice-weekly publication on 7 July 1679. In September Henry Care revived his popular weekly, *Poor Robin's Intelligence*, and in November Robert Harford began publishing his *Mercurius Anglicus* twice a week. Once the Petitioning Movement got under way in January, Harris's and Harford's newspapers became an indispensable part of the campaign by reporting the petitions, printing them, and fostering the impression of widespread popular agitation for the meeting of Parliament.

The government attempted to suppress the Whig newspapers, but its efforts in this direction dragged on through the winter and early spring without visible success. In February 1680 Harris was convicted of publishing a pamphlet, *An Appeal from the Country to the City*, for which he was fined and imprisoned.[33] After two months' confinement in the King's Bench, he was at last reduced to abandoning his newspaper in mid-April, but with the satisfaction of seeing it immediately replaced by the *True Protestant Domestick Intelligence*, started by an anonymous Whig bookseller hard on the heels of Robert Everingham's *Mercurius Civicus*, another Whig newspaper that had begun appearing in March. It was not until 12 May 1680 that a royal proclamation against unlicensed newspapers succeeded in silencing all but one of the Whig periodicals: Henry Care's serial book, the *Weekly Pacquet of Advice from Rome*, which had been appearing since December 1678.[34] When Care was convicted in July of continuing to publish in defiance of a court order, he simply renamed his weekly and proceeded without interruption.

In the face of all this vigorous Whig journalism continued for ten months, the Tories were forced to rely on a single newspaper, besides the official *London Gazette* (published since 1665), with which to oppose them. This was Nathaniel Thompson's *Domestick Intelligence*, as it was called at first, whose origin shows how far the Tories were reduced to a defensive position during 1679 and 1680, responding to events but seldom initiating them. Thompson's paper began as a hoax. Its first issue, as the *Domestick Intelligence*, "No. 16," appeared on 29 August 1679, the same date as Harris's newspaper with the same title and number, and was designed to sow confusion among the Whigs. When the joke had worn thin after three numbers, Thompson changed the title of his paper, which now claimed to be the *True Domestick Intelligence* and continued to appear twice weekly, while Harris was eventually forced to change the title of his paper to the *Protestant Domestick Intelligence* to prevent confusion. But for the first four or five months Thompson refrained from attacking the Whigs, devoting his efforts to defending the Tories. This was the period of the Meal Tub Plot, the attempt by Elizabeth Cellier to father on the Whigs a Protestant plot that had recently been exposed as fraudulent, and Thompson's paper was kept busy condemning this sham plot as a trick of the Papists that the government abhorred as heartily as did the opposition. It was only in early 1680 that he at last began denouncing "tumultuous petitions" and attacking Harris's paper. His tardy offensive would be short-lived, for the *True Domestick Intelligence* fell victim, along with its more numerous opponents, to the royal proclamation against unlicensed newspapers in May.

If the government succeeded in imposing a temporary silence on the newspapers, they could boast no such success with the tide of pamphlets and broadsides that continued to pour from the Whig presses. Typical of the vigorous offensive carried on so successfully by the Whig presses in 1680 was the popular series of *Legorn Letters*. These were based on the genuine letters from Leghorn which, like those from correspondents in other foreign cities, were frequently quoted in the newspapers as sources of foreign news. The *Legorn Letters*, ostensibly a correspondence exchanged between merchants in Leghorn and London, were broadsides and pamphlets concerning affairs on board the "Van Herring" that used the traditional metaphor of the ship of state as a means of describing the perilous situation of the English nation from a Whig perspective. The first of these letters, published on 12 January 1680, announced the discovery of a plot among the Mohammedans aboard the ship to mutiny, kill the captain, and place the lieutenant, a coreligionist of theirs, in command. The captain, however, had stubbornly ignored these threats to the ship's safety, dismissed the council of officers, and rejected petitions from the sailors to allow the council to meet and deal with the emergency.[35] This letter proved so popular that within a week two more had appeared, and another the following week.[36] These later installments related the captain's unaccountable disregard for the crew's safety, his leniency toward the purser and five Mohammedan rogues confined to the gun room by the council of officers, and his refusal to allow the lieutenant to be deprived of his right of succession to the ship's command. The Tories responded with a hoax, as they had done in reaction to Harris's newspaper, publishing a sham *Legorn Letter* shortly after the first of them appeared, which discounted the fears it had raised about the ship's safety.[37] But they made no immediate attempt to continue the hoax, and the Whigs were encouraged to launch a second and bolder series of *Legorn Letters* in the autumn of 1680 after an event occurred that was to hamper seriously the government's strategy since June 1679 of prosecuting London booksellers in the courts.[38]

The responsibility for choosing jury panels for London and Middlesex belonged to the two sheriffs, acting jointly as one officer, who were elected annually by the Corporation of the City of London on Midsummer Day (24 June) and entered office each year on the Vigil of Michaelmas (28 September). In the Midsummer Day election of 1680, the Common Hall of the Corporation, the majority of whose members were Whigs, chose as sheriffs Henry Cornish and Slingsby Bethel (Dryden's

"Shimei"), both avid Exclusionists. Their responsibility for selecting juries was supposed to be delegated to certain minor officials: in the case of the Middlesex Sessions, held at Hicks Hall and at Westminster Hall, to the under sheriff; in that of the London Sessions, held at the Guildhall and at the Old Bailey, to the secondaries of the two city prisons. But since Bethel and Cornish appointed as under sheriff Richard Goodenough, an eager collaborator, Middlesex juries would be regularly assured of a Whig complexion. The two officials charged with the selection of the London juries, Normandsell and Trotman, while politically independent, were personally timorous, so that under duress they could be expected to surrender their responsibility to the two sheriffs.[39]

From the end of September 1680, when the new sheriffs entered office, the attorney general would be frustrated again and again by the famous *Ignoramus* juries: grand juries of accommodating Whigs, impaneled under the direction of Bethel and Cornish, who predictably rejected bills of indictment from the government by returning them endorsed *Ignoramus*. These juries are best remembered for their actions in mid–1681 toward the end of Bethel's and Cornish's term of office when, as we shall see, they would obstruct the king's efforts to obtain justice in certain cases of treason. But they were no less effective in the autumn and winter of 1680 in providing what the government considered a cloak for sedition: protecting Whig booksellers from prosecution and ensuring that there would be no interruption of their presses.[40]

Hopelessly outnumbered by the Whig journalists and helpless to stem the flow of Whig pamphlets and broadsides after June 1679, the Tories were already tacitly admitting their serious disadvantage in the propaganda war by their bitter complaints against the freedom of the press long before the new sheriffs demolished the remaining barriers in the early autumn of 1680. As one Tory poet protested in February 1680:

What has our Law no limits for our words?
And shall our Pens cut like two-edged Swords,
And none regard them? shall our Libels swarm,
And will no Judge take notice of the harm?
Seditious Libels surely have a Charm,
There's not one Judge that dare put forth his arm.[41]

The same month two other Tory poets offered advice to the king that shows how far they had been driven back to a defensive position from which they could only warn against any further retreat. The first begs the king to "Stand firm; the times now come to shew thy skill," and portrays the ship of state tossed "By Winds and Storms" in which the king must "Keep fast the Helm, on either side to err, / Is alike dangerous, in the middle Stear." The second poet implores the king: "Lose not your Friends in hopes your Foes to gain," but "Cherish your Friends if Scepters you

will sway." His image of a land assaulted by a tidal wave expresses the
desperate tone of much Tory propaganda in this bleak season: "The
Bulks are yet intire, 'tis not too late / To stop another Deluge o're the
State."[42]

.　.　.　.　.

This is not to say that the Tory presses were inactive during the long
interval between parliaments in late 1679 and most of 1680. They kept
up a steady stream of lampoons attacking the Whig opposition. But this
simply confirms the impression of their essentially defensive position, responding to the Whigs by ridiculing their leaders, disparaging their motives, and questioning their numbers. The same is true of the Tory pamphlets and broadsides of 1679–80 defending the duke of York, warding
off attacks on the Succession, justifying the king's delay in summoning
Parliament, and appealing to some of the leaders of the opposition to
desist from their assaults on the government. All of them took their cue
from the enemy.

It is in this period of Whig aggressiveness and Tory reaction that we
find the earliest use of biblical parallelism in party warfare since the beginning of the political crisis. There are only two instances of any importance in the period we are now considering: *Naboth's Vinyard* and *Absalom's Conspiracy*, the first occasioned by the Popish Plot, and the second
by the Exclusion Crisis that succeeded it.

*Naboth's Vinyard* is neither Whig nor Tory, although some Tories
would have been sympathetic to its viewpoint. This poem was the work
of John Caryll, a member of the Catholic gentry whom Titus Oates had
implicated in the Popish Plot as early as October 1678 during one of his
first appearances before the House of Commons. It was written in 1679
during Caryll's long imprisonment in the Tower and, according to Anthony Wood, was "published by stealth in the beginning of October."[43]
The poem relates the familiar story of Naboth and Ahab found in 1
Kings, chapter 21. Ahab, king of Israel, covets Naboth's vineyard and,
when Naboth refuses to sell it to him, becomes disconsolate. Jezebel,
Ahab's wife, thereupon arranges an assembly of the elders at which two
false witnesses accuse Naboth of having blasphemed God and the king.
Naboth, being condemned, is stoned to death and Ahab takes possession
of his victim's vineyard, but Elijah is sent by God to curse Ahab and
Jezebel for their wickedness.

In relating the story of Naboth and Ahab, Caryll amplifies the historical account in 1 Kings by inventing scenes and speeches, but these are on
the whole faithful to his source. In fact he emphasizes his close adherence
to the Bible by announcing on the title page that his poem is "copied from

the original of Holy Scripture in heroick verse," and by providing cita-
tions of chapter and verse at appropriate points in the margin. Nevertheless, he modifies the biblical account in two respects. First, in his description of the two false witnesses mentioned in the Bible, to whom he
gives the invented names of Malchus and Python, Caryll alludes unmistakably to Titus Oates and Israel Tonge, the two originators of the Popish
Plot hoax, while his introduction of Arod, a corruptible judge who pre-
sides over a court of law, probably alludes to Lord Chief Justice Scroggs,
notorious for his harsh behavior toward the defendants in the early Popish Plot trials, although he had recently been treating them with greater
leniency.[44] Second, he replaces the biblical accusation that Naboth had
blasphemed God and the king with the particulars of the Popish Plot that
Oates claimed to have learned from his espionage work among the
Jesuits. Malchus is shown before the court:

> Then he the Story of his Plot at large
> Unfolds, and lays to guiltless *Naboth*'s charge,
> How with the *Aramites* he did conspire,
> His Country to invade, the City fire,
> The Temple to destroy, the King to kill,
> And the whole Realm with Desolation fill:
> He told, how he himself the *Agent* was,
> In *close Consults* to bring these things to pass;
> Nor did he fail with proper Circumstance
> Of Time, and Place, to garnish his Romance.[45]

By introducing these allusions to the present, Caryll supplies the familiar biblical story with an implicit context that transforms it into a metaphor for Protestant victimization of English Catholics accused in the
Popish Plot. Just as Ahab, although possessed of a kingdom, is driven by
covetousness of his neighbor's pitiful inheritance to acquiesce in judicial murder in order to seize Naboth's estate, so the Protestant majority,
not content to leave in peace a small and oppressed Catholic minority,
had now resorted to the testimony of false witnesses by which to deprive
their neighbors of their lives and remaining estates, both forfeited by
their condemnation for treason. The story of Naboth's vineyard thus becomes a parable in which the familiar biblical characters suggest groups
among Caryll's contemporaries, only his invented characters alluding to
individuals.

The tide of the Popish Plot had already turned when *Naboth's Vinyard*
was published, and Caryll would be released from the Tower on bail in
May 1680, a few weeks before the appearance of the second parallel,
*Absalom's Conspiracy*. By that time the Exclusion Crisis had been usurp-
ing public attention for nearly a year, and the duke of Monmouth, defy-

ing his father's wishes, was seeking the public limelight by appearing at every opportunity in company with the Whig magnates, eager enough to exploit his popularity without committing themselves to his designs on the Succession.

It was in this atmosphere of Monmouth's unofficial candidacy for a position that had not yet fallen vacant that an anonymous Tory writer published *Absalom's Conspiracy; or, The Tragedy of Treason* on 1 July 1680. This prose broadside is cast as a lay sermon against the sin of ambition, which begins by declaring that "There is nothing so dangerous either to Societies in General, or to particular Persons, as Ambition; the Temptations of Sovereignty, and the glittering Lustre of a Crown, have been guilty of all the fearful Consequences that can be within the compass of imagination." After a paragraph developing this general theme, the writer turns, in the tradition of such homilies, to a cautionary example from the Old Testament.

> Instances both Modern and Ancient of this, are innumerable; but this of *Absalom* is a Tragedy whose Antiquity and Truth, do equally recommend it as an Example to all Posterity, and a Caution to all Mankind, to take care how they imbarque in ambitious and unlawful Designs; and it is a particular Caveat to all young men, to beware of such Counsellors, as the old *Achitophel*, lest while they are tempted with the hopes of a Crown, they hasten on their own Destiny, and come to an untimely End.[46]

The remainder of the broadside recounts the entire story of Absalom's rebellion, defeat, and death, closing in the usual homiletic manner: "Whatsoever was written aforetime, was written for our Instruction: For Holy Men of God, spake as they were moved by the Holy Ghost."

As was the case with *Naboth's Vinyard*, however, *Absalom's Conspiracy* introduces a minor discrepancy into the biblical account. In relating how Absalom stole the hearts of the people, this writer amplifies the young man's words to allude to the Petitioning Movement of the previous winter: "He depraved [defamed] his Fathers Government; the King was careless, drown'd in his Pleasures; the Counsellors were evil; no man regarded the Petitioners; *Absalom* said unto [those he met], See thy matters are good and right, it is but reason that you petition for; but there is no man that will hear thee from the King; there is no Justice to be found; your Petitions are rejected." Like *Naboth's Vinyard*, therefore, *Absalom's Conspiracy* relies on its timeliness as well as a few deliberate discrepancies to alert the reader to the presence of an implicit parallel. These discrepancies are allusions to the present that in each case transform a story about the historical past into a metaphor for current affairs.

*Absalom's Conspiracy* in some respects recalls those thanksgiving sermons in which the preacher expounds the story of Absalom's rebellion before accommodating it to the Restoration. But this broadside invites an entirely different application, which is left to the readers to make for themselves, as in most political parallels.[47] In both cases the latter part of the biblical story is an important ingredient, but for completely different reasons. In the case of the thanksgiving sermons, it is the collapse of an actual rebellion and David's triumphant return that provide the closest parallel to Charles's restoration. In *Absalom's Conspiracy*, on the other hand, the parallel with Monmouth's case is found only in the early part of the story where Absalom "steals the hearts of the people" before he takes up arms against his father, while the shameful death of David's son after openly rebelling offers Monmouth a cautionary example in hopes that he will desist before this becomes his own fate. It is Absalom the seditionist, not Absalom the traitor, who affords a parallel to Monmouth at this stage in the developing political crisis, and it is he and his evil counselors, rather than David, who now become the central figures of the story.

In this earliest accommodation of the Absalom story to Monmouth's case, the anonymous author introduces two explicit exegeses of the biblical text that are absent from previous applications of the story to Charles's restoration, where they would have been irrelevant. But once the familiar history was recycled as a parallel to the Exclusion Crisis, they became indispensable to this and every succeeding appearance of the story in Tory propaganda.

Most biblical commentators on 2 Samuel believed that Absalom's mother, Maachah, was one of David's wives, and that her son therefore enjoyed all the rights of inheritance denied to the offspring of David's concubines.[48] Hence they concluded that Absalom, as his father's eldest surviving son after the death of Amnon, was David's heir both in law and in popular estimation, and that his rebellion must be ascribed to impatience to enter into his lawful inheritance, not to any wish of supplanting the rightful heir.[49] In that case, Absalom's situation is not really analogous to Monmouth's at all. But the author of *Absalom's Conspiracy* offers a diametrically opposite conception of Absalom's status and motives: "*Absalom* was the third Son of *David* by *Maachah*, the Daughter of *Talmai*, King of *Geshur*, who was one of *David*'s Concubines; he seeing his Title to the Crown upon the score of lawful Succession would not do, resolves to make good what was defective in it, by open force, by dethroning his Father." The author of a parallel of this kind is not free to alter a familiar historical episode at will, wrenching it to fit a modern counterpart, for this would be a tacit admission that no genuine analogy can be found in the original. But in the case of Absalom's rebellion the biblical text does not contradict either of the two interpretations above. Maachah may be David's wife or only his concubine, and Absalom may as easily be his heir as not, but the solution to these dilemmas cannot be found in 2 Samuel, where the events related are compatible with either interpretation, both of which are perfectly plausible.[50] Yet since the reading of the text given in *Absalom's Conspiracy* is the only one compatible with the Exclusion Crisis, this was to be the choice of all subsequent Tory propagandists.

In 2 Samuel, chapter 15, Absalom "stole the hearts of the men of Israel" and went to Hebron, taking with him two hundred men with the design of waging war against David. Only then did he send for Achitophel to come to him from Giloh. Not surprisingly, therefore, most preachers, as we noticed in the last chapter, had assumed Absalom to be the instigator and head of the rebellion. But although in *Absalom's Conspiracy* the rebellion is already under way before we meet "one *Achitophel*, an old Man of a Shrewd Head, and discontented Heart," the author argues that "no doubt can be made, but he was of the Conspiracy before, by his ready joyning with *Absalom* so soon as the matters were ripe for Execution," and he ends by referring to "*Achitophel* the Engineer of all this Mischief." In the peroration, with its cautionary application of the scriptural example, Achitophel is frankly assumed to have been the instigator of the rebellion. "Thus ended [Absalom's] youthful and foolish Ambition, making him an Eternal Monument of Infamy, and an instance of the Justice of Divine Vengeance, and what will be the Conclusion of Ambition, Treason and Conspiracy against Lawful Kings and Governours; A severe Admonition to all green Heads, to avoid the Temptations of grey *Achitophels*." Once again the events related are compatible with either interpretation, and at least one biblical commentator favored the latter, declaring that Achitophel "is thought to have been the Author, or, at least, the fomenter of this Rebellion."[51] In view of Monmouth's marginal role in the Exclusion Crisis, the popularity of this latter interpretation among succeeding Tory propagandists was inevitable.

Only a fortnight after *Absalom's Conspiracy* appeared, *A Letter to His Grace the D. of Monmouth*, published on 15 July, was applying to him once again the story of an ambitious young man seduced by "grey Achitophels" into joining them in the defamation of his father. This pamphlet is a direct appeal to Monmouth to dissociate himself from the Whig magnates who are encouraging his disobedience to his father. But in one of the last paragraphs the anonymous author resorts to biblical metaphor to castigate the prominent Whigs who had urged Monmouth to return from Holland and were now capitalizing on his popularity with the masses.

These are the Men, that would (with *Joab*) send for the Wise Woman, to per-swade King *David* to admit of a Return for *Absalom* his Son; and . . . These are the Men, that would have advised *Absalom* to make Chariots. . . . In short, these Principled Men were they that set on *Absalom* to steal away the Hearts of the People from the King; These are they that advised him to go to *Hebron* to pay his Vow; And These were the Men that led him into Actual Rebellion against his Father, and to be destroy'd by some of the very Hands that had assisted him in those pernicious Councels.[52]

As with *Absalom's Conspiracy*, the earlier part of the story affords the parallel with Monmouth's present behavior, while the ending offers him a warning to desist before this too becomes his own case: Absalom's later career shows how sedition leads insensibly to treason, disobedience and defiance precede open rebellion, and destruction inevitably follows.

I have not mentioned the name of Shaftesbury in discussing these two applications of the Absalom story in the summer of 1680, and for good reason. He is never alluded to as an individual in either of them, where the repeated use of the plural—"grey Achitophels" or "these men"—to de-scribe Absalom's seducers shows that the Whig magnates as a group are intended. This is consistent with the practice of all the authors of Tory pamphlets and broadsides throughout the entire period of the Exclusion Crisis, from the spring of 1679 to that of 1681. As early as 1679, Mon-mouth was being portrayed as a "flexible Prince" whom all the Whig leaders "would willingly have" to serve their purpose.[53] A year later, in October 1680, *The Progress of Honesty* would again describe him as a gull exploited by the entire Whig leadership.

> None Favour'd more, nor none more Great than he,
> Till Hells curst Agents caus'd his Sense to stray,
> Out of his once lov'd Path, his Loyal Way,
>     And counsell'd him to disobey;
> Friendly to his Destruction him advise,
> That on his Ruine they might rise;
> And more the weakness of his Youth to try,
> And swell his Illegitimate Ambition high,
>     With hopes to gain a Crown,
> Which they (by right) knew ne'er could be his own.[54]

And at the beginning of 1681 another Tory pamphleteer would describe Monmouth as "drawn in by designing Politicians for ends of their own, who never intended him more than as an useful Tool, afterwards to be laid aside," expressing the hope that he would soon "quit the Counsels of those men."[55]

As we would expect, Shaftesbury was a frequent target of Tory satirists throughout the Exclusion Crisis, but he was singled out from among the other Whig leaders chiefly in one respect. As early as 1679 he was being stigmatized as "a Politick Statesman, of body unsound," who had contrived the Popish Plot hoax to further his own designs:

> Pretending a Plot, under which he doth Lurk,
> To humble the Miter, while he squints at the Crown;
> Till fairly and squarely he pulls them both down.

For this purpose his tool was not Monmouth, of course, but Titus Oates:

> He had found out an Instrument fit for the Devil;
> Whose mind had been train'd up to all that was evil:
> His Fortune sunk low, and detested by many;
> Kick't out at St. *Omers*, nor pitty'd by any.[56]

Not until the early spring of 1681 brought new developments would Shaftesbury acquire a special relationship with Monmouth in the writings of Tory propagandists.

. . . . .

The king held out until the autumn of 1680, but at last he could delay the meeting of Parliament no longer. By now he was pressed for money with which to conduct his foreign affairs: an alliance with Spain concluded the previous summer, the refurbishing of the fleet, and the relief of Tangier, ceded to him under his marriage settlement with Portugal in 1661 but now besieged by the Moors. He sent his brother out of the way as he had done on the eve of the last session, and on 21 October, the day after the duke of York set off for Edinburgh, the king finally met his Parliament. His opening speech showed that he had decided to adopt new tactics to ward off Exclusion. Besides asking the members for supplies and repeating his promise to consider any expedients that would not alter the Succession, he urged them to pursue the further examination of the Plot and to that end expressed a wish "that the Lords in *The Tower* be brought to their speedy Trial, that Justice may be done."[57] This did not necessarily mean that he had decided to sacrifice the five Catholic peers to save his brother, since the death of William Bedloe the previous summer had removed the necessary second witness against most of them, but it was certainly an attempt to divert Parliament from Exclusion into an impasse over the trials like that of May 1679.

The Whigs, however, were not to be so easily distracted from what had now become their principal objective. On 2 November, less than a fortnight after the session had opened, the Commons debated and adopted a motion to bring in an Exclusion Bill, which passed its first reading two days later and its second in another two days. On 9 November the king made a last effort to divert them from their course, sending down a message urging them again to expedite the prosecution of the Plot. By an unlucky accident, a new witness, Edward Turberville, appeared before the Commons the same day, implicating one of the Catholic peers, Lord Stafford, against whom Stephen Dugdale and the late Bedloe had testified long before. Irritated by the king's attempt to seize the center of the stage and his "imputation," in Richard Hampden's words, "that you are slack in prosecuting Popery and the Plot," the members resolved to bring Stafford to trial as soon as their present business was concluded, and voted an address to the king coolly reminding him that if the trials had not yet taken place it was because of his dissolution of the last parliament and his repeated prorogations of the present one.[58] Without pausing further, the Commons on 11 November passed the Exclusion Bill on its third reading without a division and promptly sent it up to the House of Lords. There on 15 November, under the watchful eye of the king, it was debated and rejected on its first reading by a sizable majority of 63 to 30.

With the defeat of the second Exclusion Bill three and a half weeks into the session, it was now in the Whigs' interest, for once, to see Parliament prorogued quickly so that a new bill could be introduced in the next session. Just as surely, it now seemed to be in the king's interest to prolong the session, postponing as long as possible the inevitable renewal of their campaign to exclude his brother from the throne.

But the king figured without the advantage a parliamentary session offered the Whigs as the best of all public forums. As long as the session continued—and it was to drag on for nearly two more months—the Commons could "expect not much good from Bills we are like to pass," as Ralph Montagu reminded them. Therefore, "we have nothing left us but Votes."[59] And vote they did: resolutions, addresses to the king, impeachments, none of them requiring the concurrence of the Lords and all of them carrying an authority as official motions by the Commons that no other propaganda could enjoy. When the king sent them a message the same day the Exclusion Bill was lost, requesting supplies for the relief of Tangier, they returned him an address on 27 November rehearsing the long list of their complaints in recent years, deploring the protection afforded the Catholics and "the Duke of *Yorke*, under whose Countenance all the rest shelter themselves," and informing him that they would have to find the nation "effectually secured from Popery" before they were prepared "to assist Your Majesty in Defence of *Tangier*."[60] They passed a resolution demanding that Lord Halifax, who had led the debate against Exclusion in the Lords, be removed "from his Majesty's Presence and Councils for ever," which the king ignored.[61] They voted impeachments of Edward Seymour, one of the leading opponents of Exclusion in the Commons, and of Lord Chief Justice Scroggs, the king's chief supporter in the courts, and the Lords, as expected, ignored them. And every vote was preceded by angry speeches in which, as Sir Nicholas Carew remarked, "the burden of the Song is the Bill we lost in the Lords House."[62] But they avoided angering the Lords with fruitless recriminations because they suspected, as William Leveson Gower observed, that "if the Lords had been left to themselves, they would have passed this Bill as well as we."[63] The king was their stumbling block. When he came down to Westminster on 15 December and again asked for money for the relief of Tangier, repeating his promise "to concurr with you in any Remedies which might consist with preserving the Succession of the Crown in its due and legal Course of Descent," the Commons voted him an address on 20 December that was even more explicit.[64] Only the exclusion of the duke of York would preserve the safety of the realm and the security of the Protestant religion; first, then, let a bill "be tendered to Your Majesty, in a parliamentary Way, to disable the Duke of *York* from inheriting the Crown" and let the king "give Your Royal Assent thereto. . . . These our humble Requests being obtained, we shall, on our Part, be ready to assist Your Majesty for the Preservation of *Tangier*."[65]

In the Lords the king's latest speech was the subject of an equally unwelcome debate on 23 December, for the Whigs were using the upper house as a forum for speeches as bold as those in the Commons, even if they were unable to carry votes against the duke of York. Shaftesbury was unusually outspoken on this occasion, and his speech was published on 31 December as *A Speech Lately Made by a Noble Peer of the Realm*. The Lords ordered it burnt by the hangman, but by this time the damage was done, and Shaftesbury's daring words were on public record:

My Lords, 'Tis a very hard thing to say *that we cannot trust the King*; and that we have already been deceived so often, that we see plainly the apprehensions of *Discontent* in the People, is no Argument at Court. . . .

How the King hath behaved himself ever since the breaking out of [the Plot], the World knows; we have expected every hour that the Court should joyn with the Duke against us. . . .

The *Prorogations*, the *Dissolutions*, the Cutting *short* of *Parliaments*, not suffering them to *have time* or opportunity *to look into any thing*, hath shew'd what reason we have to have confidence in this *Court*. . . .

In the mean while where's *this Duke*, that the King and both Houses have declared unanimously *thus dangerous*? Why he is in *Scotland raising of Forces* upon the *Terra firma*, that can enter dry-foot upon us, without hazard of Winds or Seas, the very place he should be in to raise a party there, to be ready when from hence he shall have notice: So that this being the case, *where is the trust*?

We all think the business is *so ripe*, that they have the *Garrisons*, the *Arms*, the *Ammunition*, the *Seas* and *Souldiery* all in their *hands*; they want but one good *Summe of Money to set up*, and *Crown the Work*, and then they shall have *no more need* of the *People*; and I believe whether they are pleased or no will be no great trouble to them.

My Lords, I hear of a *Bargain* in the House *of Commons*, and an *Address* made to the *King*; but this I know, and must *boldly say it* and *plainly*, that the Nation is *Betray'd* if upon any Terms we part *with our Money* till we are *sure the King is ours*; have what *Laws* you will, and what Conditions you will, they will be of *no use* but *wast Paper* before *Easter*, if the Court have *Money to set up for Popery and Arbitrary Designs* in the mean while.[66]

A month earlier, responding to the demand of the Commons, the Lords had brought Stafford to Westminster Hall on 30 November to undergo the first of the long-awaited trials of the Catholic peers. It was to last seven days, during which the bishops absented themselves according to custom. Once they turned their attention from Exclusion to the Popish Plot, always their weak side, the Lords grew as undependable as the Commons. With the king looking on helplessly, they voted Stafford's condemnation by a majority of 55 to 31, almost the reverse of their vote against Exclusion only three weeks earlier. In the face of popular passions, the king dared not intervene beyond the usual commutation of a peer's sentence from hanging to beheading, and Stafford went to his death on Tower Hill on 29 December, vainly protesting his innocence to the last.[67]

By this time the Lords were deeply embroiled in a whole new chapter of the Popish Plot obligingly provided them by Shaftesbury. Realizing that endlessly repeated stories of the English Plot were beginning to pall and that Oates and the other English witnesses could not embroider their accounts indefinitely, Shaftesbury had sent his agent William Hetherington to Ireland in the spring of 1680 to find witnesses to an Irish Plot, the existence of which he had dramatically revealed to the Privy Council in March. In May the first of these disreputable witnesses had been brought over to testify before the Council, but the effect was not as great as Shaftesbury had hoped for, and they had been sent back to Ireland to await the meeting of Parliament.[68] In September, fourteen Irish witnesses had appeared in London in expectation of the approaching session, and Shaftesbury was now bringing one after another before the Lords to tell their stories of a conspiracy to massacre the Irish Protestants. The Lords listened with mounting alarm and on 4 January they passed and sent the Commons a resolution, in which they requested their concurrence, "That they do declare, They are fully satisfied, that there now is, and for divers Years last past there hath been, a horrid and treasonable Plot and Conspiracy, contrived and carried on by those of the Popish Religion in *Ireland*, for massacring the *English*, and subverting the Protestant Religion, and the ancient established Government of that Kingdom."[69] The Commons were happy to concur and to follow their vote with another resolving to impeach the earl of Tyrone, who had been implicated by the Irish witnesses.

There was an ominous echo to this day's proceedings. Two years earlier, on 31 October 1678, the two houses had concurred in a similar resolution attesting their belief in the English Plot, and the Commons, who had initiated the resolution on that occasion, had accompanied it with a vote the next day to impeach the first of the five Catholic peers, Lord Arundell of Wardour. The whole cycle was beginning again, but with a menacing difference. This time the Commons amended the Lords' resolution with the addition of almost the same words they had used in their own resolution on the eve of the first Exclusion Bill in April 1679: "And that the Duke of *York*'s being a Papist, and the Expectation of his coming to the Crown, hath given the greatest Countenance and Encouragement thereto, as well as to the horrid Popish Plot in this Kingdom."[70] This time there would be no six-month delay in exploiting the new plot to hasten Exclusion. Once the predictable wave of hysteria had convulsed the nation at the news of this fresh conspiracy, the Lords might prove vulnerable on what had always been their weakest side. As Sir Francis Winnington told the Commons during their debate on the resolution they had received from the upper house, "If the Lords had sooner been of this opinion, it may be, we had not lost our Bill."[71]

Next day, 7 January, the Commons took up a message they had received from the king three days earlier in which he had replied to their address of 20 December by reiterating his refusal to consider an Exclusion Bill and again asking for supplies. This occasioned the bitterest and most outspoken debate of the entire session. "Arbitrary Power has been setting up ever since King *James*'s time," Henry Booth told the House, "and Arbitrary Power will be set up with Popery; and there is no means but this Bill of Exclusion, without which, Popery and Arbitrary Power will be set up; and it is the more dangerous, because carried on so in the Court, that one would think the King had a hand in it."[72] In speeches such as this, and Shaftesbury's to the Lords two weeks earlier, the long-standing circumlocution of attacking the king's evil counselors rather than his person was gradually being abandoned, and Charles himself stood accused as a willing collaborator with his brother in a design to establish absolute monarchy on the French model in England. Under the protection of parliamentary privilege, the slogan "Popery and Arbitrary Power," long associated with the prospect of a Popish Successor, was being applied to the present reign.

At the conclusion of this important debate, the Commons voted a series of angry resolutions denouncing a number of the king's supporters by name; affirming "That there is no Security or Safety for the Protestant Religion, the King's Life, or the well constituted and established Government of this Kingdom, without passing a Bill for disabling *James* Duke of *York* to inherit the Imperial Crown of *England* and *Ireland*"; and firmly declaring "That, until a Bill be likewise passed for excluding the Duke of *York*, this House cannot give any Supply to his Majesty, without Danger to his Majesty's Person, extreme Hazard of the Protestant Religion, and Unfaithfulness to those by whom this House is intrusted." Finally, lest the king try to borrow money to relieve his financial straits, they resolved "That whosoever shall hereafter lend, or cause to be lent, by way of Advance, any Money, upon the Branches of the King's Revenue arising by Customs, Excise, or Hearth-Money, shall be judged to hinder the Sitting of Parliaments; and shall be responsible for the same in Parliament."[73]

The situation, which had been worsening since 15 November, was now getting completely out of hand. On 10 January 1681 the king came down to Westminster and, using his now familiar tactic, prorogued Parliament to 20 January, dissolving it a few days later and ordering elections for a new parliament to meet at Oxford on 21 March.

One important consideration in the king's decision to dissolve the second Exclusion Parliament may have been recent improvements in the machinery of Whig propaganda whereby, under the cloak of parliamentary privilege, the deliberations of the House of Commons were more easily carried beyond the confines of Westminster to the nation at large.

Early in 1680, an enterprising Whig bookseller had published the Journal of the House of Commons for the first of the parliamentary meetings related here, that of 21 October to 30 December 1678.[74] This proved to be so popular that he soon followed it with the same journal for the first Exclusion Parliament of 6 March to 27 May 1679.[75] As a means of publicizing the activities carried on inside St. Stephen's Chapel, the Journal of the House of Commons had its limitations, however. The resolutions, orders, and votes of the Commons were of course included, as well as the more copious addresses of the House to the king, but not the speeches and debates of the members, until then the principal source of parliamentary accusations and complaints against the Crown. Furthermore, the immediacy of the daily sittings was entirely lost in publishing their record as a single retrospective volume, and then only after an interval of a year or more.

By the time the second Exclusion Parliament met in the autumn of 1680, the new members of the lower house had obviously given some consideration to the second of these drawbacks, and to the importance of ensuring the accuracy of their reported proceedings as well as their immunity from interruption by publishing them under their own authority. On 30 October, only ten days after the opening of Parliament, the members of the Commons passed a resolution "That the Votes of this House be printed, being first perused and signed by Mr. Speaker: And that Mr. Speaker nominate and appoint the Persons to print the same."[76] From then until the dissolution of Parliament the following January, the votes, orders, and resolutions of the Commons, as well as their addresses of expostulation to the king and the articles of impeachment against such royal supporters as Seymour and Scroggs, continued to appear daily as half-sheets that could be read by the public all over the kingdom within a very short time of the events they related.[77]

It is probably a safe hypothesis that the excited rhetoric and mounting frequency of votes, resolutions, and addresses to the king passed by the House of Commons after 15 November can be explained not simply by the anger of the members over the defeat of the Exclusion Bill in the Lords, but by their awareness that every maneuver was now being reported to a national audience on a scale unprecedented since the beginning of the Exclusion Crisis. It only remained to bring before the public the speeches of the members preceding these votes, not as single orations, as in the case of Shaftesbury's speech of 23 December before the Lords, but in the context of the heated debates in which they had been offered. Early in 1681, after the dissolution of this parliament, the Whig bookseller Richard Baldwin collected the speeches in all the most important debates in the Commons and published them in a single volume, indicating the speakers by their initials and including at the end a list of the members of the House of Commons that simplified the task of identification.[78] In several important respects, therefore, the second Exclusion Parliament had developed into a public forum for the Whigs on a far greater scale than either of its two predecessors, making its dissolution even more imperative to the court than the earlier ones had been.

The Whigs, who had eagerly awaited a prorogation, were angered to find the prospect of a new session snatched from them by a dissolution, but they were not discouraged. Emboldened by their recent onslaught, they saw the king caught between the twin prongs of popular clamor and financial need, unable to escape. Each new election would authorize them to carry their appeal to the country, each new parliament recall them to the public forum, each new dissolution drive the king deeper into an indefensible position toward his subjects. Meanwhile, his financial plight would reinforce the pressure of public opinion. Unable to live without Parliament and denied any relief when it met, he must ultimately give way and sacrifice his brother.

In spite of Whig propaganda, therefore, portraying this as a time of national mourning in which, if we are to believe *England's Mournful*

*Elegy for the Dissolving the Parliament*, published on 21 January, the nation was overcome with grief, "Tears of Sorrow trickling from our Eyes, / Follow'd with Tempests of Heart-breaking sighs," the Whig politicians entered the new elections buoyed by hopes of increasing their momentum.[79] The outcome itself was never in doubt, most of the same Whigs being elected as before, but their return to the hustings in February and March 1681 offered them an even better opportunity than the Petitioning Movement the year before to create a mass movement that they could exploit as valuable propaganda. Each Whig victory at the polls was now accompanied by a public ceremony in which the electors presented the successful candidate with an address specifying the "particulars" he was expected to support in the new parliament and pledging "to stand by You with our Lives and Fortunes." In return, the member made a speech in which he thanked the electors for their support and promised to carry out their mandate.

This new mass movement, like the Petitioning Movement the previous winter, depended for its success on the existence of Whig newspapers to give national prominence to these local events. In December, through the connivance of the Whigs, Benjamin Harris had been released from the King's Bench prison, and five days later the *Protestant Domestick Intelligence* was again being offered for sale. The same day, 28 December, witnessed the first appearance of Langley Curtis's *True Protestant Mercury*, which would prove to be one of the most effective Whig newspapers and would continue to be published twice weekly for nearly two years. In another month, on 1 February 1681, *Smith's Protestant Intelligence*, from the hands of the notorious antigovernment printer Francis "Elephant" Smith, would join the growing ranks of Whig newspapers.

These journalists made sure that the ceremonies at the polling places would not remain local events. From mid-February to mid-March, issue after issue of Harris's *Protestant Domestick Intelligence* carried the news of these elections and printed the addresses, most of which included among their particulars the passing of an Exclusion Bill, while some carried an instruction like that of the Essex electors to their knights of the shire "that You will not consent to the disposal of any of our Monies, till we are effectually secured against *Popery* and *Arbitrary Power*."[80] The lone exception reported by Harris, emphasizing its deviation from the norm, was a Tory victory at Cricklade, in Wiltshire, where the address omitted the usual particulars, substituting an instruction to the burgesses that they "endeavor the preservation of His Sacred Majesties Royal Prerogative."[81]

The third dissolution of a parliament in two years had hastened the process by which the issue of the king's prerogative came to share equal attention with Exclusion in the mind of the public. The two Whig pam-

phlets that created the greatest stir in the weeks preceding the Oxford
Parliament, significantly enough, were *The Character of a Popish Successor* and *Vox Populi; or, The Peoples Claim to Their Parliaments Sitting,
to Redress Grievances, and Provide for the Common Safety*, which divided between them the two topics of most pressing importance in the late
winter of 1681. The former repeated with greater urgency the now familiar theme that Exclusion was the only practical means "to disable a Tyrant from wearing a Crown" in the next reign.[82] The latter, addressing
itself to the present reign, dismissed the claim that proroguing or dissolving parliaments "before Grievances were Redressed, and Publick Bills of
Common Safety Passed" was "a Priviledge, belonging to the Royal Prerogative" by declaring that "Prerogative [cannot] be pleaded to Justify
such Practices, because the King has no Prerogative, but what the Law
gives him; and it can give none to destroy its self, and those it protects, but
the contrary." Indeed, "not to suffer Parliaments to sit to answer the great
ends for which they were Instituted, is expressly contrary to the Common
Law, and so consequently of the Law of God as well as the Law of Nature, and thereby Violence is offered to the Government it self, and In-
fringement of the Peoples fundamental Rights and Liberties."[83] The king
had overtaken the duke of York as a second target whom the Tories must
cast about to defend in an unequal contest before the public.

Small wonder that, in the face of this flood of Whig propaganda, sedition became a favorite topic of the anniversary preachers, mindful of their
duty to discourage disobedience among the faithful. Thus, for his thanksgiving sermon on 29 May 1680, Thomas Long had chosen to preach *A
Sermon against Murmuring*, citing the dreadful fates of Corah, Absalom
and Achitophel, and Shimei, and lamenting in the "Epistle Dedicatory"
to his bishop how men were now grown so presumptuous that "they are
not afraid to insinuate as if the King favoured the Plot, which hath been
declared to be against His Majesties person, and the Established Religion.
They quarrel the Succession, and would put by the true and undoubted
Heir. They insinuate that His Majesty is no friend to Parliaments, and
would Rule us by an Arbitrary power."[84] The following January, Samuel
Crossman preached his martyrdom sermon for 1681 on the same topic,
using as his examples Absalom, who "had perfectly learned this knack of
popular wheedling," and "*Corah* a very busie seditious Stickler," and
sending his congregation away with the assurance that "the Mercies we
enjoy under our Government, they are many, even to the envy of other
Nations. And oh that we did but understand our own Happiness! it might
fairly silence our Murmurings."[85] On the same day, Francis Turner,
preaching a martyrdom sermon before the king, used the occasion to de-
nounce "so many *Absoloms* and *Shimeis* and *Shebas* that have rebell'd
and rail'd and blown the Trumpet of Sedition against their Kings."[86]

This was the low tide of the Tories' fortunes. In the face of a mounting outcry against Popery and Arbitrary Power, their propaganda was reduced to a feeble defense in which they were forced to evade Whig charges instead of answering them and to adopt a kind of secular quietism. A typical expression of Tory low spirits in January appears in *A Letter from a Citizen of Oxford to a Citizen of London, concerning the Dissolution of the Parliament*, whose author weakly suggests, "I think it would become us Citizens much better to mind our Trades, and our Shops, then to meddle with State-affairs: For no doubt those at the Helm know better what to do, then we can tell them"; expresses pained surprise that "You daily acquaint me with the Fears you are in of Arbitrary Government, and yet I cannot see what Reasons and Grounds you have for them"; and counsels "a perfect Resignation and Submission."[87] The same attitude appears in another Tory pamphlet of this period, *A Letter from Scotland, Written Occasionally upon the Speech Made by a Noble Peer of This Realm*, which can find no better response to Shaftesbury's aggressive speech in the Lords the previous month than to lament "such Reflections made with impunity upon the Kings Person and Government," and to express the pious sentiment that "the Calling, the Proroguing, and the Dissolving of Parliaments, are so absolutely in the King, that they ought to be Riddles to a Subject."[88]

Yet arguments such as these unwittingly reinforced Whig propaganda. A king who possesses "absolutely" the prerogative of acting from caprice as easily as from reasons of state, and whose actions are riddles to his subjects, is exercising arbitrary power in fact if not in name. The crucial issue that Tory propagandists needed to address if they were to exonerate the king from charges of despotism was not whether he had a right to dissolve parliaments but whether his motive in exercising that prerogative so frequently was to destroy the laws or to protect them. And until the king chose to reveal that motive in unambiguous terms, Tory propagandists were at a serious disadvantage in trying to defend him.

. . . . .

It is time to turn to Dryden's activities during all this excitement and to consider what role, if any, he was taking in the party propaganda I have discussed. Throughout the period of the Popish Plot hysteria and the Exclusion Crisis, from the autumn of 1678 to the beginning of 1681, Dryden was pursuing his career as a playwright, as he had been doing, almost exclusively, since 1667: producing plays for the stage, writing dedications and prefaces to them when they were published, and composing prologues and epilogues both to his own plays and to those of his fellow dramatists. Between the outbreak of the Popish Plot hysteria and the end

of the Exclusion Crisis, he wrote two plays: *Troilus and Cressida*, produced in March or April 1679, during the early weeks of the first Exclusion Parliament, and *The Spanish Fryar*, first performed in November
1680, several weeks after the second Exclusion Parliament had commenced.[89]

There have been various attempts in recent years to find political content in these plays. One method has been to single out the political issues
discussed by the characters in the course of the play.[90] These are not difficult to find, since, like most of Dryden's serious plays written at any period of his career, *Troilus and Cressida* and *The Spanish Fryar* represent
public events that inevitably involve political issues. But as Irvin Ehrenpreis has observed,

> In trying to decide whether the doctrines expressed in a play are those of Dry-
> den or of his characters, one meets tantalizing difficulties. First, Dryden pro-
> duces his allusions or doctrines spasmodically. Every now and then he breaks
> into a passage of political implication, then returns simply to the action of his
> play. What is worse, he sometimes gives his own doctrines to evil characters.
> For one cannot be sure, simply because a character is reprehensible, that he
> always quarrels with the playwright. Besides, Dryden simply enjoyed arguing
> on both sides of a question. He prided himself on his ability to defend a point
> of view which in fact he disagreed with. As a result, one hears characters speak-
> ing very persuasively indeed for doctrines which the play invites us to resist.[91]

An alternative method is to search for political meaning in the dramatic
action of the plays rather than the speeches of the characters. Critics have
been especially prone to look for overt political partisanship in *The Spanish Fryar*, encouraged by the fact that its first performance took place
during the turbulent fortnight in which the second Exclusion Bill passed
through the House of Commons, only to be defeated in the upper house.
The comic plot from which the play takes its title uses the figure of Father
Dominick to ridicule Catholicism mercilessly. The serious plot of this
tragicomedy set in Spain presents a kingdom in which the rightful ruler
has been deposed and imprisoned, while a usurper, the daughter of the
rebel who had ousted him, occupies the legitimate king's throne. Believing she has succeeded in arranging the royal prisoner's murder, the queen
marries Torrismond, one of her generals, who subsequently learns to his
horror that his wife's supposed victim is his own father, and finds himself
torn between the claims of justice and his love for the queen. Eventually,
however, the king is discovered to be alive. He is restored to his throne by
universal acclamation and the play ends in general forgiveness.

The comic plot, deriding Catholicism at a time when the outcry over
the Popish Plot was serving Whig interests, excited comment even in Dryden's lifetime. In *The Laureat*, an attack on the poet published in 1687,

Robert Gould charged that he had written *The Spanish Fryar* when the government stopped payment on his pension, which led him to join the opposition for a while in disgust.

> That lost, the Visor chang'd, you turn about,
> And strait a True Blue Protestant crept out;
> The Fryar now was writ: and some will say
> They smell a Male-content through all the Play.
> The Papist too was damn'd, unfit for Trust,
> Call'd Treacherous, Shameless, Profligate, Unjust,
> And Kingly Power thought Arbitrary Lust.[92]

The absurdity of this charge has been demonstrated repeatedly by Dryden's biographers from Malone and Scott in the nineteenth century to Louis I. Bredvold in our own.[93]

The latest, and most interesting, attempt to discover political significance in the dramatic action of *The Spanish Fryar*, since it takes into account both the comic and the serious plots, is that of Judith Milhous and Robert D. Hume, who argue that the serious plot is "a blunt and timely warning against rebellion and usurpation," while the comic plot "uses blatant satire on Dominic to dissociate the Tories from Catholicism." Thus "Dryden loudly reaffirms legitimacy, while firmly underlining his 'Protestant' loyalty." They conclude, therefore, that "*The Spanish Fryar* is a first-rate piece of Tory propaganda, and one cleverly calculated to resist Whig objections or reinterpretation."[94]

This recognition that there is no political inconsistency between Dryden's two plots is certainly a welcome one. But to call such a play "Tory propaganda" is to use both these terms so loosely that they become meaningless. We have seen what the task of Tory propagandists was in November 1680, and how, in a beleaguered situation, they attempted to carry it out by opposing the Exclusion Bill, attacking its supporters, and defending the royal policy. The topics Milhous and Hume identify in the two plots of *The Spanish Fryar*, on the other hand, are not issues that divided the two parties or were seriously questioned by either side. No respectable Whig writer at this time can be found espousing "rebellion and usurpation," to say nothing of attempted regicide, and when such ideas appeared the following year in Stephen College's *Ra-ree Show* and Edward Fitzharris's *True Englishman*, they were quickly denounced as treasonable by both parties. Similarly, anti-Catholic sentiments were affirmed as widely by Tories as by Whigs, not only because they were eager to dissociate themselves from charges of complicity with the Catholics, but because they were genuinely susceptible to inherited religious prejudice. Some Tory writers, as we have seen, believed the Popish Plot a hoax contrived by Shaftesbury, although the official position represented by the king's own speeches accepted it as a genuine conspiracy. But all Tories, practically without exception, whether or not they believed in the Plot, shared with Whigs the national hostility toward the Catholic religion and its priesthood.

Susan Staves has cautioned that "it cannot be stressed too often how frequently practical Whigs and practical Tories agreed on important issues, how ideology shifted with the new illuminations of new circumstances, and how fluid political alliances were throughout the Restoration." As she observes,

> Most Whigs and most Tories protested their devotion to monarchy and to protestantism, abhorred the thought of another civil war, considered the law a relevant curb on policy, and claimed that a study of British history showed their position to rest on tradition and their opponents' position to be an innovation. Both sides tended to idealize a harmonious mixed monarchy in which parliament respected the king's prerogative and the king valued parliamentary counsel and respected parliamentary privilege. Division occurred when it was necessary to determine precisely what these prerogatives and privileges were.[95]

When Whig writers label the Tories the "Popish Party" and Tory writers respond, as we have seen, by equating Whigs with biblical rebels, both groups are using the hyperbole of party propaganda to stigmatize their opponents with those very images that both abhor. No reasonable partisan for either side could be expected to equate deposing, imprisoning, and conspiring to murder a king with the attempt in November 1680 to pass into law, by parliamentary means, a change in the Succession. On the contrary, Dryden gives every sign here of deliberately avoiding controversial topics that could have alienated any part of his audience, and of choosing to represent in his play those very aspects of both politics and religion that were least likely to give offense to the spectators. There could have been few members of his audience who would have questioned those commonplaces on the stage which they were accustomed to hearing without protest from the pulpit: that rebellion, usurpation, and regicide were heinous crimes in the sight of God, and that the hypocrisy, lust, and venality widely credited to the Catholic clergy were a scourge from which the Reformation had mercifully delivered them. But *The Spanish Fryar* is not a sermon, nor even a thesis play, much less "a topical partisan document." It takes for granted a system of values that all members of the audience can be expected to share in despising Dominick, sympathizing with Torrismond's moral dilemma, and welcoming the rightful king's restoration.[96]

As a professional man of the theater, Dryden's primary interest at this time was in ensuring the success of his plays by appealing to all members of his prospective audience and by avoiding overt political partisanship that would have alienated any considerable segment. Obviously, such neutrality implies nothing about Dryden's private loyalty to the court in its struggle with Parliament, for it is based on pragmatic rather than political considerations. Indeed, the prologues and epilogues he was writing at this same time for his own plays and for those of other dramatists confirm the impression that his political stance in the theater was tailored to those prejudices held in common by most of the audience.

It is common practice in Restoration prologues and epilogues to allude to contemporary events of interest to the audience, and those which Dryden wrote during the excitement over the Popish Plot and the Exclusion Crisis are no exception. Many, though not all of them, mention the public events taking place during these months. By paying exclusive attention to a few of them and extracting certain lines from their context, it is possible to piece together ostensible evidence that Dryden was openly expressing his own political sentiments in the theater at this time. But Dryden wrote some twenty-seven prologues and epilogues to his own plays and those of his fellow dramatists between the supposed discovery of the Popish Plot and the end of 1682. In using them, it is essential to pay close attention to their chronology and to consider as well the audience for whom each of them was written. Approximately half of these prologues and epilogues, those written before early 1681 with which we are concerned here, are markedly different from the remainder, composed after that time, which I shall consider in the next chapter. And throughout these four years Dryden was writing his contributions to the theater for two very different audiences. The majority were designed for regular performances of plays during the season at one or the other of the two London theaters. But during the summer when the London theaters were closed, Dryden also wrote prologues and epilogues for special performances at Oxford before the members of the university.

The prologues and epilogues that Dryden wrote before early 1681 display the usual characteristics of that minor genre. Rather than being either personal testaments or political propaganda, they are addresses by one of the players to the audience, attempting to win their good will. They create in advance a favorable frame of mind among the spectators about to watch the play, or send them home afterward in a contented mood, prepared to recommend the play to their friends. Dryden employs a dramatic voice in each of these prologues and epilogues that is adapted to its particular audience. For an academic audience at Oxford, he adopts a humorous tone tempered by a subtle deference that is always gratifying to an assembly of scholars. At Drury Lane or Dorset Garden, he adopts a bantering tone toward his audience of Londoners, producing the kind of comic raillery that in the epilogue to his own *Troilus and Cressida* was appropriately spoken by Cave Underhill, who played Thersites. This

good-humored abuse had long been part of the recognized contract between the players and the London audience, amused without being of-
fended by the expected banter, and won over by rough camaraderie.

> The most compendious method is to rail:
> Which you so like, you think your selves ill us'd
> When in smart Prologues you are not abus'd.
> A civil Prologue is approv'd by no man;
> You hate it as you do a Civil woman.[97]

All Dryden's prologues and epilogues before early 1681, however different the tone in which he solicits the audience at Oxford or London, aim
at the same objective: to create a bond of mutual interest between players
and spectators by exploiting a shared contempt or hostility toward some
alien group. Before the university audience at Oxford, that bedrock of
allegiance to the religious and political establishment, Dryden's prologues in the summers of 1679 and 1680 express a mutual antagonism
toward dissenters from the Established Church, dissidents from the court,
and promoters of the Popish Plot hysteria that implies a firm alliance
between scholars and players.

> But 'tis the Talent of our *English* Nation,
> Still to be Plotting some New Reformation:
> And few years hence, if Anarchy goes on,
> *Jack Presbyter* shall here Erect his Throne.
>
> .  .  .  .  .  .  .  .  .  .  .  .  .  .  .
>
> Then all you Heathen Wits shall go to Pot,
> For disbelieving of a Popish Plot.

This is a prospect as dreadful for the players as it is for their academic
audience. "Nor shou'd we scape the Sentence, to Depart, / Ev'n in our
first Original, A Cart." Actors and scholars would be common sufferers
in a fate where "Religion, Learning, Wit, wou'd be supprest." Therefore
they are natural allies in opposing any change in church or state:

> This is our comfort, none e're cry'd us down,
> But who dislik'd both *Bishop* and a *Crown*.[98]

Back in London, however, Dryden caters to very different sympathies
in his prologues and epilogues for the spectators at Dorset Garden in
these same years, 1679 and 1680. Here the shared attitudes that create a
strong bond between the players and the London audience are chiefly
xenophobia and anti-Catholic prejudice.

> When Murther's out, what Vice can we advance?
> Unless the new found Pois'ning Trick of *France*:

And when their Art of *Rats-bane* we have got,
By way of thanks, we'll send 'em o'er our *Plot*.[99]

Poisoning is, in fact, endemic to foreigners, especially those who live in Catholic lands:

They have a civil way in *Italy*
By smelling a perfume to make you dye,
A Trick would make you lay your Snuff-box by.
Murder's a Trade—so known and practis'd there,
That 'tis Infallible as is the Chair—
But mark their Feasts, you shall behold such Pranks,
The Pope says Grace, but 'tis the Devil gives Thanks.[100]

It would be a mistake to assume that these appeals to religious and national prejudice were attempts to appease the Whigs in particular. Unlike the academic audiences at Oxford—stable, fairly homogeneous, and widely recognized as Tory sympathizers—the audiences in London were a heterogeneous lot who would have included many supporters of both parties. In choosing to make comic butts of Catholics and foreigners and to appeal to the widespread agreement between both parties on the existence (though not necessarily the extent) of the Popish Plot, Dryden identifies an alien group that is best calculated to promote a spurious feeling of cohesiveness among a diverse audience who, whatever their political differences among each other, can momentarily join forces as Protestant Englishmen sharing a common prejudice.

The dedications Dryden provided to his two plays of this period show the same refusal to identify himself as a captive of the Tories as long as he continued his career as a professional man of the theater. Earlier, in March 1678, in dedicating *All for Love* to Danby, he had shown no compunction in parading his own political sympathies. At a time when the king's chief minister was beset with difficulties created by the war with France and facing enemies at home who were determined to bring him down, Dryden warmly defended him, supported his administration, and assailed his opponents. Once the Popish Plot hysteria had broken out the following autumn, however, Dryden appears to have been less willing to alienate a faction that, with far different issues at stake, now included a considerable part of the nation, and consequently of the audience in the theater.

*Troilus and Cressida*, published in the autumn of 1679 during the long interval between the first and second Exclusion Parliaments, was dedicated to the earl of Sunderland, one of the principal secretaries of state. A nephew by marriage of Shaftesbury, with whom he was on good terms, Sunderland also enjoyed the favor of the king. At this time, in fact, he was widely regarded as a well-intentioned mediator between the two parties, and this is the role in which Dryden presents him in his dedication, where he declares "that his principles were full of moderation, and all his Councils such as tended to heal and not to widen the breaches of the Nation," that he was "chosen out in the necessity and pressure of affairs, to remedy our confusions by the seasonableness of his advice, and to put a stop to our ruine, when we were just rowling downward to the precipice." Dryden's studied neutrality here is suggested not only by his choice of this preeminent moderate as the recipient of his dedication but by his reticence in assigning blame for "our confusions." As a concerned bystander, he is satisfied to deplore "the breaches of the Nation" and to hope for an end to them: "the quiet of the Nation must be secur'd; and a mutuall trust, betwixt Prince and people, be renew'd: and then this great and good man [Sunderland] will have leisure for the ornaments of peace."[101]

In his dedication to *The Spanish Fryar*, Dryden carries his pose as an indifferent bystander exhibiting goodwill toward all parties to a point where he runs the danger of being misunderstood. Published in the second week of March 1681, during the excitement created by the elections for the Oxford Parliament, *The Spanish Fryar* is ostensibly dedicated to John Holles, Lord Haughton. This youth, who had only recently celebrated his nineteenth birthday, was as yet an insignificant figure, however, and in his final paragraph Dryden reveals that he has chosen the young man as the occasion for praising his family.

> 'Tis difficult to write justly on any thing, but almost impossible in Praise. I shall therefore wave so nice a subject; and onely tell you, that in recommending a Protestant Play to a Protestant Patron, as I doe my self an Honour, so I do your Noble Family a right, who have been alwaies eminent in the support and favour of our Religion and Liberties. And if the promises of your Youth, your Education at home, and your Experience abroad, deceive me not, the Principles you have embrac'd are such as will no way degenerate from your Ancestors, but refresh their memory in the minds of all true *English-men*, and renew their lustre in your Person; which, My Lord, is not more the wish than it is the constant expectation of your Lordship's *Most obedient, faithfull Servant*, John Dryden.[102]

Who were the members of this noble family of Holles who had been "alwaies eminent in the support and favour of our Religion and Liberties?" The patriarch of the family was Denzil Holles, still remembered today as one of the five members whom Charles I tried to arrest on the floor of the House of Commons in January 1642 on the eve of the first Civil War. Raised to the peerage after the Restoration, Lord Holles was instrumental in helping to organize an opposition among the members of the upper chamber, and it was at his house in early 1674 that Shaftesbury and his fellow peers held the meetings at which they began to formulate a concerted policy against the administration.[103] Lord Holles died in February 1680, but as his last public action he was one of seventeen Whig peers, including Shaftesbury, who led off the great Petitioning Movement in December 1679 by calling on the king to allow Parliament to meet to redress the nation's grievances, just as, some forty years earlier, he had supported the Grand Remonstrance to the king's father.[104] This parting shot earned Holles a final resting place in a Tory broadside published the day after his death, where he rounds out a satiric gallery of Shaftesbury and the other Whig leaders:

> And last, behold in Triumph to their Follies,
> In *Nol*'s own Coach of State, comes Loyal *Hollis*,
> Who sold the Father by an old Commission,
> And purchases the Son with a Petition.[105]

The second member of the family, Denzil's son and heir, Sir Francis Holles, was elected to his father's old seat in the House of Commons in the spring of 1679 and was promptly marked down by Shaftesbury on his famous list of "worthy" and "honest" men on whom he could depend in the approaching session.[106] His hopes were not misplaced. In May 1679, Sir Francis Holles voted for the first Exclusion Bill.[107]

But for dedicated service to the Whig cause carried out in the limelight, no other member of this noble family could equal Lord Haughton's father, Gilbert Holles, earl of Clare. He too had been one of the signers, along with his uncle Denzil, of the petition to the king in December 1679, and, as a Whig pamphlet immediately made public, was one of a smaller number of peers who presented it in person to Charles II.[108] On 30 June 1680, Lord Clare was one of nineteen Whig leaders, including Shaftesbury, who appeared before the grand jury of Middlesex and sought to have the duke of York indicted as a Popish recusant. The attempt failed, but it was well publicized in a Whig broadside giving the names of those who had taken part.[109] Lord Clare was not a man to make a secret of his political sympathies. In the great debate in the House of Lords on 15 November 1680, he not only voted for Exclusion but was one of a smaller number of Whig peers, Shaftesbury among them, who signed a protest against the rejection of the bill, thus ensuring that their support of the second Exclusion Bill would be made a matter of public record.[110] Most recently, Lord Clare had been one of sixteen Whig peers, again including Shaftesbury, who on 25 January 1681 signed a petition calling on the king to allow the approaching parliament to meet at Westminster rather than at Oxford, "where neither Lords nor Commons can be in safety, but will be daily exposed to the Swords of the Papists and their adherents, of whom to many have crept into Your Majesties Guards." The king ignored this provocation, but again a Whig broadside immediately appeared, listing the names of the signers.[111]

That parliament, where the Whigs were expected to make their third attempt to pass an Exclusion Bill, was about to meet at Oxford on the twenty-first of the month when Dryden's play and its dedication went on sale in the second week of March 1681. We can easily believe that Dryden esteemed the Holles family on personal grounds and that he may have been obliged to them for favors he wished to repay. But in deciding at this moment to single out for public praise their "support and favour of our Religion and Liberties" and to express the hope that the young Lord Haughton would embrace their principles, he carried his public stance as a playwright indifferent to party divisions to a point where it must have raised doubts in some minds about the image of neutrality he was apparently cultivating.

These doubts would have been compounded by the manner in which his new play was publicized. At the time of the Exclusion Crisis, books reflecting support for either party were normally offered for sale in a newspaper sharing the same political sympathies. Jacob Tonson chose to advertise *The Spanish Fryar* not in the *London Gazette*, which was carrying book advertisements regularly at this time, but in Langley Curtis's stridently Whig newspaper, the *True Protestant Mercury*, where in the following year would be advertised such angry Whig rejoinders to Dryden as *Azaria and Hushai*, *The Medal Revers'd*, and *Absalom Senior*. The issue of the *True Protestant Mercury* for 12 March 1681 carried advertisements for only two books: Dryden's Protestant play and the second edition of Henry Care's *History of the Damnable Popish Plot*, the popular Whig answer to Roger L'Estrange's Tory *History of the Plot*.

This is a curious incident that has not previously attracted comment, and it would be a mistake to make too much of it, or to consider it in isolation from Dryden's other dedications. In the span of exactly three years, he had dedicated plays to three individuals who either alone or in company with their families covered the entire political spectrum: Danby in March 1678, before the beginning of the crisis, Sunderland in the autumn of 1679, and the scion of the Holles family in March 1681.[112] This is simply further evidence of Dryden's public stance throughout the hysteria over the Popish Plot and the Exclusion Crisis as a playwright who solicited the approbation of the public for his theatrical productions by expressing good will to all parties while deploring the confusions in the nation created by their differences. His temporary withdrawal from the theater after *The Spanish Fryar* appeared, just at the time the political tide was about to turn, marked a critical change in his career, and when he returned to the stage at the end of November 1682 with *The Duke of Guise*, it would be as a Tory propagandist who had been actively engaged on the side of the court for over a year, but in the different medium of poetry.

This was no comfort to the Tories, however, in the bleak winter of 1680–81. At the low tide of their fortunes, when they would have welcomed support, and indeed from the very beginning of the political crisis two and a half years earlier, Dryden had not been at their side to encourage them. But Whig hopes and Tory discouragement at the time of elections for the Oxford Parliament were both misplaced. Events were about to take a turn that the propagandists on neither side could foresee in January and February 1681. The approaching parliament and its abrupt demise would mark a final stage in the history of the Exclusion Crisis as crucial as the beginning of the crisis produced by the dissolution of Parliament in the summer of 1679. This time, however, the initiative would come from the king rather than his antagonists.

## Chapter 3

## THE NATION'S SAVIOR

THE SAME CONSIDERATIONS from which the Whigs drew fresh hope in early 1681 could only convince the king and his advisers that he must bring a halt to the cycle of summoning, proroguing, and dissolving parliaments in which, as recent experience proved, his position was rapidly deteriorating. He must find the means of dispensing with parliaments, abandon his delaying tactics, and overcome his inertia. Matters had reached a critical stage in which his only hope for escape lay in finding ways of relieving both kinds of pressure—financial and popular—responsible for his present plight.

.  .  .  .  .

The easier of these two tasks was to find relief from his financial straits. The Commons had always been hampered in applying to Charles their traditional means of influencing the executive through their right to originate money bills. In the era of good feeling following the Restoration, Parliament had ensured that the king's ordinary revenue would be largely independent of its control. The Convention Parliament in 1660 had awarded him the yield from the customs and excise for life, and two years later the Cavalier Parliament had voted him the revenue from the hearth tax in perpetuity. Thanks to the financial reforms introduced by Danby as lord treasurer, the king's income from these principal sources of his revenue had been doubled since the mid-1670s.[1] His expenses had usually been great and he had been forced again and again to turn to Parliament for additional revenues nominally intended for his foreign policy but sometimes, as had happened at the time of the first Disbandment Act, diverted to other purposes. Recently, however, he had been practicing economies, and £100,000 a year to supplement his ordinary revenues would spell the difference between financial independence and reliance on Parliament with whom his credit was exhausted. The solution was a French subsidy of the kind Danby had been caught trying to negotiate in 1678. This had its dangers, as his disgraced minister could testify, but Charles could not afford to be squeamish at this juncture, and the resource he was now again considering had already proved successful in the past. A subsidy of £100,000 from the king of France had provided him with a fifteen-month respite from Parliament between November 1675 and February 1677. Now, in January and February 1681, he negotiated with Barrillon, the French ambassador, for another and larger subsidy from Louis XIV that would give him an indefinite term of freedom from Parliament. Louis welcomed the prospect of being able to carry on his foreign policy without fear of English interference, and the only differences needing to be worked out concerned the size of Charles's annual allowance. Well before Parliament met in March, the king was assured of a French subsidy although its terms were not yet settled, and the day after it opened he concluded the secret verbal agreement with Barrillon whereby he would receive a generous allowance over the next three years in return for not allowing Parliament to meet. Seldom can a beneficiary have been more eager to carry out the donor's conditions.

Recent historians have been practically unanimous in regarding this arrangement as the decisive event freeing Charles from any further need to call parliaments. In this view, the Oxford Parliament, summoned before the conclusion of the French treaty, had become an anachronism by the time it met, forcing the king to produce the semblance of a session before dissolving it at the earliest opportunity. But depriving the Whigs of the public forum offered them by parliamentary sessions was no longer an adequate solution to the king's difficulties. Whig propaganda had by now achieved sufficient momentum, and popular excitement a critical stage, in which the king could not again ignore public opinion while he stubbornly lived without Parliament as he had found it possible to do between May 1679 and October 1680. It would be fruitless for Charles to relieve his financial pressure if he did not find the means of reducing popular pressure as well. He could now manage to live without Parliament only if he found it possible to live with his people. The Crown's course, once it had solved its financial difficulties, must be to turn at once to the task of reducing popular fears and restoring public calm. The French subsidy was a necessary but not a sufficient condition for the king's dispensing with Parliament.

In summoning a new parliament in mid-January before he could be sure of the subsidy from Louis XIV, Charles may have been acting from recent habit without having perfected his plans. But he had no reason to doubt that the repeated promises made by the late Commons to vote him no money without Exclusion were every bit as firm as his own promises to them never to assent to the same. He also had no reason to expect the new elections to change the composition of the Commons, nor to be surprised when they returned another massive Whig majority. From the very outset, therefore, he could have been swayed by neither of his two motives for summoning the earlier parliaments: the hope of obtaining supplies and the slim prospect of a more amenable House of Commons. In any case, once the French subsidy and the Whig majority in the new Commons became practical certainties by early March, his obvious course, if he now regretted having summoned Parliament and could have ignored public opinion with impunity, would have been to prorogue it in advance of its opening, and to continue to prorogue it thereafter as he had done in 1679 and 1680. Instead, he allowed Parliament to meet at the earliest opportunity: 21 March, the date originally set for its opening. This strongly suggests that at some time over the preceding weeks the king had settled on a goal more ambitious than a financial bargain, and had decided on adopting a new policy in which the Oxford Parliament could be used to his advantage.

Charles's policy since 1678 had been one of dissimulation in which he had adopted a posture of good will toward Parliament that at times was almost fawning, while yielding as little as possible. This had served him well enough as a delaying tactic, and while he expressed eagerness to prosecute the Plot, protect the Protestant religion, and consider any expedients short of surrendering his prerogative and altering the Succession, he had made sure that Parliament accomplished little. But it was a tactic that no longer deceived his antagonists and had begun to dishearten his supporters. The Whigs saw through his professions of good will, and Shaftesbury spoke for many of them when he told the Lords that "we cannot trust the King." Meanwhile his posture was perceived as weakness by his supporters throughout the country, badly disorganized, increasingly discouraged, and driven back to a defensive position that seemed about to crumble. They desperately needed effective leadership from the court and something more than a defensive policy if they were to avoid imminent defeat. The author of a Tory poem, *The Country-mans Complaint, and Advice to the King*, published on 9 February while the Whigs were sweeping to victory at the polls, spoke for many adherents of the court when he bitterly complained of the state of the nation in these unhappy times: "Poor Land! whose Folly to swift Ruine tends, / Despis'd by Foes, unaided by its Friends." The poem ends with an appeal "To the King" that is openly critical of Charles's failure to bestir himself and provide his supporters with the leadership they had a right to expect from him:

> Arise, O thou once Mighty *Charles*, arise,
> Dispel those mists that cloud thy piercing Eyes;
> Read o're thy Martyr'd Father's Tragick Story,
> Learn by his Murder, different ways to glory.
> How fatal 'tis, by him is understood,
> To yield to Subjects, when they thirst for Blood,
> And cloak their black designs with Publick Good.
> As thou art God-like by thy *Pity*, show

That thou art God-like by thy *Justice* too:
Lest we should count thy greatest Vertue, Vice,
And call thy Mercy, servile Cowardise.
Of old, when daring Giants skal'd the Skie,
The King of Gods ne're laid his Thunder by,
To hear Addresses for their Property.
But quell'd *His* Rebels by a stroke Divine,
And left example how to deal with *Thine*.[2]

Complaints of this kind do not suggest that the king's supporters were wavering, but that they were impatiently awaiting a signal to take the offensive. Propagandists can only be effectively employed as supporting forces, not as advance battalions; it is not their business to make policy but to justify it. Clearly the king must exert himself and take the initiative if he was to rally his supporters and launch the propaganda effort necessary for dispensing with Parliament. For this purpose, the Oxford Parliament would serve as a brief dramatic performance in which the king could appear in a new role while the Whigs unwittingly cooperated by playing their customary parts.

.   .   .   .   .

The performance opened in the Geometry School on Monday, 21 March, with a speech by the king. In its substance, this speech could not be expected to differ much from his earlier ones. Once again he asked for supplies with which to cement his foreign alliances, recommended "the further Prosecution of the Plot, the Tryall of the Lords in the Tower," and warned them that "what I have formerly, and so often Declared, touching the Succession, I cannot Depart from," but professed himself "ready to hearken to any such Expedient, by which the Religion might be preserv'd, and the Monarchy not Destroy'd." Nevertheless, its aggressive tone marked a sharp departure from the conciliatory, almost obsequious speech with which he had opened Parliament the previous October. From the outset he adopted an accusatory manner in which he turned his opponents' charges back upon themselves:

> The unwarrantable Proceedings of the last House of Commons, were the occasion of My parting with the last Parliament; for I, who will never use Arbitrary Government My Self, am resolv'd not to suffer it in Others: I am unwilling to mention Particulars, because I am desirous to forget faults; but whosoever shall calmly Consider, what Offers I have formerly made, and what Assurances I renew'd to the last Parliament . . . and shall then reflect upon the strange unsuitable Returns made to such Propositions, by Men that were call'd together

> to Consult; perhaps may wonder more, that I had patience so long, then that at
> last I grew weary of Their Proceedings.
>
> I have thought it necessary to say thus much to You, That I may not have any
> new Occasion given Me to remember more of the late Miscarriages.

Having issued this clear warning in the tone of one whose patience is
nearly exhausted, the king made a point of mentioning three "late miscarriages" that the new Commons would be well advised to avoid repeating:

> I would have you likewise be Convinc'd, that neither Your Liberties nor
> Properties can subsist long, when the just Rights and Prerogatives of the Crown
> are invaded, or the Honour of the Government brought low and into Dis-
> reputation. . . .
>
> . . . And that the just Care, You ought to have of Religion, be not so manag'd
> and improv'd into unnecessary Fears, as to be made a pretence for changing the
> foundations of the Government. . . .
>
> . . . I must needs desire you, not to lay so much weight upon any One Expe-
> dient against Popery, as to determine that all Other are ineffectual.

Finally, having given notice that he would tolerate no further encroachments on his prerogative, seditious encouragement of public fears, or bills
of Exclusion, the king went on to "conclude with this One Advice to you,
That the Rules and Measures of all your Votes, may be the Known and
Establish'd Laws of the Land, which neither can, nor ought to be departed from, nor chang'd, but by Act of Parliament; And I may the more
reasonably Require, That you make the Laws of the Land your Rule,
because I am resolv'd they shall be Mine."[3] He was alluding of course to
the behavior of the late House of Commons in substituting "votes"—
resolutions and addresses—for the bills they despaired of seeing approved
by the Lords and the king. This opening speech was immediately printed
at the Sheldonian Theatre next door and given to the public.

The scene now shifted to Convocation House, where, after several days
spent in choosing a speaker and attending to other preliminary business,
the Commons proceeded immediately to ignore the king's warnings and
to behave in their usual manner. On Thursday they passed a resolution
"That the Votes and Proceedings of this House be printed: And that the
Care of the Printing thereof, and the Appointment of the Printers, be committed to Mr. Speaker."[4] As had proved so successful a tactic during the
meeting of the previous parliament, the votes, orders, and resolutions of
the Commons immediately began to appear daily as half-sheets published
under parliamentary privilege by Langley Curtis in London and disseminated throughout the kingdom.[5]

On Friday the Commons turned its attention to "Fitzharris's Plot," a
new chapter to the Popish Plot teeming with possibilities of reviving "un-

necessary fears" and further implicating the duke of York. Edward Fitz-harris, an Irish adventurer who had tried his luck with both parties, had recently been arrested as the author of a treasonous libel against the king. In hopes of saving his life, he offered to reveal new and spectacular details of the Plot. Up to now, the king had been sufficiently intimidated by pub-lic reaction to the Plot to grant immunity to the witnesses, routinely offer-ing them pardons at the request of Parliament. This time, however, strengthened by his more aggressive mood, he refused a pardon to Fitz-harris and ordered him committed to the Tower to await indictment for his libel. Amid outcries that the Plot was being stifled, the Commons pro-ceeded to impeach Fitzharris so that his case could be transferred from the king's courts to Parliament, where he might be given ample opportunity to provide the public with new details of the Popish conspiracy.

On Saturday, the Commons were ready to debate Exclusion and to listen to the expedients they had been promised as an alternative. In the event, the Tories had nothing to suggest but a regency during the next reign in which James's daughter Mary would rule in his name. This sug-gestion was quickly dismissed and the Commons agreed without a divi-sion to bring in a third Exclusion Bill. In the afternoon they learned that the Lords had refused to proceed upon their impeachment of Fitzharris, deciding to leave him to the king's courts. Infuriated by this message, the Commons plunged headlong into a new confrontation with the upper house, voting a series of resolutions charging the House of Lords with "a Denial of Justice, and a Violation of the Constitution of Parliaments."[6]

The king now had the cue he had been awaiting from the Commons to bring the performance to a spectacular close. The well-known dissimula-tions by which he staged his surprise—setting workmen to prepare larger quarters for the Commons in the Sheldonian Theatre, coming down to the Lords on Monday morning in his street clothes while his robes of state were smuggled in behind him—all testify to his intention of producing a coup de theatre to highlight his new role. The Commons barely had time to pass the first reading of the Exclusion Bill before they were summoned to the Geometry School to hear the king order: "That all the World may see to what a Point we are come, that we are not like to have a good End, when the Divisions at the Beginning are such: Therefore, my Lord Chan-cellor, do as I have commanded you." Whereupon Heneage Finch stepped forward and declared: "That it is His Majesty's Royal Pleasure and Will, that this Parliament be dissolved: And this Parliament is dis-solved."[7] The show had been closed after a week's run, but not before it had achieved its purpose: "That all the World may see to what a Point we are come."[8]

Nothing remained but to follow this curtain scene with an epilogue soliciting the audience's approbation. The king hurried back to London and set about choosing among several versions of an appeal to the nation prepared for his use. The longest of these had been written by Danby, who had more time on his hands than other courtiers, but the king selected a shorter version from the pen of Francis North, chief justice of the Common Pleas, which he issued on 8 April, less than a fortnight after he had dissolved Parliament, as *His Majesties Declaration to All His Loving Subjects, Touching the Causes and Reasons That Moved Him to Dissolve the Two Last Parliaments*. It was "published by His Majesties Command" and ordered to be read "in all Churches and Chappels throughout this Kingdom," an unusual measure testifying to the great importance attached to it by the king, and ensuring that the maximum number of his subjects should read or listen to it.

*His Majesties Declaration* is a brief, cogent pamphlet, which in the space of ten pages presents the king as a man whose patience has been exhausted by the unjust, arbitrary actions of a House of Commons to whom blame must be solely imputed for the breakdown of the process by which the government of the country normally operates:

> It was with exceeding great trouble, that We were brought to the Dissolving of the Two Last Parliaments, without more benefit to Our People by the Calling of them: But having done Our part, in giving so many opportunities of providing for their Good, it cannot be justly imputed to Us, that the Success hath not answered Our Expectation.
>
> We cannot at this time but take notice of the particular Causes of Our Dissatisfaction, which at the beginning of the last Parliament, We did recommend to their care to avoid, and expected We should have had no new Cause to remember them.

In reciting now a bill of particulars enumerating the "most unsuitable Returns from the House of Commons" during the second Exclusion Parliament, the pamphlet skillfully concentrates on the angry votes they had been reduced to passing after the Exclusion Bill was rejected by the Lords: "Addresses, in the nature of Remonstrances, rather than of Answers; Arbitrary Orders for taking Our Subjects into Custody, for Matters that had no relation to Priviledges of Parliament; Strange illegal Votes, declaring divers eminent Persons to be enemies to the King and Kingdom, without any Order or Process of Law, any hearing of their Defence, or any Proof so much as offer'd against them." The pamphlet singles out, and quotes in full, those resolutions in which the Commons had behaved most intemperately: the two aimed at preventing the king from borrowing against his ordinary revenue, "not onely exposing Us to all Dangers that might happen either at home, or abroad; but endeavouring to deprive Us of the Possibility of Supporting the Government it self, and to reduce Us to a more helpless Condition then the meanest of Our Subjects"; and another, passed in the closing moments of the session, which denounced the prosecution of Protestant Dissenters under the Elizabethan Penal Laws, "by which Vote, without any regard to the Laws establish'd, they assumed to themselves a Power of Suspending Acts of Parliament."

"These," the pamphlet declares, "were some of the unwarrantable Proceedings of that House of Commons, which were the occasion of Our parting with that Parliament. Which We had no sooner Dissolv'd, but We caus'd another to be forthwith Assembled at *Oxford*; at the Opening of which, We thought it necessary to give Them warning of the Errors of the former, in hopes to have prevented the like Miscarriages." In showing that the new House of Commons had immediately plunged into the same errors against which he had cautioned them, the king naturally turns to the Exclusion Bill. But he carefully avoids being drawn into arguments over the legality of altering the Succession. Instead he merely reminds his subjects of his repeated declarations that Exclusion "was a Point, that in Our Own Royal Judgment, so nearly concern'd Us both in Honour, Justice, and Conscience, that We could never consent to it"; warns of the catastrophe he foresees from such an act, in light of which "We cannot, after the sad Experience We have had of the late Civil Wars, that Murder'd Our Father of Blessed Memory, and ruin'd the Monarchy, consent to a Law, that shall establish another most Unnatural War"; and suggests that Exclusion was not, in any case, the ultimate objective of the Commons, but only the first step in altering the constitution: "And We have reason to believe, by what pass'd in the last Parliament at *Westminster*, that if We could have been brought to give Our Consent to a Bill of Exclusion, the Intent was, not to rest there, but to pass further, and to attempt some other Great and Important Changes even in Present." The pamphlet then quotes in full the resolutions the Commons had voted against the Lords for refusing to act on Fitzharris's impeachment, and widens the division between the two houses by declaring that "certainly the House of Peers did themselves Right in refusing to give countenance to such a Proceeding." This action of the Commons, the king concludes, had put "the two Houses out of capacity of transacting business together," so that, with "every day's continuance being like to produce new Instances of further Heat and Anger between the two Houses . . . We found it necessary to put an end to this Parliament likewise."

After this recital of the reasons justifying the recent dissolution, the pamphlet now alludes to the charges that the king intends to rule without Parliament, characterizing them as seditious rumors spread by those who are motivated by a hatred of monarchy or by self-interest.

> But notwithstanding all this, let not the restless Malice of ill Men, who are labouring to poyson Our People, some out of fondness of their Old Beloved Commonwealth-Principles, and some out of anger at their being disappointed

in the particular Designs they had for the accomplishment of their own Ambition and Greatness, perswade any of Our Good Subjects, that We intend to lay aside the use of Parliaments. . . .

. . . We are Resolved, by the Blessing of God, to have frequent Parliaments; and both in and out of Parliament, to use Our utmost Endeavours to extirpate Popery, and to Redress all the Grievances of Our good Subjects, and in all things to Govern according to the Laws of the Kingdom.

The king's peroration skillfully picks up the strands scattered earlier in the pamphlet—the Commons' championing of the Dissenters in defiance of the law, the reminder of the Civil Wars and the martyrdom of his father, the "Old Beloved Commonwealth-Principles" of his opponents— to present himself as the champion of church and state who has rescued his subjects from the brink of another national catastrophe like the one many of them still remembered with dismay.

And We hope that a little time will so far open the Eyes of all Our good Subjects, that Our next meeting in Parliament, shall perfect all that Settlement and Peace which shall be found wanting either in Church or State.

To which, as We shall Contribute Our utmost Endeavours, so We assure Our Self, That We shall be Assisted therein by the Loyalty and good Affections of all those who consider the Rise and Progress of the late Troubles and Confusions, and desire to preserve their Countrey from a Relapse.

And who cannot but remember, That Religion, Liberty and Property were all lost and gone, when the Monarchy was shaken off, and could never be reviv'd till that was restored.[9]

This appeal to the twenty turbulent years preceding the Restoration, artfully disseminated throughout the king's *Declaration* and reiterated at its close, was an effective tactic. It struck a responsive chord in the hearts of many Englishmen who still retained an instinctive loyalty to their king, while appealing to those very fears for "religion, liberty and property" on which the Whigs had been capitalizing recently, but which found their deepest roots in the memory of the Civil Wars and Commonwealth. The Restoration Settlement was about to come undone, and the same king who had made that settlement possible was now appealing to his subjects to help repair it.

To Englishmen who had reached middle age, the king's reminder of "the Rise and Progress of the late Troubles and Confusions," following hard on his recital of such "unwarrantable Proceedings" of the House of Commons at Westminster as "Addresses, in the nature of Remonstrances," "Arbitrary Orders for taking Our Subjects into Custody," and "Strange illegal Votes," would have recalled above all 1641, the year when the Long Parliament impeached the king's advisers and passed the

Grand Remonstrance; when they intimidated Charles I into assenting on the same day to the bill of attainder against Strafford and the bill against the dissolution of Parliament depriving him of his ancient prerogative; and when they began passing ordinances into law without the king's concurrence.

In suggesting that history was repeating itself, the king's *Declaration* was not, of course, taking a new line. The annual recurrence all over the kingdom of sermons commemorating the martyrdom of Charles I and the restoration of his son had long ensured that, should the occasion arise, these reminders of "the late troubles and confusions" could be applied to a current emergency. The time was now at hand, and for several years the preachers of anniversary sermons had exploited the opportunity, while propagandists had followed their lead in drawing more explicit parallels between past and present, arguing that today's Whigs were yesterday's commonwealth men, and noting, in the words of a poem of February 1680, "how far those Dismal Times and ours agree."[10] By the end of 1680, a Whig pamphleteer was complaining bitterly that "it hath been all the Clamour of late, *Forty one, Forty one*, is now coming to be acted over again. . . . These are the daily and weekly Cries of several Pamphleteers, to amuse the Loyal Subjects of His Majesty."[11] The real innovation of *His Majesties Declaration* lies not in its skillful use of this already familiar theme but in its introduction of two fresh tactics.

The first was its portrayal of the House of Commons as the real culprit. Most earlier government propaganda, published in 1679 and 1680 during the long interval without a parliament, had laid stress on the private scheming of dissidents intent on reviving "their old beloved Commonwealth," and had placed the scene of their activities in "Clubs, and Coffee-houses," as one pamphlet declared, "Taverns, and other publick Houses."[12] By laying exclusive emphasis on the obstreperous behavior of the Commons over the past few months, the king's *Declaration* transformed the principal scene of sedition to St. Stephen's Chapel and, more recently, Convocation House. The guilty party in this attempt to "shake off the monarchy" was the House of Commons, regarded as a corporate body whose character and behavior were those of its majority, ignoring such faithful supporters of the king as Jenkins, Seymour, and Hyde, whose numbers had been too small to challenge a division on most motions. In contrast, the House of Lords emerged in the king's *Declaration* as a loyal body in which the presence of Shaftesbury, Monmouth, Essex, and other prominent Whigs was ignored in considering only the characteristic motions passed by its majority of bishops and courtiers. Tory propagandists would soon follow the king's lead, casting the House of Commons as a defendant that must stand trial in the public press, having concealed its guilt for too long by deflecting attention to the king and charging him with its own crimes of arbitrary government. Within six weeks the Middlesex grand jury, that body of stalwart Whigs chosen by Sheriffs Bethel and Cornish, was bitterly complaining of "endeavours to make breaches between His Majesty and the Commons of *England* in Parliament by Printed Papers and otherwise, to bring the Commons in Parliament into the hatred and contempt of the Nation."[13]

Second, in citing the behavior of the Commons over the past few months as "proof" that the revival of past misfortunes had been imminent, *His Majesties Declaration* buttressed these conclusions with the king's own authority. For too long a time, it had been possible for the Whigs to argue that the king was being misled by his ministers, that he failed to perceive the dangerous designs of the court party, and that he must eventually cast them aside and agree to Exclusion. But the king had now spoken, identifying his own policy with that of his ministers, and disclosing that it was his subjects who had been misled by their common enemy.

More perceptive than many of his subjects, the king, in this view, had drawn back on the brink to which his rebellious Commons had pushed him. He had exercised his prerogative of proroguing and dissolving parliaments not arbitrarily and despotically but for deliberate reasons of state in order to protect the laws from those who would have used Parliament to destroy them. His *Declaration* gave fair warning that while he hoped to have frequent parliaments in the future, he would never again tolerate such a House of Commons as he had endured in recent sessions. His subjects had no way of knowing that his reign would end four years later without his ever meeting another parliament, but it could hardly have escaped their notice that whereas he had followed each of the previous dissolutions by summoning a new parliament within a few days and ordering elections for it, this time he had omitted doing so. Instead, he had expressed a "hope that a little time will so far open the Eyes of all Our good Subjects" as to send him a House of Commons with which he could work in harmony to redress the nation's real, rather than its pretended, grievances. He, not his opponents, would set the terms on which any future parliaments would meet, and the time that must elapse before their meeting would be determined by the interval necessary for his subjects to open their eyes to the real dangers confronting them.

.  .  .  .  .

The Whig propagandists failed to perceive that *His Majesties Declaration* had altered the situation by carrying an appeal directly from the king to the nation, and by casting the House of Commons as the culprit which had previously escaped detection by accusing Charles of its own crimes.

Assuming that they still held the offensive, the Whigs responded to the *Declaration* by rehearsing the old charges of arbitrary power, now grown stale by repetition. *A Letter from a Person of Quality to His Friend concerning His Majesties Late Declaration* complained that

> it hath long been the advice of some of the Wisest and Ablest of the Popish and Arbitrary Party, that the King should call frequent, short and useless Parliaments, until the Gentry, weary of the great expence, of so many fruitless Journeys and Elections, should sit at home, and trouble themselves no more, and leave the People expos'd to the practices of them and their Party; who if they carry one House of Commons for their turn, will in few Months do the Nations business for ever; and make us slaves and Papists by a Law.[14]

*A Just and Modest Vindication of the Proceedings of the Two Last Parliaments*, on the other hand, openly doubted the king's promise to call frequent parliaments in the future, pointing out that "he hath nevertheless been prevailed upon to Dissolve four in the space of 26 Months without making provision by their advice suitable to our dangers and wants."[15] Both pamphlets assumed—rightly, in fact—that the king's *Declaration* had been written for him by one of his advisers, but drew the specious inference from this that he was not to be identified with the sentiments in it that they were attacking. "'Tis rather some base Fav'rites Vile Pretence, / To Tyrannize at the wrong'd King's Expence," as a Whig versifier suggested ten days after the *Declaration* appeared.[16]

To some degree this was a circumlocution common among Whig pamphleteers, who did not enjoy the protection of parliamentary privilege; but it was also, as we have noticed, a Whig propaganda tactic that in the past had allowed them to attract support by holding out the hope that under popular pressure the king would eventually come round. The fiction, expressed both in the press and in votes by the Commons, that in his speeches and messages to Parliament the king was a figurehead echoing the words of his advisers had already worn thin and been undermined by some of the franker speeches of the Whigs in both houses of Parliament. But after *His Majesties Declaration* appeared, attempts to question the king's own position were no longer credible.

Another sign that the Whigs failed to perceive the change in the situation was their ill-fated attempt to launch a second Petitioning Movement calling on the king to summon a new parliament for which, according to a Whig broadside published on 30 March, "all *England* weeps, and doth in Sack-cloth Groan."[17] To publicize this fresh campaign they would again require the assistance of Whig newspapers, but it was unluckily at just this juncture in mid-April that both Harris's *Protestant Domestick Intelligence* and *Smith's Protestant Intelligence* succumbed to government pressure. Harris had been returned to prison on orders of the Privy

Council in February, and once again, after two months in the King's Bench, he found it impossible to continue publishing his newspaper. Francis Smith was imprisoned by the Privy Council in April, but immediately released on the condition, reluctantly accepted, of discontinuing his newspaper at once. Nevertheless, Langley Curtis's *True Protestant Mercury* continued to appear and was joined, toward the end of April, by Richard Janeway's *Impartial Protestant Mercury*; both would manage to survive until 1682. They would be needed to publicize another mass movement like that of the electors' addresses to their members during the elections in February and March. These were now collected and published on 13 April, less than a week after the king's *Declaration*, as *Vox Patriae; or, The Resentments and Indignation of the Free-born Subjects of England against Popery, Arbitrary Government, the Duke of York, or Any Popish Successor.*[18] The book came as a forceful reminder of the popular mandate behind the "miscarriages" of the Commons during the Oxford Parliament, and was probably timed as a counterblast to *His Majesties Declaration* that could signal the opening of another mass movement. Two weeks later, on 28 April, Richard Baldwin, as he had done when the previous parliament at Westminster was dissolved, collected and published the debates in the House of Commons at Oxford, again indicating the speakers by their initials, and supplying the evidence for a Whig defence of the proceedings of the late parliament against the king's recent charges.[19]

But the Whigs had failed to reckon with the king's new policy of firmness. He was no longer prepared, in the words of *The Country-mans Complaint*, "to hear Addresses for their Property" while he "laid his Thunder by."[20] When, in the middle of May, they succeeded in getting from the London Common Council a petition calling for a new parliament, with which they hoped to lead off their new campaign, that long-reliable source of support passed the petition by a slim majority of fourteen votes. And when the lord mayor, sheriffs, and aldermen presented it to the king at Hampton Court, he ordered the lord chancellor to deliver them his answer in a scathing speech reproving them for "medling with *Matters of State* and *Government*, Things which do in no sort appertain to you, but are quite out of your Sphere," telling them that "you are not the Common-council of the Nation, and yet you behave your selves so, as if you thought you were," and ordering them roughly to "*Study to be quiet* and to do *your own* Business."[21] This rude rebuff was quickly published by the king's printers on 24 May to give public notice of the kind of reception any further petitioners could expect from him. It was scarcely surprising that after such a reception very few wished to risk the king's displeasure further, and the new petitioning movement foundered a few days after launching. The tide of Whig propaganda was already running out while the Tories had been at work for the past month exploiting the advantage given them by *His Majesties Declaration*.

.  .  .  .  .

The basis of that advantage was the attitude of strengthened resolution the king had shown in dissolving the Oxford Parliament and announcing what amounted to a new policy in his *Declaration*. But an episode that took place during the session at Oxford a few days before the dissolution heralded the king's new stance that was destined to play so important a part in Tory propaganda for the remainder of the year. It is best to read it in the version given to the public shortly afterward by a Tory pamphlet ironically called *The E. of Shaftsbury's Expedient for Setling the Nation*.

> The 24th of *March*, the great Patriot, and next under God and Dr. *Oates*, the supreme Saviour and Defender of the Nation, the Earl of *Shaftsbury* receiv'd, or pretended that he receiv'd a Letter written in an unknown Hand, containing an Expedient for the setling and composing the Differences between the *King* and *Parliament*. With this he made a great noise, . . . bustling about as fast as his leggs, and man, and stick, could carry him. . . .
>
> The little Lord very busy, and desirous to speak with the *King*, was told by the Earl of *Feversham*, that . . . he would conduct him to His Majesty. . . .
>
> Well, he is brought to the *King*, and there broach'd. The Letter of Expedients is produc'd; and what do you think was this grand Secret of securing our Peace and Religion, but a Proposal for the settling the Crown on the Duke of *Monmouth*? The *K.* surpriz'd, told the Earl, that he wonder'd that after so many Declarations to the contrary, he should press him upon that Subject, . . . That his Majesty was none of those that grew more timorous with age, but that rather he grew the more resolute the nearer he was to his grave.
>
> At that word the Loyal Earl was mightily concern'd, and cry'd out that it chill'd his blood to hear of such an expression; Telling the *King* how earnest the whole Nation was for His Preservation.

The king's rejoinder to this was a stern speech in which he brushed aside Shaftesbury's expressions of concern for his safety and declared that "I intend to take a greater care of my Own Preservation, and in that of my Peoples, than any of You all that pretend to so much concern for the Security of my Person. And yet as careful as I am of my Own Preservation: Yet I would much sooner lose this Life, of which you pretend to be so watchful Preservers, than ever part with any of my Prerogative, or betray this Place, the Laws, or the Religion, or alter the true Succession of the Crown, it being repugnant both to Conscience and Law." The pamphlet concludes by observing that the king spoke on this occasion "with so much Resolution and Courage, as gave the greatest assurance and encouragement to all the Loyal Lords in the House, and all honest Subjects that could be; but to the Factious, the greatest Confusion imaginable."[22]

It is easy to understand why this episode, of no great importance in itself, should have been eagerly taken up by the Tory propagandists. Made public immediately after the king's dissolution of the Oxford Parliament, his private speech to Shaftesbury in the Geometry School epitomized the new image of the king that would be the keystone of the approaching Tory offensive: a monarch who "grew the more resolute the nearer he was to his grave," who promised to take a greater care of his own preservation and that of his people, and who was prepared to sacrifice his life, if necessary, to safeguard his prerogative and the true Succession.

If it was the king's response that made this episode immediately useful to the Tory publicists, Shaftesbury's proposal for settling the crown on Monmouth was to have an equally important effect on their propaganda. For the first time since the beginning of the Exclusion Crisis, the chief Whig magnate had personally associated himself with the duke's aspirations to the crown and had publicly come forward as his patron. For Shaftesbury this may have been no more than a temporary expedient, a means of probing and testing the king's resolution two days before the third Exclusion Bill was introduced. But his action created in the mind of the public an indelible association between the king's former counselor and his disobedient son that the Tory propagandists would not hesitate to exploit.

The first satire casting Shaftesbury in his new role as Monmouth's evil genius was a poem, *The Deliquium*, published on 8 April, the day on which *His Majesties Declaration* was issued. This is a dream vision, a popular vehicle for Tory satire at the time, which is set in Hell, where a devil reports to Lucifer how he and Capricio (Shaftesbury) conspired to destroy the English state.

> With this half Fiend I many Consults had,
> And we at last this Resolution made:
> *Almanzor*'s due Succession to oppose,
> Among his many unprovoked Foes:
> We chose young *Marcion*, not for any love,
> But to undo the Youth, as time will prove:
> Poor easie Prince, he little thinks that we
> Prostitute this his weak Credulity
> To our own use, to Anarchize the State,
> And hasten his too soon intended Fate.[23]

In another dream vision published on 30 April, *Poor Robins Dream, or The Visions of Hell*, Shaftesbury's long-standing role in Tory propaganda as the contriver of the Popish Plot hoax is joined to his new role as Monmouth's evil genius. The ghost of Israel Tonge, who had died the previous December, tells the ghost of William Bedloe:

> *Tony* was the cause of my Damnation,
> It was his malice that enflam'd the Nation.
> 'Twas He, under pretence of doing good,
> That squeez'd poor Innocents, and broacht their bloud.
> 'Twas He that made His *Grace* a stalking Horse,
> And hid himself behind his pocky Arse.[24]

April also saw the appearance of *The Waking Vision*, a popular poetic broadside in which the names of Achitophel and Absalom were applied to Shaftesbury and Monmouth in order to suggest, for the first time, their relationship as master and disciple. The poem is yet another dream vision, this time of the Whigs sowing disaffection among the rabble. "Their Leader was an Old man, known too well / By that false Trayterous name *Achitophel*," who appears in company with his crony, "Lieutenant *Absalom*," while the latter's royal father is referred to as "*David*."[25] As in the Tory propaganda of the previous year discussed in the last chapter, Monmouth is still being paralleled with Absalom the seditionist who "stole the hearts of the people" before making any attempt on his father's throne, but Achitophel now serves as a metaphor not for the Whig magnates as a group but for Shaftesbury alone. This is the only suggestion of 2 Samuel in the poem, however. The setting for the vision is the streets of London in 1681, and the remaining English persons and institutions in the poem are given their proper names.

By the end of April, therefore, Monmouth had assumed a new role in Tory propaganda as Shaftesbury's zany. *Grimalkin; or, The Rebel-Cat*, a beast fable in prose that appeared on 4 May, exploited this relationship between the two in a comic satire portraying Shaftesbury as the rebel cat of the title, scheming against the royal lion, and accompanied everywhere by a "Bastard *Leopard*," of whom we are told that "this Base Son of the Lyon is esteemed a pure Property of the Cat's, insomuch as, even in common Discourse, he ordinarily passes under the Name of the Cats-Foot."[26]

Late in the following month another Tory pamphlet appeared that epitomizes the special relationship now assumed between Monmouth and Shaftesbury. *A Seasonable Invitation for Monmouth to Return to Court*, published on 23 June, is a prose appeal addressed directly to Monmouth. Like the similar appeal that had appeared the previous summer, *A Letter to His Grace the D. of Monmouth*, it alludes to Absalom's fate as a warning to his modern successor. But on this occasion Achitophel becomes a metaphor not for the Whig grandees as a whole but for Shaftesbury alone, "a little Crooked, Hucked-back *Devil*," who "useth you for no other end, than to compleat his own Hellish Designes." The Tory author ends by urging Monmouth to free himself from Shaftesbury's tutelage and to seek his father's forgiveness: "And when *Absolom* dispiseth the Counsels of *Achitophel*, and returns to *David*, the Wicked Counsellor shall despair, be his own Executioner, and Hang himself."[27]

.   .   .   .   .

If the momentum recently created by the king was to be maintained, it was essential that the Tories have newspapers and other periodicals with which to present the king's case on a regular and continuing basis. After May 1680, when Nathaniel Thompson's *True Domestick Intelligence* had ceased publication, the government had been reduced during the slack period of Tory propaganda to relying on the dull, official *London Gazette*. Now this situation was quickly remedied. *Heraclitus Ridens* had started to appear on 1 February, and in the same week Benjamin Tooke began publishing the *Weekly Discovery of the Mystery of Iniquity*, a serial book to counterbalance the Whigs' *Weekly Pacquet of Advice from Rome*. Early March witnessed the beginning of Thompson's new venture, the *Loyal Protestant and True Domestick Intelligence*, which, unlike his previous paper, was aggressively Tory from the outset. Now Roger L'Estrange's *Observator* and John Smith's *Currant Intelligence* both began publication in April, and Thomas Benskin's *Domestick Intelligence* in May. These last two newspapers can be taken as weather vanes indicating the shift in the political winds. John Smith (not to be confused with his Whig namesake, Francis Smith) had published the *Currant Intelligence* the previous year, between February and May 1680, when it had been silenced along with its competitors by the proclamation against newspapers. In its earlier incarnation it had been the most important of the nonpartisan newspapers that managed to maintain neutrality between the two parties. Now, in reviving his newspaper in April, Smith immediately joined the ranks of the Tory journalists. Another new recruit was Thomas Benskin. As recently as January and February 1681, his imprint had appeared on several Whig pamphlets and broadsides. In March and early April, he published two short-lived newspapers, the *Protestant Oxford Intelligence* (at the time of the Oxford Parliament) and the *Impartial London Intelligence*, which cautiously avoided political partisanship. He now moved to the other side, and from its first number, on 13 May, his *Domestick Intelligence* adopted a strongly Tory stance.

*Heraclitus Ridens* and the *Observator* were not really newspapers but lively commentaries for which the Whigs had no counterpart. The first of these, as its name implied, was a humorous periodical, a running "Dialogue between Jest and Earnest." The *Observator* used a bantering manner for examining serious political issues, also through dialogue, at first in the form of questions and answers, but, after the beginning of July, in a lively interchange between a witty Tory and a Whig who showed alarming signs of mental confusion and lost every argument. The first issue of the *Observator* appeared less than a week after *His Majesties Declaration*, and quickly became the mainstay of Tory propaganda. Its purpose from the outset was to assist the king to "open the Eyes of all Our good Subjects," as he had said in his *Declaration*, to the deceptions into which they had been misled by his enemies. L'Estrange began his new paper by announcing:

> 'Tis the *Press* that has made 'um *Mad*, and the *Press* must set 'um *Right* again. The Distemper is *Epidemical*; and there's no way in the world, but by *Printing*, to convey the *Remedy* to the *Disease*.
> Q. *But what is it that you call a* Remedy?
> A. The *Removing* of the *Cause*. That is to say, the *Undeceiving* of the *People*: for they are well enough Disposed, of themselves, to be Orderly, and Obedient; if they were not misled by *Ill Principles*, and Hair'd and Juggled out of their Senses with so many Frightful *Stories* and *Impostures*.
> Q. *Well! to be Plain and Short; You call your self the* Observator: *What is it now that you intend for the Subject of your* Observations?
> A. Take it in few words then. My business is, to encounter the *Faction*, and to Vindicate the *Government*; to detect their *Forgeries*; to lay open the Rankness of their *Calumnies*, and *Malice*; to Refute their *Seditious Doctrines*; to expose their *Hypocrisy*, and the *bloudy Design* that is carry'd on, under the Name, and Semblance, of *Religion*.[28]

L'Estrange kept his promise, and thereafter was to be found several times a week "detecting forgeries" in Whig newspapers and pamphlets, arguing that "it is the main scope of their Papers to possess the People with Fears of *Arbitrary Power*, and *Popery*, and to reflect scandals upon the very *Frame* of the *Government*, and all that *serve* it," and carrying on the new offensive launched by *His Majesties Declaration*.[29]

The first number of Thompson's *Loyal Protestant and True Domestick Intelligence* also announced that "it is Publisht for no other end, but to undeceive His Majesties Loyal Subjects, and to discover to the world the notorious *Forgeries* & *Impostures* both of *Papists* and *Fanaticks* daily invented to amuse the unthinking multitude, thereby to facilitate the carrying on their own hellish Designs."[30] His periodical and Benskin's, which also appeared twice a week, were genuine newspapers that could compete with the Whig papers of Curtis and Janeway for a readership eager to learn about the latest events. Like their Whig competition, these Tory newspapers gave more space to domestic occurrences than to foreign affairs, selected the items for inclusion according to their political bias, and accompanied them with a generous amount of commentary. They were to prove indispensable as a means of publicizing the mass movement the court was now preparing to launch.

.   .   .   .   .

The Loyal Address Movement has received little attention from historians, properly cautious about using it as evidence of a genuine change in national feeling. Considered as a successful propaganda effort, however, it was enormously important, for it was the greatest mass offensive that had yet been conducted by either side until now, lasted far longer than any of the others had done, and provided a stable basis for the picture of altered conditions portrayed by Tory writers during the rest of 1681.

The loyal addresses to the king were supposedly spontaneous expressions of gratitude for *His Majesties Declaration*, pledging him support. They came from the common councils, corporations, grand juries, justices of the peace, and lieutenancies of the counties and boroughs of England and Wales: bodies of responsible citizens in marked contrast to the "rabble" who had signed the Whig petitions early in 1680. They were modeled after the Whig addresses from electors to their members of Parliament in the recent elections that had been collected and published in *Vox Patriae* on 13 April, and were designed as a direct rejoinder to them. Those addresses had been made to individual candidates for the Commons, instructing them to support a policy of Exclusion, and promising in return "to stand by You with our Lives and Fortunes." The loyal addresses were directed to the head of the nation, supported his announced policy of governing according to the laws of the kingdom and protecting their religion, liberty, and property, and closed with a similar formula offering "Your Majesty, the Command of our Lives and Fortunes."

The first loyal address came from the justices of the peace of Middlesex and was presented to the king on 18 April, ten days after *His Majesties Declaration* was issued. It may have been spontaneous, for the court apparently did not at first realize the possibilities this held for a mass movement, and several weeks were to elapse before any sequels appeared. Sir John Reresby recorded a conversation the following year in which the king told him "that when the late addresses did first begin he was not much satisfyed with them," mindful no doubt of the embarrassingly few abhorrences of the Petitioning Movement in 1680, "but when they began to encrease he was glad to find them soe numerous."[31] Their increase was no accident, for once the court awakened to their potential value, they were not only encouraged but actively solicited. A sure sign of the superior organization behind the movement was the fact that the loyal addresses did not come in to the king in a flood that would have spent its force in a month or two, but arrived in a carefully regulated flow that maintained a steady, though eventually diminishing, volume for nine months.

In the case of each loyal address, there was a short ceremony, reminiscent of those carried out by the Whigs during the recent elections, in which the presentation of the address was accompanied by a short speech, which was answered with a gracious reply from the king. The *London Gazette* regularly printed the loyal addresses, which were soon filling its columns to the exclusion of most other news, and by July it was necessary to print double issues of the *Gazette* from time to time to accommodate the backlog. Thompson and Benskin also printed many of the addresses or summarized them in their newspapers, reporting the ceremonies accompanying them and offering appropriate comments. By the middle of July Benskin was announcing that "it is verily supposed there remains not ten places of Importance or any note in this Kingdome of *England* and Dominion of *Wales*, but what have presented their dutiful and Loyal Addresses, expressing their great satisfaction in the enjoyment of so good a King"; but the supposition was wide of the mark, and the following month he was reporting that the addresses "continue to Flow (as it were daily) from all parts."[32] They would go on appearing for another four months, finally coming to an end with the year itself. The loyal addresses, numbering over two hundred in all, were then collected and published as *Vox Angliae; or, The Voice of the Kingdom*, an impressive counterweight to the Whigs' *Vox Patriae*.

The Loyal Address Movement took its cue from both the great mass movements engineered by the Whigs in the two previous winters. The Whig instructions to the newly elected members of Parliament in early 1681 find their closest parallel in the final paragraphs of most loyal addresses, where the signers promise that when the king sees fit to call his next parliament they will elect members who are committed to preserving the Succession in its rightful line and to voting the king supplies. But the Petitioning Movement of early 1680, with its bulky rolls containing thousands of signatures, also had its mirror image in the new Tory mass movement. The loyal addresses themselves were of course formal resolutions voted by comparatively small official bodies. Early in the course of the movement, however, the court seems to have awakened to the advantage of using it as evidence of widespread popular support for the king's policy. By the end of May, therefore, the practice had begun of collecting additional subscriptions to the loyal addresses, and as the custom spread the list of signatures became ever longer until they soon came to resemble the monster petitions of 1680. The loyal address from the Assizes for the County of Durham was presented to the king in a roll containing over twelve thousand signatures, and the various towns and counties were soon competing to see which could collect the greatest number. The total for each loyal address was duly reported in the Tory newspapers.

The importance of the Loyal Address Movement was that it offered the king expressions of popular support of a kind that heads of state even in our own day welcome in times of crisis, not so much because such tokens afford them personal encouragement, as because they can be used as evidence of a public mandate for their actions. In the words of one Tory pamphleteer, the loyal addresses were a "sort of Petitioning, and do express to his Sacred Majesty the desires of many Thousands of his Loyal Subjects, who take this Method to let their Sovereign know . . . how earnestly they desire the Monarchy, and Protestant Religion by Law established, may be defended."[33]

In expressing gratitude for *His Majesties Declaration*, in which the king had informed his people that they had been deceived by his enemies and expressed the hope that a little time would "open the Eyes of all Our good Subjects," the loyal addresses offered welcome testimony that they were now becoming enlightened. As early as May, Thompson was announcing in the *Loyal Protestant*: "It doth now appear that those Petitions and Addresses published in the Names of several Counties and Corporations were Mis-*Representatives*, and not *Vox Populi*; For we now abound with Addresses, Letters and Congratulations of a different nature . . . which we hope will occasion the like from all parts of *England*, and by that means convince the Hot-spurs that the Body of the People are not so disaffected as some would make the world believe they are."[34] The nation's growing enlightenment was a frequent theme with Benskin. In the first issue of the *Domestick Intelligence* he followed his summary of several of the loyal addresses by commenting "that by this we may see the faction is grown odious and Mens eyes at last are open." Two months later his report of ten more addresses led him to remark "that by this we may see that God has bowed the Hearts of all the People, unless it be of such as love to fish in Troubled Waters."[35] By the middle of August a Tory pamphleteer was gloating, "that His Majesty should condescend to undeceive his people, but much more that a great part of the people should be undeceived, and give His Majesty thanks for that gracious condescention . . . makes [the Whigs] stand as uneasie, change feet as often as an Elephant learning to dance upon hot Stones."[36]

Besides their cumulative value as a mass movement in the king's support, the loyal addresses served as individual pieces of Tory propaganda.

Their general tenor is repetitive, and it would have taken a brave Englishman to read *Vox Angliae* from cover to cover. But many of them show a
determined effort to sharpen the polemics in the king's *Declaration* and
make them more explicit. This probably accounts for the fact that a great
many of them were published as separate broadsides before appearing
once again in the newspapers and a third time in *Vox Angliae*.

A constant burden in the loyal addresses is the charge of sedition in the
king's *Declaration*, and its conversion of Whig complaints against arbitrary power into attempts to subvert the government. Thus the address
from the city of Hereford declares that "however some ill Men, to accomplish their black designs, by attempting to subvert the Government, slily
insinuate to the Credulous People, causeless Fears, and false Jealousies of
Arbitrary Power growing upon us," the people of Hereford are "as safe
from such mean apprehensions, as we are secure from the dismal Effects
of such a way of Government, which we have no cause to suspect, unless
it be from those that suggest it, nor from them neither, till they have
subverted a well temper'd Monarchy, and introduc'd their belov'd Tyrannical Republick." The address from the town of Wigan deplores "those
causeless fears and jealousies wherewith designing and ill-meaning Men,
have endeavoured to possess the minds of your People," while that of the
borough of New Radnor declares that "several foul Fogs and dark Mists,
have been rais'd of causeless jealousies, and needless fears; the Authors
insinuating to us their great apprehensions, that Arbitrary Power and
Popery were growing upon us (and indeed from some of our fellow-Subjects we had just cause to fear the first) but your Sacred Majesty in pitty
to our deluded Ignorance . . . hath enlightened our Minds, and enliven'd
our Hearts."[37]

Another tactic of *His Majesties Declaration* adopted by some of the
loyal addresses is the portrayal of the House of Commons as the guilty
party responsible for the perils from which the king has now rescued
them by a timely dissolution. Thus the Corporation of Ripon declares
that "the delivering us from the unwarrantable Proceedings of the House
of Commons, is matter of the highest joy and satisfaction to us," while
the town and borough of Chesterfield boldly returns "our Loyal Thanks
to your most Sacred Majesty for your most Gracious Declaration, and
principally for asserting and supporting your Royal Prerogative, in Calling, and Dissolving Parliaments at your Princely Pleasure, and thereby
preserving us from the late growing Usurpation, of Arbitrary Government, by imprisoning your Majesties Subjects, and other irregularities,
committed by the late House of Commons."[38]

Finally, the address from the city of Gloucester sounds a note that was
to be heard many times throughout 1681: "And we have reason to believe, the same deadly Poison [as led to the Civil Wars] was again prepar-

ing, and had certainly been given, had not God put it into your Majesties Heart timely, and most prudently, to prevent it. . . . So we make our most humble and grateful Acknowledgment to your Majesty, for your most intent Vigilence to save Us from so portentous a Storm."[39]

.    .    .    .    .

This notion that the king had saved the nation by dissolving the Oxford Parliament and by issuing *His Majesties Declaration* was to become one of the most frequent themes of Tory poems, pamphlets, and broadsides for the remainder of the year. It is a heroic theme constructed, like those of many historical romances, from fairly slender strands. A speech, a dissolution, and a declaration are not quite the ingredients of epic, but they could be made the stuff of heroic legend by a group of determined propagandists. Such legends require a heroic scene: a specific place and a limited time in which great danger threatens and the hero suddenly averts it. Oxford during the last week in March was to become, in retrospect, the scene of Charles's heroic action with which his issuing a declaration at Whitehall some ten days later would come to be fused. Some of the loyal addresses, in fact, express profound gratitude not only for *His Majesties Declaration* but for the king's aggressive opening speech to the Oxford Parliament.[40] As early as April, *Heraclitus Ridens* was proclaiming "an Epitaph upon *Arbitrary Government*," slain by the king.

> Here lies Old Nab,
> The Common-wealth Drab,
> That with her old Cause enslav'd us.
> Great *Charles* with a Speech,
> Has damn'd the Old Witch,
> And from her clutches has sav'd us.[41]

This may be the speech with which the king opened the Oxford Parliament (since he made none in closing it), but it is more likely his *Declaration* on 8 April. In any case, heroes do not issue pamphlets, though they often make speeches haranguing their followers and berating their foes. A legend was being born that would soon appear in every variety of government propaganda from the newspapers to the pulpit.

The order in council requiring that *His Majesties Declaration* be read in every church and chapel in the kingdom provided a timely opportunity for sermons to reinforce its message. Edward Slater's choice of a scriptural text for his sermon on this day is probably fairly typical. He chose to preach on Corah's rebellion, the outstanding example in the Old Testament of an insurrection averted by timely action, since the resolute behavior of Moses (with a generous amount of divine assistance) put a stop to the rebellion while it still amounted only to sedition. The purpose of his sermon, Sclater told his congregation, was "to encourage you to Obedience" by denouncing those "who undertake to perswade a People there are Distempers in their Government." As examples of such seditionists in the Old Testament he discussed not only Corah in his text but "*Absolom the fair spoken Hypocrite*" who stole the hearts of the people from his father David.[42]

The next occasion for an anniversary sermon, the commemoration of the king's birthday and restoration on 29 May, afforded further opportunities for celebrating Charles's decisive behavior in saving the nation. Henry Anderson chose to preach his sermon this day on the blessings of "Contentment," implying an Old Testament parallel in exhorting his congregation:

> O then pray for the Peace of *Jerusalem* that love her; and consequently, for the Life and Prosperity of the Monarch of Great *Britain*, King *Charles the Second*, our dread Soveraign, the light of our Eyes and the breath of our Nostrils; who causes malignant vapours to vanish, and dispels those clouds of mischief by his Princely power that would turn Religion into Rebellion, and Faith into Faction, cry up priviledge to invade Regal Prerogative, and under the notion of the Preservers of our Peace, and Defenders of our Liberties, reach out their hand to turn the stream of Royalty, and subvert an excellent Monarchy into a Tyrannical Republick.[43]

A king who causes malignant vapors to vanish and dispels clouds of mischief by his princely power has already become the stuff of heroic legend.

The king's "heroic" actions at Oxford and Westminster in March and April by which, in Benskin's words, he had "plucked us as it were out of the Jaws of a Tyrannical Common-wealth," were of course only the visible embodiments of his inauguration of a more resolute policy that Tory propagandists credited with the return of public tranquillity.[44] In midsummer one of them boldly revived the *Legorn Letters*, issuing a sham sequel to that popular Whig series of the previous year that joyfully announced to the "London merchant" that "since my last to you, it is almost impossible to believe what an Alteration there is in the state of our Ship; for since the dissolution of our Council of Officers, all things seem to contrive the welfare of the Captain," who has issued "out his Royal Declaration," which has "met with general Applause and acceptation from all the Sailers: Every Cabbin in the Ship have most humbly Addressed the Captain to accept of their most unfeigned Thanks."[45] This time it was the Whigs who were in no mood to publish a rejoinder.

As the months passed, it became increasingly clear that the political situation had radically altered, however little the Whigs were disposed to accept it in silence. The king's dissolution of the Oxford Parliament on 28

March marks the end of the Exclusion Crisis in a strict sense, the two-year effort to pass or prevent an act of Parliament excluding the heir from the throne: two years of debates, dissolutions, campaigns, and elections in which the Whigs had held the initiative. But in the wider arena of public debate carried on in the press, the Exclusion Crisis also began rapidly to fade in the spring of 1681 as the numerous pamphlets of the previous two years arguing over the merits and legality of altering the Succession gave place to others whose consuming interest lay in deciding whether the king or his House of Commons was to blame for the recent turbulence that came to be increasingly accepted as a period already concluded. For the remainder of 1681, Whigs and Tories alike would find themselves involved in a historical debate that looked to the past and endlessly reviewed the events since 1678.

It was a sign of how completely the initiative had now passed to the Tories that they were able to dictate the terms of that debate. By portraying Exclusion as the first step in a concerted effort by members of the House of Commons to subvert the government in the interest of their "old beloved Commonwealth principles," the Tories forced the Whigs into a defensive position where they must devote their greatest efforts to justifying the motives from which they had been acting. In the first stage of this debate, before the midsummer of 1681, the absence of any evidence of overtly treasonable activities on their part was assumed to prove the insidious nature of the Whigs' threat to the constitution, and invited reminders of 1641. By making Parliament the scene of their operations, the Whig leaders, according to this version of events, had hoped to accomplish their treasonable aims under the cloak of legality, content to rely on sedition to create popular pressure on the king for consenting to their pernicious measures. By dissolving Parliament instead of bowing to it, the king, according to Tory propaganda, had frustrated their evil plans, and his subjects, at last awakened to their danger, were daily expressing their gratitude to him in the form of loyal addresses.

.  .  .  .  .

If the Oxford Parliament and its immediate aftermath marked the opening phase of the Tory propaganda campaign of 1681, the allegation in the course of the summer that a treasonable conspiracy against the king had been hatching at Oxford at the time he dissolved Parliament there inspired a second phase of that campaign which supplemented the earlier one without in any way supplanting it. Under the cloak of sedition, it now appeared, the Whig leaders in Parliament had been engaging in treason, laying a plot that, if successful, would have made unnecessary any further pretense of legality.

It is a curious irony that the same disreputable figure, Edward Fitz-harris, should have played so important a role in both phases of the campaign. It was, as we have seen, the quarrel between the two houses over his impeachment that gave the king the excuse he needed to dissolve the Oxford Parliament. None of the participants in that drama, however, could have foreseen that Fitzharris would be responsible, three months later, for transferring the struggle between the government and the opposition from Parliament to the king's courts.

The evidence against Fitzharris was so strong that not even a panel of Whig jurors could fail to indict him at a grand inquest, or to convict him if he were brought to trial. A month before the Oxford Parliament met, he had approached a certain Edmund Everard, offering him money to write a libel against the king; Everard had planted witnesses in the next room to watch and overhear Fitzharris's subsequent interviews with him; when Fitzharris was arrested on 27 February he was carrying the libel and admitted that parts of it were in his own handwriting; finally, the libel itself, which advocated armed rebellion against the king, was unquestionably treasonable.[46] Fitzharris's only hope of escape lay in making himself indispensable to the Whigs by agreeing to offer sensational discoveries about the Popish Plot. The king's refusal to grant him immunity as a Plot witness was a setback, but his impeachment by the late House of Commons seemed to promise him a respite, since this could proceed no further until the meeting of a new parliament.

But the government moved swiftly to bring him to justice in the king's courts. On 27 April his indictment was presented to a Middlesex grand jury. When the foreman, Michael Godfrey, brother of the Whig "martyr," expressed scruples about proceeding against a defendant lying under impeachment by the House of Commons, the lord chief justice dismissed his objection, and the grand jurors reluctantly indicted Fitzharris. On 30 April he was arraigned before the Court of King's Bench, where for nearly a fortnight arguments were presented for and against Fitzharris's plea on the question "Whether an Impeachment for Treason, by the House of Commons and still depending, be a sufficient matter to oust the Court from proceeding upon an Indictment for the same Offense."[47] This was a test of strength between the powers of king and Parliament that generated intense public excitement. By early May Thompson was reporting in his newspaper that "*Fitz-Harris*'s Case is now the only Subject of all Peoples Discourse, both in City and Country, and all are big with expectation to see the issue of this Cause."[48] Much more than Fitzharris's life depended on its outcome. If the Whigs were unable to save this new witness to the Popish Plot, Shaftesbury's Irish witnesses, kept in London on a slim allowance paid them by John Rouse, servant to the Whig magnate Sir Thomas Player, might soon conclude that both their safety and their advantage lay in testifying against their former masters. On 11 May the justices ruled against Fitzharris's plea and ordered him to stand trial; on 9 June, confronted with the overwhelming evidence against him, a Whig jury found him guilty of treason.[49]

Frantically casting about for some means of saving his life, Fitzharris seems to have decided at this juncture to turn against his Whig supporters and to try making himself indispensable to the government as he had hoped earlier to serve the opposition. It was a futile attempt, born of desperation, for his testimony might implicate others, but it could do nothing to save himself. His first impulse, apparently, was no more than to accuse one of the Whigs of the crime for which he stood condemned. On 14 June Janeway reported that Fitzharris's wife, "discoursing with Mr. *Whitaker*, her Husband's Solicitor," told him "that the Lord *Howard* of *Escrick* did give her Husband the Heads of the Libel"; when this evidence was conveyed to one of the principal secretaries of state, Lord Howard had been arrested and committed to the Tower for treason.[50] But Fitzharris seems to have been meditating more sensational revelations by the time he was brought to the Court of King's Bench for sentencing on 15 June and pleaded that "he thought it was more for the King's Service, to respite his Judgment, till he had perfected his Evidence against the Lord *Howard*."[51] The court brushed his plea aside, however, and pronounced sentence of death.

Returned to the Tower to await execution, Fitzharris quickly "perfected" his evidence in consultation with his wife, who was allowed to visit him freely. On 21 June Lord Howard's indictment was presented to a Middlesex grand jury, the majority of whom were Whigs. After listening to the testimony in secret, they were preparing to bring in a finding of *Ignoramus* when the attorney general, learning of their intentions, withdrew the bill and returned Howard to the Tower to await a more favorable opportunity. The foreman, Sir Charles Lee, and three other members of the grand jury were Tories, however, and these four gave the evidence they had taken down at the inquest to a bookseller, Samuel Carr, who immediately published it as *Notes of the Evidence Given against the Lord Howard of Escrick*. Reprinted verbatim in the *Impartial Protestant Mercury* on 24 June by Janeway (who questioned its accuracy) this broadside is a crucial document for understanding the Tory propaganda of the next five months that reaches its climax in *Absalom and Achitophel*, for it first revealed to a startled public the treasonable conspiracy in which not only Howard but the rest of the Whig leadership, including Shaftesbury, would soon be implicated.

The two principal witnesses at the inquest were Anne Fitzharris and her maid, Theresa Peacock. Besides supporting the charge on which Howard had been arrested, testifying that they had been present when he gave Fitzharris the "heads" of the libel, they now added a sensational revelation he had supposedly made on the same occasion. In nearly identical words they testified that Howard had told Fitzharris in their hearing: "If this were once Published about, the People would rise, and then we will seize upon the King, and keep him, until such time as he passes the Bill, concerning the Exclusion of the *Duke of York*; and settle the Crown upon the *Duke of Monmouth*."[52]

This single sentence was the seed from which would rapidly grow the "Protestant Plot" of 1681. Like the earliest revelation of the Popish Plot by Oates and Tonge three years earlier, it would inspire additional informers to embellish the tale and to implicate others. Ironically, it would be taken up and used against their Whig masters by some of the Irish informers, who had been casting about for employment ever since the Oxford Parliament was dissolved and were now finding themselves in legal jeopardy. The first of them to be arrested, a few days after Howard's inquest, was Bryan Haines, who immediately gave evidence against their paymaster, John Rouse, and another minor Whig, Stephen College, the "Protestant Joiner." These two were arrested on 29 June, and Haines was given immunity as a witness. He had saved himself, it would soon emerge, by implicating them in the same plot that Mrs. Fitzharris and her maid had just made public.[53]

It would not save Fitzharris, however, who had waited too long to produce his latest plot testimony. On the morning of 1 July he was drawn to Tyburn where, a few moments before he was hanged, he called attention to a paper he had given Francis Hawkins, the chaplain in the Tower, informing the spectators that it contained his last declaration.[54] The next day the Privy Council took two actions that were closely connected, although this did not immediately appear. The first was to order Shaftesbury's arrest on charges of treason, the exact nature of which would not be made public until his grand inquest some five months later, but which was widely assumed—and rightly as it proved—to be connected with the plot about which Mrs. Fitzharris and her maid had testified at Howard's inquest. The council's second action was to order the official publication of *The Confession of Edward Fitz-harys*, the paper he had given Hawkins before his execution, and of *A Narrative: Being a True Relation of What Discourse Passed between Dr. Hawkins and Edward Fitz-Harys*, Hawkins's own account of his conversations with Fitzharris in the Tower at the time he was writing his confession. By arranging to have both works published by order in council, the government conferred an official sanction on these publications similar to that which *His Majesties Declaration* had been given three months earlier. This was altogether appropriate, for these two publications launched the second phase of the government's propaganda campaign in 1681, just as the king's *Declaration* had inaugurated the first of them. The Privy Council's two actions on 2 July were actually two prongs of the same weapon they would employ against the Whigs over the next five months: propaganda capitalizing on the conspiracy first divulged by Fitzharris, and attempts to prosecute Shaftesbury and several other Whigs for their part in the same plot.

Fitzharris's *Confession* and Hawkins's *Narrative* confirmed the testimony of Anne Fitzharris and her maid at Howard's inquest, added a few details, and affirmed that the conversation the two women claimed to have overheard was but one of several in which Howard had revealed his part in an existing conspiracy involving others besides himself. In the first of these documents Fitzharris repeated his charge that Howard had been responsible for the libel, and revealed that it was Sheriffs Bethel and Cornish, visiting him in the Tower after his arrest, who had persuaded him that if he would "make so much as a plausible Story to confirm the [Popish] Plot" and incriminate the queen and the duke of York, Parliament would save him and restore his estate. But what followed was of far greater importance: "I do further confess and declare, That the Lord *Howard* told me of a Design to seize upon the King's Person, and to carry him into the City, and there detain him till he had condescended to their Desires. *Heyns* and my self were privy to this Design, and had several Meetings with the Lord *Howard*."[55]

Hawkins was still more explicit. He declared that Fitzharris had told him of

> the design to seize the King; of this he spoke often, and said, when they (the party he always called them) had seized the King, they would have obliged him to call a Parliament, which should sit until the Bill of Exclusion against the Duke was passed; all evil Counsellers removed; and men of their chusing put into places of trust; the Militia setled, and the Navy put into good hands; all Grievances redressed, and all things ordered to their own liking: And had this Design succeeded, (he said) the Bishops and others of the Clergy would have suffered severely. The Party that were engaged in this Design (he said) were men of Interest, and had 60000 Men at command, at very short warning. . . . he told me, that himself was to have had a Company of Foot, *Heyns* a Company, and . . . a person whose name he purposely concealed, was to have had the command of a Man of War.[56]

By making Bryan Haines, who had already accused Rouse and College, a fellow witness to the "design," these two documents established his credentials as a second informer who would survive Fitzharris, adding details to the latter's story and incriminating others besides Lord Howard.

These two publications aroused an immediate furor, and the same Whigs who had formerly championed Fitzharris as a dependable witness to the Popish Plot now denounced him as a liar whose greatest libel was not the paper for which he had been executed but the confession he left behind him.[57] By 7 July a Whig verse broadside was representing Fitzharris's ghost as already remorseful for having invented a sham Protestant Plot.[58]

Unwilling to lose the momentum created by public excitement over Fitzharris's confession, the government waited only a week to bring Stephen College's indictment before a London grand jury at the Old Bailey on 8 July. It soon appeared that Bethel and Cornish had chosen its members with their usual care, and a finding of *Ignoramus* was speedily returned. Once again, however, as with Howard's inquest a fortnight earlier, a pamphlet immediately appeared disclosing the secret testimony, which the newspapers publicized further, and the public now learned for the first time that College was being charged with complicity in the same plot that Fitzharris and his wife had recently revealed: "He was one that was to seise the King at *Oxford*: and . . . unlese he would comply with his *Parliament*, there would be ready thousands to secure him."[59] This was also the first intimation the public received of a specific time and place at which the king was to have been seized: Oxford during the meeting of Parliament there in late March.

Since College's accusers alleged that Oxford had been the scene of some of his treasonable activities, he was now taken to that city, where a grand jury of a very different complexion proceeded to indict him on 14 July. For the second time in six months, Oxford became the center of the nation's attention, and Londoners would soon be pouring into the city for College's trial, due to take place on 17 August. But Tory propagandists did not await the transfer of the case to Oxford. As soon as the testimony at the London inquest linking College to the plot to seize the king became public, they began capitalizing on it. On 13 July, five days after the London inquest, L'Estrange, who until now had been filling the *Observator* with defenses of *His Majesties Declaration* and comments on the loyal addresses, first alluded to the "Design *to Seize the Person of the King*," which would consume his attention for the next few months. Within a fortnight other Tory propagandists followed in L'Estrange's wake, issuing verse broadsides that rejoiced, in the words of one of the earliest, at "the happy discovery of the hellish fanatick plot."[60]

At this point occurred the first of those defections among the witnesses to the new plot that would embarrass the government several times over the next few months. As early as 24 July, L'Estrange was privately informing Sir Leoline Jenkins, one of the principal secretaries of state, that "the widow Fitzharris is certainly tampered with and shuffles in her tale."[61] On 13 August Thompson's newspaper announced: "It's certain Mrs. *Fitz-Harys* has withdrawn her self from the Messenger that had her in Custody, and that she has retracted her Evidence before a great Magistrate in the City, and (as is given out) is gone for *Holland*; And the Commonwealths men at *Richard*'s [coffee house] boast much of their having outbidden for her Evidence," adding, however, that "it's certain she is still in Town, and Warrants are issued out to apprehend her." The king was sufficiently concerned at this defection to instruct Jenkins that it was "his pleasure that you order Dr. Hawkins to go to Oxford to be at College's trial that, in case Mrs. Fitzharris be set up to destroy her husband's last confession, he may be there to support it."[62] But his fears were groundless. Anne Fitzharris and her maid faded into obscurity once more, and though the government had lost its first two witnesses and executed the third, there seemed to be no shortage of new informants to take their place.

College's trial at Oxford began on 17 August and lasted two days. Bryan Haines, his original accuser, appeared as a witness in company with three former witnesses to the Popish Plot, John Smith, Stephen Dugdale, and Edward Turberville, all three of whom had testified at Stafford's trial the previous December. They now swore that College had boasted to them that, in the words of the indictment, "it was purposed and designed to seize the Person of . . . the King at *Oxford*" and that he would "be one of them who should seize" him. Dugdale testified that College had told him: "If the King did not yield to the Parliament, he should be forced to it," while Smith asserted that "he told me, the Parliament were agreed to secure the King, and that in order to it, all Parliament-men came very well Armed, and accompanied with Arms and Men; and he told me of a great Man [Shaftesbury] that had notice from all the Gentlemen of *England* how well they came armed." Turberville quoted College as telling him that "there are several Brave Fellows about this Town that will secure him till we have those Terms that we expect from him," and Haines explained that once this was done, according to College, "the Parliament shall sit at *Guildhall*, and adjust the Grievances of the Subject, and of the Nation." On the basis of this testimony and of Lord Chief Justice North's instruction to the jury that "a Seizing of the King, and an endeavor to do that, is a constructive Intention of the Death of the King; for Kings are never Prisoners, but in order to their Death," College was convicted of treason and sentenced to hang.[63] On 31 August he was executed before the castle gate at Oxford, protesting his innocence to the last and declaring to the spectators: "I cannot charge any man in the world with any design against the Government . . . or against his Majesty," for "I know of no Plot in the world but the Popish Plot."[64] This was a disappointing anticlimax to the government's victory in the courtroom, but a Tory pamphleteer did what he could to repair the damage by publishing a bogus speech in which College supposedly died confessing the crimes of which he had been convicted.[65]

As "perfected" by the witnesses at College's trial, this became the final version of the new Protestant Plot, which would preempt public attention for the next three months until Shaftesbury's grand inquest in late November. The individual agents in the story I have been piecing together here—Fitzharris, Howard, College, and Shaftesbury—have all figured separately in modern historical accounts of 1681, but the strand connecting them—the alleged conspiracy to seize the king at Oxford—has been ignored. Fitzharris and Howard are usually linked in these accounts only by the treasonable libel for which both of them were arrested but which was quickly forgotten in the excitement over more important revelations. College too has been chiefly remembered as the alleged contriver of a libel that was only a minor count among the charges upon which he was convicted.[66] Shaftesbury's arrest for treason has been tied so exclusively to the government's unsuccessful efforts to indict him that the specific charges against him have been largely ignored. But this is not the light in which contemporaries saw these men. To the public in the latter part of 1681 they were all alleged agents in the unfolding drama of a conspiracy to seize the king that now appeared to have been taking place behind the scenes at Oxford in late March and which could be seen as further justifying the monarch's actions at that time.[67]

The importance of the Protestant Plot first disclosed by Fitzharris, his wife, and her maid and finally "perfected" at College's trial by other witnesses was that it appeared to confirm the suspicions and innuendos the government had been propagating ever since *His Majesties Declaration* appeared in April. Thus the second phase of the Tory campaign of 1681 did not supplant the first but reinforced it, complementing the loyal addresses, which would continue to appear until the end of 1681. As early as the second week in July, indeed, some loyal addresses began referring with shocked dismay to "Plots and Conspiracies against your Royal Crown and Dignity, which under colour of securing us in our Religion and Liberties, are manifestly tending to the destruction of both."[68] The disclosure of the Protestant Plot offered "proof" of the king's hints in his *Declaration* that more lay behind the Exclusion movement than the alteration of the Succession. It revealed that the perilous situation from which the king had rescued the nation was far more serious than had previously been realized, enhanced the king's role as the nation's savior, and gave even greater importance to Oxford in March as the specific place and time of his heroic action.

In the first place, it encouraged the idea that the king, far more astute than his subjects, was already aware at the time he dissolved Parliament of a plot that would only become public some months later. This was an inference L'Estrange was drawing in the *Observator* as early as 16 July, on the strength of the testimony at College's Oxford inquest:

WH[IG]. They talk of Seizing the King at *Oxford*; Had he not his *Guards* about him?

TO[RY]. Yes, and so he had at *Windsor*, when the *Papists* should have Executed *their Plot* too.

WH. Why did not the Witnesses acquaint the King with it sooner?

TO. Why did the King make so much hast from *Oxford*, but upon that *Information*?

Later in the summer two Tory versifiers took up this theme of the king's prescience at Oxford and its heroic aftermath. The first related how, at the moment when the conspirators at Oxford were preparing to

> take him Prisoner be Sure,
> Unto *Guildhall*;
> Where he shall Endure,
> Till he yield to the Parliaments ALL,

Charles suddenly foiled their plans:

> The Parliament soon He Dissolved,
> Preventing our being Involved,
> In the Old Snare,
> As 'twas Resolved;
> You see what such Traytors will dare.

In the second author's account of events at the end of March,

> *Rowley* now with Wisdom and grave Reason,
> To prevent the swift approaching Treason,
> In season
> Put a period to their strife;
> In *Oxford* all their Stratagems confounded,
> The Roguish *Joyner* too.[69]

By dissolving Parliament and hurriedly returning to London, it now emerged, the king had managed to escape imprisonment and perhaps the fatal sequel to his father's confinement. The contingency contained in Dugdale's testimony that "if the King did not yield to the Parliament, he should be forced to it" implied an intention to seize him as soon as the third Exclusion Bill had passed through the Commons and, predictably, had been defeated by the Lords, responding once again to the king's wishes. In that case, the king had acted not a moment too soon in dissolving Parliament when he did. Thus with the public's tardy discovery of what the king was assumed to have known, or at least suspected, as early as March, his subjects could at last appreciate the magnitude of the danger from which he had delivered them and the full extent to which he was

entitled to be regarded as the nation's savior. Their growing enlightenment, initiated by *His Majesties Declaration*, had been further enlarged
by Fitzharris's confession and College's trial.

Secondly, the emergence of the Protestant Plot of 1681 reinforced the
effort to make the late House of Commons the culprit behind the recent
crisis: a tactic that the king had adopted in his *Declaration* and which
Tory propaganda and some of the loyal addresses had been promoting
throughout the spring. At College's trial, we have noticed, John Smith
had testified that "the Parliament were agreed to secure the King," and
"in order to it, all Parliament-men came very well Armed, and accompanied with Arms and Men." A writer for the Whigs had already perceived
the direction in which such revelations were leading in a pamphlet published on 12 July, as soon as the testimony at College's London inquest
pointed to Oxford during the meeting of Parliament as the scene of the
alleged conspiracy:

> For according to the Evidence which *Smith* and others gave in Court, it is no
> less than a Plot, wherein not only *City* and *Country*, but the very *Parliament*
> are all embark't and engaged. But as the naming and interesting the Parliament
> in a Conspiracy, is enough to satisfie any reasonable man that there is none at
> all; so it enlightens us upon what Motive and Inducement all this is invented
> and contrived. For the *Papists* . . . have therefore no other course to steer, but
> to render *Parliaments* suspected to his Majesty, that he may call no more. Ac-
> cordingly after they had hired a company of rascally scriblers to defame *Parlia-
> ments*, especially the *House* of *Commons*; they now assume the impudence
> openly to arraign them of a Treasonable Design of Deposing the King and
> altering the Government.[70]

The author of *Truth Vindicated*, the most important of the Whig pamphlets denouncing Fitzharris's confession, also recognized that the conspiracy to seize the king would, if true, implicate no less than Parliament
itself, and on these grounds dismissed it as a fabrication: "Surely the In-
venter of this, never considered that such a design was of a thing impossible, unless the Parliament did concurr and Act in such a Treason, and
prepare and frame their desires into Bills for that purpose; and unless the
Government, and also the force of the City did joyn with the Parliament
to detain the King in Custody for the same ends."[71] But if one were disposed to credit Fitzharris's confession and the testimony at College's trial,
the same reasoning suggested that the Whig-dominated House of Commons was fully prepared to concur in such a treason, and was prevented
from doing so only because the king took its members by surprise, dissolving Parliament before their plans could be perfected. In that case, his
"arbitrary" actions could be justified as emergency measures essential to
the survival of the legal government. Even a Whig propagandist conceded

that if the king and his ministers "were informed of such a Plot so long ago" as March (which he doubted), "this one thing had been a more justifiable reason of the speedy dismissing that Parliament, than all that are in the Declaration which was published upon that occasion."[72]

Meanwhile, Tory propagandists were already at work linking Fitzharris's confession to Shaftesbury's arrest the following day. Although Howard's had been the only Whig name to appear in that document, a Tory pamphlet quickly added another: "Sure at his Death, under the awe of a terrifi'd Conscience, in the last Agonies of Contrition and Repentance, he may be allow'd to speak Truth of a L[ord] H[oward] and E[arl] of S[haftesbury]." Referring to Shaftesbury's arrest, this writer asks indignantly, "Can it do less than strike astonishment into the heart and mind of every honest man, to find him accused of no less Crimes than *High-Treason* at last? The Conspiring to seize upon and secure the King's Person by violence; the subverting the Government, and raising Men and Arms to that purpose?"[73] Tory broadsides drew the same connection between Fitzharris's confession and Shaftesbury's arrest. One of them presents the latter in the Tower, lamenting that "*Fitz-Harris* like an *Irish* Sot, / Has me betray'd, and *H[owar]d* too, / And now we know not what to do."[74] Another, addressing Shaftesbury, declares: "Had not *Harris* spoke truth at's last Hour; / Thou ne're hadst been sent to the *Tower*."[75]

Fitzharris's confession followed by College's conviction had, for the purposes of Tory propaganda, already proved conclusively the existence of a plot involving the Whig members of the Oxford Parliament. Since Shaftesbury was their acknowledged leader, his guilt as the head of the conspiracy was assumed from the outset, even though he had not yet been indicted for the crime. In the endless flood of vituperation that appeared against Shaftesbury following his arrest, he figures repeatedly as "the Foreman" now "caught in his own Snare," the "Plotting head," the showman who "behind the *Curtain* sate" manipulating College as his "active *Puppet*," "the Head of the Crew," or the "Chief Work-man" for whom "the *Joyner* work't."[76]

Monmouth's possible involvement in the new plot, on the other hand, was generally ignored, for none of the testimony that had come to light had implicated him as an active conspirator. At Lord Howard's inquest, as we noticed, Anne Fitzharris and Theresa Peacock had quoted the Whig peer as revealing that the ultimate objective of seizing the king was to "settle the Crown upon the *Duke of Monmouth*," but no evidence had been offered of the latter's consenting to his father's confinement. Ever since March, when Shaftesbury had broached Monmouth's succession as an "expedient to save the nation," Tory propagandists had made capital of his hopes of making the young man a puppet king. It now appeared that Shaftesbury had been willing to accomplish by force what he failed to achieve by parliamentary means. Confiding his designs to one of the

Popish lords, now his fellow prisoner in the Tower, Shaftesbury declares in a Tory broadside published on 13 July:

> The Duke of *York* I would Exclude in Season,
> And set up M[onmouth] without Sense or Reason.
> I with the Godly ones will once more Joyn,
> To darken and destroy the Royal Line.[77]

But Monmouth was not openly accused of being aware of the plot to seize his father.

Bryan Haines's testimony at College's trial, on the other hand, denied that the conspirators seriously intended to make Monmouth king. He related a conversation he had initiated with College: "You pretend, you say, to the Duke of *Monmouth*, that he is a fine Prince, and stands up for the Protestant Interest: Alas, said [College], we make an Idol of him to adumbrate our Actions, for fear we should be discovered. Do you think the wise People of *England* shall ever make a Bastard upon Record King of *England*; No, said he, for tho' we praise his Actions, yet we cannot endure him, because he is against his own Father."[78] This of course supported the portrayal of Monmouth as a temporary tool that Tory propagandists had been repeating since the beginning of the Exclusion Crisis, and they continued, therefore, to exploit this image after the disclosure of the conspiracy to seize the king. As a verse broadside described him on 9 September:

> *Perkin* makes fine Legs to th' shouting Rabble,
> Who to make him King he thinks are able;
>> But the Bauble
> Is only shew'd for use:
> The silly Idiot serves but for a Tool still,
>> For Knaves to work their Feats,
> And will remain a dull mistaken Fool still,
> For all their damn'd Cabals and *Wapping* Treats.[79]

Whether or not the Whigs had seriously intended to make him king, then, the part assigned to Monmouth by Tory propagandists exploiting the Protestant Plot was that of a fool among knaves, still assuming that sedition alone would be enough to create popular pressure on Lords and king to pass his succession into law, and oblivious to the treasonable conspiracy in which he was serving as a gullible pawn. [80]

. . . . .

The Tory offensive against Shaftesbury in the press was a weathercock responding to the government's fluctuating hopes of indicting him. The summer had begun with two events that discouraged the king and his party even before they had ordered his arrest. On 21 June, as we have seen, the attorney general had failed to obtain an indictment against Lord Howard when this was offered to a Middlesex grand jury selected by Richard Goodenough, the under sheriff to Bethel and Cornish, whose terms of office were due to expire the following 28 September. At the shrieval elections for the next year held on 24 June, three days after its defeat at Howard's inquest, the government put up its own candidates, Ralph Box and Humphrey Nicholson, in hopes of bringing the era of *Ignoramus* juries to an end. But to its mortification, the Whig candidates, Thomas Pilkington and Samuel Shute, were elected by an overwhelming majority. A fortnight later, with Shaftesbury now lodged in the Tower, the government suffered another setback when, as we have noticed, a London grand jury returned an *Ignoramus* at College's inquest.

Before another week had passed, however, the government's mood changed abruptly. Its success in obtaining College's indictment from an Oxford grand jury after the earlier failure in London suggested a similar maneuver against Shaftesbury if his own activities at the time of the Oxford Parliament in March could yield charges of treason. Rumors that he would be presented before an Oxford grand jury began to circulate among the members of the king's party and even to appear in the newspapers.[81] In any event, witnesses were prepared to testify to his treasonable activities in Thanet House, his home in the City, and it might yet prove possible to reform the sheriffs' jury panels there. An attempt of this kind at Hicks Hall on 26 August proved futile in the face of Goodenough's obstinacy, but the new sheriffs, who were to take office in another month, might prove less resolute. Reflecting this hopeful mood, Tory broadsides began confidently prophesying that before long the public would see Shaftesbury's "Head fixed fast on a Gate."[82]

Throughout September and the early part of October, Tory optimism continued while the Whigs showed signs of fear at the outcome. On 8 October Shaftesbury petitioned the king to allow him to retire into exile on his plantations in Carolina. But the king, sharing his advisers' exaggerated confidence, replied that the law must be allowed to take its course.[83] His hopes were misplaced, for the next fortnight was to witness an unbroken series of defeats for the king and his friends.

Events would soon prove that the new sheriffs were as firmly committed to the cause of Whig justice as Bethel and Cornish had been. Once installed, they proceeded to appoint as under sheriff Goodenough's brother Francis, who proved in every respect as obdurate as Richard had been. For nearly two weeks the justices of the Middlesex sessions wrangled with him first at Westminster Hall and then at Hicks Hall over the panel of forty Whigs he had chosen for jury duty. At last, on 17 October, they had to admit defeat. No good could be expected of a Middlesex grand jury this term. The following day the government tried its fortunes with a London grand jury by attempting to indict John Rouse at the Old Bailey. "It was resolved," the earl of Longford explained to the duke of Ormond, "to taste the temper of this Jury by preferring an indictment against Rouse, in which if there were success, it was believed the bill against my Lord Shaftesbury was to follow."[84] The witnesses against Rouse included Haines, Smith, and Turberville, but the new sheriffs had packed the grand jury with reliable Whigs who quickly returned the bill endorsed *Ignoramus*.[85]

Matters would quickly grow worse for the government. On 24 October, the justices at Westminster Hall, worn down by repeated appeals from Shaftesbury and Howard for a writ of habeas corpus, at last ruled that they must be indicted before 28 November, the last day of Michaelmas term, or be set at liberty. The same day the attorney general gave his opinion that, since it had been impossible to discover any treasonable actions committed by Shaftesbury outside London, all hopes of indicting him at Oxford must be abandoned.[86]

Shaftesbury's victory in the king's courts was now a foregone conclusion. The unwelcome prospect was confirmed for the government a few days later when its informers reported the new sheriffs' private assurance to Shaftesbury's agents that their master had nothing to fear.[87] Halifax declared despondently that it was now pointless to proceed with plans for a grand inquest, suggesting that "he had as good be set at liberty upon terms as by a jury, which would be sure to acquitt him."[88]

But most of the king's advisers, while no less disappointed than Halifax by the recent turn of events, still hoped to wrest an important advantage from their approaching defeat in the courts. In spite of their reluctant conclusion that Shaftesbury could not be indicted, they decided, as Longford declared, "to let the world see that the King had reason for his lordship's commitment"; therefore, "it is resolved that the evidence against his lordship shall be exposed" at a grand inquest.[89] Like the setting for the Oxford Parliament the previous March, the Old Bailey in November could be turned into a theater where the Whigs' wrongdoing would be bared to public view. If the king was unable to obtain justice in his own courts, as he was fond of complaining to his adherents at this time, he could at least hope to use the inquest as a public forum at which Shaftesbury's treason might be proved to the satisfaction of his subjects if not to that of the grand jurors.

For a month preceding the inquest on 24 November, therefore, the propaganda warfare between Whigs and Tories grew more heated than ever over an approaching event in which Shaftesbury's escape from legal prosecution was already taken for granted by both sides. But since it was agreed by all parties that the verdict they were seeking would ultimately be decided by the public, they conducted an inquest of their own in the press, where Tories and Whigs sought to indict, respectively, the grand jurors or the witnesses against Shaftesbury.

In support of this new objective, Tory propagandists quickly changed their tactics in order to ensure that the government would not appear to be taken by surprise by the outcome of the inquest. They now prophesied Shaftesbury's acquittal as confidently as they had earlier predicted his conviction. A Tory broadside published on 4 November, for instance, ends with a peroration addressed to his fellow Whigs by the persona of the poem:

> Our Common-Councel lets Summon together,
> To Pannel pack't Jury's, Let's mak't our endeavour,
> For an *Habeus Corpus*, insist on our Power;
> To fetch our Great Patriots out of the *Tower*;
> And then we'le Dispute the Case, for Reformation,
> And make the proud *Torys* Resign us the Nation.[90]

And a few days later *Heraclitus Ridens* published another poem, "The Whigs Save-All," in which a second Whig persona declares:

> If we're sworn of a Jury,
> To Try a rank Tory,
>    Though no proof, we'l find him ne'r fear it,
> But if by the By,
> A Whig we must Try
>    We'l clear him though th' Apostles themselves did swear it.

> If *Tapsky* comes to 't
> I'le warrant ye we'l do 't
>    For the Sheriffs have by their *Mandamus*
> Pick'd up such a Crew
> Of Protestants True
>    That ne'r doubt it the Bill will be found *Ignoramus*.[91]

On the other side, during the weeks preceding Shaftesbury's inquest, Whig propagandists were intent on undermining the credibility of the expected testimony against the leader of their party. Robert Ferguson's *No Protestant-Plot*, published in mid-October, attacked the veracity of the eight witnesses already slated to appear at Shaftesbury's inquest, denouncing most of them as "men Infamous and Unworthy to be believed."[92] When, shortly afterwards, it was learned that another witness, John Booth, had come forward, the Whigs lost no time in publishing *The Information of Capt. Henry Wilkinson*, in which a debtor imprisoned in the King's Bench claimed that he had recently been approached by Booth, his fellow prisoner, with a promise that "I might have five Hundred

Pounds *per Annum* setled upon me and my Heirs, or Ten Thousand Pounds in money, which I pleased," on condition that he join Booth in testifying against Shaftesbury at his approaching inquest.[93] Ferguson quickly followed this pamphlet with *The Second Part of No Protestant Plot* in which he denounced Booth as "one who had ere this been Hanged for Coyning and Murder, if His Majesty had not vouchsafed him his gracious Pardon."[94]

The one point of agreement between Whigs and Tories was that, since there was no longer any doubt of Shaftesbury's acquittal by the grand jury, the objective of both parties at the approaching inquest must be to obtain a true bill or an *Ignoramus* from the public at large, not simply on the Whig nobleman's involvement in the plot to seize the king at Oxford but on the very existence of that plot. This of course, as its title proclaimed, was the subject of Ferguson's *No Protestant-Plot*, in which he systematically challenged every allegation of its existence since the earliest of these at Lord Howard's inquest in June by publicizing Anne Fitzharris's later retraction of her testimony on that occasion. He also claimed to have seen a paper written the night before his execution in which Fitzharris allegedly repudiated his famous confession, and he disparaged the testimony at College's trial before proceeding to attack the witnesses expected to appear against Shaftesbury.[95] The most important rebuttal to Ferguson, L'Estrange's *Notes upon Stephen College*, published the first week in November, also stressed the essential coherence of these allegations while insisting on their veracity. In showing the close correspondence between Fitzharris's confession and the testimony at College's trial, L'Estrange insisted that all this evidence (and, by implication, that which could be expected to follow at Shaftesbury's inquest) proved conclusively that "there was a Design upon the King at *Oxford*," as must be granted "by any man that has but eyes in's head, and looks that way."[96]

Ultimately, the importance to both sides of convincing the public that there had, or had not, been a plot to seize the king turned not only on implicating or exonerating Shaftesbury as its principal instigator but on justifying or discrediting Charles's action in dissolving the Oxford Parliament and failing to summon another, the central issue of political debate since March. Ferguson in mid-November echoed the earlier Whig propagandists of July by reminding his readers of the essential link between the king's actions at Oxford and the details of the supposed Protestant Plot about to be rehearsed once again at the Old Bailey:

In the first place, they who advised the Dissolution of the last Parliament, do by obtruding upon the world the belief of a *Protestant Plot*, hope to justifie their Wisdom and Loyalty in giving His Majesty so unseasonable and pernicious Counsel. For as they cannot but observe, that that effort of Royal Power, which

they put the King upon, hath 'tis feared, diminished the confidence which the
people put in his Prudence and Conduct, and not only embroiled his affairs at
home, but lessened his Interest and Reputation abroad; so they could think of
no other means to vindicate themselves from the many imputations which they
lye under, for influencing His Majesty to so hasty and prejudicial an act of
Prerogative and Royal Authority, but by ascribing it unto an indispensable
Necessity, occasioned by a Conspiracy of seising His Person.[97]

For the Tories, if all went as expected, the great government propaganda
campaign of 1681 would close as it had opened with a public performance staged for the benefit of the public and designed to show once
again that the king's recent actions, far from being arbitrary, were necessary to the continued existence of the lawful government.

A week before that spectacle was due to take place, *Absalom and
Achitophel* appeared.

.   .   .   .   .

Before turning to *Absalom and Achitophel*, however, we must first consider the role Dryden had been playing between early March and late
November 1681, the months we have been reviewing in this chapter.

At Oxford on 19 March 1681, the Saturday before Parliament was to
open there the following Monday, the king and members of both houses
met on neutral ground to witness a performance of Charles Saunders's
*Tamerlane the Great*, and to hear an epilogue that Dryden had written
specially for this occasion. Before such a mixed audience neutrality was
more than ever necessary, and the epilogue he produced for it would
again be designed, like those discussed in the last chapter, to please all his
spectators without exception.

For this epilogue, coming two days before Charles was to address the
two houses, Dryden understandably took his cue from the conciliatory
speech with which the king had opened the preceding parliament on 21
October 1680. On that occasion, Charles had reminded the members that
"all *Europe* have their Eyes upon this Assembly, and think their own
Happiness or Misery, as well as Ours, will depend upon it." Dryden in
turn employs a theatrical image to tell the members,

> *Oxford* is now the publick *Theater*;
> And you both Audience are, and Actors here.
> The gazing World on the New Scene attend,
> Admire the turns, and wish a prosp'rous end.

The king had assured the members that what "I value above all the Treasure in the World . . . is a perfect Union amongst Our Selves. . . . Let Us
therefore take care that We do not gratifie Our Enemies, and Discourage

Our Friends by any unseasonable Disputes. . . . But from so great Prudence and so good Affections as yours, I can fear nothing of this kind; but do relie upon you all, that you will use your best Endeavours to bring this Parliament to a good and happy Conclusion." Dryden expresses a similar hope for the new Parliament, assembled in a setting so conducive to harmony:

> This Place the seat of Peace, the quiet Cell
> Where Arts remov'd from noisy buisness [sic] dwell,
> Shou'd calm your Wills, unite the jarring parts,
> And with a kind Contagion seize your hearts:
> Oh! may its Genius, like soft Musick move,
> And tune you all to Concord and to Love.

Charles had declared that "nothing but this [perfect union] can Restore the Kingdom to that Strength and Vigour which it seems to have lost, and Raise Us again to that Consideration which *England* hath usually had."[98] Dryden, adopting the Ark in the Flood as a secondary image for that of the ship of state tossed in a storm, represents concord and love as a safe harbor beckoning the members:

> Our Ark that has in Tempests long been tost,
> Cou'd never land on so secure a Coast.
> From hence you may look back on Civil Rage,
> And view the ruines of the former Age.
> Here a New World its glories may unfold,
> And here be sav'd the remnants of the Old.[99]

Like most of his audience, Dryden could scarcely be expected to foresee that the king's stern speech opening the new Parliament two days later would replace fawning condescension with harsh admonishment and signal the beginning of a new policy.

It was only after that new policy had been in operation for a few weeks that Dryden began to abandon the nonpartisan stance he had cultivated until now as a professional man of the theater. By this time he was no longer writing plays himself, but he continued to write prologues and epilogues for the plays of other dramatists, and it is in these that we can detect the first signs of a change. The epilogue to John Banks's *The Unhappy Favourite*, produced at Drury Lane in April or May, is another piece of banter in the usual vein, but the targets of Dryden's ridicule on this occasion are the Whig booksellers:

> 'Tis not our want of Wit that keeps us Poor,
> For then the Printers Press would suffer more:
> Their Pamphleteers each day their Venom spit,
> They thrive by Treason and we starve by Wit.

> Confess the truth, which of you has not laid
> Four Farthings out to buy the *Hatfield Maid*?
> Or which is duller yet, and more wou'd spight us,
> *Democritus* his Wars with *Heraclitus*?[100]

The implied relationship between players and audience here has subtly shifted. The tone is still playful, but in place of a spurious cohesiveness between the two, achieved by laughing at a common target, the players now jibe at a group that includes not only the Whig booksellers but that portion of the audience which buys and reads their productions so avidly. In relation to the latter, this is good-humored abuse in the tradition of comic raillery expected in London prologues, but for the first time political differences among the audience supply the basis for this raillery and ally the players with one segment against another.

Again, in the prologue he wrote for the performance of a play at Oxford in the summer of 1681, Dryden praises the university for its loyalty to the Crown, a frequent topic in addressing this academic audience, but the tone has grown more serious:

> What e're the Story be, the Moral's true,
> The Wit we lost in Town, we find in you.
> Our Poets their fled Parts may draw from hence,
> And fill their windy Heads with sober Sense.
> When *London* Votes with *Southwark*'s disagree,
> Here they may find their long lost Loyalty.
>
> . . . . . . . . . . . . . .
>
> He, whose undaunted Muse, with Loyal Rage,
> Has never spar'd the Vices of the Age,
> Here finding nothing that his Spleen can raise,
> Is forc'd to turn his Satire into Praise.[101]

The first unequivocal sign of a decisive change, however, appears in Dryden's prologue for a command performance of *The Unhappy Favourite* before the king and queen at Drury Lane, given either toward the end of the season in the spring of 1681, or, just as probably, the following autumn.[102] This prologue, like the one he had produced for the Oxford performance before the king in March, ignores the play it ostensibly introduces to pursue a serious subject. Dryden also returns here to the complex image of the Ark for the ship of state he had used so skillfully in March. But the use to which he now puts it is radically different.

> When first the Ark was Landed on the Shore,
> And Heaven had vow'd to curse the Ground no more,
> When Tops of Hills the Longing Patriark saw,
> And the new Scene of Earth began to draw;

The Dove was sent to View the Waves Decrease,
And first brought back to Man the Pledge of Peace:
'Tis needless to apply when those appear
Who bring the Olive, and who Plant it here.
We have before our eyes the Royal Dove,
Still Innocence is Harbinger to Love,
The Ark is open'd to dismiss the Train,
And People with a better Race the Plain.[103]

In using the Ark on Mount Ararat as a parallel that he proceeds to "apply" to the political situation of England in the late spring or autumn of 1681, Dryden presents it as already "landed on the shore" and "opened to dismiss the train" who in March were still afloat in the midst of tempests, and still clinging to a hope that the approaching Parliament would unite in concord to bring them to safe harbor. Now, the tempests ended, it is Charles, the "Royal Dove," who has brought the "Pledge of Peace" to his relieved subjects, prepared at last to "people with a better race the plain." It is an image of the land already restored to tranquillity through the good offices of the king that accords exactly with the line taken since April by Tory propagandists and by the numerous loyal addresses.

The following October, Dryden wrote both the prologue and epilogue for a revival of Nathaniel Lee's *Mithridates* at Drury Lane. These return to the bantering manner of all his London theater pieces up to this time (with the exception of the prologue to *The Unhappy Favourite*), but now, instead of Popish plotters at home and other Catholics abroad, it is the witnesses to the Popish Plot, particularly Oates, on whom the players pour scathing ridicule, and in choosing a target that a part of their audience would have found offensive, they abandon all pretense to a common bond with the spectators as a whole.

The Plot's remov'd, a Witness of Renown [Oates]
Has lodg'd it safe, at t' other End o' th' Town,
And that it ne're may fail, some pious Whore
Has cast her Mite, and fairly at his Dore
Laid two small squalling Evidences more;
Which well instructed, if we take their words,
In time may come to hang two Popish Lords.[104]

We have the testimony of Richard Janeway, the Whig bookseller, that these pieces had the divisive effect on the audience that Dryden must have foreseen and deliberately fostered. In his *Impartial Protestant Mercury* Janeway wrote: "There is a Report that a Revived Play was some days since Acted on an Eminent Publick Theatre, and the Prologue is extreamly talked of, some Verses of which are these that follow." He then quotes, without of course naming the still unknown author, the last half of the prologue with its sharp jibes at Oates and the other witnesses, and comments: "Many are pleased to *Applaud* these Lines for the *Wit*, but *many more* extreamly admire at them for diverse other reasons."[105] The following day Nathaniel Thompson responded to Janeway in his own newspaper: "Whereas Mr. *Janeway* in his *Partial Protestant* of yesterday, is pleased to make use of part of a *Prologue* to a reviv'd Play lately acted at the *Theatre Royal*, with his grave Authors Animadversions upon the same. By his good leave, I'll incert a part of the *Epilogue* to the same Play, and leave it to the chewing of the Brotherhood."[106] And he proceeds to quote some more of Dryden's lines ridiculing Oates. Clearly, Thompson had found an unknown ally in the author of the prologue and epilogue.

These theater pieces that follow the Oxford epilogue at the time of the Parliament there show Dryden abandoning, at last, the pose of a neutral bystander to cultivate the sympathies of one part of the audience at the expense of the other. But we must remember that, while these more partisan prologues and epilogues were being heard at Drury Lane from April or May 1681, the audience in the theater was of course unaware of their authorship, and not a single one was published under Dryden's name or publicly attributed to him before the appearance of *Absalom and Achitophel* in November.[107] Until the publication of that poem, therefore, and the rapid spread of rumors that he was its author, Dryden's emergence at the eleventh hour as a Tory spokesman remained unknown to the public at large.

The anonymous prologues and epilogues for theater productions beginning in April or May 1681 represent Dryden's only demonstrable publications between that date and mid-November.[108] By late summer he was almost certainly, in view of its length, at work on *Absalom and Achitophel*. With this work, because of events he could not foresee, the Tory propaganda campaign of 1681 would reach not only its climax but also its conclusion.[109]

. . . . .

Coming late in the campaign of 1681, *Absalom and Achitophel*, published on 17 November, pursues the same goal as practically all Tory propaganda since March. Like these earlier newspapers, pamphlets, broadsides, and loyal addresses taking their cue from *His Majesties Declaration* over the past eight months, Dryden's poem is designed to show that the king's recent actions, far from being arbitrary and tyrannical, were emergency measures adopted in the face of a grave crisis that had imperiled the continued existence of the lawful government.[110] Its originality lies not in its purpose, but in the means Dryden chose to adopt for accomplishing this common design.

Any estimate of Dryden's originality must take into account his being the first to write a narrative poem about the recent dangers confronting the nation from which the king had finally rescued his subjects after matters had been allowed to drift to the very brink of disaster, and his making the familiar history of Absalom's rebellion instrumental to this new design. The story from 2 Samuel, already employed as a parallel for Charles's restoration in so many thanksgiving sermons, for Monmouth's disobedience to his father in the Tory propaganda of 1680, and for the duke's unequal alliance with Shaftesbury in other Tory broadsides in the spring of 1681, was now enlisted for a more complex function. In the story's latest incarnation, Absalom and Achitophel would continue to serve as analogues for Monmouth and Shaftesbury, but David would acquire greater importance than either in keeping with the central place accorded to Charles in Tory propaganda ever since he dissolved the Oxford Parliament in March 1681.

In *Absalom and Achitophel* Dryden employs a method the exact opposite of that found in earlier biblical parallels. Whereas a poem such as *Naboth's Vinyard* relates an Old Testament story in which the presence of a few discrepancies directs the reader's attention to an analogous contemporary situation, *Absalom and Achitophel* does just the reverse. It recounts the Tory version of the Exclusion Crisis and its resolution, but by setting the narrative in biblical times and employing biblical names, Dryden compels the reader to recognize unfolding analogies with the past. The modern allusions in *Naboth's Vinyard* implicitly invoke a contemporary parallel to this ancient story; the biblical allusions in *Absalom and Achitophel* explicitly recall a historical parallel to this account of English rebelliousness late in the reign of Charles II. Instead of accommodating a biblical narrative to a contemporary situation in the homiletic manner borrowed from the pulpit by earlier Tory propagandists, Dryden has accommodated his contemporary narrative to the biblical past in a manner all his own.

Dryden's preface "To the Reader" gives no indication of the changed direction the familiar Old Testament parallel will take in his poem, nor of David's increased importance there. In what is designed as an ethical appeal to unimpassioned readers on behalf of his anonymous poem, Dryden presents himself as a moderate Tory who bears no personal animus toward the Whigs, least of all the duke of Monmouth. He therefore focuses exclusively on the satirical aspects of his poem in an attempt to justify his attacks on the king's opponents, while referring to Charles only in the course of expressing a wish that Monmouth may yet be reconciled with his father: "Were I the Inventour, who am only the Historian, I shoud certainly conclude the Piece, with the Reconcilement of *Absalom* to *David*. And, who knows but this may come to pass? Things were not brought to an Extremity where I left the Story: There seems, yet, to be room left for a Composure; hereafter, there may only be for pity."[111] As a result he sounds here much like the Tory authors of those cautionary appeals in biblical guise like *Absalom's Conspiracy* and *A Seasonable Invitation for Monmouth to Return to Court* that had been written for a very different purpose. But the impression created by this somewhat disingenuous apologia from one who had formerly enjoyed Monmouth's patronage is an inadequate image of *Absalom and Achitophel*, which, as Narcissus Luttrell noted on his copy of the poem, is not just "agt ye Duke of Monmouth, Earl of Shaftsbury & that party," but "in vindication of the King & his freinds."[112]

What is commonly overlooked in discussions of *Absalom and Achitophel* is that Dryden's parallel between Charles and David, like all the other historical parallels he would draw as a Tory propagandist over the next few years, employs Plutarch's method of singling out disparities as well as similarities in the course of comparing the two figures. In the "Life of Plutarch" he was to write for the translation of *Plutarchs Lives* published two years later in 1683, Dryden would freely paraphrase the words of Montaigne to emphasize this very method as one of Plutarch's greatest and most characteristic achievements.

> But an equitable Judge who takes things by the same handle which *Plutarch* did, will find there is no injury offer'd to either party, tho there be some disparity betwixt the persons: For he weighs every circumstance by it self, and judges separately of it: Not comparing Men at a lump, nor endeavouring to prove they were alike in all things, but allowing for disproportion of quality or fortune, shewing wherein they agreed or disagreed, and wherein one was to be preferr'd before the other.[113]

At a time when the preachers of thanksgiving sermons had become adept at using Plutarch's method to show how Charles II "was to be preferr'd before" David on such scores as birth and personal courage, we should not be surprised to find Dryden implying more important differences between the two besides drawing significant likenesses. The very complexity of the biblical David's character and behavior encouraged this kind of treatment.

The fascination with David as a type of Christ and a model for Christian kings in some studies of Dryden's political poetry has created a one-sided picture at odds with the rounded image of him portrayed in 2 Samuel and conveyed to seventeenth-century readers through not only the Bible but also numerous scriptural commentaries and sermons.[114] As these readers could hardly avoid noticing, the qualities and achievements responsible for David's heroic stature in the Old Testament are matched by moral transgressions of almost equal magnitude. In one of the standard scriptural commentaries popular in the Restoration period, for example, the chapter on 2 Samuel begins with a list of David's familiar virtues that is immediately followed by a reminder of his equally notorious vices:

> Yet as he was endowed with all these excellencies, he had also his failings, yea, strong corruptions, as exorbitant lusts, uncleannesse, cruelty, which discovered themselves in the matter of *Uriah*; pride in numbring of the people; partial injustice, in passing an unrighteous sentence against innocent *Mephibosheth*; lying, dissembling, which the Holy Ghost hath also recorded, not to encourage any to do the like; but as Sea-marks, that they may avoid these Rocks, against which so choice a Vessel dashed, and had surely splitted and perished, had not Gods Grace and holy Spirit, as a timely gale of winde, blown him off, and reduced him into his right course by unfeigned repentance.[115]

Thus David's role for modern times is in some respects that of an exemplary figure whose virtues invite imitation, but in others that of a cautionary example whose vices, mistakes, and weaknesses ought to be shunned.[116]

It is the fallible David of 2 Samuel, chapters 13–19, whom Dryden invokes as a parallel for Charles in *Absalom and Achitophel*. These seven chapters include Absalom's rebellion, of course, but they begin some years before that event, when the young man makes his first appearance in the opening verse of chapter 13, and they end with David mourning the death of his son in chapter 19. Taken together they form a long chain of connected events that acquire their coherence from a common theme: the relations between the king and his capricious son, and the extent to which David's own public behavior is affected by that private relationship.

It is a story in which David's foolish indulgence toward his favorite son leads him to condone or ignore Absalom's transgressions, allowing them to continue and increase until David's own life and those of his subjects are endangered, and converting what would have been shameful weakness in a private person into culpable negligence on the part of a king. Absalom slays his elder brother Amnon to avenge their sister Tamar and flees abroad. "And the soul of King David longed to go forth unto Absalom" (2 Sam. 13:39). At the solicitation of Joab, who "perceived that the king's heart was toward Absalom," David pardons his son and permits him to return to Jerusalem but not to enter his presence. Yet when Joab pleads for him a second time, David sends for his son, "and the king kissed Absalom" (2 Sam. 14:33). Emboldened by his father's lenity,

Absalom sets about publicly defaming the king and gradually winning away his subjects' allegiance, but David never lifts a finger to stop him. At last Absalom collects his rebel forces in Hebron, David flees Jerusalem with those who remain loyal to him, and both sides prepare for battle, David ordering his captains: "Deal gently for my sake with the young man, even with Absalom" (2 Sam. 18:5). There follows "a great slaughter that day of twenty thousand men" in a battle that need never have occurred if David had taken timely action during the course of several years in which Absalom was openly stealing the hearts of his people. David's forces are victorious over the rebels and Absalom is slain by Joab, but the king's only response to the messengers bringing news of their success is to inquire anxiously, "Is the young man Absalom safe?" (2 Sam. 18: 28–32). Informed of his son's death, David is inconsolable. "And the victory that day was turned into mourning unto all the people: for the people heard say that day how the king was grieved for his son" (2 Sam. 19:2). Joab bitterly reproaches David: "Thou hast shamed this day the faces of all thy servants, which this day have saved thy life . . . in that thou lovest thine enemies, and hatest thy friends. For thou hast declared this day, that thou regardest neither princes nor servants: for this day I perceive, that if Absalom had lived, and all we had died this day, then it had pleased thee well" (2 Sam. 19:5–6). Stung by this just rebuke and warned by Joab that his followers, angry at his indifference, are about to abandon him, David at last leaves off his selfish grieving and resumes his responsibilities toward his neglected subjects.

Biblical commentators on 2 Samuel, chapters 13–19, all found the same common theme running through the various episodes: "*David* was ever too indulgent a father, and smarted for it," in the words of one of them; "he was so indulgent a father," in the words of another, "that his excesse of love would make him dispence with the greatest fault, in one that was so dear unto him."[117] They condemned David's partiality as supreme magistrate when after Amnon's slaying he "reconciled himself to his wicked son, and again received him into grace and favour, neglecting to execute justice, by inflicting upon him that punishment which Gods law required, and his bloody sin deserved."[118] Instead of kissing Absalom, "he should have *kicked* him rather; and not have hardened him to further villany."[119] They reproved the king's negligence in ignoring his son's seditious behavior and failing to act before it led to insurrection, noting that "*David* was so blinded with fond affection, that he could see nothing amiss in *Absolom*."[120] And they were particularly severe on David's behavior after the battle, blaming "his excessive love and unbounded affection towards his dear Absalom, which doth so wholly engross and take him up, that he doth not so much as mention other and far

greater causes of grief, as the slaughter of twenty thousand of his subjects."[121] In every instance David had placed private feelings before public
responsibilities, leniency before justice, and the consequence was "the
indangering of all his people."[122]

.   .   .   .   .

*Absalom and Achitophel* opens with David, just as it closes with him, for
it relates the rise and progress of a crisis in the English David's kingdom,
and the means by which these perils to his own safety and that of his
subjects were finally overcome. Dryden begins by giving his contemporary narrative the biblical setting it will bear throughout its course:

> In pious times, e'r Priest-craft did begin,
> Before *Polygamy* was made a sin;
> When man, on many, mutiply'd his kind,
> E'r one to one was, cursedly, confind:
>
> (1–4)

By invoking a time "When Nature prompted, and no law deny'd / Promiscuous use of Concubine and Bride," Dryden is not seeking to excuse
Charles's promiscuity, as is sometimes said, much less to convert it into a
heroic virtue. But he does deflect the force of an awkward admission by
focusing attention on the comic incongruity of a modern history set in
biblical times. The effect is much the same as that of his later witticism
about the Popish Plotters, "Some thought they God's Anointed meant to
Slay / By Guns, invented since full many a day" (130–31). Charles cannot
be exonerated by the more tolerant standards of an earlier age, but he
benefits all the same from Dryden's reminder that it is only the accident of
having been born at the wrong time that makes him culpable for the same
behavior that carried no stigma for the biblical David:

> Then, *Israel*'s Monarch, after Heaven's own heart,
> His vigorous warmth did, variously, impart
> To Wives and Slaves: And, wide as his Command,
> Scatter'd his Maker's Image through the Land.
>
> (7–10)

With these lines Dryden begins to divert attention from the illicitness of
Charles's relationships to the sheer quantity of their results, which, while
scarcely rivaling the biblical David's record, nevertheless affords a genuine (though essentially frivolous) likeness between these two fathers of
widely different eras, and earns them the first of three epithets Dryden
uses to mark their closest similarities:

> several Mothers bore
> To Godlike *David*, several Sons before.
> But since like slaves his bed they did ascend,
> No True Succession could their seed attend.
> Of all this Numerous Progeny was none
> So Beautifull, so brave as *Absolon*.
>
> (13–18)

This first epithet for the English David, "godlike," will also be his last, in the penultimate line of the poem. But the term carries an entirely different and less serious connotation here from that which it will come to bear later. On this earlier occasion both Davids are called godlike in the facetious sense that they parody the divine plenitude by scattering their "Maker's Image through the Land."[123]

So too their offspring, following the standard Tory interpretation of 2 Samuel we noticed in the last chapter, are alike in being ineligible by birth for "True Succession" to their fathers' thrones: the one fact essential to the succeeding narrative that has made it necessary to mention Charles's promiscuous behavior at all. The groundwork is now complete for an even closer and far more significant likeness between the English David and his biblical predecessor, introduced by Dryden's second epithet for the two kings:

> With secret Joy, indulgent *David* view'd
> His Youthfull Image in his Son renew'd:
> To all his wishes Nothing he deny'd,
> And made the Charming *Annabel* his Bride.
> What faults he had (for who from faults is free?)
> His Father coud not, or he woud not see.
> Some warm excesses, which the Law forebore,
> Were constru'd Youth that purg'd by boyling o'r:
> And *Amnon*'s Murther, by a specious Name,
> Was call'd a Just Revenge for injur'd Fame.
>
> (31–40)

Nothing as serious as this charge of partiality in administering justice where his son is concerned is ever laid to Charles's account throughout the rest of the poem. He is shown at his most culpable when he is most similar to the biblical David who looked the other way at Absalom's crimes: a low point in Dryden's characterization of Charles from which any change thereafter can only raise him in the reader's estimation. It seems less likely that Dryden is alluding to a single unpunished crime of Monmouth's whose identity has never been agreed upon, than that he is assuming the contemporary reader's familiarity with any number of rumors, true or false, of the young man's escaping the rigors of the law through his royal father's notorious complaisance.

The opening verse paragraph of Dryden's poem turns last of all from the wayward sons shared by the two monarchs to the turbulent subjects both are called upon to rule:

> The *Jews*, a Headstrong, Moody, Murmuring race,
> As ever try'd th' extent and stretch of grace;
> God's pamper'd people whom, debauch'd with ease,
> No King could govern, nor no God could please.
>
> (45–48)

Dryden's language evokes those numerous reproofs to the children of Israel as "a stiffnecked people" in Exodus and Deuteronomy, or "a rebellious people" in the jeremiads of Isaiah and Ezekiel, that preachers were fond of repeating. In proceeding to trace the remarkable similarity between the monarchs in the way they came to their thrones, however, Dryden attaches a third and final epithet to the two Davids which suggests that the language used to describe the children of Israel applies with equal force to the English people.

> They who when *Saul* was dead, without a blow,
> Made foolish *Ishbosheth* the Crown forgo;
> Who banisht *David* did from *Hebron* bring,
> And, with a Generall Shout, proclaim'd him King:
> Those very *Jewes*, who, at their very best,
> Their Humour more than Loyalty exprest,
> Now, wondred why, so long, they had obey'd
> An Idoll Monarch which their hands had made.
>
> (57–64)

The youthful Charles invited to return from abroad by the Convention Parliament is like the young David brought back from Hebron by the Israelites (2 Sam. 5:1–5): not only were both of them joyfully acclaimed as kings, but each of them was also a "banisht *David*" who had earlier been rejected by the same volatile and capricious people who now reversed direction, and would later do so again.

Once Dryden takes up the relations between Charles and his subjects, however, the close similarities he has been drawing between the two Davids until now come to an end, to be replaced by the first of several implicit disparities. His poem has begun with the English David's complaisance toward Absalom, it now emerges, not because, as in 2 Samuel, it is to be the principal cause of the troubles that follow (an eventuality precluded by Monmouth's marginal role in the Exclusion Crisis), but because it epitomizes Charles's behavior toward those he governs. His indulgence of his coddled son is an exact reflection of the father-king's forbearance toward the "pamper'd people" who are his subjects, "too fortunately free" beneath his mild yoke. Each significant element in the earlier account of the spoiled Absalom now finds its exact counterpart in the description of a people "debauch'd with ease" and "less circumscrib'd and bound" by laws than any population on earth, yet petulantly dreaming that "they wanted libertie." We recall how Charles instinctively excuses or overlooks his son's transgressions:

> Some warm excesses, which the Law forbore,
> Were constru'd Youth that purg'd by boyling o'r:
> And *Amnon*'s Murther, by a specious Name,
> Was call'd a Just Revenge for injur'd Fame.
>
> (37–40)

But in the same fashion he disregards the youthful careers of his former enemies in showering them now with favors:

> Some, by their Monarch's fatall mercy grown,
> From Pardon'd Rebels, Kinsmen to the Throne;
> Were rais'd in Power and publick Office high:
> Strong Bands, if Bands ungratefull men could tye.
>
> (146–49)

Just as the English David's indulgence of his favorite son could long continue without any warning signs of danger,

> Thus Prais'd, and Lov'd, the Noble Youth remain'd,
> While *David*, undisturb'd, in *Sion* raign'd.
>
> (41–42)

so his coddled subjects continue peaceable as long as "no form'd Design, / Nor Interest made the Factious Croud to joyn" (67–68):

> And *David*'s mildness manag'd it so well,
> The Bad found no occasion to Rebell.
>
> (77–78)

But in each case the effect of the complacent couplet is at once inverted by the addition of a proverbial truth reminding us that all such peaceful appearances are misleading, since no tranquillity can be permanent. Where the English David's negligent relationship with his son is concerned, we are quickly reminded:

> But Life can never be sincerely blest:
> Heaven punishes the bad, and proves the best.
>
> (43–44)

So in the case of Charles's pampered subjects, we are told:

> But, when to Sin our byast Nature leans,
> The carefull Devil is still at hand with means.
>
> (79–80)

As anyone familiar with the biblical David could not fail to recall, his own conduct toward his subjects was quite the reverse of his indulgence of his favorite son. Quick to punish and slow to forgive, the David of 2 Samuel is normally a severe ruler who exacts strict obedience from his people and makes examples of those who fail him in their duties. As one biblical commentator remarked, David was "blinded with fond affection" for Absalom, "though otherwise he were sagacious enough, yea suspicious without cause, as of good *Mephibosheth*."[124]

In 1685, in *Threnodia Augustalis: A Funeral-Pindarique Poem Sacred to the Happy Memory of King Charles II*, Dryden would once more contrast David with Charles to the latter's advantage, this time explicitly, and again on the score of severity vs. mildness. Relating the deathbed scene in which Charles, "kind, good and gracious to the last," anxiously recommends "all that on earth he held most dear" to the care of his brother James, Dryden juxtaposes this image with another deathbed scene, that of David (1 Kings 2:5–9), whose dying charge to his own successor Solomon was to pay off his father's old scores by putting Joab to the sword ("let not his hoar head go down to the grave in peace") as well as Shimei, "which cursed me with a grievous curse" ("his hoar head bring thou down to the grave with blood"):

> That King who liv'd to Gods own heart,
>  Yet less serenely died than he:
> *Charles* left behind no harsh decree
> For Schoolmen with laborious art
>   To salve from cruelty:
>  Those, for whom love cou'd no excuses frame,
>  He graciously forgot to name.[125]

"Mildness" and "mercy," the two terms Dryden introduces early in *Absalom and Achitophel* to describe Charles's characteristic behavior toward his people, will be repeated many times and amplified later in the poem, always in respect to this same subject. The attitude Dryden adopts toward these two related qualities in *Absalom and Achitophel* is deliberately ambivalent. As a mirror image of Charles's paternal indulgence toward his son, the father-king's permissive treatment of his subjects, tacitly encouraging their insubordination, is as shortsighted a policy as the other. It is a more generous weakness than the first, since it escapes the taint of self-love inseparable from indulgence of one's offspring ("With

secret Joy, indulgent *David* view'd / His Youthfull Image in his Son
renew'd" [31–32]), but it is capable of far greater harm, to the degree that
a monarch's responsibilities for the welfare of an entire nation exceed
those of a parent for his children.

Even the first appearance of these terms in the poem, referring to the
earlier part of Charles's reign before the beginning of the Exclusion Crisis, carries this ambivalent note. That "the Bad found no occasion to
Rebell" in the previous era is credited to the fact that "*David*'s mildness
manag'd it so well"; and that quality in a ruler is always admired in the
abstract. On the other hand, the policy by which some fomenters of the
Exclusion Crisis had earlier been "rais'd in Power and publick Office
high" thanks to "their Monarch's fatall mercy" is tacitly condemned as
unwise. David's "fatal mercy" is not, however, as has been argued in
recent years, an allusion to Charles's promise of an Act of Oblivion in the
Declaration of Breda on the eve of his restoration, which all parties had
accepted at the time as an essential concession short of which Charles
could never have recovered his throne without a bloody struggle, whose
outcome would have been uncertain.[126] On the contrary, as the lines
make clear, "fatal mercy" is the king's unwise but well-meant policy during the years following the Restoration of elevating these former enemies
"from Pardon'd Rebels," the status they enjoyed unchallenged under the
Act of Oblivion, to "Kinsmen to the Throne," that is to say, peers of the
realm, by a gratuitous series of promotions through the ranks of the no-
bility; appointing them to positions of trust; and taking them into his
counsels, by which means they were "rais'd in Power and publick Office
high."[127]

But the phrase "fatal mercy" also carried a very specific connotation to
Englishmen of middle age who remembered the troubled times from
which the Restoration had seemingly delivered the nation. It referred to
the policies of the king's father, which his supporters blamed in no small
part for his eventual death, and which had consisted not in his issuing
pardons, either general or individual, but in his making concessions to his
opponents during the years immediately preceding the first Civil War that
had strengthened them to the point where they were at last able to challenge his authority successfully.

We can better understand Dryden's ambivalent attitude toward "fatal
mercy" by considering the way he treats this conception in his earliest
poems following the Restoration. In *Astraea Redux* (1660), he addresses
the newly restored king, praising him for possessing the same temperament that had proved fatal to his father, yet encouraging him to exercise
it freely:

> But you, whose goodness your discent doth show,
> Your Heav'nly Parentage and earthly too;

By that same mildness which your Fathers Crown
Before did ravish, shall secure your own.
Not ty'd to rules of Policy, you find
Revenge less sweet then a forgiving mind.[128]

The explanation of this paradox must be sought in the change of conditions between 1640 and 1660. The same mildness that ravished his father's crown will secure his son's because the temporary aberration of English loyalty that cost Charles I his throne and eventually his life has now faded into history. What was a fatal weakness in the father will be a saving grace in the son.

Returning to this subject less than two years later in *To My Lord Chancellor* (1662), Dryden tells Clarendon that

Heav'n would your Royal Master should exceed
Most in that Vertue which we most did need,
And his mild Father (who too late did find
All mercy vain but what with pow'r was joyn'd,)
His fatal goodnesse left to fitter times,
Not to increase but to absolve our Crimes.[129]

Again it is the return of fitter times and an altered mood among the people that promises opposite effects from the same family traits. Under different circumstances, the "fatal goodness" of the martyred monarch becomes a life-giving quality to be emulated by his more fortunate successor. But mercy must be joined with power if it is to be exercised wisely, as Charles I learned to his regret. Since the emergence of such a combination has been demonstrated by the universal acclaim recently accompanying his son's restoration, the conditions under which mercy becomes a blessing now exist.

As all these considerations of the subject make clear, Dryden uses such terms as "mildness" and "mercy" in two quite different, though related, senses: to refer either to temperament or to policy. As temperament, mildness and mercy carry no suggestion of blame whatever. They are virtues derived from heaven, conspicuous tokens of the martyred monarch's saintly nature, which, as congenital dispositions, have been inherited by his son. As policy, they figure as an instinctive exercise of these same inclinations that will prove wise or misguided, beneficial or dangerous to the commonwealth, depending on their appropriateness to the circumstances obtaining at any particular time.

In *Absalom and Achitophel* Dryden shows the abrupt demise of those favorable conditions that justified his recommending a policy of mildness and mercy to the newly restored king some twenty years earlier.[130] The English, a people who, like the children of Israel, "at their very best, / Their Humour more than Loyalty exprest" (61–62), have now succumbed to an opposite mood, in which "every hostile Humour, which before / Slept quiet in its Channels, bubbles o'r" (138–39). But this is no more than can be expected of a "People easie to Rebell" who, "govern'd by the *Moon*,"

> Tread the same track when she the Prime renews:
> And once in twenty Years, their Scribes Record,
> By natural Instinct they change their Lord.
>
> (217–19)

This sudden shift in the political climate is brought about by the discovery of the Popish Plot and the subsequent atmosphere of public hysteria to which it leads.

> The Good old Cause reviv'd, a Plot requires.
> Plots, true or false, are necessary things,
> To raise up Common-wealths, and ruin Kings.
>
> (82–84)

In describing the Popish Plot, Dryden does not dismiss it as a complete fabrication:

> Some Truth there was, but dash'd and brew'd with Lyes;
> To please the Fools, and puzzle all the Wise.
> Succeeding times did equal folly call,
> Believing nothing, or believing all.
>
> (114–17)

Since the king had recommended "the further Prosecution of the Plot" to his last two parliaments in a vain attempt to divert their attention from an Exclusion Bill, Dryden declines to follow most Tory propagandists who, since as early as 1679, as we noticed in the last chapter, but increasingly since the arrest of Shaftesbury the previous summer, had been ridiculing the Popish Plot as a Whig invention.[131] He presents it as having just enough truth to save the king's honesty, while making clear that Shaftesbury had exaggerated and skillfully exploited it in order to create public unrest:

> The wish'd occasion of the Plot he takes,
> Some Circumstances finds, but more he makes;
> By buzzing Emissaries, fills the ears
> Of listning Crowds, with Jealosies and Fears
> Of Arbitrary Counsels brought to light,
> And proves the King himself a *Jebusite*.
>
> (208–13)

The English Achitophel's use of these "buzzing emissaries" to convert public excitement over the Popish Plot into "jealousies and fears" directed against the king himself is simply the earliest instance in the poem of the unique skills that make him first in importance of all those "Pardon'd Rebels" whom the indulgent David has raised to a position from which they can now challenge his authority. As we noticed earlier, most Tory propagandists, while working within the tradition of derision and invective that passed for satire among the pamphleteers and versifiers of both parties, had acknowledged Shaftesbury's intellectual leadership of the Whigs under such appellations as "the Foreman" or the "Plotting head." Dryden, intent on magnifying the danger Shaftesbury had posed to the commonwealth at the height of the Exclusion Crisis, greatly enhances his managerial skills, depicting him as a master politician working behind the scenes, devising complex strategies, and choosing as his lieutenants those individuals best suited in each case to their particular assignments.

It is on these terms that Dryden represents Shaftesbury as Monmouth's evil genius, a role we have seen the Whig leader playing in Tory propaganda since the previous April, when his "expedient" of "settling the Crown upon the Duke of *Monmouth*" had first attracted wide publicity.

> *Achitophel* still wants a Chief, and none
> Was found so fit as Warlike *Absolon*:
> Not, that he wish'd his Greatness to create,
> (For Polititians neither love nor hate:)
> But, for he knew, his Title not allow'd,
> Would keep him still depending on the Crowd:
> That Kingly power, thus ebbing out, might be
> Drawn to the dregs of a Democracy.
>
> (220–27)

Here Dryden opens the pivotal scene between Achitophel and Absalom. Often referred to in recent years as the "temptation scene," this dialogue of some 250 lines—roughly a quarter of the entire poem—owes its importance, however, not only to its dramatizing the seduction of Absalom but to its disclosing Achitophel's designs that "threat the Government" until they are averted, and demonstrating the extent to which these are tacitly encouraged by David's mildness and mercy.

The Miltonic echoes of Achitophel's opening speech to Absalom (230–302) have attracted a disproportionate amount of attention to this part of their dialogue to the exclusion of the rest. The misdirected tracing of these Miltonic allusions to *Paradise Lost*, furthermore, has fostered the popular notion that Absalom's seduction by the satanic Achitophel is the central dramatic episode of the entire poem, analogous in this respect to Milton's depiction of the Fall of Man in book 9 of his epic. But this idea ignores the marginal importance of Absalom in Dryden's poem, where his role in the developing crisis in David's kingdom is no greater than that of Monmouth himself in the Exclusion Crisis. While Absalom serves an important rhetorical function in Dryden's poem, he does so not as a character about whom we are made to feel concern whether he resists or succumbs to temptation or about the moral consequences of his choice, but as an interlocutor in a dialogue with Achitophel that is unerringly focused on David from its opening lines until its close.

The misconception that Achitophel's opening speech to Absalom alludes to the temptation scene in *Paradise Lost* originates in a passage in Dryden's preface "To the Reader," where, already referring to Monmouth under the name of "Absalom," he argues that "since the most excellent Natures are always the most easy; and, as being such, are the soonest perverted by ill Counsels, especially when baited with Fame and Glory; 'tis no more a wonder that he withstood not the temptations of *Achitophel*, than it was for *Adam*, not to have resisted the two Devils; the Serpent, and the Woman" (italics reversed). But this analogical argument (alluding to Genesis as easily as to *Paradise Lost*) is introduced to support Dryden's questionable claim that he wishes "*to Extenuate, Palliate and Indulge*" Monmouth's guilt, not to provide the reader with a key to the allusions in the succeeding poem.

The Miltonic allusions in Achitophel's opening speech to Absalom, associating Shaftesbury with the Prince of Tempters as well as with the evil counselor of 2 Samuel, are in every case to *Paradise Regained*, not *Paradise Lost*. The former poem is far more appropriate to Dryden's immediate subject than would be anything found in Genesis or in Milton's longer epic, neither of which concerns a temptation that appeals to the listener's ambition by holding out the prospect of a throne.[132]

Since the imagined scene of Monmouth's seduction by Shaftesbury, like everything else in Dryden's narrative, takes place in a biblical setting, that scene too is adapted to the earlier era, and opens with a speech in which a satanic Achitophel flatters Absalom into believing himself the object of universal adulation, eagerly acclaimed by the children of Israel as their promised Messiah.

> Thy longing Countries Darling and Desire;
> Their cloudy Pillar, and their guardian Fire:
> Their second *Moses*, whose extended Wand
> Divides the Seas, and shews the promis'd Land:
> Whose dawning Day, in every distant age,
> Has exercis'd the Sacred Prophets rage:
> The Peoples Prayer, the glad Deviners Theam,
> The Young-mens Vision, and the Old mens Dream!

(232–39)

It is on these specious grounds that Achitophel urges Absalom to accede to popular demand and resolve upon ascending his father David's throne.

For such a speech there is a witty appropriateness in Dryden's alluding repeatedly to the second and longest of Satan's temptations in *Paradise Regained*, imitating "the perswasive Rhetoric / That sleekd his tongue" (4.4–5) as Milton's Tempter tries without success to awaken worldly ambition in the true Messiah by reminding him that "to a Kingdom thou art born, ordaind / To sit upon thy Father *Davids* Throne" (3.152–53), a course of action by which he can "best fulfill, best verifie / The Prophets old, who sung thy endless raign" (3.177–78). Thus, when Achitophel asks Absalom,

> How long wilt thou the general Joy detain;
> Starve, and defraud the People of thy Reign?
> Content ingloriously to pass thy days,
>
> (244–46)

we are invited to recall Satan's inquiry to the Son,

> These God-like Vertues wherefore dost thou hide?
> Affecting privat life, or more obscure
> In savage Wilderness, wherefore deprive
> All Earth her wonder at thy acts, thy self
> The fame and glory.
>
> (3.21–25)

Or when Achitophel warns Absalom,

> Had thus Old *David*, from whose Loyns you spring,
> Not dar'd, when Fortune call'd him, to be King,
> At *Gath* an Exile he might still remain,
>
> (262–64)

he echoes Milton's Tempter cautioning the Son,

> thy Kingdom though foretold
> By Prophet or by Angel, unless thou
> Endeavour, as thy Father *David* did,
> Thou never shalt obtain.
>
> (3.351–54)[133]

Achitophel's opening speech has awakened Absalom's ambitions for his father David's throne by stressing advantage ("Not barren Praise alone, that Gaudy Flower, / Fair only to the sight, but solid Power" [297–98]) and opportunity ("All sorts of men by my successful Arts, / Abhorring Kings, estrange their alter'd Hearts / From *David*'s Rule" [289–91]). What he has not touched upon is a plausible excuse for adopting the unlawful course of action he recommends. Absalom therefore begins his reply to Achitophel by asking "what Pretence have I / To take up Arms for Publick Liberty?" (315–16). Posed as a rhetorical question dismissing Achitophel's suggestion, his words are equally a disguised request to be given just such an excuse, as he hesitates in a state of indecision, "Half loath, and half consenting to the Ill" (313).

> My Father Governs with unquestion'd Right;
> The Faiths Defender, and Mankinds Delight:
> Good, Gracious, Just, observant of the Laws;
> And Heav'n by Wonders has Espous'd his Cause.
>
> (317–20)

Acknowledging his father's undisputed right to his throne, divinely sanctioned in the miraculous restoration by which he began his reign and since confirmed by the exemplary manner in which he has carried out his kingly responsibilities, Absalom proceeds to particulars by posing a series of genuine rhetorical questions.

> Whom has he Wrong'd in all his Peaceful Reign?
> Who sues for Justice to his Throne in Vain?
> What Millions has he Pardon'd of his Foes,
> Whom Just Revenge did to his Wrath expose!
> Mild, Easy, Humble, Studious of our Good;
> Enclin'd to Mercy, and averse from Blood.
> If Mildness Ill with Stubborn *Israel* Suite,
> His Crime is God's beloved Attribute.
> What could he gain, his People to Betray,
> Or change his Right, for Arbitrary Sway?
>
> (321–30)

Cast in the form of an admission privately offered by one of Charles's public critics, these lines constitute one of the crucial passages of the poem, for they directly address the charges of arbitrary power that the Whigs had repeatedly leveled against the king, and concede that they are without foundation. In returning to this, one of the central debates between the two parties for as long as the Exclusion Crisis had lasted, Dryden shows the English Absalom covertly agreeing with the Tory position on the question, and even adopting here the rhetoric of some of the king's supporters. Thus, in early 1681, shortly before Parliament was to meet at Oxford, a spokesman for the government had defended the king from the charge that he intended to introduce arbitrary government by asking just such a series of rhetorical questions about Charles's conduct as his son returns to here:

What one Illegal Arbitrary Act has he done in his twenty years Reign? Whom has he defrauded of an Ox or an Ass, of life or possession? Where has he in any one instance invaded *magna charta*, our Rights, Properties or Liberties? What Bill tender'd by Parliament, for the security of our Lives or Fortunes, has he rejected? . . . As he has freely pass'd all Laws, has he not as chearfully offer'd to enact any thing that was agreable to Justice and Reason for our further security in Religion, Liberty and Property?

From these considerations, nothing will appear more vain and idle than our *Fears* and *Jealousies*, our Factious and Seditious reflections on the Government.[134]

Absalom's testimony to his father's mildness and mercy takes into consideration both the king's temperament ("His Crime is God's beloved Attribute") and his policy. The first is a family trait, obviously inherited from the Royal Martyr, and shared by Charles's brother, whose "Mercy even th' Offending Crowd will find, / For sure he comes of a Forgiving Kind" (359–60). The second is a record of public service that, like the one sketched by the government spokesman above, emphasizes the total absence of any actions on the king's part to justify the "Jealosies and Fears / Of Arbitrary Counsels" (211–12) spread abroad by Achitophel's emissaries.

Achitophel's reply is the longest speech in the poem, and is exceeded in importance only by David's at the close. He begins by responding to Absalom's tribute to his father.

> Not that your Father's Mildness I condemn;
> But Manly Force becomes the Diadem.
> 'Tis true, he grants the People all they crave;
> And more perhaps than Subjects ought to have:
> For Lavish grants suppose a Monarch tame,
> And more his Goodness than his Wit proclaim.
> But when shoud People strive their Bonds to break,
> If not when Kings are Negligent or Weak?
>
> (381–88)

In accepting Absalom's description of David's reign, Achitophel must also implicitly concede that the people's jealousies and fears of arbitrary government, encouraged by his own efforts, are groundless. But he uses this as further evidence of David's present vulnerability by showing how, under the turbulent conditions that have obtained since the beginning of the Exclusion Crisis, the king's enemies are benefiting from his forbearance. In the present circumstances, Charles's mildness is perceived as weakness, an absence of the "Manly Force" expected of a monarch; his concessions under public pressure, by which he "grants the People all they crave," as pusillanimity. Consequently his indulgence toward a public already in turmoil encourages them to throw off their last restraints, for "when shoud People strive their Bonds to break, / If not when Kings are Negligent or Weak?" In pursuing this line of argument, Achitophel, like Absalom earlier, is adopting the rhetoric of some of Charles's own supporters at the height of the Exclusion Crisis, when the government's fortunes were at their low tide, and confirming its accuracy.

The author of *The Country-mans Complaint*, offering his "Advice to the King" on 9 February 1681 during the elections for the Oxford Parliament, had cautioned his sovereign against making further concessions to his opponents, "Lest we should count thy greatest Vertue, Vice, / And call thy Mercy, servile Cowardise."[135] Later the same month the Whig persona of a Tory broadside had boasted that "the most tempting things, /Are too much Wealth, and too Indulgent Kings," while a few weeks later the Tory author of *The Deliquium* was still complaining that "the more indulgent" Charles showed himself to be, "th' more he is opprest" by his enemies.[136] And every well-meaning Tory versifier advising the king in 1680 and early 1681 had included a reminder of the Royal Martyr's fatal mercy in the face of circumstances bearing a melancholy resemblance to those of his son. One of them, in imploring Charles to "stand firm" and "slight the Murmurs of a giddy Crew," had warned, "Thus had thy Father done, we nere had known / A Tyrant sitting on the Royal Throne."[137] The author of *The Country-mans Complaint* had exhorted him:

> Read o're thy Martyr'd Father's Tragick Story,
> Learn by his Murder, different ways to glory.
> How fatal 'tis, by him is understood,
> To yield to Subjects, when they thirst for Blood.[138]

Others had implored him to "Learn by your Father, not to trust to those / That in the end will prove confiding Foes," or had cautioned that "The Royal Martyr *Charles*, the Wise, the Just, / Commands you to forgive, but never trust."[139]

A month before *Absalom and Achitophel* appeared, a Tory pamphleteer, defending the loyal addresses that had recently been acclaiming Charles's adoption of a more resolute royal policy, commented on the king's indulgent behavior at the height of the Exclusion Crisis.

> I shall only observe the late King, and our now Gracious Soveraign; (being ever desirous to Reign in the Hearts of their people,) have too often by condescentions endeavoured a complyance with many too Stiff and Rigid Articles, which Condescentions these Stubborn Creatures have ever argued a weakness of Judgment: And can there be a greater wickedness under Heaven, then to argue

a Kings Affection, a want of understanding? . . . neither of these Kings have err'd in Politicks, except of a too great Tenderness to a Stubborn people, that instead of quelling their Hearts by these soft methods, have the more hardned themselves against Government.[140]

Encouraged by David's recent concessions to expect more in the future, Achitophel outlines the policy by which he and his confederates are determined to continue pressing the king ever further until he ends by granting them all they desire.

Let him give on till he can give no more,
The Thrifty Sanhedrin shall keep him poor:
And every Sheckle which he can receive,
Shall cost a Limb of his Prerogative.
To ply him with new Plots, shall be my care,
Or plunge him deep in some Expensive War;
Which when his Treasure can no more Supply,
He must, with the Remains of Kingship, buy.

. . . . . . . . . . . . . . . .

The next Successor, whom I fear and hate,
My Arts have made Obnoxious to the State;

. . . . . . . . . . . . . . . .

His Right, for Sums of necessary Gold,
Shall first be Pawn'd, and afterwards be Sold:
Till time shall Ever-wanting *David* draw,
To pass your doubtfull Title into Law.

(389–408)

This is of course, in every respect, a parliamentary plan of action that depends upon a pliant king who, as often as he postpones the inevitable by dissolving recalcitrant parliaments, can be expected to summon another in which his opponents will renew the same relentless pressure. The financial form that pressure takes, a refusal by the House of Commons to grant the king the money he needs to conduct his foreign policy unless he continues surrendering his prerogatives and consents at last to a Bill of Exclusion, was particularly associated, as we noticed in the last chapter, with the angry addresses to the king voted by the Commons during the closing weeks of the second Exclusion Parliament, as well as with Shaftesbury's notorious speech in the Lords on 23 December 1680. It implies a date for this imagined dialogue sometime between the dissolution of that parliament in January 1681 and the meeting of the Oxford Parliament in March.

If these parliamentary maneuvers prove successful, eventually forcing David to pass Absalom's "doubtfull Title into Law," his son will have no need "to take up Arms for Publick Liberty." But with his next words ("If not . . ."), Achitophel prepares to disclose to Absalom a contingency plan, unknown to Tory propagandists until after the Exclusion Crisis had come to an end, that can be used in the event it proves impossible to alter the Succession in a parliamentary way. Since this alternative plan must inevitably involve the use of arms by Absalom and his confederates, Achitophel begins by offering a general justification of armed rebellion:

> If not; the People have a Right Supreme
> To make their Kings; for Kings are made for them.
> All Empire is no more than Pow'r in Trust,
> Which when resum'd, can be no longer Just.
>
> (409–12)

He then proceeds to furnish Absalom with the pretext he is seeking to rebel against his own father. Arguing that "the next Heir, a Prince, Severe and Wise, / Already looks on you with Jealous Eyes" and "meditates Revenge," he appeals to the law of self-preservation.

> Your Case no tame Expedients will afford;
> Resolve on Death, or Conquest by the Sword,
> Which for no less a Stake than Life, you Draw;
> And Self-defence is Natures Eldest Law.
>
> (455–58)

Achitophel is now prepared to take Absalom into his confidence and disclose the alternative plan, should the king's opponents fail to achieve their goals in a parliamentary way:

> Leave the warm People no Considering time;
> For then Rebellion may be thought a Crime.
> Prevail your self of what Occasion gives,
> But try your Title while your Father lives:
>
> . . . . . . . . . . . . . .
>
> And who can sound the depth of *David*'s Soul?
> Perhaps his fear, his kindness may Controul.
> He fears his Brother, though he loves his Son,
> For plighted Vows too late to be undone.
> If so, by Force he wishes to be gain'd,
> Like womens Leachery, to seem Constrain'd:
> Doubt not, but when he most affects the Frown,
> Commit a pleasing Rape upon the Crown.
> Secure his Person to secure your Cause;
> They who possess the Prince, possess the Laws.
>
> (459–76)

This is an unmistakable sketch of the plot to seize the king at Oxford in the event the Whigs once again failed to pass an Exclusion Bill into law. More specifically, it adopts the version in which that plot, supposedly hatched during the weeks preceding the opening of the Oxford Parliament, had first become public at Lord Howard's inquest, where witnesses testified that the ultimate objective of seizing the king and holding him prisoner was to "settle the Crown upon the *Duke of Monmouth.*"

But whereas earlier government propagandists, as we noticed previously, had absolved the duke of any knowledge of the plot, Dryden shows Absalom both learning of the plan and consenting to it, should parliamentary methods fail: "And this Advice [to "secure his Person" without harming David] above the rest, / With *Absalom*'s Mild nature suited best" (477–78). That family trait restrains him from even greater crimes, it is true, but not from treason. In a break with Tory precedent, Dryden chooses to implicate Monmouth in the Protestant Plot by portraying him as an accessory before the fact. Viewed in that light, the following lines, which ostensibly "*Extenuate, Palliate and Indulge*" Absalom's character, as promised in the preface "To the Reader," even pleading that "'Tis Juster to Lament him, than Accuse" (486), carry little conviction, for in spite of these professions of good will the narrator has already accused him of a capital crime.

Absalom's final appearance in the poem, some two hundred lines later, is in the role of a shameless liar and sanctimonious hypocrite whose speech to the populace (698–722), portraying himself in words "colour'd with a smooth pretence / Of specious love" (745–46) as "a prey to Arbitrary laws" (701), contradicts in every detail his earlier portrayal of his father to Achitophel as "Good, Gracious, Just, observant of the Laws" (319). But even in this imagined scene, typifying all those public appearances in which the king's son had courted popular favor, Absalom is of secondary importance to the evil genius whose presence lurks behind the young man's "moving Court, that caught the peoples Eyes" (739). For we are told that

> *Achitophel* had form'd it, with intent
> To sound the depths, and fathom where it went,
> The Peoples hearts; distinguish Friends from Foes;
> And try their strength, before they came to blows.
>
> (741–44)

It is on this ominous note of impending violence between the king's enemies and his defenders that Dryden leaves the "Malecontents of all the *Israelites*" to intervene in his own person with the famous lines (753–810) against altering the Succession.[141] He begins by raising prudential considerations to which he will return later:

> Oh foolish *Israel*! never warn'd by ill,
> Still the same baite, and circumvented still!
> Did ever men forsake their present ease,
> In midst of health Imagine a desease;
> Take pains Contingent mischiefs to foresee,
> Make Heirs for Monarks, and for God decree?
>
> (753–58)

The question whether the people have a right to "Make Heirs for Monarks" had earlier been answered in the affirmative by Achitophel (409–18). Resorting to a rhetorical tactic familiar in many of his imagined debates between two speakers, Dryden here expresses in his own voice the two positions on the question; but in his usual manner he gives the side he favors himself an overwhelming advantage by reserving it for last, and presenting it in far greater detail. Thus he first epitomizes in a mere six lines (759–64) the case for allowing a people to revoke the covenant legitimizing a hereditary monarchy, before devoting thirty lines (765–94) to canvassing the arguments against a "resuming Cov'nant."

But more important than the question of whether in theory it is ever legitimate to alter the Succession, Dryden emphasizes, is that of whether, in practical terms, it is expedient. He therefore dismisses the argument over the legality of altering the Succession with a rhetorical concession permitting him to return to the prudential considerations that ought to be paramount in any case, whatever one's answer to the previous question.

> Yet, grant our Lords the People Kings can make,
> What Prudent men a setled Throne woud shake?
> For whatsoe'r their Sufferings were before,
> That Change they Covet makes them suffer more.
> All other Errors but disturb a State;
> But Innovation is the Blow of Fate.
>
> .   .   .   .   .   .   .   .   .   .   .   .
>
> The Tampering World is subject to this Curse,
> To Physick their Disease into a worse.
>
> (795–810)

Most critical observations on the so-called "discourse on government" in *Absalom and Achitophel* start from the assumption that Dryden's pragmatic and prudential perspective on the question of Exclusion is idiosyncratic.[142] Yet this had long been the perspective adopted by supporters of the government in arguing against any alteration of the Succession. Two years earlier, L'Estrange had dismissed Exclusion as an impractical remedy by asking in one of his pamphlets: "And shall we now expose and abandon our *present quiet* and *security* only for *future possibilities*, and make our selves *certainly* miserable *before-hand* for fear of being miserable herafter?"[143] The author of *A Seasonable Address to Both Houses of Parliament concerning the Succession*, directed the previous winter to the members of the approaching Oxford Parliament, had opened his own discussion of the Exclusion question by observing that "it seems hard to believe that sober men shou'd ever attempt innovations, seldom or never advantageous, always hurtful, because necessarily attended with the sad effects of *Civil War*," and had closed by declaring "That our fears [of a Popish Successor] in this point are groundless, and at best founded upon accidents, that may never happen: That 'tis the highest Imprudence to run into real, present, to avoid possible, future evils."[144] And less than a week before the Oxford Parliament was opened by the king, the Tory author of *An Answer to a Late Pamphlet, Entituled, A Character of a Popish Successor* had declared, in reference to the Whig supporters of Exclusion, that "surely those men are highly culpable, nay, the greatest Enemies of the publick good that can be imagined; who thus for an uncertainty ruine *a Kingdoms Peace and Prosperity*, and make us run into those ills which we are sure to suffer, in avoiding those which we neither know, or are certain we shall be ever so much as in danger of."[145]

The tactic by which these pampleteers, along with Dryden in his poem, assess the practical advantages and disadvantages of an Act of Exclusion by weighing the odds between "possible future evils" it may prevent, associated with a Popish Successor, and "real present evils" it is certain to bring in its wake, involving civil war, requires some explanation, since it does not figure in critical comments on *Absalom and Achitophel*. The "possible future evils" an Act of Exclusion was designed to forestall were of course the encroachments on civil and religious liberty the Whigs promised as the inevitable prospect for English Protestants once a Popish Successor had come to the throne on the death of his brother, but which the Tories discounted as improbable, though remotely possible. The "ills which we are sure to suffer" if an Act of Exclusion is passed into law pertain to the civil war which, according to the Tories, would inevitably follow from disinheriting the duke of York. "Prudence will tell us, *That this [is] an evil, that must be attended with greater*," the author of *A Seasonable Address* cautioned his readers. "For the minute that [an Act of Exclusion] passes, the Duke is at liberty to recover his Right by secret or open Violence, Foreign or Domestick," and no precautions can prevent his doing so. "The Duke will still find a party, at least if he out-lives the King, in the Three Kingdoms to fight his Quarrel; and if he comes in by Force, he may well use us like *a conquer'd Nation*, break our old, and give us what Laws and Religion he pleases; Whereas if we attempt no such thing, we shall not run the hazard of a *Civil War*."[146]

"Now if such an Act [of Exclusion] should be obtain'd," another supporter of the government had warned the year before,

> the Consequence, if the D. survive the King, (*whose Life God long continue*) must needs be War and Misery, Folly and Repentance. Our Histories are full of Tragical Events upon such Occasions. . . . The Duke cannot be supposed to want Sticklers both at home, and from abroad; few will believe the Act lawful in its own nature, nor the King's Consent free, or themselves not bound by Oath to his Assistance: *Scotland* and *Ireland* will rejoyce at another Civil War in *England*, in hopes to free themselves from the Inconveniences of being Provinces. . . .
>
>     . . . So that upon the whole, if the Duke out-live the King, I see nothing but Misery and Desolation like to ensue upon his Disinherison.[147]

Small wonder that, faced with such horrifying "ills which we are sure to suffer," the author of *An Answer to a Late Pamphlet* above implored the members of the approaching Oxford Parliament: "I conjure you as you expect to answer it to God and a whole Nation, to take care above all things that we have not a Civil War entailed upon us" by their passing an Act of Exclusion.[148]

These are scare tactics, of course, developed to offset, and outdo, the ghastly "prospect of a Popish Successor" that the Whigs had been using to frighten a nervous public since early 1679. The Tory tactics were, in fact, almost as old as their Whig counterpart, for they had been employed by the government's supporters in the House of Commons in the debate over bringing in an Exclusion Bill during the first Exclusion Parliament on 11 May 1679, when four of the speakers opposed the bill by warning that an outraged duke of York would descend upon them with an army to recover his rights should they be so foolish as to deprive him of them.[149] Eighteen months later, in the second Exclusion Parliament, five of the government's supporters in the Commons revived these same fears in the debate over bringing in an Exclusion Bill on 2 November 1680.[150] Last of all, the same argument was heard again in the Oxford Parliament during the debate in the Commons over bringing in an Exclusion Bill on 26 March 1681.[151] By the time *His Majesties Declaration* appeared in early April, therefore, the public was so familiar with the threatened prospect of a Popish non-Successor that the king had no need to explain his meaning when he declared: "In short, We cannot, after the sad Experience We have had of the late Civil Wars, that Murder'd Our Father of Blessed Memory, and ruin'd the Monarchy, consent to a Law, that shall establish another most Unnatural War, or at least make it necessary to maintain a Standing Force for the Preserving the Government and the Peace of the Kingdom."[152]

Like the king, Dryden discretely avoids any direct allusion to the duke of York as a future Bolingbroke or Richmond invading England to recover the rights of which he has been unjustly deprived. But after two and a half years in which the threat had been repeatedly publicized by both Parliament and the press, Dryden could depend upon his readers' recognizing his dark allusions to the fatal consequence of shaking "a setled Throne" and incurring evils far worse than "their Sufferings were before." And while we have noticed Absalom, in referring to his father's brother, concede "His Mercy even th' Offending Crowd will find" (359), he was describing his uncle as his subjects would experience him in the future as their unopposed king. Achitophel, however, paints a very different picture of the king's brother as excluded heir:

> Though now his mighty Soul its Grief contains;
> He meditates Revenge who least Complains,
>
> .   .   .   .   .   .   .   .   .   .   .   .   .   .
>
> Till at the last, his time for Fury found,
> He shoots with suddain Vengeance from the Ground.
>
> (445–52)

Achitophel's characterizations of the royal brothers are distortions of the truth, of course. He construes David's mildness as weakness, his brother's severity as vindictiveness. But the basis for these exaggerations remains sound, and the impression Dryden leaves of the duke of York, tactfully ascribed to an unfriendly witness, is of "a Prince, Severe and Wise" who, if driven to such a course, will recover his just rights at a terrible cost to those who stand in his way, and to a nation that once again must experience the miseries of civil war.

With this veiled prospect of what must ensue if the king's opponents succeed by any means whatever in altering the Succession, we reach the climax of a series of increasingly serious threats to the government and the public order. This is the strategic moment for Dryden to introduce Charles's friends and counselors, "a small but faithful Band / Of Worthies, in the Breach who dar'd to stand," and to sum up the gravest of those dangers that would have been apparent to them on the eve of the Oxford Parliament:

> With grief they view'd such powerful Engines bent,
> To batter down the lawful Government:
> A numerous Faction with pretended frights,
> In Sanhedrins to plume the Regal Rights:
> The true Successour from the Court remov'd:
> The Plot, by hireling Witnesses improv'd.
>
> (917–22)

Lastly, he records the advice they press upon their beleaguered monarch:

> These Ills they saw, and as their Duty bound,
> They shew'd the King the danger of the Wound:
> That no Concessions from the Throne woud please,
> But Lenitives fomented the Disease:
> That *Absalom*, ambitious of the Crown,
> Was made the Lure to draw the People down:
> That false *Achitophel*'s pernitious Hate,
> Had turn'd the Plot to Ruine Church and State.
>
> (923–30)

The king's speech from the throne that concludes the poem shows him accepting his counselors' advice and informing his subjects of the new policy he has decided to adopt after "long revolving, in his carefull Breast, / Th' event of things" (934–35). The speech is framed, at both its beginning and its end, with the same phrase, "Godlike *David*," as had been used to introduce the monarch in the poem's opening lines. Here the epithet carries a more serious connotation than earlier, as most commentators have recognized. But it would be a mistake to give it the exaggerated mystical significance it has acquired in much recent criticism.[153]

An authoritative explanation of the respects in which kings are godlike can be found in the second of the two Books of Homilies, in the first part of the "Homily against Disobedience and Willful Rebellion."

> And as God himself, being of an infinite Majesty, power, and wisdom, ruleth and governeth all things in Heaven and Earth, as the universal Monarch and only King and Emperour over all, as being only able to take and bear the charge of all: so hath he constituted, ordained, and set earthly Princes over particular Kingdoms and Dominions in Earth . . . that the Princes themselves in authority, power, wisdom, providence, and righteousness in government of People and Countries committed to their charge, should resemble his heavenly governance, as the majesty of heavenly things may by the baseness of earthly things be shadowed and resembled.[154]

While all kings, as rulers of their microcosms, bear some analogy to the King of Kings who rules the macrocosm, therefore, it is their manner of governing their subjects and realms that "should resemble his heavenly governance" if they are truly to be considered "godlike." Dryden's David recognizes this distinction in his speech when he specifies that "Gods, and Godlike Kings their Care express, / Still to Defend their Servants in distress" (997–98). The "Homily against Disobedience," referring to "that similitude of Government which [kings] have or should have, not unlike unto God their King," goes on to explain: "Unto the which similitude of heavenly Government, the nearer and nearer that an earthly Prince doth come in his regiment, the greater blessing of Gods mercy is he unto that Country and People over whom he reigneth."

Dryden reserves a serious use of the epithet "godlike" for the English David until his speech from the throne, therefore, and even emphasizes it by repetition at the end, because, in announcing his resolution to pursue a new policy, the monarch finally exhibits a balanced combination of those essential attributes that characterize "Gods, and Godlike Kings" as rulers.

> Thus long have I, by native mercy sway'd,
> My wrongs dissembl'd, my revenge delay'd:
> So willing to forgive th' Offending Age,
> So much the Father did the King asswage.
> But now so far my Clemency they slight,
> Th' Offenders question my Forgiving Right.
> That one was made for many, they contend:
> But 'tis to Rule, for that's a Monarch's End.
> They call my tenderness of Blood, my Fear:
> Though Manly tempers can the longest bear.
> Yet, since they will divert my Native course,
> 'Tis time to shew I am not Good by Force.
> Those heap'd Affronts that haughty Subjects bring,
> Are burthens for a Camel, not a King.

(939–52)

What the English David promises here is to correct an imbalance by which he has been immoderately exercising one godlike attribute, mercy ("If Mildness Ill with Stubborn *Israel* Suite, / His Crime is God's beloved Attribute" [327–28]), at the expense of other attributes required of a godlike king, justice among them. Thus an excessive concern to forgive their enemies may lead monarchs to neglect the care they ought to take "still to Defend their Servants in Distress," thereby sinning against justice. But these attributes need not be exclusive alternatives, and the proper exercise of one should not displace the other. It is certainly no part of Dryden's intention to leave his readers with the impression that a once merciful ruler has grown cruel and tyrannical in the course of saving the nation from anarchy. The author of *The Country-mans Complaint* the previous winter had advised the king, "As thou art God-like by thy *Pity*, show / That thou art God-like by thy *Justice* too."[155] This is exactly what Dryden shows him doing at last: not substituting justice for mercy, but invoking both necessary qualities. David's references in his speech to his "native mercy" and to the "Native course" he has been pursuing until now are meant to remind us that his temperament remains ineradicably merciful, offering assurance that it will restrain the severity of his altered policy lest it too should grow excessive. This tempering of justice with mercy is particularly noticeable when David promises that his new policy will apply to his son quite as rigorously as to his other subjects, "If my Young *Samson* will pretend a Call / To shake the Column, let him share the Fall," but adds (beginning with the third edition of the poem), "But oh that yet he woud repent and live! / How easie 'tis for Parents to forgive!" (955–58).

Thus we are shown the English David recognizing at last the dangers to which his indulgence toward both his wayward son and his erring subjects has exposed the nation by his allowing mercy to take precedence over his responsibility for the safety of all his people ("So much the Father did the King asswage"). But, unlike the biblical David, who carelessly allowed matters to drift until twenty thousand of his subjects must perish along with his son Absalom before order could be restored, the English David has heeded his counselors in good time and rescued his people on the brink of armed rebellion and civil strife that threatened to engulf them.

The remainder of David's imagined speech from the throne outlines the specific measures by which he intends to implement his new policy and reverse the nation's drift toward anarchy. These measures are of two kinds and are meant as remedies for two separate abuses. A failure to recognize this important distinction has led one recent commentator to characterize the king's speech as a series of "not so thinly veiled threats of judicial murder" encompassing the Whig leaders, which, if true, would certainly expose Charles as just such a tyrant and arbitrary ruler as Dryden and the other Tory propagandists were taking pains to show that he was not.[156]

David begins this last section of his speech by asking,

What then is left but with a Jealous Eye
To guard the Small remains of Royalty?
The Law shall still direct my peacefull Sway,
And the same Law teach Rebels to Obey:
Votes shall no more Establish'd Pow'r controul,
Such Votes as make a Part exceed the Whole:
No groundless Clamours shall my Friends remove,
Nor Crowds have power to Punish e're they Prove:
For Gods, and Godlike Kings their Care express,
Still to Defend their Servants in distress.

(989–98)

These resolutions, as Godfrey Davies pointed out long ago, closely echo some of those expressed by the king in *His Majesties Declaration* the previous April.[157] They include both his promise there "in all things to

Govern according to the Laws of the Kingdom," and his refusal to brook any repetition in the future of those "causes and reasons that moved him to dissolve the two last parliaments." Among these are "the most unsuitable Returns from the House of Commons" during the closing weeks of the second Exclusion Parliament, comprising "Votes . . . endeavouring to deprive Us of the Possibility of Supporting the Government it self, and to reduce Us to a more helpless Condition then the meanest of Our Subjects," as well as "Strange illegal Votes, declaring divers eminent Persons to be enemies to the King and Kingdom, without any Order or Process of Law, any hearing of their Defence, or any Proof so much as offer'd against them."[158] All these measures resolved upon by the king are preventive rather than punitive, since they are designed to halt the progress of parliamentary encroachments on his own prerogatives and on the rights of his subjects, which, for all that they are denials of justice, remain within the limits of the law.

The next lines of the king's imagined speech show him explicitly passing from preventive to punitive measures as he addresses himself to another and very different abuse.

> Oh that my Power to Saving were confin'd:
> Why am I forc'd, like Heaven, against my mind,
> To make Examples of another Kind?
> Must I at length the Sword of Justice draw?
> Oh curst Effects of necessary Law!
> How ill my Fear they by my Mercy scan,
> Beware the Fury of a Patient Man.
>
> . . . . . . . . . . . .
>
> By their own arts 'tis Righteously decreed,
> Those dire Artificers of Death shall bleed.
> Against themselves their Witnesses will Swear,
> Till Viper-like their Mother Plot they tear.
>
> (999–1013)

The king is speaking here, unmistakably, of those traitors involved in the plot to seize his person at Oxford, which he was credited with suspecting as early as March. This is confirmed by his allusion to the Irish witnesses to the Popish Plot ("their Mother Plot") who would soon turn against their former masters in exposing this new conspiracy ("Against themselves their Witnesses will Swear"). The measures he proposes to take against these intriguers are certainly punitive ("Those dire Artificers of Death shall bleed" [1011]), since they are designed to bring to justice malefactors whose crime is no less than high treason. But nothing in the king's language justifies the inference that he is threatening to commit "judicial murder." His words about being forced against his mind to draw the "Sword of Justice" and to sanction the "curst Effects of necessary Law" suggest a determination, however reluctantly reached (since severity is foreign to his temperament), to ensure that the accused are prosecuted in his courts and, if found guilty, left to their sentences. Since most readers of the poem would have been aware that from the time the plot was first disclosed in June only four persons had been implicated and arrested (three of them still awaiting indictment), the king's words, however severe, would hardly have raised a fear of wholesale proscriptions.

The sudden resolution of the nation's crisis upon the conclusion of David's speech ("Henceforth a Series of new time began, / The mighty Years in long Procession ran" [1028–29]) has been both criticized and defended on aesthetic grounds for two hundred years. But it is entirely in keeping with the way Tory propagandists had all along been picturing the prompt effect of the king's new policy in general, and *His Majesties Declaration* in particular, on a recently enlightened populace. As the author of *The True Englishman*, writing a month before the appearance of *Absalom and Achitophel*, described the abrupt transformation of his countrymen,

> Seeing we could not see, and hearing we could not understand; yet how in an instant hath a single Declaration (such is the Power of a Princes Courage joyn'd with Wisdom) given sight to our Blindness? And sense to our Understanding? For what is wonderful observable, the Rable or Multitude that could only hope by our Confusions, instead of mounting the Horse which they were ready for, are now in all Allegiance holding the Stirrop to their lawful Soveraign.[159]

Or in the words of the poem, "Once more the Godlike *David* was Restor'd, / And willing Nations knew their Lawfull Lord" (1030–31). But this is no biblical David restored by special Providence to a throne he had lost through indulgence and procrastination. The English David, speaking from a throne he has never lost, recovers his authority through his own courage and wisdom, and "th' Almighty, nodding, gave Consent" (1026) to the new policy he has announced to his people.

The imagined speech from the throne that produces this sudden resolution in *Absalom and Achitophel* represents no single action on Charles's part. It embodies his dissolution of the Oxford Parliament without summoning another to take its place, the issuing of *His Majesties Declaration to all His Loving Subjects* by which he had opened the eyes of his people, his insistence on prosecuting Fitzharris in his own courts by which the Protestant Plot had come to light when it was in danger of being stifled by a parliamentary impeachment, and, most important, the "Power of a Princes Courage joyn'd with Wisdom" exhibited in all these actions. "What a Heroe would he have been esteemed in our Chronicle," the author of *The True Englishman* exclaimed, "that should have Dissolved the

Fourty One Parliament, afore they had finisht what the King had given them leave to do, the cutting his own Throat."[160] Just such a hero, in fact, as his son now proved to be in the legend Tory propagandists had been cultivating for eight months before Dryden's David made his appearance.

# Chapter 4

## THE ASSOCIATION

SHAFTESBURY'S GRAND INQUEST on 24 November 1681, a week after the appearance of *Absalom and Achitophel*, is a turning point in Tory propaganda, marking an end to the campaign of 1681, and serving as the starting point for a new campaign, along noticeably different lines, which would capture public attention until the middle of 1683.

. . . . .

Within a few minutes of the opening of the inquest at the Old Bailey, the grand jurors found themselves overruled when they demanded that testimony should be heard in secret in accordance with "the ancient usage and custom of *England*"; instead, Lord Chief Justice Pemberton ordered that there be "an open and plain Examination of the Witnesses, that all the World may see what they say," in keeping with the strategy the government had decided to adopt in appealing to the public over the heads of the Whig jurors.[1] Yet in spite of having delayed the inquest until four days before the end of Michaelmas term, when Shaftesbury must be either indicted or released, the government had not succeeded in finding new witnesses who could add any substantial details to the account of the Protestant Plot that had been public knowledge since College was convicted in August. John Booth, the subject of so much Whig denunciation for the past month, was the only one of these late arrivals to pretend to any knowledge concerning plans to "bring the King to *London*," and his information was disappointing. He could only testify to having been enlisted as one of Shaftesbury's personal bodyguard, a small force of fifty men under the command of Henry Wilkinson, who were still in London awaiting orders when Parliament was dissolved at Oxford.[2] There was no one to corroborate his testimony, and Wilkinson, of course, had already contradicted it a month earlier, as we have seen. The other newcomers were some of Shaftesbury's Irish witnesses who only mentioned various treasonable remarks they had heard him make about the king.

The best source of information about the Protestant Plot to seize the king and bring him to London remained, therefore, the four witnesses at College's trial whose testimony on that occasion had already tied the conspiracy to Shaftesbury as well as to the House of Commons.[3] These four

men—Bryan Haines, John Smith, Stephen Dugdale, and Edward Turberville—were slated to appear again at the inquest, where they could be
expected to amplify their accounts of the plot and to implicate Shaftesbury even further. As witnesses they were not only better informed but
more credible than the newcomers. Haines, it is true, was also one of
Shaftesbury's despised Irish informers, but he enjoyed the unique advantage of having been certified as a privileged witness to the Protestant Plot
by Fitzharris both in his confession and in Hawkins's *Narrative*. The
other three, however, could boast far better credentials, earned in their
previous careers as witnesses to the Popish Plot. Even Robert Ferguson,
intent on discrediting the witnesses against Shaftesbury in his *No Protestant-Plot*, had to concede that Smith and Dugdale were the "two, who
among all those who have appeared to swear a Protestant Plot are reputed the best." In fact Ferguson remarked, not without irony, that Smith
was "a Gentleman of so celebrated a rep[u]tation, that people do commonly believe it is his Testimony upon which this Protestant Plot doth
chiefly bear."[4]

Smith had borne the nickname of "Narrative" Smith since the autumn
of 1679, when he published a "further discovery" of the Popish Plot,
which attracted considerable attention.[5] Not surprisingly, therefore, he
had been produced along with Titus Oates as a preliminary witness at
Stafford's trial in December 1680 to "give a general account of the Design
of the Papists." When, a few months later, Edmund Everard needed two
men of good reputation whom he could conceal, on separate occasions,
to overhear Fitzharris's treasonable plans, he chose Smith as a matter of
course along with the zealous Whig informer Sir William Waller. Consequently Smith had been one of the three material witnesses, along with
Everard and Waller, on whose testimony Fitzharris had been convicted at
his trial in June 1681. By the time he repeated his success at College's trial
two months later, therefore, Smith was a seasoned veteran of successful
prosecutions.

Even more reputable than Smith, however, was Stephen Dugdale, who
had been one of the earliest and most sought-after witnesses to the Popish
Plot, following close on the heels of Oates, Tonge, Bedloe, and Prance
when he made his first appearance before a parliamentary committee in
January 1679. As John Kenyon has pointed out, Dugdale's "speech and
bearing were those of a gentleman," and so convincing was the impression he gave of "blameless respectability" that he continued to enjoy the
confidence of the public long after many of his companions had lost their
credibility.[6] He had first been involved in a successful prosecution as early
as June 1679, when he appeared as a material witness in one of the most
famous of all the Popish Plot trials, that of the five Jesuits, who were
convicted and executed on his testimony along with that of Oates and

Prance. His greatest fame, however, had been won in December 1680, when he appeared as a material witness against Stafford at his trial before the House of Lords in Westminster Hall.

Compared to Dugdale and Smith, Edward Turberville was a late-comer, since he did not emerge as a witness to the Popish Plot until November 1680, when he testified before a parliamentary committee. By implicating Stafford in that testimony, however, he won immediate notoriety by making it possible for the Lords to proceed at last with the nobleman's trial, for as Stafford ruefully observed on that occasion, "I was as far from being proceeded against now, as any of the rest of the Lords in the *Tower*, till *Turbervile* came in with his Discovery."[7] In Stafford's case, of course, it was not a jury of twelve citizens but a large majority of the House of Lords whom Turberville and Dugdale had persuaded of the truth of their testimony, and hence of their reliability as witnesses. The solicitor general laid particular stress on this at College's trial nine months later, when the two men appeared together once again as material witnesses in another treason trial, but this time testifying to a very different plot:

> Gentlemen, these are the men the whole Nation have given credit to, the Parliament having impeached my Lord *Stafford* upon the credit of them (for it was upon the credit of *Dugdale* and *Turbervile* that they impeached him, for there was not two Witnesses till *Turbervile* came in and made a Second, and upon their credit) after so solemn a Tryal where all the Objections that could possibly be made were made, the House of Lords thought fit to find my Lord *Stafford* Guilty, and my Lord *Stafford* suffered for it, and dyed upon the credit of these men.[8]

Sir George Jeffreys went further, reminding College's jury of the crucial part Dugdale had played in the trial of the five Jesuits, and coupling Smith with Dugdale and Turberville as "three men upon whose Testimony the Lives of so many as have suffered, have been taken away, and as we *Protestants* do believe justly." Indeed, "if these men have not sworn true I am sure Mr. *Oates* must stand alone in the greatest point, in which all the Evidence agree, that is the *Popish* Plot." To doubt their credibility now would raise disturbing questions about that plot and about English justice. "And I hope we do not live to that Age, that any *Protestant* whatsoever should come to trip up the Heels of the *Popish Plot*, by saying, that any of them who suffered for it, did die contrary to Law, or without sufficient proof."[9]

Perhaps most important, the allegations these three witnesses had already made concerning a Protestant Plot to seize the king at Oxford with the active participation of the Whig members of Parliament were internally consistent and had supplied Tory propagandists throughout the autumn of 1681 with a plausible, coherent account of recent events that could be used to justify the king's behavior. If Dugdale, Smith, and Turberville, with their successful record of convictions in some of the great Popish Plot trials and, more recently, those of Fitzharris and College, were to do no more than repeat at Shaftesbury's inquest the same story they had told at College's trial, as they were expected to do at the very least, Tory hopes, not of an indictment from such a grand jury, of course, but of another propaganda victory, would be justified. But this was not to be.

It is quite possible that the resolution of these three men had been gradually weakening during the weeks leading up to Shaftesbury's inquest, but it was the threatening behavior of the London mob on the day itself that seems to have been responsible for the sudden collapse of the sensational story that had been making its rounds, in some form at least, since June. In an account he gave Sir Leoline Jenkins the following April, Smith related how their confederacy began to crumble before the three star witnesses had even entered the courtroom:

> The day the Earl was tried, Turberville, Dugdale and myself went together to the Old Bailey but going thence to the Fountain tavern, the place appointed for all the witnesses to meet, the rabble followed us, crying out, There go the rogues, the perjured rogues, that swear against the Earl, which caused Dugdale to say, I wish I were at home, for we shall have our brains knocked out before we can give our evidence. . . . As soon as we entered with much ado into a room, the rabble came to the court[yard] after us, often saying, hang them rogues, perjured rogues and villains. . . . On this outcry of the rabble, I perceived Mr. Dugdale to be much afraid. I used all endeavours to persuade him there was no danger and that the rabble were but like little curs that barked but dared not approach to bite. Dugdale replied, every one of us will be knocked in the head for this day's work at one time or other, yet I am resolved, happen what will, to give my evidence, but at last, he, seeing the rabble in that rage and fury and their number increasing, declared he had nothing to say against the Earl.[10]

Smith claimed to have quarreled with Dugdale for his cowardice, but to no purpose; when the witnesses were finally summoned to the Old Bailey to give their testimony, "Dugdale went another way" and was seen no more in any courtroom, bringing his three-year career as a star witness to an inglorious close.

In spite of Smith's bravado, he and Turberville were obviously shaken by Dugdale's flight and by the mob scene that had led to it. When Smith was called as a witness, he took the court by surprise, announcing that he wished to make a preliminary statement before testifying, and although the lord chief justice tried to prevent him, telling him "you may take

another time for that" and ordering him to "go to your Evidence," he
insisted on being heard: "My Lord, it hath been reported about in Coffee-
houses and Taverns, that I should Swear there was a general Design
against his Majesty; and that I Swore it before the King and Secretary of
State; and that I also Swore it at the Tryal of Mr. *College* and Mr. *Rowse*:
I take it upon my Oath I never Swore any such thing, neither can I Swear
there was a General Design by the City, or the Parliament against the
King."[11]

After this unexpected disclaimer repudiating his most significant testimony at College's trial, Smith confined his allegations against Shaftesbury to some intemperate remarks he had heard him make about the
king. Turberville and Haines adopted the same policy, carefully avoiding
any mention of the plot to seize the king they had testified to in August
and merely quoting Shaftesbury as making random threats against the
government that, like those reported by the other witnesses, were certainly treasonable, but completely contradictory, and impossible to make
consist with any "General Design by the City, or the Parliament against
the King." The Whig author of a verse broadside, published ten days after
the inquest, nicely summarized the wildly conflicting allegations made
there:

> ONE Swears this EARL aim'd to Depose the King,
> And Inthrone *Buckingham*, a likely Thing!
> Another Swears, This Earl would Crown Himself,
> Yet ALL *Depos'd*, He's for a COMMON-WEALTH:
> Lo, th' Inconsistency of th' Evidence,
> Both with it Self, with Truth and Common Sense,
>
> . . . . . . . . . . . . . . . .
>
> If He design'd to set up *Buckingham*,
> Then to Inthrone himself must be a Sham;
> For a Republick if he did pursue,
> Then neither of the former can hold True.[12]

This proved to be the end of the Protestant Plot in the version that
had served Tory propagandists so well in 1681: a conspiracy by Shaftesbury and the Whig members of the House of Commons to seize the king
at Oxford during the last week in March, to carry him to London, and
to keep him prisoner there until he agreed to a Bill of Exclusion. Its
demise at Shaftesbury's inquest followed by almost exactly five months
its first appearance at another inquest, the equally unsuccessful attempt
to indict Lord Howard of Escrick on 21 June. It had depended entirely
on the testimony of witnesses and, with the exception of Fitzharris,
who was dead, every one of those witnesses, beginning with his wife, had
eventually repudiated that testimony either directly or implicitly. It is

small wonder that the government decided to place its reliance for the future on a new version of the Protestant Plot that would be based this time on documentary evidence rather than the shifting sands of oral testimony.

.  .  .  .  .

The Association, which was soon to monopolize public attention, was first divulged in the early moments of the inquest at the Old Bailey. As soon as the indictment was read, but before the evidence to support it was heard, a paper in an unknown hand was produced, and testimony given to authenticate it as one of the documents seized in Shaftesbury's house at the time of his arrest. This paper, which was read in open court, consisted of a preamble proposing "to all true Protestants an Union amongst themselves by solemn and sacred promise of mutual Defence and Assistance," and an oath to be taken by all those agreeing to join the Association. While the preamble merely repeated many of the commonplaces of Whig propaganda about the dangerous prospect of a Popish Successor, it was the oath that was to create the greatest stir, for it included a vow that "I will never consent that the said *J. D.* of *Y.* . . . . be admitted to the Succession of the Crown of *England*; But by all lawful means and by force of Arms, if need so require, according to my Abilities, will oppose him, and endeavour to Subdue, Expel and Destroy him . . . and all such as shall Adhere unto him"; and a solemn promise to "follow such Orders as we shall from time to time receive from this present Parliament, whilst it shall be sitting, or the Major part of the Members of both Houses subscribing this Association, when it shall be Prorogued or Dissolved."[13] It was widely assumed that "this present Parliament" referred to the Oxford Parliament, although possibly to the last Westminster Parliament, and that the draft had been prepared, therefore, sometime between December 1680 and late March 1681.

The government's purpose in first producing the Association at Shaftesbury's inquest was presumably to make it a matter of public record and to ensure that it would receive maximum publicity by coming to light at the spectacle on which the nation's attention was now riveted. It was nowhere mentioned in the bill of indictment, which related strictly to the oral testimony against Shaftesbury, and the grand jury's proper course, if it had been so disposed, would have been to make the Association the subject of a separate presentment. In the event, to no one's surprise, the jurors ignored the Association and returned the bill of indictment against Shaftesbury marked *Ignoramus*. It was now the turn of the government to recover the initiative and to try to convert this day's work to its own advantage.

Following what was by now the established procedure for launching a new campaign, the government's first step was to issue a publication under its particular authority. Like *His Majesties Declaration* the previous April, *The Proceedings at the Sessions House in the Old-Baily, London . . . upon the Bill of Indictment for High-Treason against Anthony Earl of Shaftsbury*, which went on sale the day after the inquest, was "published by His Majesties Special Command."

In keeping with the plans the government had laid some weeks before the inquest, at a time when at least four of the witnesses were expected to make a consistent and plausible case against Shaftesbury, the *Proceedings* were to have allowed "all the World" to recognize his guilt and the partiality of the London grand jury that had refused in the face of such evidence to indict him. Except for the authors of a few verse broadsides, however, Tory propagandists following in the wake of the *Proceedings* wisely avoided the disappointing allegations against Shaftesbury, who had been released from the Tower on 28 November along with Lord Howard and would soon be bringing actions of *scandalum magnatum* against his accusers.[14] The safer course was to argue, as L'Estrange and other Tories would do over the next few months, that an inquest was not the place to assess the credibility of testimony against the accused, and to condemn the grand jurors for dereliction of duty in not "*Finding the Bill*, even in the Case of a *False Oath*," leaving it to a court of law to weigh the evidence and decide the "Issue upon a Fair and Legall Tryall."[15] Another favorite tactic that ignored the specific allegations at Shaftesbury's inquest was to defend the general truthfulness of the witnesses by arguing, as had been done earlier at College's trial, that their testimony at the Popish Plot trials had been readily accepted. Hence the grand jurors had no right, in L'Estrange's words, "to Disparage the *Kings Evidence* in *One* Case more then in *Another*."[16]

Fortunately, the *Proceedings* offered Tory propagandists a second resource that would prove far more useful than the contradictory oral testimony against Shaftesbury. In making public the text of the Association, the official record of the inquest seemed to provide documentary evidence of a general design against the Crown that, while not the same as that which Smith and the other witnesses had failed to corroborate, provided a satisfactory substitute in the form of a new and perhaps better version of the Protestant Plot. In less than a fortnight the Tory newspapers were busy helping the government publicize this latest evidence of Whig culpability. Thompson printed the text of the oath to the Association in the *Loyal Protestant* on 6 December, and the next day L'Estrange opened his attack on the Association in the *Observator*. In mid-December *Remarques upon the New Project of Association* appeared, providing an authoritative commentary, paragraph by paragraph, on the now familiar text and completing the groundwork for a new Tory campaign that would differ in many important respects from the earlier one.

Coming in the wake of *His Majesties Declaration* and the Loyal Address Movement, the earlier discovery of a plot to seize the king at Oxford had seemed to offer additional evidence that in dissolving the parliament there Charles had wisely averted a threat that could have succeeded only if the session had been allowed to continue. A parliamentary design of holding the king prisoner in London until he had assented to an Exclusion Bill, while obviously treasonable, suggested a bizarre attempt to break the two-year stalemate between a Whig House of Commons determined to achieve Exclusion by parliamentary means and a king equally resolved to prevent this eventuality by a series of prorogations and dissolutions. It bolstered, however inexactly, the already familiar parallel between 1681 and 1641 when Charles I, although not a prisoner, was coerced under pressure from the London mobs into making concessions to the Long Parliament that sapped his remaining prerogatives. No wonder that L'Estrange, three weeks before Shaftesbury's inquest, had gleefully called that version of the Protestant Plot "the History of *Forty-One* over again, to a single Circumstance, and Syllable. . . . the Stile of *One and Forty*, to a hair."[17]

The Association, on the other hand, was viewed by Tory propagandists as an act of desperation contrived by men who, foreseeing another legislative defeat at Oxford, had been at last prepared to dispense with even the semblance of parliamentary forms requiring the king's assent and to take the direct route to Exclusion by open warfare. As the author of *Remarques upon the New Project of Association* glossed its oath, "[We] do Declare, and Swear, that what we cannot Compass in a Parliamentary-way, We will endeavour to bring about by force of Arms." The draft found among Shaftesbury's papers represented no more than the design for an Association, of course, which had not materialized, presumably because the sudden dissolution of the Oxford Parliament had dispersed the Whig members before they could subscribe their names to the paper. But once it was in place, those who had joined the Association would have been prepared to bear arms against the king as well as his brother, the author of the *Remarques* insisted, since the offending paper included a "Sacred Promise to Destroy [the duke], and his Adherents, without exception to His Majesty himself, who for Refusing to Exclude his Royal Brother, is declared to be one of the Party." If the earlier design had seemed to recall the uneasy state of affairs that preceded the first Civil War, this latest plan had offered a prospect more reminiscent of 1643, the year of the Solemn League and Covenant to wage to a finish the war already begun against the king's forces. As the author of the *Remarques* declared, "this Form of Association is only the Covenant

Reviv'd, with the same Licence, Limitations, Reserves, and Equivocations; and to the very same End and Purpose. . . . and there needs no more then Dipping any where in the Records of the Late Times to F[urn]ish the Parallel."[18]

But the Tories had no intention of leaving it to students of history to seek out the parallel for themselves. *The Two Associations*, published on 19 December, explicitly furnished the parallel with 1643 in matching columns, the new Association appearing alongside the oath and covenant among themselves signed by 156 members of the House of Commons on 6 June 1643, some three months before the more famous Solemn League and Covenant.[19] A far more ambitious use of historical analogy to discredit the Association followed on 6 February 1682. This was *The Parallel; or, The New Specious Association an Old Rebellious Covenant*, by Dryden's friend John Northleigh, for whom three years later he would write his verse epistle "To My Friend Mr. J. Northleigh, Author of *The Parallel.*" This substantial book drew a double parallel between the Association and both the oath and covenant of the House of Commons printed in *The Two Associations* and the Solemn League and Covenant concluded with the Scots on 25 September 1643, juxtaposing the relevant paragraphs of all three covenants and on each occasion following this with an elaborate commentary explaining the remarkable similarity between past and present. Indeed, the prospect envisioned by the draft of an Association mirrored 1643 so closely, according to Northleigh, that "there remains nothing to do but to drive the King out of his Palace, Proclaim all his followers Delinquents; all his *adherents* Enemies to King and Countrey; send post to *Scotland*, Messengers to the Field-Conventicles, get another Army from the North, swallow a *second Solemn League*; and then we shall have exactly a *second* 43, the perfect Revolution of a sad *Platonick* Year."[20]

One significant difference between 1643 and the prospect offered by the intended Association, as even the Tories must admit, was that Charles II would never have found himself in the exact situation of his father, at war with a parliament that could not be dissolved without its own consent. "The obeying of the Parliament in Forty two, and Forty three without a King, was pretended somewhat warrantable," Northleigh conceded, "because his Majesty had unhappily passed an Act for Triennial Parliaments, and then another afterwards for their perpetual sitting."[21] But the present king's readiness to exercise his restored prerogative of dissolving parliaments had been proved too often to allow anyone to suppose that in this respect history would have repeated itself. The antagonists of Charles II in a new civil war would not have been another Long Parliament but "the Major part of the Members of both Houses subscribing this Association, when [Parliament] shall be Prorogued or Dissolved," as specified in the offending paper. These "Disbanded Members of our own Fellow Subjects," deprived of any legal standing once the parliament was dissolved, would act, declared the author of the *Remarques*, "as a Standing Committee, and to Exercise an Arbitrary Power over their Fellow-Subjects, to the Subversion of the Common Rights, and in Defiance of the Fundamental Privileges of King, Parliaments, and People."[22] Northleigh agreed, describing these new masters as "*Disbanded Members* that have no more share in the Government then a petulant Officer in the Company from which he is cashiered."[23]

From the very outset, the Whigs countered this latest version of a Protestant Plot as vigorously as they had challenged its predecessor, but with greater ingenuity than before, when their only defence had been to deny the truth of Fitzharris's confession and the credibility of the witnesses. Many Whig rejoinders did, it is true, include a similar denial that the Association was genuine, usually coupled with a suggestion that it had been written by agents for the government who had thrust it in among Shaftesbury's papers after they were seized. A more resourceful tactic, however, was to accept the intended Association as genuine and to defend it as a perfectly legal, and indeed loyal, design openly broached nearly a year before it was produced at Shaftesbury's inquest. The first time L'Estrange mentioned the Association in the *Observator*, on 7 December, his doughty Whig interlocutor declared: "There is a Paper abroad, I am told, that bears the Title of such an *Association*: But that, they say, was only a Draught of a *Bill* for the *House of Commons*." He was parroting a suggestion made at Shaftesbury's inquest by the foreman of the grand jury, Sir Samuel Barnardiston, who, in questioning the officials who had seized the paper, tried to associate it with "a Debate in Parliament of an Association."[24]

On 15 December 1680, a month after the defeat of the second Exclusion Bill in the Lords, an angry House of Commons had passed a resolution "that a Bill be brought-in, for an Association of all his Majesty's Protestant Subjects, for the Safety of his Majesty's Person, the Defence of the Protestant Religion, and the Preservation of his Majesty's Protestant Subjects, against all Invasions and Oppositions whatsoever; and for the preventing the Duke of *Yorke*, or any Papist, from succeeding to the Crown."[25] No such bill was introduced during the few remaining weeks of the session, but on 20 December the House, voting a reply to the king's speech of five days earlier, requested that the next time an Exclusion Bill was offered, the king should assent both to it, "and, as necessary to fortify and defend the same," a Bill of Association "for the Defence of Your Majesty's Person, the Protestant Religion, and the Security of Your Kingdoms."[26] The wording of this request, as well as the debate over the earlier resolution, shows that such an act could only have followed an Act of Exclusion and was meant to enforce it, should the duke of York try to recover his inheritance by force of arms.[27]

In the weeks following Shaftesbury's inquest, however, the Whigs came to lay particular stress on the projected bill's concern "for the Safety of his Majesty's Person" in the face of the designs against the king's life uncovered by the revelations of the Popish Plot. The model for such an Association, they insisted, was the act of 27 Elizabeth, passed in 1585, by which Parliament had ratified the Bond of Association formed the previous year to protect the queen's life against the attempts on it feared from the partisans of Mary Queen of Scots. In trying, therefore, to pass off the Association found among Shaftesbury's papers as no more than a draft of the Bill of Association called for by the House of Commons in December 1680, the Whigs were pursuing a double advantage. Its legality could be sanctioned by the vote of the Commons ordering the preparation of such a bill, its loyalty by the model of the Association passed into law by an earlier parliament to protect Queen Elizabeth. In fact the Elizabethan association of 1585 offered the Whigs a rival historical parallel which they could oppose to the two rebellious associations of 1643 exploited by the Tories.

The upshot of this maneuver was that historical parallelism came to acquire a greater importance than at any time since the beginning of the Exclusion Crisis, each party as eager to disprove its opponent's parallel as to establish its own. "There remains yet another Abuse to be Clear'd, wherein they Impose upon the people, that this Association is founded upon the same Grounds and Considerations with that of the 27th of the Queen," declared the author of the *Remarques upon the New Project of Association*. In the usual fashion, he provided his readers with the texts of both associations so that they could "better judge whether it be so or no," but in this case in order to reveal their disparity before drawing a series of antitheses between the two: the one "a Solemn Acknowledgement of Soveraign Power in the Queen, and Indispensible Obedience in the Subject," the other "a Vow of Conspiracy to Oppose [the king] by Force; and set up an Inconsiderable part of the people, Masters of the Government."[28]

The Tories' determination to distance the Whig Association from parliamentary legality in 1680 as well as Elizabethan loyalty in 1585 created an important difference between the new campaign and that of the previous year. In their earlier offensive initiated by *His Majesties Declaration* and promoted by the loyal addresses, the principal culprit responsible for the political crisis, as we saw in the last chapter, had been the House of Commons, encouraging popular fears of arbitrary power, reducing the king's prerogatives, and withholding treasury grants until he would assent to an Exclusion Bill "in a parliamentary way." The revelation a few months later that "the Parliament were agreed to secure the King" at Oxford in order to coerce his assent to such a bill had served to cast further odium on the Commons in particular.

But in the face of Whig attempts to identify the paper found in Shaftesbury's closet with the Bill of Association proposed by the House of Commons in December 1680, Tory propagandists now found themselves denying that the Commons could possibly have harbored such treasonable
designs as were disclosed by the notorious paper. "But to imagine, that
the Honorable House of Commons would ever have endur'd the Starting
of a Project to overturn the very Foundations of Government," the author
of the *Remarques* declared, "were to do them the greatest Indignity in the
world. The late Usurpers themselves were half way through the Rebellion, before they arriv'd at that degree of Boldness."[29] "I confess we had
a Parliament that did all this, raised an Army, made their Generals,
fought their King," Northleigh declared, "but sure this *Associator* can't
be such a Villain to think the late Representatives of the Nation, would all
have commenced Traitors; and after a most inconsistant rate, imitated
that Parliament in 41."[30] "I know," he added later, "that which makes
them so Impudent to slur this *Association* on that honourable Assembly
are those Votes that were passed" in December 1680 to bring in a Bill of
Association. But these resolutions, like the act of 27 Elizabeth passed by
an earlier parliament, were designed "to associate themselves for the Preservation of the Defender of their Faith," quite the reverse of "Subverting
the State, and ruining the Church, (the clear intent of this discovered *Association*)."[31] If we recall that the votes whose loyalty Northleigh was
now defending were some of the "unsuitable Returns from the House of
Commons" at Westminster deplored in *His Majesties Declaration*, we
can appreciate the distance that Tory propaganda had traveled in the
course of a few months.

. . . . .

By mid-January 1682 it was becoming clear that the government's new
campaign was in danger of dwindling into an inconclusive debate between Whig and Tory propagandists over their respective interpretations
of the Association and its most appropriate historical parallel. It was
time, therefore, to bring into action a far more powerful resource than
newspapers and pamphlets, one already developed in its previous campaign against the Whigs.

The second Abhorrence Movement was a deliberate sequel to the
Loyal Address Movement that had proved so successful the previous
year. The latter had finally exhausted itself at a time when every corporate
body in England and Wales appeared to have addressed the king by the
end of December, thanking him for *His Majesties Declaration*. The appearance of the *Proceedings against Shaftesbury* could scarcely have been
more timely, providing many of the same corporate bodies with a fresh
topic on which they could express their support to the king under the

appearance of responding to another official publication. As the author of a Whig pamphlet observed once the new movement was under way, "the Operation and Efficacy of the *Declaration* against the two last Parliaments being wholly spent, I am not surprised to find an advantage taken from a pretended Paper, importing an Unlawful *Association* against the Government."[32]

It was in its logistics rather than its immediate purpose that the Abhorrence Movement was patterned most closely after the Loyal Address Movement, profiting from some of the lessons learned in that campaign. The first two abhorrences were presented to the king on 13 January 1682 and came from the grand jury for the county of Dorset and the general sessions of the peace for the county of Somerset. This time there would be no such awkward delay as had followed the appearance of the first loyal address the preceding April. In a memorandum by Sir John Reresby dated 17 January we catch a glimpse of the lessons government officials were now putting to use in orchestrating "spontaneous" movements:

> The same day I moved the justices of the peace for Middlesex, at the adjournment of the sessions at noon, to this purpas, that the first address of thankes to the King for his gracious declaration had been offered by them, and since followed from all parts of England; but that the justices of the peace for the countys of Dorset and Sommersit had now been before them in another address to his Majesty, wherby they did express their detestation of an association lately produced upon the tryall of my Lord Shaftsbury, and said to be found in his closit, conteaning absolute rebellion and subversion of the government; but that I hoped they would follow at least the exemple of the said countys by the like application to his Majesty, which they unanimously consented to, and ordered Sir William Smith, the then chairman, to draw up an address accordingly.[33]

That evening the king told Reresby he "should be pleased that this intended abhorrancie of the association might proove as generall as the former addresses," and thanks to such energetic courtiers as this he would not be disappointed. But by this time the identity of those responsible for the efficient operation of these movements was an open secret, and their "spontaneity" was growing less credible. The Whig pamphleteer quoted above accounted for the success of both mass movements by exposing L'Estrange as "the very person that is not only principally employ'd in framing the draughts which are remitted into the Countrey, where Lieutennants, Justices and Curates, are commissioned to procure subscriptions to them, but whose Province it is to publish their usefulness to the Government, and to make the world believe what security the State receiveth from them in order to its support in the pursuance of present Councels."[34]

As had been the case with the loyal addresses, the texts of all the English and Welsh abhorrences were printed in the *London Gazette*, and the ceremonies in which they were presented to the king were duly publicized in the *Loyal Protestant* and Benskin's *Domestick Intelligence*, although not as regularly as had been the case with the earlier movement. In addition, numerous abhorrences from Ireland were listed in the *London Gazette* without being printed. Most important, the flow of these new addresses was regulated just as carefully as in 1681 to ensure that they would not spend their force at once. By 23 February Thompson was reporting in his newspaper that "there are *Addresses* daily presented from several parts of *England*, in abhorrence of the late Damnable *Association* found in the Earl of *Shaftsbury*'s Closet," and in March the *London Gazette* began appearing in double issues, as in 1681, to accommodate the backlog of abhorrences. By the time they dwindled to an end in September the abhorrences, some two hundred in all, had been appearing in the *London Gazette* for nine months, the same space of time allotted the year before to the loyal addresses.

This is not to say that the Abhorrence Movement was simply a repetition of the Loyal Address Movement, for each of these two campaigns served a distinct purpose related to different circumstances. The loyal addresses, thanking the king for *His Majesties Declaration* and pledging him support, ratified Charles's justification of his own actions in dissolving the last two parliaments by testifying that his subjects' eyes had at last been opened to the perils from which he had saved them. Hence the importance of the additional subscriptions that had figured so prominently in the earlier movement. The abhorrences, on the other hand, came mostly from grand juries, justices of the peace, inns of court, general sessions of the peace, and assizes, and were cast as official reactions to the record of the inquest, expressing outrage at the Association and pronouncing it treasonable. They did not pretend to be expressions of a broad popular movement as in 1681 and, except for an abhorrence signed by twelve thousand freemen and apprentices of London, there was seldom any attempt to collect additional signatures. In some cases the abhorrences served as substitute presentments of the Association testifying to the action that could have been expected from a grand jury impaneled any place in the kingdom but London. The abhorrence from the grand jury of Wiltshire is typical in this respect:

> Having perused a Book set forth by His Majesties special Command, Entituled, *The Proceedings at the* Sessions-House *in the* Old Bailey, London . . . we find therein mentioned a certain Paper which was positively sworn to be found in the Earl of *Shaftsbury*'s House, which . . . towards the end . . . is High Treason, and may be parallel'd with a like Paper, called *An Association*, Subscribed by 156 Members of the *House of Commons*, in the year 1643 which . . . by sad

experience produced a Rebellious, Inhumane, and Bloody War in this Kingdom; and also that most execrable and horrid Murther of our late Sovereign
and Blessed Martyr King *Charles* the First, and to the grief of our Hearts, we
fear the like Events may follow such an unwarrantable *Association* as is mentioned in the Paper found in the said Earl's House, and do Present it as a Treasonable and Malicious Design against the Kings Majesties most Sacred Person
and Government.[35]

Where they originated with justices of the peace or inns of court, on the
other hand, the abhorrences served as legal opinions enjoying a quasi-
official status. Thus the abhorrence from the Middle Temple declared
that its members,

conceiving our Selves, by reason of our profession more obliged then others of
Your Majesties Subjects, to offer to Your Sacred Majesty our Sense of that
execrable Paper, purporting the frame and form of a *Traiterous Association*,
produced at the late Proceedings against the Earl of *Shaftesbury* at the *Old
Baily*; Do therefore Declare it our Opinion, that the same contains most gross
and apparent Treasons, more manifestly tending to the ruine of Your Majesties
Dominions, then the old Hypocritical *Solemn League and Covenant*.[36]

Besides their cumulative value as a unanimous expression of legal opinion on the treasonable nature of the Association possessing far greater
authority than the views of pamphleteers, the abhorrences also served as
reminders, week after week, of the principal debating points in the new
Tory campaign. Most of them, like the examples quoted above, drew a
parallel between this association and those of 1643, especially "that pernicious *Solemn League and Covenant*, which that Paper does not only
Coppy, but Exceed," if we are to believe the abhorrence from the Lieuten-
ancy of the City of London. Many emphasized that the principal target of
the Association would have been the king, the abhorrence from the City
of Hereford warning him that "if You oppose the Exclusion, You are to
expect the same Measure as [the duke of York's] Adherents, to be
Subdu'd, Expel'd, and Destroy'd." Another subject stressed by the same
abhorrence was that "Allegiance is to be Sworn to a pack of our Fellow
Subjects, substituted and impower'd to Direct and Govern the People, not
only in time of Parliaments." The abhorrence from the City of Norwich
emphasized both points with greater economy, declaring that the aim of
the Association was "to Destroy both Your Majesty and Monarchy it
self, by Levying War upon no other Authority, but the Arbitrary Orders
of a Disaffect, though Dissolv'd part of Parliament." Another favorite
topic of debate with the Whigs was introduced by the abhorrence from
the Society of Gray's Inn, which condemned those defenders of the Association who were "falsly recommending it to the Nation, as a design of

the late *House of Commons*, as if they intended Treason should have been Enacted by a Law."[37]

What may have been the most important contribution of the Abhorrence Movement to the new Tory campaign, however, was not the substance of its familiar charges but the rhetoric of outrage it adopted as its peculiar keynote. As the very term "abhorrence" suggests, these new addresses to the king assumed a posture of acute indignation that deliberately raised the temperature of political debate and created an atmosphere distinctively different from that of the previous campaign. Such phrases as "Horror and Amazement" or "Detestation and Abhorrence" recur constantly in the abhorrences; as pained expressions of loathing and disgust by corporate bodies enjoying a privileged legal and social standing in the nation, they show that ethical and pathetic appeals were being deliberately substituted for argument. These modes of persuasion were obviously adopted as most appropriate to a debate that turned not so much on matters of fact as on opposing and equally subjective interpretations of a project for an Association whose existence was accepted by most of those engaged on both sides. As a bid for winning acceptance of the government's interpretation of the Association, the rhetoric of outrage employed by the abhorrences was an effective tactic, and it is not surprising that it was widely imitated by Tory propagandists in their newspapers and pamphlets as well.

Northleigh revealed a special talent for this kind of rhetoric. The opening sentence of *The Parallel* epitomizes the new tactic, for besides offering a particularly good example of the rhetoric of outrage, it seeks to justify its use by the circumstances that occasioned it:

Never did a piece of Villany deserve sharper Animadversion, or the Contriver of it more severity; and both I fancy might have had their deserts already, did not the grossness of the Treason, almost supersede reflection, and the greatness of the Traytor exempt him from Punishment; so that there is even a sort of necessity severely to reflect on such a horrid Contrivance; as onely by the boldness of its being undertaken, seems to dare and provoke it; and presume upon an *Impunity*, from the very *greatness* of its *guilt*; and this enormity of the Subject may serve to make this Paper a palatable sort of scribble, though the superfluity of so many Pamphlets is enough to make it nauseous: But the Author of it desires as little to be known, as that of the *Association*; and therefore comes into the World, as some late Criminals out of Prison, with an *Ignoramus*.[38]

.   .   .   .   .

As Northleigh's oblique allusions to Shaftesbury suggest, the Whig leader had not lost his importance to Tory propaganda once the plot to seize the king passed into oblivion and the Association came to monopolize attention. True, he had never been officially accused of any responsibility for the Association, the earlier charges on which the government had sought to indict him had been finally dismissed on 13 February, and he was still bringing actions of *scandalum magnatum* against his former accusers that would not be decided against him until May. Meanwhile, in the absence of a parliamentary forum he remained in seclusion, avoiding occasions for fresh notoriety. But, like Northleigh, most Tory writers were convinced that Shaftesbury was the author or contriver of the Association found among his papers at the time of his arrest, and that, as the acknowledged leader of the Whigs, he would have been the chief of those disbanded members of both houses of Parliament from whom the Associators would have taken their marching orders. And of course every abhorrence carried a sly reminder that Shaftesbury was the person in whose closet the paper of Association had been found, and at whose inquest it had been produced.

On similar grounds now that the Association had come to eclipse the earlier plot to seize the king, Shaftesbury's grand jurors remained as notorious as ever, Tory propagandists denouncing them for having shielded the Association and prevented an inquiry that might have discovered its suspected author. "To reflect here a little on the proceedings of our late *Juries*," Northleigh declared without specifying his particular target, "is so far pertinent to this discourse, as they themselves seem a band of covenanting *Associators*, such as would have acquitted the Factious Inditer of this *Association*, had they found him musing on it at his Desk, with an imperfect draught of the bloody Scheme in his hand, and blowing up the Government with his dangerous Ammunition of Pen, Ink, and Paper."[39] Two weeks later the abhorrence from the Middle Temple made a similar accusation against the grand jurors, charging that they had countenanced the "*Rebellious Association*" by preventing "the Authors and Promoters thereof" from "being brought to a fair Tryal," which drew an angry rebuttal from the Whigs.[40]

But if Shaftesbury and his grand jury provided a bridge between the older and the newer versions of the Protestant Plot, both versions having figured in the notorious inquest, the more lenient treatment of the late House of Commons in recent Tory propaganda created a vacancy in the role of chief culprit that would not long remain empty. In the new Tory campaign against the Association this role would now be shared by the City of London and the Dissenters.

This shift of priorities in Tory propaganda reflected the changing political realities of 1682. As the first anniversary of the king's dissolution of the last parliament approached, the prospect of his having to summon another in the foreseeable future receded, and with it the likelihood of any more Exclusion bills. Unable to launch another Petitioning Movement, and reduced to a posture of habitual defense as one version of the Protestant Plot gave place to another, the Whigs could no longer hope to recover their parliamentary forum, much less to achieve their principal legislative goal. Meanwhile, the government's campaign to justify the king's behavior in dissolving his last two parliaments had apparently succeeded. It was time to abandon an obsessive attention to the recent past and to turn to more current concerns.

This did not represent a change in government policy, only in the means of implementing it. That policy was consistently to suppress or at least to control dissidents from the Restoration Settlement in church and state. When the most active of those dissidents controlled the Commons and used the House of Lords as a political forum, suppression had taken the form of dissolving parliaments and of conducting a propaganda campaign to justify those dissolutions as a necessary means of preventing anarchy. Now the government was at leisure to devote greater attention to other long-standing sources of disaffection with the civil and ecclesiastical establishment.

The most pressing objective was to exert greater control over the City of London, that permanent source of political and religious dissent. A month after Shaftesbury's inquest, the government began its quo warranto proceedings by which it hoped to withdraw the City's charter, and the newspapers were already reporting the early stages of the maneuver. The connection between the two events was obvious. To the Tories, Shaftesbury's acquittal by a Whig grand jury was simply the latest proof that the king could not obtain justice in his own courts as long as the choice of officials, especially that of the two sheriffs, was left to a Common Hall that was sure to be dominated by Whigs. Every assault in the Tory press on Shaftesbury's grand jurors was intended as a reminder of "*Ignoramus* justice" and of the London charter under which it flourished. Appropriately enough, *The Two Associations* printed not only their names but those of the Whig grand juries of London that had thrown out the bills on College and Rouse, further testimony to the City's perpetual interference with the administration of justice in the king's courts.[41] It made a plausible sorites, Northleigh suggested, that "if we find a Factious City, then a Factious Sheriff; If a Factious Sheriff, then a Factious Jury; If a Factious Jury, then all the Factious Fellows are acquitted."[42]

The action of Shaftesbury's grand jury in refusing to indict him or to present the Association gave Northleigh just such a pretext for questioning the privileges London enjoyed under its charter. "What wonder is it," he asked, if the detection of their Conspiracies, and the Punishment of the Delinquents be so difficult to be compass'd, when both must lye in the breast of such as seem to espouse the Prisoner's Cause, and with a resolved sort of incredulity to believe neither Evidence on Oath, matter of Fact, or their own Sences? What wonder is it if His Majesty, cannot have the Common Justice they distribute to their private selves; to every *Tyler*, or *Jack Straw*, that has but a Property to a Stall, a Shop, a Tool, or a green Apron; when these Gentlemen of the Yard and Tool, themselves must decide the Controversie; who I warrant you will be sure to take more care of their own *Propertie*, than of his *Prerogative*? But are these all the thankful Acknowledgments His Majesty must expect for His Gracious Charter? . . . And must those Immunities, and Priviledges he gives them for their Liberty, be used by those ungrateful Wretches as *Spoils* and *Trophies* of his *Prerogative*?[43]

The City of London was in fact one of Northleigh's principal targets in *The Parallel*. This perennial source of disaffection with the government purported to be "*His Majesties Loyal City*," he observed wryly, "yet I think seldome call'd so, but in some *Appeal from the Countrey*, or in the head of their own *Petitions*." More realistically, London was "that *Bedlam* of deluded Fools and Mad-men, gull'd always with the specious names of *Liberty* and *Religion*." He denounced the citizens of London repeatedly, declaring that "I am sure this Instrument [the draft of the Association] expresses more the sense and clamour of their mighty *Babylon*, than of the Countrey *Representatives*," and suggesting that it "was first hatch't when the last Parliament sate at *London*, when the Licentiousness of the *City* was such, as nothing but the Tumults in the late Times could exceed it."[44]

Another festering source of disaffection with the Restoration Settlement was to be found in the Dissenters, a standing reproof to the Act of Uniformity who constituted a permanent opposition insistently pronouncing, as L'Estrange declared, "upon the Church of *England*, to be *Popish*, for Agreeing with the Church of *Rome* in that which is *Orthodox* and *Sound*."[45] Freed from more pressing concerns, the government had begun enforcing the penal laws against them more rigorously, and nearly every issue of Benskin's *Domestick Intelligence* now carried news from all over the kingdom of constables dispersing conventicles. The new campaign could perform valuable service in justifying this course of action as a necessary means of preventing another civil war. "The *United Dissenters*," L'Estrange warned his readers, "are *Separating* themselves *together*; and the keeping up of *Conventicles* is the very Soul of the *Conspiracy*."[46]

One of the most significant ways in which the abhorrences supported the new Tory campaign was in their repeatedly singling out the Dissenters, either alone or in combination with republicans, as the culprits who, according to the grand jury of the County of Northumberland, were contriving "the ruine of our Glorious Church and the antient Monarchy of this Kingdom." Thus the authors of the abhorrence from the Corporation of Wigan, "finding (to our grief) that the restless attempts of Factious Republicans, and Undermining Dissenters, are still vigorously carried on against the Government, both in Church and State," condemned "all such Contrivances as shal any way tend to the Subversion of the antient Monarchical Government of this Nation, or the alteration of Religion, as 'tis now by Law established in the Church of *England*," while assuring "your Majesty that we will never take part with them that joyn in the Rebellion of *Absolom*, or follow the Counsels of *Achitophel*."[47] It comes as no surprise, then, to find some abhorrences urging that the laws against conventicles be put into execution more vigorously.[48]

An effective means of encouraging suspicion of the Dissenters was the parallel the Tories were drawing with 1643. The language of the intended Association, which "began in piety but ended in treason," according to the popular formula, did in fact encourage comparisons with the Solemn League and Covenant. In proposing a union of "all true Protestants," the notorious paper assigned primary importance to maintaining and defending "the true Protestant Religion" against not only Popery but "all Popish Superstition, Idolatry, or Innovation," those very faults that Puritans of every hue had always professed to find in the Established Church. Tory propagandists had no difficulty, therefore, in associating this program with that of the Solemn League and Covenant concluded with the Scottish Presbyterians: "the preservation of the reformed religion in the Church of Scotland," and "the reformation of religion in the kingdoms of England and Ireland in doctrine, worship, discipline and government," beginning with the extirpation of prelacy.[49]

Small wonder, then, that Tory propagandists were able to exploit the intended Association as evidence of another threat to the Established Church posed by the spiritual heirs of the Puritans, "the *Sects*, and the *Heads* of them," who, in L'Estrange's words, "all Joyn as *One Man*, in *One Common Project*, and *Determination*, for the Overthrowing both of the *Church*, and the *State*." The Dissenters, in fact, appeared on center stage in L'Estrange's campaign against the Association week after week in the *Observator*. His favorite tactic was to profess agreement with Ferguson that there was "No *Protestant-Plot*, for the *Protestant Religion* does not allow of any disorderly Practices to disturb the Government under any Colour whatsoever." It was in truth "a *Phanatical Plot*," which he described in its broadest terms as "a *Downright Conspiracy*, and *Conjunction* of *Republicans*, and *Fanaticks* against the Constitution of the *Church* and *State*," but more narrowly as "a *Schismatical Conspiracy* against the *Doctrine*, and *Discipline* of the *Church Establish'd*."[50]

The author of *Billa Vera; or, The Arraignment of Ignoramus*, published in February, agreed, declaring that "a *Protestant Plot*, I do confess, is a Title I do not well relish," all true English Protestants being loyal members of the Church of England, whereas this latest plot was the work of "some *Zelots* of Reformation" who "have spread their pretensions much wider than the *Protestants*."[51] Northleigh, in turn, referred habitually to "the *Presbyterian Plot*," which he described as "a complicated Conspiracy, though not proved with an actual Rebellion, and which I am apt to believe has been carrying on, ever since the death of the *Protector*."[52]

Since London was the Nonconformists' seat of power, in practice the two offered Tory propagandists a single target.[53] To L'Estrange, for example, the Dissenters and the City that was their stronghold were both tarred with the same seditious brush.

> Or is it not an Insufferable thing rather that your *London-Schismatiques* cannot content themselves to *Damn, Poyson*, and *Seduce* within the sound of *Bow-Bell*; but that they must, (like the *Doctors [Oates's] Jesuites*) run tampering of his Majesties People into Seditious, and Schismaticall Practices against the Government, from one End of the land to the other? Nay, and at a time too when the Factious Teachers have as good as abandon'd their Flocks, and the whole project had already fallen to the ground, if it had not been for Supply's from your *Metropolis*.[54]

Ferguson had been preparing his response to the latest version of the Protestant Plot for several months, and when it finally appeared in mid-February as *The Third Part of No Protestant Plot, with Observations on the Proceedings upon the Bill of Indictment against the E. of Shaftsbury*, it came as no surprise to find this deprived minister championing the beleaguered Dissenters. Much of the book was devoted, as one might expect, to attacking the credibility of the witnesses at the inquest, showing the contradictions in their testimony, and defending the Association. But these particulars were instrumental to his purpose of showing that this sham Protestant Plot, like its predecessors of 1679 and 1681, had been concocted by the Papists to divide the English Protestants while distracting attention from their own genuine plot. Their most successful attempt to create such divisions "since His Majesties Restoration," Ferguson argued, could be seen in the penal laws passed in recent years against "those that are called Protestant Dissenters," because "it is to the influence which the *Papists* have had upon our Publick Ministers, that we owe the Enacting of those Laws, which as they were directly calculated to ruin many of His Majesties *Protestant* Subjects, so they have weakned the whole Reformed Interest in these Kingdoms, by encreasing our Differences, and inflaming Jealousies, Heats and Animosities amongst us." But "now when neither the Church can be able to subsist, nor are any means left to the preservation of the *Protestant* Religion, unless Moderation and Lenity be exercised to Dissenters," the Papists had contrived this latest means of setting "one half of the Protestants against the other." If the Dissenters were "left destitute of all other means of relieving themselves," he hinted darkly, they might "become so far exasperated and incensed" as to challenge "the validity of the principal Laws upon which they suffer," and then "no man can undertake what a rich and courageous people may do."[55]

L'Estrange, who began answering Ferguson in the *Observator* on 20 February, took these words as an admission that the Dissenters were "already *Prepar'd*, and *Resolv'd* to follow the *Word* with a *Blow*: the Rel[en]ting of the rigour of the Law upon these Menaces," he warned, "were to lay the Government at their feet."[56] But the principal Tory rejoinder to Ferguson came on 4 March with the publication of *A Protestant Plot No Paradox; or, Phanaticks under That Name Plotting against the King and Government*, which implied another historical parallel to the new Protestant Plot by reprinting the "Indictment, Arraignment, Tryal and Sentence" of six Protestant Dissenters executed in late 1662 for one of the numerous sectarian conspiracies that had bedeviled the government during the early years following the Restoration.[57]

A timely opportunity for flogging the Dissenters appeared when the date for the annual martyrdom sermons fell early in the new campaign. Just as the Gunpowder Plot sermons on 5 November were traditionally the occasion for attacking the Catholics, the martyrdom sermons provided a similar excuse each 30 January for assailing the Dissenters. In 1682, however, some prominent Anglican preachers went further, turning the anniversary into an occasion for reinforcing Tory propaganda tying the Dissenters to the new Protestant Plot. In such sermons the pulpit became practically indistinguishable from the government press. These homilies were more overtly political than before, and they reversed the direction of the historical parallels that had long been familiar in anniversary sermons. Traditionally these parallels were used, as we noticed earlier, to liken the martyrdom of Charles I to previous instances of such crimes in both sacred and profane history. But some preachers now turned the rebellion leading up to his death into a historical parallel of its own for 1682, when the same religious sects were attempting once again to subvert the Established Church and the monarchy. In their sermons the times of Charles II came to replace those of Abel and Zedekiah, or of Edward II and Richard II, as the closest analogue to the later reign of the Royal Martyr.

The sermon George Hickes preached on 30 January before the lord mayor and aldermen at Bow Church must have tried the patience of a congregation long hardened to these rituals, for he liberally quoted, "without any other Apology, but what the Day will make for me," forty seditious principles taught by antiepiscopal writers "not only in the time of the late Rebellion, but since the late liberty of the Press. And from the men of these Principles it is, that we have had within these Three last years so many Impious and Treasonable books Printed." These are the men "that have made so many Protestant Plots," and indeed

> they are so far from undoing what they formerly did, and abhorring themselves for their former practices; that if you compare the former, and these later things, which have hapned together, you will find them speaking to the people in the very same Prologue, and already entred upon the same prelude that pre-ceeded the beginning of that Execrable Tragedy which they concluded this day. Search in the books of the Records of your fathers, and you shall find and know, that the men of these unchristian principles have been a rebellious peo-ple, hurtful to Kings and Princes, and that they have of old time moved Sedition within this City and Kingdom, and turned the world upside down.[58]

In much the same fashion, Edward Pelling exploited the subject of this day to show how "the Same Pretences which are so *Rife* in *this Age*, were so *Fatal* in that" of Charles I. In those days as in these, "the World was filled with Insinuations and Complaints, as if the *Liberties* of the People were in *Danger*; as if *Religion* was going out of the Land, and *Arbitrary Power* coming in; as if his Majesties *Counsellors were Evil*; as if the Intro-duction of *Popery* and *Tyranny* were the *Design*, and the King *himself* were *consenting* to the *Plot*."[59]

As L'Estrange was doing in the case of contemporary Dissenters, Pell-ing stressed the essential link between the earlier fanatics and their Lon-don stronghold when he reminded his City congregation "that the *Origi-nal* and *Growth* of our Late Troubles, and the *Sin* of *This Day*, were all in a great measure owing to the wicked Practices of a prevailing Party *here*, whose Confederacies in Treason did help strongly to give the Fatal blow to Three Kingdoms," and suggested that they "do but Look into the Annals of the Times, and you will *Blush* to see, that so much *Guilt* was contracted within the Walls of *London*."[60]

What is most remarkable about the new government offensive against the Whigs, firmly in place before the beginning of March, is the consis-tency with which various groups—Anglican clergy, pamphleteers, news-paper publishers, and legal bodies throughout the land—pursued the same essential program. In a matter of a few weeks the concerns of 1681—the obstreperous behavior of recent parliaments, the justification of the king's action as a last-minute rescue operation, the plot to seize him and keep him prisoner until he had assented to Exclusion—had been put behind in favor of a new plot centered on the Association, supported by Dissenters with the encouragement of the City of London, and designed not to alter the Succession but to destroy both the monarchy and the Established Church.

.    .    .    .    .

The foregoing account of important changes that were taking place in Tory propaganda at the very time Dryden was writing *The Medall* should help clear up certain misunderstandings about that poem, published on 16 March 1682. Two assumptions in particular that have beclouded discussions of *The Medall* can be traced to a failure to perceive the new political climate out of which it emerged.

Critics of *Absalom and Achitophel* who comment on *The Medall* at all (they are a minority) usually stress the surprising differences between two poems written by the same hand, dealing with the same ostensible subject—Shaftesbury and the Whigs—and published within four months of each other. They are particularly struck by the change in Dryden's tone, the note of harsh invective that marks off *The Medall* from the earlier poem. It is customary to see this as a reflection of Dryden's surprise and alarm at Shaftesbury's acquittal. One modern critic, for example, writes that "after Shaftesbury's temporary triumph, Dryden seems to have been thrown off balance, put on the defensive. The tone of *The Medall* lacks the poise of *Absalom and Achitophel*, perhaps because his fear of incipient chaos is now too strong." Another concludes that "Dryden did not appreciate the King's astute tactics [against the Whigs]; and his concern over Shaftesbury's not very meaningful acquittal led to his writing the harsher and more polemical poem *The Medall*."[61]

To read *The Medall* as evidence of Dryden's rising alarm in contrast to the confident mood he had shown in *Absalom and Achitophel*, however, is to confuse his rhetorical stance in these poems with his emotional state at the time he wrote them. His tone of anger and exasperation in *The Medall* (it is anything but fearful) is an effective rhetorical tactic to which his real feelings, whatever they may have been, are irrelevant. Along with other Tory propagandists in the winter of 1681–82, Dryden has raised the pitch of his discourse and adopted what I have been calling the rhetoric of outrage. *The Medall* and its preface adopt the same note of shocked resentment at *Ignoramus* justice and the Whig Association as had been struck by so many Tory jeremiads over the preceding four months.

The other important difference between the two poems that has attracted critical comment is the greater simplicity and brevity of *The Medall* in contrast to the complexity and length of *Absalom and Achito-*

*phel.* Such comments usually assume from the proximity of the two poems in time and subject that their purpose is also the same. One critic, for example, remarks that "[*The Medall*'s] simplified use of the complex procedures of *Absalom and Achitophel* suggests that Dryden, intent on repeating the success of the first poem, self-consciously condensed his proven methods and reproduced them, almost according to rule and formula, in the second."[62]

What such comments fail to consider, however, is that the greater simplicity and brevity of *The Medall* are inevitable in view of rapidly changing conditions following Shaftesbury's inquest, which in a few weeks had altered the thrust of political propaganda on both sides. If *The Medall* is shorter and simpler than *Absalom and Achitophel*, this is not because it is a condensed version of the earlier poem but because it is an altogether different poem, responding to different conditions, and written in a different political climate.

In the space of a few weeks, much that appears in *Absalom and Achitophel*, admirably suited to the government's campaign of 1681, had become irrelevant to the new campaign of 1682. If the Popish Plot, Charles and his supporters, the duke of York, Monmouth, Parliament, Buckingham, Bethel, Oates, the problem of the Succession, and the plot to seize the king, along with much else in the earlier poem, find no place in *The Medall*, these topics had also receded in importance or had been completely displaced in most Tory propaganda that had been appearing over the preceding four months. The reordering of priorities we have been observing in the campaign against the Association and in the Abhorrence Movement that was an important component of the new offensive had focused attention on Shaftesbury, *Ignoramus* juries, Dissenters, and the City of London that was their common stronghold. Monmouth, along with the plot to seize the king, had been quietly forgotten, while even the Exclusion Bill lost much of its former prominence. The failure to pass such a bill had supposedly occasioned the project of an Association, it is true, but since the latter was viewed as a parallel to the Solemn League and Covenant, an attempt to achieve a second Puritan Revolution that would have destroyed the monarchy as well as the church, the issue of the succession was rendered moot.

*The Medall* belongs as much to the new campaign of 1682 as *Absalom and Achitophel* does to that of 1681, although their timing differs. The earlier poem, appearing only a week before Shaftesbury's inquest, was the last significant contribution to a campaign that had been in progress since April 1681, whereas *The Medall* was written at a relatively early stage in the new campaign, less than four months old in March 1682, but destined to last until the summer of 1683. Nevertheless, it is the preface to the latter poem that most directly resembles the other prose contributions to the new campaign, while *The Medall* itself, although dealing with the same issues, shows far greater independence.

In the "Epistle to the Whigs" prefixed to *The Medall*, Dryden associates himself with the current controversy in the press far more openly than he had done in the preface to *Absalom and Achitophel*. On the earlier occasion, it is true, he had made a virtue of drawing "*his Pen for one Party*" in the debate between "Whig *and* Tory." His pose of moderation was not a claim to neutrality, therefore, but it certainly was an attempt to dissociate himself from the passions of the Tory pamphleteers and the professional commitment of such as L'Estrange. He came to the campaign as an outsider, he would have us believe, moved to intervene at last solely by the merits of the case. In the "Epistle to the Whigs," on the other hand, he changes his stance to one that is in these respects the very reverse of his earlier role. He drops any pretense of moderation, substituting the exaggerated rhetoric of outrage: "Never was there practis'd such a piece of notorious Impudence in the face of an Establish'd Government" as when the Whigs "put out this Medall."[63] Yet he no longer claims to be drawing "his Pen for one Party." In fact he never mentions the Tories or even alludes to them. There is now only one "Party," or "Faction," that of the Whigs, opposed not to another party but to the great majority of the nation, loyal to their king and determined to avoid another civil war.

Although much that Dryden says in his preface is applicable to the Whigs as a whole, his polemical epistle is particularly addressed to the Whig pamphleteers. This is a preface, after all, to a "Satyre against Sedition," and in the absence of a parliamentary forum it was the Whig press that had been most active recently in spreading what the Tories regarded as sedition. " 'Tis apparent that your Seditious Pamphlets are stuff'd with particular Reflexions [on the king]," he tells the Whigs, for he has made them his particular study. "I have perus'd many of your Papers"; so many, in fact, that he could cite "a thousand Passages, which I onely forbear to quote, because I desire they should die and be forgotten."

Dryden's polemical "Epistle to the Whigs" is written, in fact, very much in the manner of certain abusive letters to their adversaries that Tory propagandists had begun publishing in recent weeks, during the very time, presumably, when he was adding this preface to his poem. On 24 February a Whig writer published a defense of Shaftesbury and his grand jury that dismissed the Association as a forgery. It appeared under the title *A Letter from a Person of Quality to His Friend, about Abhorrers and Addressors*, supposedly replying to an earlier letter seeking advice, and was shortly followed by *A Second Letter from a Person of Quality to His Friend*.[64]

Adopting a tactic they had used with some success in answering the *Legorn Letters* at the height of the Exclusion Crisis, the Tories quickly issued a sequel, *A Letter from a Friend, to a Person of Quality*, supposedly a reply to the first letter by the "friend," who proved to be anything but amicable.[65] This time, however, they carried the hoax a step further. Since Shaftesbury was widely believed to have written the notorious *Letter from a Person of Quality* condemned by the House of Lords in 1675, the Tory "friend" pretended that his correspondent on this occasion was the same "Person of Quality," now shamelessly denying his responsibility for the Association. When a third Whig "Letter to a Friend" claiming the paper of Association to be a forgery appeared shortly afterwards, again replying to a fictitious letter seeking advice, the Tories pretended to believe it another missive from the indefatigable Whig leader.[66] Once more the "friend" answered him with *A Second Return to the Letter of a Noble Peer* even more abusive than the first.[67] Eventually the ruse exasperated the Whigs enough to draw an indignant reply from them denying Shaftesbury's part in the spurious correspondence.[68]

What distinguishes these pamphlets from most Tory propaganda of the time is the epistolary form allowing the authors to engage in a frontal attack on the supposed author of the Association and his followers. Without ever mentioning his name, the authors of these Tory letters can grossly abuse Shaftesbury to his face, relying on allusions to his speeches and past actions to disclose his identity to every reader. At the same time, under cover of an epistle to the leader of the party, they can directly assail the Whigs as a whole.

Except for the hoax of replying to Shaftesbury, Dryden's abusive "Epistle to the Whigs" follows suit, singling out two of their pamphleteers, each of whom he treats as representative of a whole group of writers for that party. The slightly earlier group consists of the Whig respondents to *Absalom and Achitophel*, most (though not all) of them having published their answers between the middle of December and mid-January, from whom he chooses the most vulnerable author to represent the lot: the "Non-conformist Parson" (Christopher Nesse) who had written *A Key (with the Whip) to Open the Mystery of Iniquity of the Poem Called, Absalom and Achitophel*, published on 13 January, a reply so doggedly literal-minded that it is often ludicrous.[69] Those who believe Dryden had succumbed to his emotions by March 1682 should consider the latter part of his preface, where he disposes of these answers to his earlier poem. His bantering tone here, oscillating between irony and open derision, shows how easily he can modulate his mood to suit his subject.

Throughout most of his preface, however, Dryden joins in the furious assault, now several months old, against the Whig pamphleteers defending Shaftesbury and the Association. The writer he chooses to represent this group is its most important member, Robert Ferguson, whose *Third Part of No Protestant Plot*, published in mid-February, he names no fewer than three times. Since Ferguson had covered the Whig territory so thoroughly, his book affords Dryden all the opportunity he needs to rehearse once again many of the points made so often by government propagandists in the paper war. He parallels the Association with the Solemn League and Covenant, of course, charging that the Whigs had stolen both "your first Covenant, and new Association, from the holy League of the *French Guisards*," a subject to which I shall return later.

Taking up the alternative parallel the Whigs had been drawing with their Association, he tells them: "In the mean time you wou'd fain be nibbling at a parallel betwixt this Association, and that in the time of Queen *Elizabeth*. But there is this small difference betwixt them," he adds, echoing Northleigh, L'Estrange, and the author of the *Remarques*, "that the ends of the one are directly opposite to the other: one with the Queen's approbation, and conjunction, as head of it; the other without either the consent, or knowledge of the King, against whose Authority it is manifestly design'd."

Turning to the other standard Whig response to attacks on the Association, he continues: "Therefore you doe well to have recourse to your last Evasion, that it was contriv'd by your Enemies, and shuffled into the Papers that were seiz'd: which yet," he adds, alluding to the abhorrences that by this time were appearing daily, "you see the Nation is not so easy to believe as your own Jury; But the matter is not difficult, to find twelve men in *New-gate*, who wou'd acquit a Malefactour."[70]

This is the familiar stuff of any number of pamphlets, as we have seen, and would scarcely have borne repeating for its own sake, since Dryden has nothing to add here to what others had said at far greater length. But it establishes the right tone of exasperation for the poem that follows, while picturing those who persist in defending Shaftesbury and his supporters as shameless scribblers who have forfeited any claim to respect.

This note of contempt is anything but fearful, however, and it is not meant to persuade the reader "that real dangers threatened, calling for a swift response."[71] *Ignoramus* justice is a grievance, certainly, which must be redressed as soon as possible by imposing greater control on the City, but neither this nor the intended Association, discovered in good time, poses any immediate danger justifying public alarm. Dryden adopts an offhand tone of dismissal in this scornful epistle to the Whigs that prepares us for the disdainful treatment of their champion and his infamous supporters in the poem. "The late Copy of your intended Association, you neither wholly justify nor condemn," he tells them before launching his poem. "So, now, when your Affairs are in a low condition, you dare not pretend that to be a legal Combination, but whensoever you are afloat, I doubt not but it will be maintain'd and justify'd to purpose. For indeed there is nothing to defend it but the Sword: 'tis the proper time to say any thing, when men have all things in their power." But the important point is that they are not in power, and he never suggests that they are about to be. As long as the nation continues to be vigilant, mindful that whenever the Whigs are again "afloat" they will maintain themselves with "the Sword," those who now possess the upper hand can make sure that their enemies remain powerless, unable to raise their affairs from the "low condition" into which they are now fallen.

It is a long way from Dryden's purpose, after all, to spread alarm among his readers and to leave them expecting a Whig revolution. For him to suggest that such a turn of events was now imminent would be to deny the whole tenor of the preceding year's campaign showing that the king had saved the nation, and to imply instead that the Tories had been deluding themselves in their complacency at what had now proved to be no more than a temporary respite. In Dryden's case, the prophetic lines at the close of *Absalom and Achitophel*, "Henceforth a Series of new time began, / The mighty Years in long Procession ran," would be quickly proved false by a new poem sounding the alarm at dangers that had been lurking undetected even as his earlier poem appeared.

In the Tory version of events, as we noticed earlier, the draft of the Association had been prepared either in December 1680, toward the end of the Westminster Parliament, if Northleigh was right, or in March 1681, before the meeting of the Oxford Parliament, but had never materialized in any case, thanks to the king's timely action in scattering the Whigs assembled at Oxford before they could subscribe to the document. Thus the discovery that a treasonable Association was being projected at the time the king dissolved the Oxford Parliament confirmed his wisdom just as much as had the earlier belief that the Whig members had been planning to seize his person on the same occasion. Indeed, the Association could have been used for the same purpose as the plot to seize the king, had it been necessary, in a continuing campaign to justify his action in March 1681 and to promote the legend that he had saved the nation by his decisive intervention on that occasion.

This seems to have been the immediate response to Shaftesbury's acquittal by Tory propagandists habituated to the campaign of 1681 and now casting about for ways of exploiting the Association. A Tory verse broadside significantly entitled *The Recovery*, published a few weeks after Shaftesbury's inquest, uses "that *Horrid Paper* . . . Which does almost exceed in *Villany*, / *Satan*, or his Vicegerent *Sh    ry*" as fresh evidence of the perils from which the king had rescued the nation.

Yet once more *Peace* turns back her head, to smile,
And take some Pity on our stubborn *Isle*;
She, and her Sister *Truth* now Hand in Hand,
Return to visit our forsaken *Land*.
I see, I see, O *Albion*! Bless the Sight!
*Truth* long Eclips'd lift up her Sacred Light,
And chase away the obscene *Birds of Night*.

. . . . . . . . . . . .

Already thy *Glad Influence* We find,
And all now see but They who will be blind:
They see whilst Thou holds't up thy *Guiding Light*,
The Dangerous Errour of their *Former Night*;

. . . . . . . . . . . .

But now the *Charm*'s Dissolv'd, and *England*'s free
From the *Enchantment*, does it's Madness see;

. . . . . . . . . . . .

Prevailing *Truth* has open'd *Britains* Eyes,
And *Folly* seen, begins to make Her wise.

. . . . . . . . . . . .

All this to thy Defender CHARLES is due,
Who now with Thee His *Glory* does renew;
Already with Fresh Beams the *Crown* does shine,
*Power* Sacred grows, and *Majesty* Divine.[72]

Except for the use of the Association, these verses could have appeared at any time between the heyday of the Loyal Address Movement and the publication of *Absalom and Achitophel*. They repeat the same familiar motifs of peace returning to the troubled land, of truth having at last "open'd *Britains* Eyes," of an evil charm suddenly dissolved, and of the king's having been responsible for all these blessings, which had been the theme of the earlier campaign.[73]

But that was not to be the theme of the campaign of 1682, which had quickly acquired a new objective. By the time this poem appeared, the Loyal Address Movement was already coming to a close, but not before it had seemed to prove once and for all that in thanking the king for saving the nation the public was firmly convinced of his wisdom and justice in dissolving the recent parliaments. There was no longer any need for Tory propagandists to continue looking to the past and endlessly to recapitulate events that by this time were receding into history. Instead, the campaign of 1682 would soon be busy exploiting the Association as evidence to prove the recalcitrance of the Whig diehards, and the true nature of their design, which had been all along to use the issue of the Succession as a blind for destroying the monarchy and the church. It focused therefore on the present and the future, on the means of preserving and extending the state of peace to which the king had restored the nation by ensuring that the factious City of London and the turbulent Dissenters were deprived of any chance to renew their treasonable machinations.

Yet the Tory propaganda did at times seem to forget the previous campaign's thesis that the king had restored peace to the nation, in its eagerness to show the urgency of curbing the City of London and the Dissenters before it was too late. When L'Estrange warns that the Dissenters are "already *Prepar'd*, and *Resolv'd* to follow the *Word* with a *Blow*"; when Northleigh infers from the draft of an Association that "there remains nothing to do but to drive the King out of his Palace," raise an army, "and then we shall have exactly a *second* 43"; or when Hickes assures his congregation that the nonconformists are "already entred upon the same prelude that preceeded the beginning of that Execrable Tragedy" of January 1649, their intent is clear: to justify the intended revocation of the City's charter and the stricter enforcement of the penal laws against the Dissenters already in progress.[74] But their alarmist rhetoric threatens to undo the propaganda of the previous year that had celebrated the blessings of civil peace the king had won for his people. In particular, it undercut that favorite theme of Charles's heroism by which at Oxford, at one stroke and with almost instantaneous effect, he had broken the Whigs' evil spell, so that, in the words of *The Recovery*, "now the *Charm*'s Dissolv'd, and *England*'s free / From the *Enchantment*." If the Whigs posed as dangerous a threat to the nation now as before, the king's heroism had proved to be an empty gesture.

It was an irony they were not prepared to appreciate that Tory propagandists were, in such unguarded moments, unwittingly agreeing with the Whigs, who refused to admit that their temporary setback the previous year was a defeat. The "Bells, Bonfires and Acclamations" proudly reported in Whig broadsides, with which they had since 24 November been celebrating Shaftesbury's "victory," had been designed to convince the public that they were as effective a political force as before, that the "recovery" to be celebrated was their own, and that it was the Tories who had now suffered a defeat.[75]

*The Medall* is a sequel to *Absalom and Achitophel* not because Dryden is trying to repeat his recent success by recasting the earlier poem in a briefer form but because it is founded on the same unchanging premise: that the king's decisive action at the height of the political crisis the previous March had indeed restored peace and stability, inaugurating a "Series of new time" that Dryden, for his part, refuses to consider once more in jeopardy. But in responding to the new political situation, *The Medall* puts that premise to new uses in the service of a different purpose.

Whereas the earlier poem had used it to justify the king's behavior toward Parliament that the Whigs had condemned as arbitrary and autocratic, the new poem uses it to deflate two reactions to the outcome of Shaftesbury's inquest that, from either camp, now threatened to revive the popular fears and disquiets of the Exclusion Crisis. The far more serious of the two, of course, which the poem openly confronts and disparages, is the triumphant mood of the Whigs, publicly celebrating their leader's release as a victory for their party and hoping to use it to rally new supporters to their ranks. But another reaction Dryden hopes to minimize is the inflated rhetoric of some Tory propagandists whose scare tactics threaten, however innocently, to undermine the success of their earlier campaign by exaggerating the Whigs' remaining power.

The fact that *The Medall* is "A Satyre against Sedition" rather than a "historical" poem like *Absalom and Achitophel* reflects Dryden's different purpose in writing his new poem. As a satire it seeks to discredit the Whigs and diminish their importance in order to forestall the revival of popular fears. Dryden has no wish to encourage complacency, of course, and in this respect he agrees with the other Tory propagandists. But vigilance is not the same as alarm, and by encouraging the former attitude he hopes to make the latter unnecessary. The impression he seeks to create with his poem is that the Whigs have been crushed and scattered as an effective political force capable of disturbing the peace by the king's actions of the previous year and by the revelations of their infamy that followed. The surviving remnant of the Whigs must still be reckoned with, of course, but now that it has lost its national power base in Parliament it is reduced to a hard core of Dissenters and adventurers sheltering themselves within the walls of London, to whose charter they owe their temporary immunity from justice.

If this was Dryden's purpose in *The Medall*, he was not the only Tory writer at this time trying to deflate the Whigs' apparent triumph as the empty boasts of a noisy minority. From the time of Shaftesbury's acquittal, *Heraclitus Ridens*, the most brazenly satirical of the Tory newspapers, had been pursuing the same objective. As early as the first week in December, the newspaper's Earnest, deriding "the Whiggs that were so scandalously stack'd about the Court t'other day, for the great end of hooping and hollowing" over Shaftesbury's *Ignoramus*, observed that this event had set in motion a series of celebrations that gave no sign of abating. "The Whiggs are triumphant now; not an honest Tory dare peep out; nothing but Bonfires and *Io Paeans*, for the victory some men have gotten over their Consciences."[76] A month later, the same paper's Jest noted that the Whigs' "forsaken Scriblers" had grown so bold that "poor *Absalom* and *Achitophel* must e'n hide themselves in the old Testament again."[77]

Only a week after Shaftesbury's release from the Tower, *Heraclitus Ridens* carried a mock advertisement: "Whereas the Wives and Children of some Artificers have shew'd a desire to kiss the hands of the Prince of *Whigg-land* since his Restauration, these are to give notice, that so soon as we understand that his Worthiness hath setled his days of appearance in publick, we shall take the pains to let the world know it."[78] The very next issue began with Jest announcing, "News! Why I know none; you hear I suppose that the K. of *Poland* is so well recover'd as to go abroad, to the great joy and satisfaction of his People," and with Earnest replying, "Yes, and some say they made Bonefires; but matters at that distance are variously reported."[79] These jeers epitomize the twofold theme that would be repeated incessantly in *Heraclitus Ridens* throughout the winter. On the one hand, the leader whose "exoneration" was responsible for the triumphant mood of the Whigs becomes a pygmy monarch: the "Roytelet of *Whigland*," or the insignificant king of Poland (sometimes "Prince Tapski"), or the elf king who receives "A Congratulatory Poem on his happy Restauration, written on the leaves of a *Medlar-Tree*, and sent by the Penny-Post" from "*Oberon* King of *Fairies* to the Prince of *Whigland*."[80]

On the other hand, the subjects of this diminutive ruler, lavishing "numerous Visits, Congratulations and *Baise-mains*" on their idol, are of corresponding importance: "the Wives and Children of some Artificers," the authors of pamphlets "printed at *Warsaw* by his Majesty of *Poland*'s special Command," or "the *Associati*, a dissatisfied and rebellious *Clan*, who have lately made him their Head."[81] Yet while "a little old, uncertain, quaking, stooping Gentleman should make but a sorry Champion in any Cause," it is a special wonder that Shaftesbury, about whom "it be questionable whether he were ever of any Religion," should be chosen as the "*Dux Phanaticorum*" or ruler of Whigland, "a kind of *gathered* Commonwealth, or a Kingdom in the Congregational way," and that he should now be represented as "an *Atlas* stooping under the weight of the *Protestant Cause*."[82] Therefore *Heraclitus Ridens* pretends to question Whig assertions that "the noble E. of *Shaftsbury* is the *Head of the Party*. . . . Let 'em prove that he goes to Conventicles, and then I'le believe something of what they say."[83]

The author of *Heraclitus Ridens* was not, of course, the only Tory satirist who was employing ridicule at the expense of the Whigs during the winter of 1681–82, but in his case it was an instrument used single-mindedly for the purpose of undercutting the attempt by the Whigs to recover their momentum, and of forestalling fears that public unrest was about to return. "'Tis a year since" there was cause for such fears, Earnest assured the readers of *Heraclitus Ridens*, "and the Case is altered; the Whigs began to have fine Projects in their Heads, and were according to very credible Evidence about to put 'em into Act," but that was before the king dissolved the Oxford Parliament and issued his Declaration. "The many honest men who by an easiness perhaps excusable were wrought upon to concur with their specious designs, are now undeceiv'd." Consequently, Jest rejoiced, "Whiggism declines sensibly; they are forc'd now to court the Ostlers and Carmen." In short, "Our Prophesie then is come to pass, that Whiggism is fallen, it is fallen. Their stock is out, and they are come to Thieving."[84]

.　.　.　.　.

The ostensible occasion of *The Medall*, the striking of a medal to commemorate the outcome of Shaftesbury's inquest and his release from the Tower, has been treated in commentaries on the poem as a noteworthy event of some importance independent of Dryden's response to it. Yet this is belied by the paucity of contemporary allusions to the event, suggesting that in fact it attracted relatively little attention—so little, in fact, that there is no surviving evidence of when exactly it occurred.[85] It seems reasonable, however, to assume that the memento was being distributed within a few weeks of Shaftesbury's inquest (the date of which, 24 November, appears on the reverse of the medal), since the Whigs probably seized the occasion while excitement over Shaftesbury's acquittal was still fresh, and at a time when they were feverishly celebrating the event with bonfires, public dinners, and other festivities. Any realistic estimate of the time Dryden would have needed for writing the poem before it was published on 16 March would also support this hypothesis.[86]

In choosing as the occasion of his poem the striking of a medal and its circulation among the Whigs as a commemoration of their leader's acquittal and release, Dryden was probably influenced by several considerations. In the first place, it was an event, scarcely noticed beyond their own circle, that could typify all those public acclamations by which the Whigs had been congratulating their leader since the conclusion of his inquest and flaunting their immunity from prosecution when shielded by a London grand jury. In this respect, the medal can serve as an appropriate symbol of *Ignoramus* justice, the repeated abuse of privilege justifying the effort to reform the City's method of choosing its sheriffs.

At the same time, the striking of the medal had been the Whigs' method of erecting a trophy to their political victory in an effort to persuade the nation that they had regained their former ascendancy. In this respect the medal allows Dryden to expose the reality behind the Whig boasts of recovered strength by using it as a symbol, appropriately miniaturized on its two opposite faces, of the superannuated leader and his negligible supporters.

Dryden's ways of introducing the medal into his preface and his poem are not the same, although they complement each other. At the beginning of his "Epistle to the Whigs" he treats the medal in the broad comic manner of *Heraclitus Ridens* and the Tory broadsides, and there he exploits both its sides simply as a joke at Shaftesbury's expense. The implicit legend behind his jeers is that the king of Poland has now been elected Prince of Whigland, and that his jubilant English subjects have struck a medal to commemorate their "New Sovereign's Coronation," where they can "admire and prize" his picture, appropriately depicted "in little." Since all the graver's "Kings are bought up already" by Shaftesbury's new Protestant subjects, "many a poor *Polander* who," being Catholic, "would be glad to worship the Image, is not able to go to the cost of him: But must be content to see him here," in Dryden's poem that presents the hero's "Picture drawn at length," and therefore includes much that is judiciously omitted in the medal's bust in profile. This is all of a piece with the harsh humor with which he concludes his first mention of the medal: "Truth is, you might have spar'd one side of your Medall: the Head wou'd be seen to more advantage, if it were plac'd on a Spike of the Tower; a little nearer to the Sun: Which wou'd then break out to better purpose." This is below Dryden's usual style of controversy, but its level is consistent with the rest of the "Epistle to the Whigs," whose tone and subject are deliberately modeled on the Tory newspapers and pamphlets of the past four months. The strain of the poem itself is of a somewhat higher mood.

In his poem, Dryden minimizes the importance of the medal from the outset by making its appearance a purely local event attracting the notice only of the rabble of the City of London:

> Of all our Antick Sights, and Pageantry
> Which *English* Ideots run in crowds to see,
> The *Polish Medall* bears the prize alone:
> A Monster, more the Favourite of the Town
> Than either Fayrs or Theatres have shown.
>
> (1–5)

This localization continues as he proceeds to describe the two sides of the medal that epitomize the subject of the poem:

> One side is fill'd with Title and with Face;
> And, lest the King shou'd want a regal Place,
> On the reverse, a Tow'r the Town surveys;
> O'er which our mounting Sun his beams displays.
> The Word, pronounc'd aloud by Shrieval voice,
> *Laetamur*, which, in *Polish*, is *rejoyce*,

The Day, Month, Year, to the great Act are join'd:
And a new Canting Holiday design'd.

(10–17)

It has been argued, with considerable ingenuity, that the significance of the medal for Dryden's purpose is in supplying the design for his poem.[87] I am not persuaded, however, that he attempts to produce a "literary medal" to complement the other, for his language is not especially pictorial or descriptive, and most of the poem does not correspond to the details on the original. After the first twenty-five lines, in fact, Dryden ignores the actual medal, for by then it has served its purpose of allowing him to specify his quarry by a description of its two faces: the obverse with its "king," Shaftesbury himself, and the reverse with its "Town" that constitutes his petty city state.

The medal Dryden describes is a perfectly creditable specimen of the medalist's art, and deserves more attention than it has usually received. Commentators have often relied on the reproduction of the medal John Evelyn used for his *Numismata* in 1697, which gives an inexact and misleading approximation of its reverse face.[88] The details actually depicted on the reverse are specific and reasonably accurate, but they combine features that were never at any date seen together. For the most part it is a view of London as it existed before the Fire of 1666. In fact, George Bower, its engraver, was almost certainly working from Wenceslaus Hollar's well-known etching of London before the Fire viewed from the tower of St. Mary Overie in Southwark, near the south end of London Bridge.[89] Bower's only addition has been to insert the Monument, finished in 1677, in its proper place close to the north end of London Bridge, in an attempt to modernize the scene in spite of the Monument's incongruous appearance among so many anachronistic details.[90]

Bower has severely compressed Hollar's vista, of course, to meet the constraints of his much smaller medium.[91] But what is more significant is the fact that he has deliberately narrowed its scope, encapsulating Hollar's etching into an iconic representation of the City of London. Like most such panoramas, Hollar's etching offers an unenclosed prospect of the north bank of the Thames.[92] It extends from a point considerably west of St. Paul's to slightly beyond the Tower on the east, its boundaries determined only by the prospect supposed to be visible from this vantage point. Bower, on the contrary, frames his picture between old St. Paul's, rising above the other buildings on the west, and the Tower, elevated above its neighbors on the east, with London Bridge beginning at the center and forming a diagonal across the foreground. By converting the two most prominent City landmarks into bastions framing his scene, Bower has transformed Hollar's open prospect into an image epitomizing the City of London within its ancient walls, Dryden's "Town" in its most literal dimension.[93]

Bower's scene is meant to convey two complementary meanings. The sun breaking forth from the clouds directly above the Tower on the extreme right, along with the date "24 Nov 1681" at the bottom, commemorates the acquittal of the noble prisoner portrayed on the obverse and his subsequent release from the scene of his confinement. The word "Laetamur" emblazoned across the sky above the City of London expresses the joy of its inhabitants, serving as a synecdoche for the people of England. Deliberately ignoring Bower's synecdoche and applying a literal interpretation, Dryden supplies alternative meanings for the same details. As the only royal palace within the City of London, the Tower is the most appropriate "regal Place" for the king of this urban realm. The word "Laetamur" signifies in turn the inauguration within his city state of "a new Canting Holiday" by the Dissenters who are his only acknowledged subjects.

Returning briefly to the obverse of the medal with its bust of the satanic king, Dryden introduces a transition from the graver's restricted medium to the greater latitude afforded the poet.

> Oh, cou'd the Style that copy'd every grace,
> And plough'd such furrows for an Eunuch face,
> Cou'd it have form'd his ever-changing Will,
> The various Piece had tir'd the Graver's Skill!
>
> (22–25)

These lines are often explained by commentators as a use of the "Advice to a Painter" tradition popular in political satires of the Restoration period. But Dryden's point, surely, is that no painter, or graver in this instance, could possibly portray his subject's inner character, which only the written word—this poem, in fact—can do. If a literary antecedent lies behind these lines, as I believe it does, it is far more likely that Dryden is playfully alluding to Ben Jonson's famous verses opposite Martin Droeshout's engraved portrait of Shakespeare in the First Folio:

> This Figure, that thou here seest put,
>     It was for gentle Shakespeare cut;
> Wherein the Graver had a strife
>     With Nature, to out-doo the life:
> O, could he but have drawne his wit
>     As well in brasse, as he hath hit
> His face; the Print would then surpasse
>     All, that was ever writ in brasse.
> But, since he cannot, Reader, looke
>     Not on his Picture, but his Booke.[94]

In both cases the subject's internal qualities—Shakespeare's wit, Shaftesbury's ever-changing will—have eluded the graver and can only be supplied by the written word—Shakespeare's plays, Dryden's poem. The implicit contrast between Jonson's illustrious subject and Dryden's infamous one is as inescapable as the overt verbal parallels.

By pretending at the outset of his poem that the medal depicts in miniature the present Whig leadership and its dwindling supporters, Dryden establishes the periphery of his satire before leaving the medal and its physical limitations behind. Thereafter, throughout the entire course of *The Medall*, he mentions no other Whig leader except Shaftesbury and no Whig supporters outside the City of London. This is not offered as a literal canvass of the remaining membership of the party, of course, which would only invite disbelief as an obvious distortion of its actual composition. But just as the two faces of the medal symbolize at the outset the persons represented in the poem, these in turn epitomize the negligible components of the party as it now exists: those unrepentant demagogues exemplified by Shaftesbury, and the mindless rabble who are their willing tools.

*The Medall* is a sequel to *Absalom and Achitophel* in another sense besides its sharing the earlier poem's premise that the king has restored peace to the troubled land. Published less than four months after *Absalom and Achitophel* at a time when that poem was still a subject of intense interest and angry Whig replies to it were continuing to appear, *The Medall* reasonably assumes the reader's familiarity with the earlier poem, depending for a good part of its effect upon the marked contrasts it creates with *Absalom and Achitophel*.[95] Among the most noticeable of these differences is precisely the complexity and wide variety of individuals and groups making up the Whig leadership and its supporters in *Absalom and Achitophel* as compared to the simplicity displayed in *The Medall*.

The very different political situations Dryden portrays in his two poems are of course poetic fictions shaped by his disparate rhetorical purposes, but they would be implausible if they were entirely divorced from the historical realities to which they refer. In comparing the two poems it is important to keep in mind that although they were published only four months apart, the situations they profess to describe are separated by an entire year: March 1681, the historical past when David resolves a grave political crisis in *Absalom and Achitophel*, and March 1682, the historical present depicted in *The Medall*. The declining fortunes of the Whigs between those two dates constitute the historical realities behind Dryden's poetic fiction, which he alters freely to fit his political purpose. The essential difference in his version of events is that the Whigs were dangerous on the earlier occasion, whereas they are now disabled.

The first significant disparity between the two poems appears in the opening verse paragraph of *The Medall*, where Dryden dismisses the inadequacies of the medal's portrait in favor of a historical account of Shaftesbury's career that can reveal his "ever-changing Will." This inevitably reminds us in some respects of the parallel narrative of his career in *Absalom and Achitophel* (150–220). Yet the differences are more remarkable than the similarities. Both poems trace the same episodes of his career under Charles II: his meteoric rise as a counselor to the king, his responsibility for the breaking of the Triple Alliance, his volte-face into political opposition, his assumption of the role of demagogue. Both also isolate Shaftesbury's ruling passion as perpetual restlessness fed by insatiable ambition. In *Absalom and Achitophel* he is "Restless, unfixt in Principles and Place; / In Power unpleas'd, impatient of Disgrace" (154–55), just as in the latter poem the one constant ingredient in Shaftesbury's inconstant career is "his ever-changing Will."

But in *The Medall* Dryden also introduces new details into both Shaftesbury's career and his character that significantly alter the resulting impression of the Whig leader. His account of that career begins not with Shaftesbury's protean history since the Restoration, as in the earlier poem, but with his service in the Parliamentary army during the Civil Wars, his experience as a counselor to Cromwell, and, most important, the allegation, here treated as a fact, that he was a Presbyterian under the Commonwealth and Protectorate.[96]

> Bar'tring his venal wit for sums of gold
> He cast himself into the Saint-like mould;
> Groan'd, sigh'd and pray'd, while Godliness was gain;
> The lowdest Bagpipe of the squeaking Train.
>
> (32–35)

To his perpetual restlessness Dryden now adds Shaftesbury's reputed lechery, a flaw that modifies his entire character.[97] In *Absalom and Achitophel* Shaftesbury's restlessness explains why a "fiery Soul" endowed with "Great Wit" and "discerning Eyes," destined by his unquestioned abilities for a brilliant career as a statesman, was driven by "wilde Ambition" to become a fomenter of mischief, an instance of the maxim *corruptio optimi pessima*. Such unpredictable behavior matched with great talents makes him all the more dangerous, a loose cannon crashing about the deck of the ship of state. In *The Medall*, on the other hand, Shaftesbury's passions are shown to have been at odds with one another from his youth, his lust frustrating his ambition at a time when it was to his advantage to appear chaste.

> But, as 'tis hard to cheat a Juggler's Eyes,
> His open lewdness he cou'd ne'er disguise.
> There split the Saint: for Hypocritique Zeal
> Allows no Sins but those it can conceal.

Whoring to Scandal gives too large a scope:
Saints must not trade; but they may interlope.
Th' ungodly Principle was all the same;
But a gross Cheat betrays his Partner's Game.

(36–43)

Thus Shaftesbury's kaleidoscopic career is now shown as the effect not just of his restless spirit fed by ambition but of his inability to control or conceal his other appetites, deflecting him from his immediate goals under the Protectorate and forcing a change in his allegiance which in that instance, at least, he would not have sought in his own interest. It is symptomatic of a fatal weakness that has frustrated his hopes in the past and may do so again in the future.

For the moment, however, that future is suspended while Dryden examines in the remainder of the first verse paragraph the reasons why so undependable a figure has enjoyed an initial success each time he has turned demagogue. The explanation is that Shaftesbury appeals to the mob who share the same base motive underlying his own volatile behavior. In all his turbulent career, "Pow'r was his aym" (50), the single unchanging goal of his driving ambition. In seeking proselytes, he fastens on the same ruling passion in the common rabble.

He preaches to the Crowd, that Pow'r is lent,
But not convey'd to Kingly Government;
That Claimes successive bear no binding force;
That Coronation Oaths are things of course;
Maintains the Multitude can never err;
And sets the People in the Papal Chair.

(82–87)

This recalls the scene in which Achitophel preaches the same political philosophy to Absalom in Dryden's earlier poem:

the People have a Right Supreme
To make their Kings; for Kings are made for them.
All Empire is no more than Pow'r in Trust,
Which when resum'd, can be no longer Just.

(409–12)

But in *Absalom and Achitophel* this philosophy is tied specifically to the policy of Exclusion:

Succession, for the general Good design'd,
In its own wrong a Nation cannot bind:
If altering that, the People can relieve,
Better one Suffer, than a Nation grieve.

(413–16)

Here the principle is extended to monarchy itself: not only "That Claimes successive bear no binding force," but, even more radically, "That Coronation Oaths are things of course." It is the prospect of reclaiming to themselves the power relinquished to a monarchical form of government that proves most alluring to those whose favor Shaftesbury solicits.

"Power" is in fact the controlling term in Dryden's characterization of "the Crowd" that follows, just as it had been in his description of Shaftesbury earlier in the same paragraph. If the latter "Maintains the Multitude can never err,"

> The reason's obvious; *Int'rest never lyes*;
> The most have still their Int'rest in their eyes;
> The pow'r is always theirs, and pow'r is ever wise.
> Almighty Crowd, thou shorten'st all dispute;
> Pow'r is thy Essence; Wit thy Attribute!
> Nor Faith nor Reason make thee at a stay,
> Thou leapst o'r all eternal truths, in thy *Pindarique* way!
>
> (88–94)

In *Absalom and Achitophel* Dryden had introduced the same ironic theme of "might makes right" in his account of Shaftesbury's career: "How safe is Treason, and how sacred ill, / Where none can sin against the Peoples Will" (182–83). Here, however, he raises the false maxim *lex populi, lex Dei* to tie rebellion to religious dissent. In the one case, "Crowds err not, though to both extremes they run; / To kill the Father, and recall the Son" (99–100). In the other, "The common Cry is ev'n Religion's Test" (103), according to the principle behind all religious dissent, with the result that "This side to day, and that to morrow burns; /So all are God-a'mighties in their turns" (109–10).

It was the realization that the power of the majority would be exercised in such an erratic manner to the disadvantage of the minority that led to the establishment of a monarchical form of government by "our Fathers,"

> Who, to destroy the seeds of Civil War,
> Inherent right in Monarchs did declare:
> And, that a lawfull Pow'r might never cease,
> Secur'd Succession, to secure our Peace.
> Thus, Property and Sovereign Sway, at last
> In equal Balances were justly cast.
>
> (113–18)

Once again, as in recounting Shaftesbury's career earlier in the same paragraph, Dryden returns to the time of the Civil Wars to illustrate the effects of a resumption of power by the people:

> God try'd us once; our Rebel-fathers fought;
> He glutted 'em with all the pow'r they sought:
> Till, master'd by their own usurping Brave,
> The free-born Subject sunk into a Slave.
> We loath our Manna, and we long for Quails;
> Ah, what is man, when his own wish prevails!
> How rash, how swift to plunge himself in ill;
> Proud of his Pow'r, and boundless in his Will!

(127–34)

Dryden's pragmatic appeal to the people's own self-interest, the argument that this is best secured by their entrusting to a monarchical form of government the power they cannot exercise responsibly themselves, and the claim that under such an arrangement they already enjoy maximum freedom ("Too happy *England*, if our good we knew" [123]) all find their counterparts in his so-called "discourse on government" in *Absalom and Achitophel* (753–810). But they serve a different purpose here as a means of examining the common motive that has brought Shaftesbury and the dregs of the people into temporary alliance.

The succeeding lines, which conclude this long verse paragraph on Shaftesbury, might under other circumstances be alarmist:

> That Kings can doe no wrong we must believe:
> None can they doe, and must they all receive?
> Help Heaven! or sadly we shall see an hour,
> When neither wrong nor right are in their pow'r!
> Already they have lost their best defence,
> The benefit of Laws, which they dispence:
> No justice to their righteous Cause allow'd;
> But baffled by an Arbitrary Crowd:
> And Medalls grav'd, their Conquest to record,
> The Stamp and Coyn of their adopted Lord.

(135–44)

In the atmosphere of early 1681 preceding the Oxford Parliament, such lines would have accorded exactly with the defeatist sentiments of such poems as *The Country-mans Complaint*, warning the king of imminent defeat unless he and his government at last arouse themselves to action. But in the far different climate of early 1682 their rhetoric serves instead to justify the quo warranto proceedings by which the government is already seeking to curb such miscarriages of justice. For it to do otherwise, Dryden's rhetoric implies, would be to act irresponsibly, and to invite a return to the times of "our Rebel-fathers" that he has just recalled, when "neither wrong nor right" was any longer in the power of a king beset on every side.

These closing lines supply a natural transition to the following verse paragraph, from Shaftesbury, the beneficiary of *Ignoramus* justice, to the the London grand jury that has dispensed it, at the same time depriving the king of "the benefit of Laws."

> The Man who laugh'd but once, to see an Ass
> Mumbling to make the cross-grain'd Thistles pass;
> Might laugh again, to see a Jury chaw
> The prickles of unpalatable Law.
>
> (145–48)

The twisting evasions of which he accuses the jurors, echoing L'Estrange and the other Tory propagandists, consist in their professing to disbelieve testimony from the same witnesses whose credibility had been acclaimed by the Whigs at the time of the Popish Plot trials.

> The Witnesses, that, Leech-like, liv'd on bloud,
> Sucking for them were med'cinally good;
> But, when they fasten'd on *their* fester'd Sore,
> Then, Justice and Religion they forswore;
> Their Mayden Oaths debauch'd into a Whore.
> Thus Men are rais'd by Factions, and decry'd;
> And Rogue and Saint distinguish'd by their Side.
>
> (149–55)

Dryden puns here on the word "Saint" (he had used it in the preceding verse paragraph, as we noticed, to refer to the Presbyterians), preparing us for the remainder of the paragraph, in which he draws an analogy between the Whig jurors' wresting of the law and the same party's treatment of Scripture.

> They rack ev'n Scripture to confess their Cause;
> And plead a Call to preach, in spight of Laws.
> But that's no news to the poor injur'd Page;
> It has been us'd as ill in every Age:
> And is constrain'd, with patience, all to take;
> For what defence can *Greek* and *Hebrew* make?
> Happy who can this talking Trumpet seize;
> They make it speak whatever Sense they please!
> 'Twas fram'd, at first, our Oracle t' enquire;
> But, since our Sects in prophecy grow higher,
> The Text inspires not them; but they the Text inspire.
>
> (156–66)

"They" are of course the grand jury with whom Dryden began his verse paragraph, and the Whig party as a whole of which they are typical members. They can wrest English law to their own purposes because, as Dissenters, they have long been accustomed to treating Scripture in the same fashion, applying the "private spirit" to the biblical text in order to "make it speak whatever Sense they please."[98] The "Cause" for which they rack both divine and civil law for their own ends is the same, for the Whigs are merely the "Sects" in their political dimension.

The transition that follows is equally natural, for if the actions of the London grand jury in a courtroom are of a piece with their religious practices, their behavior is also consistent with that of the disloyal London citizens for whom they serve as a convenient synecdoche.

> *London*, thou great *Emporium* of our Isle,
> O, thou too bounteous, thou too fruitfull *Nile*,
> How shall I praise or curse to thy desert!
> Or separate thy sound, from thy corrupted part!
> I call'd thee *Nile*; the parallel will stand:
> Thy tydes of Wealth o'rflow the fattend Land;
> Yet Monsters from thy large increase we find;
> Engender'd on the Slyme thou leav'st behind.
>
> (167–74)

The Nile image for the Thames, in which the disloyal citizens of London are likened to the plague of the frogs visited upon Pharoah in Exodus, had also been used by Northleigh to castigate the Whigs as "*Frogs*" who would "fill the King's Chambers, with their harsh and discontented Murmurings, as they did the *Aegyptians* once, with their Croakings: These little Democraticks, the scum of those beggarly Elements, Mud, and Water; still as mean as the one, and restless as the other."[99] And, like Northleigh, Dryden launches a scathing attack on the disloyal London tradesmen that serves to justify the government's efforts at gaining control over the City.

> But Wisedom is to Sloath too great a Slave;
> None are so busy as the Fool and Knave.
> Those let me curse; what vengeance will they urge,
> Whose Ordures neither Plague nor Fire can purge;
> Nor sharp Experience can to duty bring,
> Nor angry Heav'n, nor a forgiving King!
> In Gospel phrase their Chapmen they betray:
> Their Shops are Dens, the Buyer is their Prey.
> The Knack of Trades is living on the Spoyl;
> They boast, ev'n when each other they beguile.
> Customes to steal is such a trivial thing,
> That 'tis their Charter, to defraud the King.
>
> (185–96)

As in his earlier use of "Saint," Dryden exploits two senses of the term "Charter." Literally, the dishonest London tradesmen consider it their privilege to defraud the king of the customs money, but in a more specific sense they take advantage of their royal charter to rob him of his prerogative. Their greed for money is of a piece with their greed for political power: both are indulged by depriving their ruler of what is rightfully his.

Finally, Dryden ends this verse paragraph by identifying the disloyal citizens of London with the Dissenters, just as he had equated part of their number, the London grand jurors, with the same Dissenters at the end of his preceding paragraph.

> All hands unite of every jarring Sect;
> They cheat the Country first, and then infect.
> They, for God's Cause their Monarchs dare dethrone;
> And they'll be sure to make his Cause their own.
> Whether the plotting Jesuite lay'd the plan
> Of murth'ring Kings, or the *French* Puritan,
> Our Sacrilegious Sects their Guides outgo;
> And Kings and Kingly Pow'r wou'd murther too.
>
> (197–204)

Thus Whigs, Dissenters, and Londoners are merged into the same indistinct mass: the "party" or "sect" of hopeful regicides who have chosen, for the moment, Shaftesbury as their unsuitable champion to lead them to the promised land.

In the following verse paragraph Dryden supports his accusation of potential regicide against the Whigs by citing the intended Association, fortunately disclosed before it could be put into effect:

> What means their Trait'rous Combination less,
> Too plain t'evade, too shamefull to confess?
> But Treason is not own'd when tis descry'd;
> Successfull Crimes alone are justify'd.
>
> (205–8)

Returning for the last time to the London grand jurors, he repeats the frequent charge we have noticed in Tory propaganda that by refusing to present the treasonable Association the jurors had shown their support for a plot that was ultimately directed against the king himself.

> The Men, who no Conspiracy wou'd find,
> Who doubts, but had it taken, they had join'd:
> Joyn'd, in a mutual Cov'nant of defence;
> At first without, at last against their Prince.
>
> (209–12)

Dryden traces the steps whereby, "had it taken," which fortunately it did not because of its timely discovery, the Association would have led by degrees from "the cooler methods of their Crime"—depriving the king of his powers while permitting him "to exercise the Name"—to the final step of abolishing the monarchy and taking the king's life. But having raised this specter, he abruptly ends the verse paragraph on a reassuring note.

> Such impious Axiomes foolishly they show;
> For, in some Soyles Republiques will not grow:
> Our Temp'rate Isle will no extremes sustain,
> Of pop'lar Sway, or Arbitrary Reign:
> But slides between them both into the best;
> Secure in freedom, in a Monarch blest.
> And though the Clymate, vex't with various Winds,
> Works through our yielding Bodies, on our Minds,
> The wholsome Tempest purges what it breeds;
> To recommend the Calmness that succeeds.
>
> (246–55)

These lines provide a transition between the present, founded on the past, and the future, founded on both, with which the remainder of *The Medall* will be concerned. Once again, we are reminded of several passages in *Absalom and Achitophel* where Dryden traced the periodic recurrence of English political instability to occasions when "every hostile Humour, which before / Slept quiet in its Channels, bubbles o'r" (138–39). But he had raised the subject there to explain why such a people, "who, at their very best, / Their Humour more than Loyalty exprest" (61–62), are never quiet for long. He had portrayed them as an unsteady race "govern'd by the *Moon*" who

> Tread the same track when she the Prime renews:
> And once in twenty Years, their Scribes Record,
> By natural Instinct they change their Lord.
>
> (217–19)

Such images for English instability had continued to be popular more recently among Tory alarmists who viewed the Association as evidence that the cycle of periodic rebelliousness was about to recur. Edward Pelling, for example, prefaces his martyrdom sermon for 1682 by lamenting:

> But alas! since we have been healed of our Stripes, some seem to have almost forgotten the Rod, and are not only Willing, but Desirous to come under the Lash again. So unfixt and mutable are many *English* Spirits, that the only Center they can rest in, is the Grave: For as the Moon, after so many Periods,

returns into the same *Phasis*; so some Erratick Humors, after so many Years, revert into the same Motion; and the only Way to save men the Charge of being cured again of their Lunacy, is to prevent the Disease.[100]

Northleigh had used a similar image to castigate returning English rebelliousness: "Strange that this *Amazing* fit should on the sudden surprise us, of which we have had not so much as a Symptom this twenty Years. I suppose it would puzzle this *quacking Statesman* [Shaftesbury] to give the true cause of this sudden *shivering* Distemper in the Body *Politick*, as much as it doth most *Physicians* truly to define the matter of *Agues* in the *Natural*."[101]

In *The Medall*, however, Dryden uses such imagery for an exactly opposite purpose: to point not to the recurrences of English disobedience but to their reassuring counterpart: an inevitable return to loyalty as a result of the same climate that accounts for their periodic instability. Whereas the earlier poem had drawn attention to the descending hemisphere of the cycle, *The Medall* emphasizes instead the inexorable ascent into a more lasting tranquillity that succeeds these intermittent disquiets. The circle is a traditional image of change and restless movement, of course, which excludes any idea of permanent stasis. But it can serve, as in *Absalom and Achitophel*, to suggest that "Life can never be sincerely blest" (43), calm always being followed by turbulence, or, as in *The Medall*, to argue that this turbulence itself holds promise of "the Calmness that succeeds." The climatic cycle prepares us for the historical cycle with which Dryden concludes the poem.

The nation as a whole, its eyes opened at last to the delusions into which it had been led during the Exclusion Crisis, has already recovered its tranquillity. It is only the permanently disaffected—Shaftesbury and the London Dissenters—who continue turbulent, and no period of public peace is ever free of such a minority. With the opening words of the succeeding verse paragraph, "But thou, the Pander of the Peoples hearts" (256), Dryden returns in *The Medall* to Shaftesbury, "whose blandishments a Loyal Land have whor'd" in the past (258), and who still

> inspires the Tongues, and swells the Breasts
> Of all thy bellowing Renegado Priests,
> That preach up Thee for God; dispence thy Laws;
> And with thy Stumm ferment their fainting Cause;
> Fresh Fumes of Madness raise; and toile and sweat
> To make the formidable Cripple great?
>
> (267–72)

Shaftesbury had been introduced in the first verse paragraph to recount his past; here we are offered his future, where he will end as he began, his career finally coming full circle. In his youth he had failed to ally himself for long with the rebellious Saints of that time because his *practices* were at odds with theirs: "his open lewdness he cou'd ne'er disguise" (37). Now his hopes of reviving his waning fortunes, dependent on his forming a lasting alliance with the successors of those Saints, will founder on the incompatibility of his *principles* with theirs: "Religion thou hast none: thy *Mercury* / Has pass'd through every Sect, or theirs through Thee" (263–64).[102] In *Absalom and Achitophel* the existence of a wide variety of selfish and conflicting interests that go to make up the "Trait'rous Combination" of disparate rebels under Achitophel's command demonstrates his superior skill in forming them into an effective political organization: "Whose differing Parties he could wisely Joyn, / For several Ends, to serve the same Design" (493–94). In *The Medall*, on the other hand, the disparity between the "several Ends" dividing the Dissenters from those like Shaftesbury who lead them must inevitably shatter their momentary alliance:

> Yet, shou'd thy Crimes succeed, shou'd lawless Pow'r
> Compass those Ends thy greedy Hopes devour,
> Thy Canting Friends thy Mortal Foes wou'd be;
> Thy God and Theirs will never long agree.
> For thine, (if thou hast any,) must be one
> That lets the World and Humane-kind alone:
> A jolly God, that passes hours too well
> To promise Heav'n, or threaten us with Hell;
>
> . . . . . . . . . . . . . . . .
>
> A Tyrant theirs; the Heav'n their Priesthood paints
> A Conventicle of gloomy sullen Saints;
> A Heav'n, like *Bedlam*, slovenly and sad;
> Fore-doom'd for Souls, with false Religion, mad.
>
> (273–86)

As I pointed out earlier, Shaftesbury epitomizes in this poem the Whig leadership among whom he alone is individualized. The fatal incompatibility between head and members in the Whig body is not unique to the "formidable Cripple," weakened by age and ill health, whose political career cannot, in its natural course, trouble the nation much longer. Shaftesbury exemplifies the intelligentsia of republican libertines who are the ideologues of the party, intent on destroying both church and state in hopes of freeing themselves from all restraints, religious as well as civil. The religious fanatics whose support they need, on the contrary, are bent on replacing the existing church and state with a rigid theocracy like their idea of heaven, "a Conventicle of gloomy sullen Saints" presided over by "a Tyrant." As long as their "greedy Hopes" of overturning church and state are not actualized, republican libertines and religious fanatics can make common cause, but "shou'd thy Crimes succeed," their alliance would soon founder. In that event, as Dryden will shortly predict, neither libertine nor Saint will achieve his cherished aims: "Not Thou, nor those thy Factious Arts ingage / Shall reap that Harvest of Rebellious Rage" (291–92).

Like many of Dryden's poems, *The Medall* ends with a prophecy, but it is a prophecy with a difference.

> Without a Vision Poets can fore-show
> What all but Fools, by common Sense may know:
>
> (287–88)

Dryden begins by explicitly rejecting any pretense to the kind of "eschatological prophecy" that some recent critics have found in so many of his poems. He is offering a commonsense prediction based squarely on the nation's past experience, a practical application of history to its most important use that he was to describe the following year in his "Life of Plutarch":

> It informs the understanding by the memory: It helps us to judge of what will happen, by shewing us the like revolutions of former times. For Mankind being the same in all ages, agitated by the same passions, and mov'd to action by the same interests, nothing can come to pass, but some President [*sic*] of the like nature has already been produc'd, so that having the causes before our eyes, we cannot easily be deceiv'd in the effects, if we have Judgment enough but to draw the parallel.[103]

In foretelling what will happen "if True Succession from our Isle shou'd fail, / And Crowds profane, with impious Arms prevail" (289–90), Dryden draws just such a parallel. His picture of the future is simply a retelling of the past: a deliberately recognizable account of the cycle of English history between 1646 and 1660 in which "Republique Prelacy" under the Presbyterian yoke is shortly succeeded by civil war with the sects, the dictatorship of their general, and the overthrow of the Protectorate, concluding the cycle at last where it began:

> Till halting Vengeance overtook our Age:
> And our wild Labours, wearied into Rest,
> Reclin'd us on a rightfull Monarch's Breast.
>
> (320–22)

Dryden's predictive use of history in foretelling the future through the past depends on his being able to establish a probable parallel between a series of completed events, as mediated by his own political vision, and an analogous series of contingencies, still unrealized and therefore incapable of being tested by experience. Its persuasiveness must therefore depend on the only parallel open to experience, not between the events themselves but between their agents. In his "Life of Plutarch" this takes the form of an axiom: "Mankind being the same in all ages, agitated by the same passions, and mov'd to action by the same interests, nothing can come to pass, but some President of the like nature has already been produc'd." In *The Medall*, however, Dryden does not need to rely on a general axiom. The same discordant factions that failed to work harmoniously in pursuit of a common aim during the late rebellion are once again pursuing the same divided aims, with easily predictable results. The entire poem has been establishing this parallel from the start. That is another important reason, besides suggesting their dwindling numbers, why Dryden has so relentlessly reduced the Whig supporters to those very elements—factious Londoners and religious fanatics—who had their closest counterpart among the various groups involved in the late rebellion and Civil Wars, while he individualizes the leadership of the party under Shaftesbury, whose progression in the poem from Roundhead adjutant to Whig demagogue, hoping to foment another rebellion like the earlier, encompasses in his own person both poles of the historical parallel between actual past and contingent future.

The prophecy with which Dryden concludes *The Medall* differs in another important respect from those with which some of his other political poems end. It is a contingent prophecy like that of Jonah to the people of Nineveh, which does not foretell what must inevitably take place but warns of what will follow from a course of action that can still be abandoned in time to avert its evil consequences. What is most dissuasive about Dryden's picture of an England torn once again by civil war is not the sufferings it would entail, for a nation has often been willing to endure the greatest sufferings for the sake of an important goal. What Dryden emphasizes is the uselessness of suffering for the sake of changes that will prove impermanent, and in pursuit of innovation that for this people is only a profitless dream. Often as they forget their allegiance, they eventually return to it, "Secure in freedom, in a Monarch blest" (251). Therefore Dryden's description of where a successful rebellion would ultimately lead brings *The Medall* to exactly the same point as his narrative of an aborted revolution in *Absalom and Achitophel*:

> And our wild Labours, wearied into Rest,
> Reclin'd us on a rightfull Monarch's Breast.

(321–22)

But that comforting assurance, like the spectacle of possible rebellion that precedes it, is also contingent on the resolution of the English people: a warning as well as a prophecy. To the Whigs the impossibility of ever permanently achieving their goals should induce any who are still open to argument to abandon their futile efforts. More realistically, to the remainder of the nation, that purported majority of loyal Englishmen newly conscious of their blessings, it stands as a warning that the fanatic Dissenter, sheltered within the protective walls of London and exploiting its royal charter to his advantage, must never again be allowed the opportunity "to take the Bit between his teeth and fly / To the next headlong Steep of Anarchy" (121–22). Without ever mentioning the stricter enforcement of the penal laws and the continuing effort to revoke the City's charter, Dryden implies that the nation's remedies are already at hand for those willing to use them.

.   .   .   .   .

By his own account, Dryden's collaboration with Nathaniel Lee on *The Duke of Guise* began as soon as he had finished *The Medall* and occupied him until sometime in the spring of 1682. In the normal course of events, the play would have been produced on the stage toward the end of July and published several months later, allowing Dryden, his promise to Lee fulfilled, to put the matter behind him.[104] But unforeseen circumstances were to prolong the business of *The Duke of Guise* for more than a year following the appearance of *The Medall*. In the event, the play did not receive its first performance at Drury Lane until the end of November; it was published in February 1683, and Dryden's *Vindication* of the play followed in April of that year. In the rapidly changing circumstances of 1681, such a delay would have led to the play's being overtaken by subsequent events long before Dryden had seen it staged and published and had tardily defended it. But in the absence of any significant change in the political climate between the end of 1681 and mid-1683, a play that recapitulated the subject of *Absalom and Achitophel* and employed the rhetoric of *The Medall* retained its timeliness in the face of these delays.

Thanks to Dryden's *Vindication*, for which he could not have foreseen the necessity at the time he was working on the play, we know a good deal about the time *The Duke of Guise* was written, his share in it, and its subsequent fortunes. He declares that "after the writing of *Oedipus* [in 1678], I pass'd a Promise to joyn with [Lee] in another; and he happen'd to claim the performance of that Promise, just upon the finishing of a Poem [*The Medall*], when I would have been glad of a little respite before the undertaking of a second Task."[105] We also learn from Dryden's *Vindication* a year after the event that "the Play was wholly written [i.e., completed] a month or two before the last Election of the *Sheriffs*" (p. 44), which took place on 24 June 1682, although its outcome was not decided until the end of the summer. This would place the composition of the play between early March and perhaps early May, and as James Winn points out, the "Epistle to the Whigs" prefixed to *The Medall* suggests that "Dryden was clearly now reading (or rereading) the main source for the new play, the historian Davila, whom he specifically cites in the 'Epistle.' "[106] As a result, there is a seamless continuity between Dryden's work on *The Medall* and his contribution to *The Duke of Guise*, both of them reacting to precisely the same political circumstances.

The extent of that contribution was probably greater than Dryden allows in the *Vindication*, however, where he minimizes his share of the play—less out of modesty than to redress the exaggerated role his enemies were giving him as the play's principal author: "I know very well, that the Town did ignorantly call and take this to be *my Play*; but I shall not arrogate to my self the Merits of my Friend." Actually, he claims, "*Two thirds* of it belong'd to *him*; and then to *me* only the *First Scene* of the Play; the whole *Fourth Act*, and the *first half*, or somewhat *more* of the *Fifth*" (p. 3). But the first scene of the play comprises nearly half of act 1. Act 4, which is wholly Dryden's, and act 5, where somewhat more than half is his, are longer by some distance than the other three. By his own reckoning, then, Dryden was probably responsible for more like half than a third of *The Duke of Guise* in addition to the prologue and epilogue.[107]

The accusations against *The Duke of Guise* that delayed its stage production for four months and led Dryden eventually to publish his *Vindication* are all variations on a single theme: that, in Dryden's words, "some Great Persons were represented or personated in it" (p. 2). The first such charge, that Monmouth was represented in the play under the character of Guise, began before the play had even been performed, when rumors to this effect reached the ear of the lord chamberlain about a fortnight before it was due to appear on the stage, and led him to issue an order prohibiting it from being acted until further order.[108] Since this rumor was grounded on act 4, scene 1 (by Dryden) in which Guise returns to Paris against the king's orders (as Monmouth had disobeyed his father in returning to London in November 1679), Dryden was commanded to wait on the lord chamberlain, "which I did, and humbly desir'd him to compare the *Play* with the *History*, from whence the Subject was taken . . . and leaving *Davila* (the *Original*) with his Lordship." Consequently "a strict Scrutiny was made, and *no Parallel* of the Great Person design'd, could be made out. But this Push failing, there were immediately started some terrible Insinuations, that the *Person* of his *Majesty* was *represented* under that of *Henry the Third*; which if they could have found out, would have concluded, perchance, not only in the *stopping* of the *Play*, but in the *hanging up* of the *Poets*" (pp. 2–3).

By the time the authorities had satisfied themselves of the falsity of this second rumor, Dryden continues, "the *Play it self* was almost *forgotten*," but at last "there were Orders given for the *Acting* of it," and it made its belated stage appearance on 28 November. But next, before the play was even published, it had to contend with two Whig pamphlets, by Shadwell and Thomas Hunt respectively, which revived the accusations reponsible for the play's postponement and amplified their gravity. Dryden, they charged, ignoring Lee, had "malitiously and mischievously represented the King, and the Kings Son" under the play's two most vicious characters. "He puts the King under the person of *H. 3d.* of *France*, who appeared in the head of the *Parisian* Massacre [of Saint Bartholomew]. The Kings Son under the person of the Duke of Guise, who concerted it with the Queen Mother of *France*, and was slain in that very place by the righteous judgment of God, where he and the Queen Mother had first contrived it."[109] And in depicting the latter's murder by the French king in a justifiable light, they charged, Dryden had "invited, commended and encouraged" a repetition of the like crime: "the Assassination of the Duke of *Monmouth*."[110] When *The Duke of Guise* was finally published about 13 February 1683, Dryden added an advertisement promising that his answer to these "*two scurrilous Libels*" would be "*printed by it self*" (p. 76). He was already at work on his *Vindication*, which followed sometime in April.

Dryden begins his *Vindication* by declaring: "In the Year of His Majesty's Happy Restauration, the First Play I undertook was *the Duke of Guise*, as the Fairest way, which the *Act of Indempnity* had then left us, of setting forth the *Rise* of the *Late Rebellion*; and by *Exploding* the Villanies of it upon the *Stage*, to *Precaution Posterity* against the Like Errors." He goes on to recount that on the advice of friends to whom he showed the play he set it aside, and to claim that "the *Scene* of the Duke of *Guise*'s *Return* to *Paris*, against the King's *Positive Command*, was then written; I have the Copy of it still by me, almost the same which it now remains, being taken *Verbatim* out of *Davila*" (p. 1).[111] Inasmuch as Dryden asserts that this earlier play was entirely his own work, it obviously must have differed in many respects from the later play on which he collaborated with Lee. We can assume, for example, that it did not include such invented characters as Malicorne, Melanax, and, especially, Marmoutier, whose romantic relationship with Guise is so important in the plot of the later play.

There is no reason to disbelieve Dryden's assertion that he had written a different play on the same subject as a parallel between the French and English civil wars in 1660 during the first flush of enthusiasm over the Restoration. He had, after all, drawn that parallel the same year in *Astraea Redux*, where, comparing Charles to Henri IV, he had written:

In such adversities to Scepters train'd
The name of *Great* his famous Grandsire gain'd:

Who yet a King alone in Name and Right,
With hunger, cold and angry *Jove* did fight;
Shock'd by a Covenanting Leagues vast Pow'rs
As holy and as Catholique as ours:
Till Fortunes fruitless spight had made it known
Her blowes not shook but riveted his Throne.

(97–104)

As Charles H. Hinnant has shown, the parallel between the two "Covenanting Leagues" in France and England had been used by others in the immediate aftermath of the Restoration.[112] I would add that Sir William Dugdale had revived the same parallel in May 1681, realizing its timeliness in the critical state of current affairs, to which, implicitly, it bore a further resemblance.[113]

Some critics, surprisingly, have taken Dryden's claim that he wrote an earlier version of this play as a parallel between the French and English civil wars to mean that "he essentially denies any intention to draw a parallel between the story of the House of Guise and contemporary English politics" in the play he later wrote with Lee.[114] Yet Dryden repeatedly insists throughout his *Vindication* that the play he and Lee had now written about the French Leaguers *is* intended as a parallel to the Whigs. "For this Play does openly discover the Original and Root of the Practices and Principles, both of their Party and Cause" (p. 4). The Whigs are angry, he declares, because the play is a "Glass, which has shewed them their own Faces" (p. 14). He tells them that "your Party are certainly the men whom the Play attaques; and so far I will help you: the Designs and Actions represented in the Play, are such as you have Copyed from the *League*; for though you have wickedness enough, yet you wanted the *Wit* to make a *new Contrivance*" (p. 42).

Dryden seems to have had two reasons for revealing that he had written an earlier version of the play in 1660. The first, and much the more valid, reason was to affirm, at a time when the Whig Association was repeatedly being paralleled with the Solemn League and Covenant, that a play about the Holy League could serve equally well as a parallel to either of them. Dryden specifically says so shortly afterwards when he states the purpose for which he and Lee wrote their play: "Our intention therefore was to make the Play a Parallel, betwixt the *Holy League* plotted by the House of *Guise* and its *Adhaerents*, with the *Covenant* plotted by the *Rebels* in the time of King *Charles* the *First*, and those of the *new Association*, which was the Spawn of the *old Covenant*." He also points out in the same paragraph that the opening words of his prologue to the play had confirmed this intention: "The first words of the *Prologue* ['*Our Play's a Parallel*'] spake the *Play* to be a *Parallel*, and then you are immediately inform'd how far that *Parallel* extended, and of what it is so. *The*

*Holy League begot the Covenant, Guisards got the Whig, &c"* (p. 7). That is to say, the Holy League spawned both the Solemn League and Covenant and the Whig Association. Yet of the two English parallels to the Holy League, the Whig Association is obviously the more central to the purpose of Dryden and Lee, as the other expressions of their intention, quoted in the last paragraph, make clear.

This complex parallel of the Holy League, the Solemn League and Covenant, and the new Association had suggested itself to Tory propagandists almost from the time that the last of these had become public at Shaftesbury's grand inquest. The abhorrences, which as a matter of course drew a parallel, as we have seen, between the Association and the Solemn League and Covenant, often took care to suggest as well a further parallel between the Association and the Holy League in France. According to the Common Council of the City of Hereford, whose abhorrence was published in February 1682, the Association "outstrips the Holy League in *France*, outdoes the Solemn League and Covenant in *Scotland*," while the Artillery Company of the City of London, later in the same month, declared that the "*Accursed Conspirators*" responsible for the Association "have much outdone the Originals after which they Copied: *The Solemn League and Covenant*, and the *Holy League of* France."[115] But the most detailed use of this further parallel at the time Dryden was at work on *The Medall*, and about to collaborate with Lee on a new play, was made by his friend John Northleigh in *The Parallel*, published on 6 February. Throughout most of his book, as we noticed earlier, Northleigh had drawn a double parallel between the Association, the oath and covenant of the House of Commons signed in June 1643, and the Solemn League and Covenant drawn up the following September. But having finished that task, he then turned to another: "And now we are in the Vein and Humor of drawing *Parallels* between *Covenants*, I shall give them a tast too, of that in *France* against the poor *Hugonots* . . . and let these deluded Zealots see," he adds with unconcealed irony, "that they tread not only in the footsteps of the *true Protestants* of *Charles* the *First* in *England*, but also of the *rank Papists* of *Henry* the *Third* in *France*." And he proceeds to print the articles of the French Holy League beside those of the English Association in parallel columns.[116]

Dryden's second, and more questionable, reason for disclosing his authorship of an earlier play about the League is to deny that the scene in which Guise returns to Paris in defiance of the king's orders, written in 1660, could have been designed as an allusion to Monmouth's reappearance in London against his father's wishes in 1679, "unless they will make the *pretended Parallel* to be a *Prophecy*, as well as a *Parallel* of *Accidents*, that were *twenty years after to come*" (p. 2). But this ignores the real issue, which is whether, in choosing to include this scene in their play of 1682, Dryden and Lee did not purposely allude to Monmouth's similar escapade of three years earlier. This rather disingenuous argument is only the first of many such attempts throughout the *Vindication* to answer Hunt's and Shadwell's charges of defaming the king and his son by denying that *The Duke of Guise* contains any allusions to individuals. "So then it is not, (as the snarling Authors of the *Reflections* tell you) a Parallel of the *Men*, but of the *Times*. A Parallel of the *Factions*, and of the *Leaguers*" (p. 7). Two months earlier, in dedicating the printed quarto of *The Duke of Guise* to Lawrence Hyde, earl of Rochester, Dryden had made a similar denial in assuring him that the play "*was neither a Libel, nor a Parallel of particular Persons.*"[117] And even before Hunt and Shadwell published their charges, Dryden had responded in much the same fashion to the rumors of the previous summer with a new epilogue to *The Duke of Guise*, where the actress Sarah Cooke assured the audience:

> Yet no one Man was meant; nor Great, nor Small;
> Our Poets, like frank Gamesters, threw at All.
> They took no single Aim:
> But, like bold Boys, true to their Prince and hearty,
> Huzza'd, and fir'd Broad-sides at the whole Party.
>
> (Sig. A4)[118]

But Dryden's distinction between individuals and parties is impossible to maintain in practice, since any dramatic parallel of "the times," or public events, must inevitably touch on not only the "factions" and "parties" involved, but also the "particular persons" who play a significant role in them. The point is nicely illustrated by a Tory pamphlet published on 30 May 1682, at about the time Dryden and Lee finished writing their play. In the course of drawing a parallel of his own between the Holy League and the Whig Association, the author declares:

> The *Guises* were a *bloody Faction* indeed, and design'd the overthrow of that Monarchy, by the same means and measures your *Associators* do that of ours. It was *they* deluded a youthful Prince with the hopes of a Crown, and *strengthen'd* their Party by the *weakness* of a young Duke: It was *they* made the *profess'd Religion* a pretence for all the Desolations that attended a miserable War: It was *they* drew up the *primitive Association*, and were the *first* Founders of an *Holy League*.[119]

This certainly begins as "a Parallel of the *Factions*, and of the *Leaguers*," but it slides almost imperceptibly into "a Parallel of particular Persons" with an allusion to the duke of Guise that evokes Monmouth as a matter of course.

By its very nature, the parallel drawn in *The Duke of Guise* between the Holy League and the Whig Association embraces much else besides the factions themselves. The French history related by Davila concerned a Catholic country with a king who shared the religion of his countrymen but had no children, his collateral heir, the king of Navarre, being a Protestant; where the Leaguers, who wished at any cost to exclude that heir from the throne because of his religion, controlled the Estates General and enjoyed the support of the people of Paris; where civil war threatened, the king being forced to summon the Estates General to meet at Blois when he no longer dared trust his capital; and where peace was restored only when the indolent king, at the urging of his loyal supporters, resolved to "put on the Lyon," by which he recovered his authority. The remarkable parallel between this series of actual events and the recent history of the Exclusion Crisis that had reached its climax in the Oxford Parliament was unmistakable, and by dramatizing the French episode so soon after the conclusion of its English analogue, Dryden and Lee could be sure that their audience would recognize at least the most important respects in which "Our Play's a Parallel."

It is quite beside the point, therefore, for Dryden to deny that the scene in which Guise returns to Paris against the king's orders can possibly allude to Monmouth because it is "taken *Verbatim* out of *Davila*" (p. 1), or to assert in more general terms: "That which perfectly destroys this *pretended Parallel*, is that *our* Picture of the *Duke of Guise* is exactly according to the *Original* in the *History*; his Actions, his Manners; nay, sometimes his very Words, are so justly copied, that whoever has read him in *Davila*, sees him the same here" (p. 6). Like *Naboth's Vinyard* and indeed most parallels (except *Absalom and Achitophel*), *The Duke of Guise* portrays a historical episode whose contemporary analogue is only implicit. Just as Caryll's poem relates the story from the first book of Kings concerning Naboth's judicial murder by Ahab and Jezebel, all the while encouraging the reader to infer the obvious parallel with the persecution of the English Catholics in the Popish Plot trials, so *The Duke of Guise* dramatizes, often quite literally, the French political crisis related in Davila's history, at the same time alluding to the more recent political crisis in England by drawing the audience's attention, as we shall see, to some uncanny similarities with persons and events nearer home.

Actually, Dryden acknowledges as much in his *Vindication*, where, ignoring the apparent inconsistency with his own words, he readily admits in three different places to having implied throughout the play a parallel between the king of Navarre and his grandson the duke of York.[120] That of course had been meant as a flattering analogy, like the one Dryden had earlier drawn between Navarre and Charles in *Astraea Redux*. But his refusal here to concede the presence of unflattering analogies between the rebel duke of Guise and Monmouth is of a piece with his dubious claim in "To the Reader," prefixed to *Absalom and Achitophel*, that he had sought "*to Extenuate, Palliate and Indulge*" Monmouth's character in that poem. In both cases Dryden seeks to clear himself "from the imputation of an ungrateful man, with which my enemies have most unjustly tax'd me" (p. 20) for having turned against his former patron. The fact that Dryden goes out of his way in the *Vindication* to insist that he is "very far from detracting from him [Monmouth]" and to acknowledge "the Obligations I have had to him," which "were those, of his Countenance, his Favour, his good Word, and his Esteem" (p. 20), suggests the embarrassment he must have suffered on this sensitive topic ever since joining the ranks of the Tory propagandists.

.  .  .  .  .

By choosing to dramatize what had figured in the abhorrences and in Northleigh's book as a fairly simple parallel between the Holy League and the Whig Association, Dryden and Lee created something altogether different and far more complex. "*This Parallel* is plain," Dryden pointed out in his *Vindication*, "that the *Exclusion* of the *Lawful Heir* was the main design of *Both Parties*" (p. 7). By deciding to portray the crises that had torn both France in the 1580s and England in the 1680s as a consequence of this same issue, the playwrights expanded the scope of the original parallel to a considerable degree.

The result of that decision was that *The Duke of Guise* would offer a parallel with precisely the same subject as *Absalom and Achitophel*, allude to many of the same actions and agents, and recall the identical chronological period covered in the poem. The differences would be considerable, of course, since the poem had recounted the Tory version of the Exclusion Crisis while alluding to a biblical parallel, whereas the play would present a dramatized version of French history that implied numerous analogues to the Exclusion Crisis. Nevertheless, one important benefit for Tory propaganda in a play suggesting another parallel with the Exclusion Crisis and its outcome would be to allude once again to Charles's decisive action of the previous year, and we may wonder why Dryden should have undertaken it at a time when writers for the government, having exhausted that topic, had already embarked on a new campaign in which he had just participated himself with the publication of *The Medall*. The answer is that *The Duke of Guise* is not simply an inferior recycling of *Absalom and Achitophel*. It would be closer to the mark to say that it is an updating of his earlier parallel with the Exclusion Crisis, allowing him to allude to the role played in that crisis by the Association, which had not become public until after the publication of his poem, and to give it corresponding importance. Furthermore, it allows Dryden and Lee to exploit the rhetoric of the new campaign by alluding much more frequently to the City of London and the Dissenters than

Dryden had done in *Absalom and Achitophel*. As a result, *The Duke of Guise*, while inviting a parallel with the previous year's events, is very much a part of the new propaganda campaign of 1682.

As Dryden's various editors have pointed out, he speaks no more than the truth when he claims that most of the incidents in *The Duke of Guise* (except those involving Marmoutier, Malicorne, and Melanax) are closely modeled on Davila. But as any good parallelist must do, the playwrights select and emphasize those historical episodes that bear most closely on their implicit subject, the Exclusion Crisis in England. The majority of such instances occur in the parts of the play for which Dryden was responsible, and it should come as no surprise that in some cases this selection and emphasis brings to mind *Absalom and Achitophel*. On occasion, Dryden (and in one instance, even Lee) seems to have introduced into *The Duke of Guise* deliberate verbal echoes of his poem, thus exploiting the public's familiarity with *Absalom and Achitophel* as a means of enhancing the parallel with the subject shared by both his poem and his play. More often, of course, he and his collaborator simply rely on the audience's acquaintance with recent events to insure their recognizing the suggested analogues. By noticing some of these instances of deliberate parallelism, we can better understand the political rhetoric of the play.

In the opening scene Dryden wrote for the play, a consultation among the conspirators, Polin, who is secretly acting as the king's spy, declares that "one prime Article of our Holy League, / Is to preserve the King, his Pow'r and Person," which the curate of St. Eustace dismisses as "a pretty Blind to make the Shoot secure" (p. 2), recalling the Whig pretense that their Association was designed to insure the king's safety. Polin then turns to "the next Article in our Solemn Covenant":

> POL. That in case of Opposition from any person whatsoever—
> CUR. That's well, that's well; then the King is not excepted, if he oppose us—
> POL. We are oblig'd to join as one, to punish
>     All, who attempt to hinder or disturb us.
>
> (P. 2)

This recalls the Tory debating point we noticed earlier, that the paper of Association included a promise to destroy all opponents "without exception to His Majesty himself." In the play, of course, the League is already in operation, whereas the intended Association had never actually materialized. But it was supposedly being planned during the weeks before the Oxford Parliament, a period corresponding to the development of the French conspiracy represented in the play.

Dryden also draws particular attention in this scene to the abortive scheme, which he had found in Davila, to kidnap the king while he was taking part in the Lenten procession. The cardinal asks, "What hinders us to seize the Royal Penitent, / And close him in a Cloyster?" Guise, agreeing to the plan, orders his confederates to "guard him safe":

> Thin Diet will do well; 'twill starve him into Reason;
> Till he exclude his Brother of *Navarre*,
> And graft Succession on a worthier Choice.
>
> (P. 4)

By reminding his audience of the plot to seize Charles at Oxford and hold him prisoner in London until he would agree to the exclusion of his brother, the duke of York, Dryden ensures their recognizing that there were analogies in the French political crisis for both versions of the Protestant Plot: that which the Whig grand jury had refused to believe at Shaftesbury's inquest, and the Association that had replaced it in Tory propaganda. Since both plots were supposed to be forming at the same time preceding the Oxford Parliament, it is appropriate that these allusions to them appear together in the first scene of the play.

James Winn has pointed out that in act 1 Marmoutier's words accusing Guise of courting popularity—"But, Sir, you seek it with your Smiles and Bows, / This Side and that Side congeing to the Crowd" (p. 9)—are "a close parallel to Dryden's description of Monmouth in *Absalom and Achitophel*, 'On each side bowing popularly low' (l. 689)."[121] He surely is correct, and I would add that there are other such deliberate reminders of Absalom in act 1. In the opening speech of the play, Bussy refers to "glorious *Guise*, the *Moses*, *Gideon*, *David*, / *The Saviour of the Nation*" (p. 1), while Marmoutier, in the speech to Guise I have just quoted, continues:

> You have your Writers too, that cant your Battels,
> That stile you the New *David*, Second *Moses*,
> Prop of the Church, Deliverer of the People.
>
> (P. 9)

These epithets are almost certainly meant to recall the similar language used of Absalom, whom Achitophel proclaims

> Thy longing Countries Darling and Desire;
> Their cloudy Pillar, and their guardian Fire:
> Their second *Moses*, whose extended Wand
> Divides the Seas, and shews the promis'd Land:
>
> .  .  .  .  .  .  .  .  .  .  .  .  .  .  .  .  .  .  .
>
> Thee, *Saviour*, Thee, the Nations Vows confess;
> And, never satisfi'd with seeing, bless.
>
> (232–41)

Act 5 of the play, for which Dryden wrote "somewhat more" than the first half, takes place at Blois, where Henri III has just opened the meeting of the Estates General, here regularly referred to as the "Parliament." Alphonso Corso, referring to the king's behavior at this ceremony, declares that "I have heard, he made a sharp reflecting Speech upon their Party at the opening of the Parliament, admonish'd Men of their Duties, pardon'd what was past, but seem'd to threaten Vengeance, if they persisted for the future" (p. 56). This is clearly meant to recall Charles's severe speech opening the Oxford Parliament, which, as we noticed earlier, covered exactly the same points except for the threat of vengeance at the close.

Shortly afterward, the deputies of the Estates General appear before Henri III, and the cardinal, acting as their spokesman, tells the king that "the Commons will decree to exclude *Navar* / From the Succession of the Realm of *France*" (p. 61). The king replies,

> Decree, my Lord! What one Estate decree,
> Where then are the other two, and what am I?
> The Government is cast up somewhat short,
> The Clergy and Nobility casheer'd,
> Five hundred popular Figures on a Row,
> And I my Self that am, or should be King,
> An o'regrown Cypher set before the Sum.
>
> (P. 61)

This echoes rather closely one of David's arguments in his speech from the throne at the end of *Absalom and Achitophel*:

> Would *They* impose an Heir upon the Throne?
> Let Sanhedrins be taught to give their Own.
> A King's at least a part of Government,
> And mine as requisite as their Consent.
>
> (975–78)

Refusing to endorse the king of Navarre's exclusion, Henri III goes on to praise his heir's qualifications for the crown:

> I know my Brother's nature, 'tis sincere,
> Above deceit, no crookedness of thought,
> Says, what he means, and what he says, performs:
> Brave, but not rash; successful, but not proud,
> So much acknowledging that he's uneasie,
> Till every petty service be o're paid.
> . . . . . . . . . . . . . .
> He can forgive, but you disdain Forgiveness.
>
> (P. 62)

This speech includes many of the same qualities found in Absalom's grudging praise of the lawful successor in *Absalom and Achitophel*:

> His Brother, though Opprest with Vulgar Spight,
> Yet Dauntless and Secure of Native Right,
> Of every Royal Vertue stands possest;
> Still Dear to all the Bravest, and the Best.
> His Courage Foes, his Friends his Truth Proclaim;
> His Loyalty the King, the World his Fame.
> His Mercy even th' Offending Crowd will find,
> For sure he comes of a Forgiving Kind.
>
> (353–60)

The most consistent use of deliberate parallelism, however, occurs in the opening scene of act 1, in act 4, and in the early half of act 5—that is to say, in every portion of the play for which Dryden was responsible— where he repeatedly emphasizes the major role played in the French crisis by the Parisians, incited by their religious leaders, in order to suggest an analogy with the central role in the Exclusion Crisis attributed by Tory propagandists to London and the Dissenters. This theme is so frequent in Dryden's share of the play that selective quotation will have to suffice.

The curate of St. Eustace boasts of having overcome the scruples of some "weak Brothers of our Party" by producing arguments from a book written by a "Calvinist Minister"

> to justifie the Admiral [Coligny]
> For taking Arms against the King deceas'd [Charles IX]:
> Wherein he proves that irreligious Kings
> May justly be depos'd, and put to death.
>
> (Pp. 1–2)

"The Author," the curate concedes, "was indeed a Heretick," but "the Matter of the Book is good and pious." In his "Epistle to the Whigs" preceding *The Medall*, Dryden had already applied this parallel to the English faction:

> Any one who reads *Davila*, may trace your Practices all along. There were the same pretences for Reformation, and Loyalty, the same Aspersions of the King, and the same grounds of a Rebellion. I know not whether you will take the Historian's word . . . that it was a *Hugonot* Minister, otherwise call'd a *Presbyterian*, (for our Church abhors so devilish a Tenent) who first writ a Treatise of the lawfulness of deposing and murthering Kings, of a different Perswasion in Religion: But I am able to prove from the Doctrine of *Calvin*, and Principles of *Buchanan*, that they set the People above the Magistrate; which if I mistake not, is your own Fundamental; and which carries your Loyalty no farther than your likeing (p. 40).

As the consultation among the conspirators proceeds, Bussy predicts:

Our Charters will go next: Because we *Sheriffs*
Permit no Justice to be done on those
The Court calls Rebels, but we call them Saints.

(P. 3)

In tallying their supporters, the cardinal boasts that "all the Saints are Cov'nanters, and Guisards," while Bussy announces that

Our City Bands, are twenty thousand strong;
Well Disciplin'd, well Arm'd, well season'd Traitors;
Thick rinded heads, that leave no room for *Kernel*;
Shop Consciences, of proof against an Oath,
Preach'd up, and ready tin'd for a Rebellion.

(P. 4)

In act 4 the king exclaims, "O *Paris, Paris*, once my Seat of Triumph; / But now the Scene of all thy King's misfortunes" (p. 40), while a citizen reminds his fellow Parisians, "We have all profited by godly Sermons that promote Sedition" (p. 48). Dryden returns to the theme at the beginning of act 5, where Grillon declares that "*Paris* is a damn'd, unweildy Bulk, and when the Preachers draw against the King, a Parson in a Pulpit is a devilish Fore-horse," adding contemptuously, "what dangerous Beasts these Townsmen are" (p. 56). This is the rhetoric of 1682, not 1681, and it finds its closest echoes not in *Absalom and Achitophel* but in *The Medall*.

Since history never repeats itself exactly, there were of course important differences as well as similarities between the two exclusion crises. The civil disorders in France had no counterpart even in the Tory version of recent English history. Act 4 of *The Duke of Guise* dramatizes the return of Guise to Paris and its sequel, the Day of the Barricades, in which fighting took place in the streets of Paris and Henri III was besieged in the Louvre, barely escaping with his life by fleeing to Blois. Dryden and Lee make no attempt to suggest English parallels for these disturbances, since there were none. " 'Tis true, there was no *Rebellion*," Dryden pointed out in his *Vindication*, "but whoever told [the Whigs], that I intended this *Parallel* so far?" (p. 44). Obviously, the king's authority had deteriorated much farther in France than in England a century later, and this is confirmed in act 5 when the deputies brusquely inform the king that the Estates General intend the next day to appoint Guise lieutenant general of the kingdom, effectively depriving Henri III of his royal powers, a far more serious crisis than that with which Charles was confronted at Oxford. But the most important difference of all between the two exclusion crises is suggested by the manner in which the French emergency is resolved, through the murder of Guise and, subsequently, his brother the cardinal on the orders of the king.

The parallel between the crises confronting Henri III and Charles II, as well as their different ways of resolving them, is central to the political design of *The Duke of Guise*. It is again, as in *Absalom and Achitophel*, a parallel of the kind that, a year later, Dryden would commend Plutarch for writing: "Not comparing Men at a lump, nor endeavouring to prove they were alike in all things, but allowing for disproportion of quality or fortune, shewing wherein they agreed or disagreed, and wherein one was to be preferr'd before the other."[122] The closest resemblance lay in the crises confronting the two kings and in their initial reluctance to act decisively in the face of national emergency, by which they allowed the crises to grow more serious. Grillon, who plays Ventidius to the French king's Antony, warns his royal master: "If Kings will be so civil to their Subjects, to give up all things tamely, they first turn Rebels to themselves, and that's a fair example for their Friends" (p. 63). Marmoutier urges the king to "resume, my Lord, your Godlike temper, / Yet do not bear more than a Monarch should" (p. 30). Their words recall the advice of the indulgent David's "faithful Band of Worthies" in *Absalom and Achitophel*:

> They shew'd the King the danger of the Wound:
> That no Concessions from the Throne woud please,
> But Lenitives fomented the Disease.

> (924–26)

Yet the French king's dilatory behavior had allowed matters to slide much farther—to the very brink of the precipice, in fact—than Charles's hesitation had done, and this is the first of the implicit differences in the behavior of the two rulers that far outweigh the resemblances. Dryden and Lee evoke these differences particularly in the ways the two kings responded to their respective crises, and in the course of doing so they leave no doubt how greatly the English king "was to be preferr'd before the other." These widely different responses are shown to be the result of sharp disparities in both personal character between the two monarchs and national character between the two countries.

In his *Vindication*, Dryden observed that the greatest difference in personal character setting the two kings apart lay in the contrast between Charles's merciful nature—so great that "*Plutarch* himself, were he now alive," could not have found his equal "in that eminent vertue of his *Clemency*"—and the opposite temperament of the French king, among whose virtues, he remarked drily, "I do not find his *forgiving qualities* to be much celebrated. That he was deeply engag'd in the bloody *Massacre* of *St. Bartholomew*," he adds, "is notoriously known" (p. 9). Dryden and Lee emphasize this implicit contrast in their characterization of the French king.

Henri III's vindictive feelings toward Guise are stressed repeatedly throughout the play. Early in act 2 he tells the queen mother, "Know then I hate aspiring *Guise* to Death," while at the end of act 3 he vows before her, "My Heart has set thee down, O *Guise*, in Blood, / Blood, Mother, Blood, ne're to be blotted out," adding, "If I forgive him, may I ne're be forgiv'n" (pp. 14, 36). In resolving at last that "'Tis time to push my slack'nd vengeance home, / To be a King, or not to be at all," he reveals the uneasy balance between reasons of state and hatred for his rival underlying his decision, in which the latter is never far from the surface: "My vengeance, ripen'd in the womb of time, / Presses for birth, and longs to be disclos'd" (p. 63).

In emphasizing the crucial role played by the queen mother in that decision, Dryden and Lee underscore the differences in national character between France and England to the advantage of the latter. Early in the play, Henri III asks, "What Honours, Interest, were the World to buy him, / Shall make a Brave Man smile, and do a Murder?" and he goes on to condemn "sneaking *Brutus*, / Whom none but Cowards and white-liver'd Knaves / Would dare commend" (p. 13) for having acted toward Caesar in this fashion. By a fine stroke of dramatic irony, this is precisely the course he will come to adopt himself toward Guise, under the tutelage of the queen mother: Catherine de Medici, the principal contriver of the Massacre of St. Bartholomew and, to English minds, the personification of Catholic duplicity and Latin cruelty, Italian as well as French. Her prominence in the play exemplifies the process of selection available to the parallelist in emphasizing similarities or, in this case, differences between the historical past and its contemporary reflection. Catherine de Medici did of course exert an important influence on Henri III, as she had done on his two brothers who preceded him on the throne. But the dramatic representation of that influence, by which she and her clerical confidant Abbot Delbene are shown as instrumental in shaping the king's policy at every turn, is an important means by which Dryden and Lee guide the audience's attitude toward his actions. It is from her "Cruel Wit" (p. 13) that he learns the "Arts" of outward friendship and secret intrigue, inviting Guise to "take this Embrace: I court you for my Friend" while all the time meditating revenge, and promising his mother that "here your part of me will come in play; / Th' *Italian* Soul shall teach me how to sooth" (pp. 20, 41).

That policy, by which he arranges to have assassins murder the unsuspecting Guise, is bluntly condemned by the two most sympathetic characters in the play, both of them loyal supporters of the king's cause. Marmoutier has personal reasons for urging the king to spare Guise's life, since she loves him, but when she realizes what the king intends to do it is moral revulsion that leads her to exclaim, "you would murder *Guise*," and to brush aside his plea that she "use a softer word" (p. 59). Later, when Henri orders Grillon to assassinate Guise, his faithful soldier refuses, in part because he owes his life to Guise. But again it is moral outrage at such a request that leads him to blurt out, "Now I understand you; I shou'd murder him: / I am your Soldier, Sir, but not your Hangman," and to ask indignantly, "how have I / Deserv'd to do a Murder?"

> As for Cutting off a Traytor, I'le execute him lawfully
> In my own Function, when I meet him in the Field;
> But for your Chamber-practice, that's not my Talent.
>
> (Pp. 63–64)

What is most significant, perhaps, is the accurate parallel Marmoutier draws between the king's intended action and the Massacre of St. Bartholomew, to English Protestants the most heinous crime in French history. When Henri professes to her that "I am reconcil'd" with Guise at the very time when he is already planning his brutal murder, she declares, "These are your Arts to make [Guise and his friends] more secure, / Just so your Brother [Charles IX] us'd the Admiral [Coligny]" (p. 58). Although the king protests that "this is no Vigil of St. *Bartholmew*," the audience would have recognized the justice of the analogy, for it was the duplicity of the French court in professing amity with the Huguenots that exacerbated the enormity of the crime that followed. If Henri intended fewer victims on this occasion, he was employing the same "Italian" arts as his brother previously, in which both had been well schooled by their mother, Catherine de Medici.

To the French king, his assassination of the unsuspecting Guise is not murder but "Soveraign Justice," the term he uses to both Marmoutier and Grillon, for he is an absolute ruler who believes, "I'm born a Monarch; which implies, alone / To weild the Scepter, and depend on none" (p. 36). As a Frenchman, even Grillon must grudgingly accept the legality of an action that he regards as morally repugnant. This is how matters are handled abroad, Dryden and Lee suggest, where French absolutism and Catholic cruelty prevail. In *The Duke of Guise* France finds itself "betwixt the two encroaching Seas of Arbitrary Power, and Lawless Anarchy," as Dryden called them in dedicating *All for Love* to Danby in March 1678, and the playwrights leave no doubt that where these are the only alternatives, the former, which has been restored at the end of the play, is preferable to the latter. But no better can be expected, their audience would agree, of a people who are not endowed with those "properly

*English* Virtues" that Dryden commended to Danby, artfully appealing to the chauvinism shared by most of his readers, however great their differences on other grounds:

> No People in the World being capable of using them, but we who have the happiness to be born under so equal, and so well-pois'd a Government; a Government which has all the Advantages of Liberty beyond a Commonwealth, and all the Marks of Kingly Sovereignty without the danger of a Tyranny. . . . The Nature of our Government above all others, is exactly suited both to the Situation of our Country, and the Temper of the Natives . . . and therefore, neither the Arbitrary Power of one in a Monarchy, nor of many in a Commonwealth, could make us greater than we are.[123]

The playwrights' implicit contrast between the French king's way of resolving the exclusion crisis at Blois and the English king's at Oxford is unmistakable. Charles, while slow to act at first, had done so in good time before matters had slipped beyond his control; he had exercised no more than his lawful prerogative in dissolving Parliament; and he had restored peace without shedding blood. The contrast was much on Dryden's mind at this time, as we might expect. In the "Prologue to His Royal Highness" he wrote for a special performance of *Venice Preserv'd* at Dorset Garden on 21 April 1682, while he and Lee were still at work on their play, Dryden uses the same theme again in general terms whose application to Charles is obvious: "A Tyrant's Pow'r in rigour is exprest: / The Father yearns in the true Prince's Breast."[124]

The aftermath to Charles's decisive action, in which he sought to punish the traitor chiefly responsible for the crisis, afforded as striking a contrast with the behavior of Henri III. When the French king responds to Marmoutier's accusation that "you would murder *Guise*" by exclaiming "Murder! what Murder! use a softer word, / And call it Soveraign Justice," Marmoutier replies:

> Wou'd I cou'd:
> But Justice bears the Godlike shape of Law,
> And Law requires Defence, and equal Plea
> Betwixt th' Offender, and the righteous Judge.

(P. 59)

Her words are surely meant to remind the audience that this was precisely the way in which Charles and his administration had meted out English justice to Shaftesbury, who had been placed under arrest for treason, brought before a grand jury, and, when the jurors refused to indict him, released by the government in spite of official unhappiness over the outcome.

If Charles contrasts favorably with David in *Absalom and Achitophel* in respect of responsible action versus fatally protracted indulgence toward a rebellious son, he contrasts even more favorably with Henri III in *The Duke of Guise* in respect of moderate and lawful action versus the harsh and morally reprehensible conduct of a tyrant. By encouraging a mood of self-congratulation in the audience at the superiority of English law to French absolutism, Dryden and Lee hope to make Charles himself a beneficiary of those patriotic feelings while associating his enemies with the foreign cabals of religious zealots.

*The Duke of Guise* takes its rhetoric, then, from both Tory campaigns, that of 1681 as well as the later one of 1682. By its tacit reminders of Charles's legitimate actions in March 1681, it once more justifies his behavior as reasonable and proper. By its implicit parallels between two rebellious capitals bursting with religious fanatics, it contributes to the ongoing attack on London and the Dissenters by sounding once more a warning Dryden had offered at the beginning of 1682 in *The Medall* and, regarding the Dissenters, would repeat yet again toward the end of the year.

In the Preface to *Religio Laici*, published on 28 November 1682, the day on which *The Duke of Guise* received its delayed premiere, Dryden quoted the "Prophetick speech" of "our venerable *Hooker*" about the Puritans of his own day: "There is in every one of these Considerations most just cause to fear, lest our hastiness to embrace a thing of so perilous Consequence (*meaning the Presbyterian Discipline*) should cause Posterity to feel those Evils, which as yet are more easy for us to prevent, than they would be for them to remedy." Dryden comments: "How fatally this *Cassandra* has foretold we know too well by sad experience: the Seeds were sown in the time of Queen *Elizabeth*, the bloudy Harvest ripened in the Reign of King *Charles* the Martyr: and because all the Sheaves could not be carried off without shedding some of the loose Grains, another Crop is too like to follow; nay I fear 'tis unavoidable if the Conventiclers be permitted still to scatter."[125] But that too is more easy to prevent than to remedy, and the means are already at hand in the penal laws against Dissenters, if only magistrates throughout the land will be diligent in enforcing them, insuring that the conventicles are dispersed before another bloody harvest can take place.

# Chapter 5

## A SECOND RESTORATION

IF, AS DRYDEN AND LEE implied, Charles's action in saving his country from possible anarchy in 1681 was more just and lawful than Henri III's, it also promised to be more lasting than that of the French king, who within a few months of arranging Guise's murder would "dye a violent Death himself; murder'd by a *Priest*, an *Enthusiast of his own Religion*" (pp. 9–10) while investing his still rebellious capital: the judgment of Providence, Dryden suggested in the *Vindication*, for his part in the Massacre of St. Bartholomew.

Yet Charles's capital, while not in open rebellion, still provided a refuge for Whig diehards, offering them immunity from prosecution while its presses, evading legal restraints, multiplied seditious pamphlets and newspapers: abuses condemned explicitly or implicitly in both *The Medall* and *The Duke of Guise*. Until these lingering ailments were cured, the nation's widely heralded recovery would remain incomplete.

. . . . .

The first encouraging sign from London had appeared even before *Absalom and Achitophel* was published. As early as October 1681, a month after the two newly elected Whig sheriffs, Pilkington and Shute, had taken office, the court had the satisfaction of seeing a more accommodating lord mayor, Sir John Moore, installed at the Guildhall. Tory propagandists were quick to proclaim this a victory for their party, boasting that "Sir *John* is for Allegiance, which Rebels wou'd destroy."[1] But with the sheriffs enjoying exclusive control over the selection of jury panels, Moore's election could have no effect on *Ignoramus* justice. "The Head is loyal which thy Heart commands," Dryden conceded in *The Medall* in March 1682, "But what's a Head with two such gouty Hands?" (181–82).

That disability would be cured more quickly than Dryden could have expected: almost as soon as he and Lee finished writing *The Duke of Guise* "a month or two before the last Election of the *Sheriffs*," and well before their play made its delayed appearance on the stage. In the midsummer election of 1682 to which Dryden refers, the king's party again put up its own candidates for sheriff, Dudley North and Ralph Box, against the Whig nominees, Thomas Papillon and John Dubois, both of whom had been members of Shaftesbury's grand jury. Once again the Whig candidates polled a majority of votes from the Common Hall, but on this occasion, after a series of adjournments and contested tallies protracted throughout the summer, the pliable lord mayor, acting under instructions from the court, declared North and Peter Rich elected, the latter having replaced Box, who had earlier withdrawn from the embarrassing contest. On 28 September the new sheriffs were installed and during the night or early the following day Shaftesbury, his immunity from indictment at an end, went into hiding. The behavior of the new London and Middlesex juries, now packed with dependable Tories, soon confirmed his fears, and some two months later Shaftesbury slipped away to Holland, there to die in exile. True, the government to all appearances had only gained a year's respite from *Ignoramus* justice and must expect to renew the struggle each summer until a favorable outcome of the quo warranto proceedings afforded them permanent relief. But to the Tories it denoted an important victory marked by triumphant broadsides rejoicing that "*Ignoramus* is out of Doors."[2] Counting over the recent improvements to London in his *Vindication* in April 1683, Dryden was able to include "the last and the present Lord Mayor [the Tory Sir William Pritchard, who had succeeded Moore in October 1682], our two Honourable Sheriffs," and "the rest of the Officers, who are generally well affected, and who have kept out their factious Mem[bers] from its Government" (p. 54). Toward Shaftesbury, who had died in Holland on 21 January, he could afford to deal charitably now that he posed no further threat, dismissing him as "a Noble Peer deceas'd: the Case is known, and I have no quarrel to his memory: let it sleep; he is now before another Judge" (pp. 45–46).

At the same time as its offensive against *Ignoramus* justice throughout the summer of 1682, the court renewed its efforts against the London press that it held responsible for the spread of sedition. Determined to deprive the Whigs of the most important public forum remaining to them in the absence of a parliament, the government now took steps to silence the two Whig newspapers that had survived the pressures under which, as we noticed earlier, Benjamin Harris and Francis Smith had been forced to discontinue their own publications in mid-April 1681. At the end of May 1682 Richard Janeway was imprisoned and forced to purchase his freedom by agreeing to discontinue the *Impartial Protestant Mercury*, succumbing to the same tactic the government had used successfully against Francis Smith the previous year. Shortly afterward Langley Curtis went into hiding to avoid a similar fate, his wife continuing to publish the *True Protestant Mercury* for another five months, until her arrest and imprisonment at the end of October 1682 brought this last of the Whig newspapers to an end. As had been the case with the proclamation against newspapers in May 1680, the Tory journalists suffered along with their Whig opponents. John Smith's *Currant Intelligence* had died of natural causes at the end of December 1681 and *Heraclitus Ridens* came to a close in August 1682 on the grounds that its mission was no longer necessary, the Whig faction having grown so feeble. But it was under pressure from the government, wishing to appear impartial in its suppression of the newspapers, that Thompson's *Loyal Protestant* and Benskin's *Domestick Intelligence* vanished together on 16 November 1682. By the beginning of 1683, therefore, only the official *London Gazette* and L'Estrange's *Observator* remained, neither of which had ever made any pretence of reporting domestic news, and the public was reduced once more to depending on rumors and private newsletters for its information.[3]

No wonder, then, that Dryden expressed so much satisfaction at the nation's rapid convalescence when *The Duke of Guise* was finally published in February 1683. As he assured Lawrence Hyde, earl of Rochester, in dedicating the play to him, the Whigs "can make the major part of no Assembly, except it be a *Meeting-House*. Their Tyde of Popularity is spent, and the natural Current of Obedience is in spight of them, at last prevalent" (sig. A2v).

Two months later, when his *Vindication* appeared, Dryden's assurances that the Whigs had been put to flight carried even greater conviction. "The quarrel of the Party to [L'Estrange in the *Observator*]," he declared, "is that he has *undeceiv'd* the *ignorant*, and laid open the shameful contrivances of the *new vampt Association*" (p. 40). Their late hopes "of altering the *Succession*," he explained, returning to the theme of *Absalom and Achitophel*, concealed mischiefs to the nation "which our Gracious King, in his Royal Wisdom well forsaw; and has cut up that accursed Project by the Roots; which will render the memory of his *Justice* and *Prudence*, *Immortal* and *Sacred to future Ages*, for having not only preserv'd our present quiet, but secur'd the Peace of our Posterity" (p. 35). Consequently, the Exclusion Crisis has passed into history. "Neither is it any way probable, that the like will ever be again attempted: For the *fatal Consequences*, as well as the *Illegality* of that Design, are seen through already by the People" (p. 32).

As a result, the Whig party is now reduced to libertines and religious fanatics, the same two incompatible groups among the surviving Whigs whom Dryden had portrayed as the irreligious Shaftesbury and his godly supporters in *The Medall* the year before.

And indeed, to look upon the whole Faction in a lump, never was a more pleasant sight than to behold these builders of a new *Babel*, how ridiculously they are mix'd, and what a rare confusion there is amongst them. One part of them is carrying Stone and Mortar for the building of a *Meeting-house*, another sort understand not that Language; they are for snatching away their Work-fellows materials to set up a *Bawdy-house*: some of them *blaspheme*, and others *pray*; and both I believe with equal godliness at bottom: some of them are *Atheists*, some *Sectaries*, yet *All True Protestants* (p. 23).[4]

"But, the truth is," Dryden concludes his *Vindication*, "their contrivances are now so manifest, that their Party moulders both in Town and Country: (for I will not suspect that there are any of them left in Court.) Deluded *well-meaners* come over out of *honesty*, and *small* offendors out of common *discretion*, or fear. None will shortly remain with them, but men of *desperate fortunes* or *Enthusiasts*" (pp. 59–60).

Dryden's tactic has a familiar ring, for it is the same he had used some twenty years earlier in his poem celebrating the Restoration, where he proclaimed the nation's near unanimity in welcoming that event. Indeed, these last sentences from his *Vindication* could be a paraphrase of his triumphant lines in *Astraea Redux* in 1660:

> The discontented now are only they
> Whose Crimes before did your Just Cause betray:
> Of those your Edicts some reclaim from sins,
> But most your Life and Blest Example wins.
>
> (314–17)

Once again, as on the earlier occasion, Dryden portrays the nation as already experiencing the consensus he hopes it will soon achieve. His commitment to this tactic over the past year and a half beginning with *Absalom and Achitophel* ("And willing Nations knew their Lawfull Lord") explains the hostility he, in company with other Tory propagandists, expresses at this same period toward the Trimmers.

Dryden's harsh attacks on these individualists begin in November 1682, the same month in which L'Estrange replaced Tory and Whig with Observator and Trimmer as the interlocutors in his newspaper, whose readers now learned that "a Trimmer is a kind of a *State-Otter*, neither *Fish*, nor *Flesh*, and yet he Smells of *Both*."[5] In the new epilogue Dryden wrote for the delayed premiere of *The Duke of Guise* on 28 November, the actress Sarah Cooke relates a dialogue with a Trimmer who is shocked by her severe language against the Whigs and exclaims, "Fie, Mistress *Cooke*! Faith you're too rank a Tory!" In times like these, "Lenitives, says he, suit best with our Condition," the direct reverse of the advice given David in *Absalom and Achitophel* by his "faithful Band of Worthies," according to whom "Lenitives fomented the Disease." Cooke concludes the dialogue by giving a scornful character of the Trimmers.

> Damn'd Neuters, in their middle way of steering,
> Are neither Fish, nor Flesh, nor good Red-Herring:

Not Whiggs, nor Tories they; nor this, nor that;
Not Birds, nor Beasts; but just a kind of Bat:
A Twilight Animal; true to neither Cause,
With Tory Wings, but Whiggish Teeth and Claws.

(Sigs. A4–A4v)[6]

Five months later Dryden returned to the Trimmers in his *Vindication*, where he seems especially irritated that Thomas Hunt "calls the *Trimmers*, the *more moderate sort of Tories*. It seems those Pollticians are odious to both sides," he observes, "for neither own them to be theirs. We know them, and so does he too in his Conscience, to be *secret Whigs*, if they are any thing. But now the designs of *Whiggism* are openly discover'd, they tack about to save a Stake, that is, they will not be villains to their own ruine" (p. 26). As in his epilogue, where the Trimmers are denounced as "Damn'd Neuters" who are "true to neither Cause," it is their professed neutrality rather than their moderation that most offends Dryden in his *Vindication*: "*Loyal* men may justly be displeas'd with this *Party*, not for their *Moderation*, as Mr. *Hunt* insinuates; but because, under that Masque of *seeming mildness*, there lies hidden either a deep *treachery*, or at best, an *interressed luke-warmness*" (pp. 27–28). Indeed he discovers a historical parallel for the Trimmers in the civil wars of fourteenth-century Castile, where a group of "*Neuters*" had "*neither Courage enough* " to engage on one side, "*nor Conscience enough*" to support the other (pp. 26–27).

Dryden's dislike for the Trimmers is sometimes taken as evidence that his own political position was hardening at this time. Since the Trimmers were moderates, according to this view, Dryden's distaste suggests that he was coming to ally himself ever more closely with the extremists in the Tory party. But his attacks on the Trimmers tell us less about his ideological position as a Tory than about his tactics in support of the government and his unwillingness to see that strategy lose its effectiveness. Dryden detests the Trimmers because they spoil his picture of the English as a cohesive people who, now that they are undeceived and "the designs of *Whiggism* are openly discover'd," are universally acclaiming the king and flocking to his standard, the only exception being a small band of unrepentant Whigs, "men of *desperate fortunes* or *Enthusiasts*," who are already so tarred with treason that for them there is no turning back. As neutrals who decline either to condemn the Whigs completely or to commend the government without reservation, the Trimmers continue to withhold the support that would lend credence to Dryden's picture of unanimity. His irritation is understandable. From a tactical point of view, the Trimmers are worse than the Whigs. "The [Whig] *Party* indeed speaks out sometimes," Dryden declares in his *Vindication*, "for wickedness is not always so wise, as to be secret, especially when it is driven to despair" (p. 17). That is a consistent part of the picture of the nation we have seen him drawing, a small minority of shameless reprobates still preaching sedition when there are none to hear. But there is no place on his canvas for a group of independents who disclaim the Whig label yet stubbornly refuse to join the swelling chorus hailing the king "for having not only preserv'd our present quiet, but secur'd the Peace of our Posterity." To Dryden they are an embarrassment, and when he accuses the Trimmers of "deep *treachery*" he seems to sense that they threaten to betray not so much the government itself as the impression of growing unanimity created with such effort by its dedicated publicists.

But only a few months after Dryden published his *Vindication* in April 1683, new and surprising developments may have led even his most skeptical readers to admit the essential accuracy of his optimistic picture.

·  ·  ·  ·  ·

By a remarkable coincidence, the two events that would crown the government's long struggle against the Whigs with a conclusive victory in 1683 occurred on the same day. Under the heading "*Westminster*, June 12," the *London Gazette* informed the public: "This day the Court of *Kings Bench* unanimously gave Judgment for the King upon the *Quo Warranto* against the City of *London, That the Franchises and Liberties of the said City be seized into the King's hands.*"[7] The same day Josiah Keeling, a common oilman, was brought at his own request before Sir Leoline Jenkins, one of the principal secretaries of state, to begin disclosing the last and most conclusive of the Protestant Plots that had been monopolizing the public's attention ever since the first of them emerged at Lord Howard's inquest in June 1681.

The Rye House Plot was not only the last but also the most complex of the Protestant Plots, and the one that would be exploited most skillfully by members of the government who had by this time acquired considerable experience in propaganda. Unlike the earlier Protestant Plots, this conspiracy did not come to light all at once because of a single confession or the discovery of a single document. It unfolded piecemeal, and as new facts came to light the government recognized fresh possibilities that it could put to its own use. In retrospect it is possible to detect three phases of the climactic propaganda campaign the government would mount over the summer of 1683, and it is best to follow them in their proper sequence.

The aspect of the Rye House Plot best remembered today is the assassination scheme from which it acquired its name. This was the earliest discovery to be made and appeared at first to be the entire substance of the conspiracy. As Keeling revealed to Jenkins in the series of depositions he began making on 12 June, a consortium of forty obscure Whigs, many of them drawn from such humble occupations as joiners, distillers, salters, and dyers, had devised a bold plan for assassinating the king and the duke of York the previous 7 April while the royal brothers were returning to London from their spring visit to Newmarket for the races. The conspirators' rendezvous was appointed at the Rye House in Hertfordshire, where one of their number, Richard Rumbold, carried on his trade as a maltster, and from which they could ambush the royal pair on the Saturday before Easter as their coach passed the house on its way back to London. The outbreak of a fire at Newmarket, which destroyed much of the town, forced the king and his brother to return to London four days earlier than expected, however, and the plans of the conspirators were for the moment defeated, although they continued to meet in hopes of finding another means of carrying out the assassination.

For the first week after Keeling began making his disclosures the government kept the matter a close secret while he continued to attend the meetings of the conspirators and to report their substance to Jenkins. It was not until 18 June, when the conspirators learned of warrants for their arrest, that they hastily dispersed, some to be seized, others to go into hiding, and still others to make their escape to Holland. But a gratifying number surrendered themselves during the following days, offering, like most of those unfortunate enough to be arrested, to turn king's evidence in hopes of saving their lives. The government, on its part, soon came to realize that a small number of prosecutions, abundantly supported by testimony from a large number of witnesses, would be the best means of reaping political profit from the chance discovery. In a matter of a few days, therefore, Jenkins and other government officials were busy taking depositions from a steady procession of informants, and word of the conspiracy was rapidly spreading in spite of the absence of genuine newspapers.

On 23 June the government first took public notice of the plot in a royal proclamation, published immediately afterwards in the *London Gazette*, offering in the king's name a reward of £100 apiece for the arrest of nine fugitives from justice, most of them unknown to the general public, who "have Traiterously Conspired together, and with divers other ill-affected and desperate Persons of this Our Kingdom, to compass the Death and Destruction of Our Royal Person, and of our Dearest Brother *James* Duke of *York*; And to effect the same, have held several Treasonable Consultations, and made great Provision of Arms."[8] The same day Sir Leoline Jenkins sent off letters to the lords-lieutenant of all the counties in England informing them of "a horrid design on his Majesty's and his Royal Highness' life having been discovered, which should have been executed in his return from Newmarket," had not "the accident of the fire there hastened his coming for London sooner than the time appointed."[9] In short order a correspondent was writing him a letter from Gloucester to describe the "bonfires and ringing of all the bells in the city" occasioned by "the good news received to-day of the preservation of his Majesty and his Royal Highness."[10]

The initial phase of the new Tory campaign could now begin in earnest. On 28 June L'Estrange first took notice of the latest Protestant Plot in the *Observator*. "The *Town* I know is almost all *Mad* upon the Noise on't," Trimmer remarked, "and let a man walk the *Streets* from *Westminster* to *Billingsgate*, he shall Scarce hear any thing else." For the next few months little else would be heard from the *Observator* itself. To L'Estrange the discovery of a new Protestant Plot, whoever the particular Whigs behind it, strengthened the credibility of all the earlier plots. "I need not tell you how I have been Mumbled for *Shamming* of *Plots* upon the *Protestants*," Observator reminded Trimmer a few days later. "I was not much out in my *Guesse*, you see; for (God be Praised) we are now come to the *Revelation* of the *Roguery*; and we have *the Devil Dancing naked before us*."[11]

On 30 June the appearance of three verse broadsides within a matter of hours marked the beginning of a flood of Tory propaganda rejoicing at the latest discovery. The popularity of such ironic titles as *The Last and Truest Discovery of the Popish Plot* and *No Protestant Plot; or, The Whigs Loyalty* indicates that, like L'Estrange, most Tory publicists were behaving as if their entire series of allegations against the Whigs in recent years had been confirmed at a single stroke.[12]

Meanwhile, preparations were being made for a sequel to the Abhorrence Movement that had played so important a part in the campaign against the Association the previous year. Two days later, on 2 July, the submissive lord mayor, aldermen, and Common Council of the City of London appeared in a body at Whitehall to present the king not with an unwelcome petition, as on so many earlier occasions, but with the first abhorrence of the Rye House Plot. The ceremony was repeated by another delegation before the day was over, and in rapid succession by other official bodies from all parts of the kingdom during the weeks and months that followed.

In mounting the fourth addressing movement in as many years, the government could by this time make use of officials who were seasoned veterans of such campaigns.[13] Once again the texts of all the English and Welsh abhorrences were printed in the *London Gazette*, while the Irish abhorrences were simply listed, but the effect this time was different. In each of the previous two movements the volume of addresses and abhorrences had mounted slowly, so that only after several months did it become necessary to publish double issues of the *London Gazette* to accommodate their numbers. Again, by carefully regulating their volume, those responsible for the addresses and abhorrences of 1681 and 1682 had managed to prolong each movement for nine months. On this occasion, however, greater importance was attached to the quantity of the abhorrences, and to the speed with which they appeared. So great was their flood from the very start that only a week after the king received the first of them the *London Gazette* began appearing in double issues to handle the unprecedented volume. At this rate, most of the abhorrences had come in by the end of four months, although they would continue until the end of the year, while the number eventually printed in the *London Gazette* (well over three hundred) would exceed the total reached in either of the two previous campaigns by some 50 percent.

The logistics of the last of the address movements suggests that it was designed for a different purpose from those of its two immediate prede- ·cessors. The loyal addresses of 1681 with their additional subscriptions of hundreds or thousands of signatures had passed for popular expressions of support ratifying the king's actions in dissolving the last two parliaments which some had been condemning as an abuse of the royal prerogative. The abhorrences of 1682 had served as official expressions of legal opinion on the treasonable nature of the Association which Whig propagandists were denying. In both cases they were meant to promote political beliefs on which the public was divided. But the new abhorrences, coming from many of the same official bodies as before, expressed a reaction that would have been instinctive to most Englishmen on first learning of the Rye House Plot or of any other scheme to assassinate their king. Their authors evinced horror and amazement at the news, congratulated the royal brothers on their happy escape, and offered thanks to Heaven for this deliverance. As such, they were expressions of support, certainly, but of a kind that said as much about the government's ability to command such endorsements on brief notice as about the public's willingness to offer them. The very rapidity with which they were organized and produced was apparently intended to suggest not so much spontaneity, as on the earlier occasions, as predictable submission. If so, they may have been meant less to persuade the public at large than to intimidate stragglers by an open display of the government's increased power. This impression is borne out by their language, noticeably more obsequious than that of the earlier addresses to the king.[14]

．　．　．　．　．

On 28 June the government unexpectedly issued a second royal proclamation that, like its predecessor, was immediately published in the *London Gazette*.[15] This was worded exactly like the royal proclamation of 23

June except that it substituted the names of four new fugitives from justice, far better known to the public than those they replaced: Monmouth, his henchman Sir Thomas Armstrong, Lord Grey of Warke, and the irrepressible Robert Ferguson. The rewards for their capture were also suitably increased to £500 apiece.

The explanation for this new development is that, only a few hours after the appearance of the first royal proclamation on 23 June, the influx of informers eager to confess to the new Protestant Plot in hopes of saving their lives had begun to produce a more substantial class of witnesses than before, knowledgeable about much else besides the plans for assassinating the king and his brother at the Rye House the previous April. The first of these to come in was the barrister Robert West, a member of the Middle Temple whose appearances before Jenkins beginning on 23 June would be repeated daily for almost a week. He was followed on 25 June by Colonel John Rumsey, and on 27 June by Thomas Shepherd, a prominent wine merchant in the City who had been a member of Shaftesbury's grand jury. The last of these valuable new informers to appear would be none other than Lord Howard of Escrick, discovered hiding in a chimney on 8 July and brought before the king three days later, only too happy to implicate his friends in hopes of a royal pardon.[16] But, thanks to the three new informers who preceded him, the government did not have to await Howard's tardy arrest to learn that the latest Protestant Plot had already been in existence for six months before the king's return from Newmarket in April, and that it had begun under the direction of six of the most prominent Whigs in the kingdom: the four fugitives named in the royal proclamation of 28 June, William Lord Russell, son and heir of the earl of Bedford, who had been arrested and sent to the Tower two days earlier, and Shaftesbury, who had died five months before in Holland.

Except to issue the proclamation calling without explanation for the arrest of some of the principals involved, the government made no effort to publicize the flow of new information its officials would continue to be offered for another fortnight. Some word of the new developments leaked out, of course, but the fact that they were studiously ignored by the Observator and the abhorrences during this period suggests that the government wished to choose its own time for revealing these developments to the public in what would become the second phase of its new campaign, once it was satisfied of being in possession of all the facts.[17]

That time had come once Howard finished telling his story to the king. The next morning, 12 July, twenty persons whom the informers had implicated in the conspiracy were indicted for high treason at the Old Bailey.[18] Fifteen of those named in the indictments had already fled from justice, but the remaining five were in custody, and their trials began in the same courtroom that very afternoon. The accused included three obscure participants in the assassination scheme—Thomas Walcot, William Hone, and William Blague—in addition to the better-known John Rouse, who, like Shaftesbury and Lord Howard, had been a beneficiary of *Ignoramus* justice in 1681, and, most important, Russell, the only one of the six Whig principals mentioned earlier on whom the government was able to lay hands, since Monmouth was in hiding, Shaftesbury dead, and Armstrong, Grey, and Ferguson safe in Holland.

Like the Oxford Parliament, College's trial, and Shaftesbury's grand inquest on earlier occasions, the trials of these five men were intended above all as a theatrical performance where the government's latest propaganda campaign could be staged with the maximum publicity. The five trials followed one another in steady succession like the five acts of a play, and the star performers were Keeling, West, Rumsey, Shepherd, and Howard, aided by a supporting cast of lesser informers. Their testimony, mutually consistent, was disclosed in a coherent scenario designed not only to convict the prisoners but, perhaps more important, to reveal for the first time in public the nature and complexity of the design behind the new Protestant Plot.

As the attorney general, Sir Robert Sawyer, announced by way of prologue in his opening speech to the jury for the first trial, "Gentlemen, this design was for a general Rising, and at the same time to assassinate the King and the Duke of *York*: this is the design which the whole course of our Evidence will open to you." That is to say, the drama of conspiracy that the government was about to unfold in the courtroom had a double plot, the main one consisting of plans for a general insurrection, the under-plot involving plans for assassinating the royal brothers, and each with its own cast of characters, "for every one had their particular part; some for the great design of the rising, some for the killing of the King." The two plots were in fact concurrent, both dating from early October 1682, and both directed from behind the scenes by "a Noble Lord, that is gone now to his own place"—Shaftesbury, acting in the safety of his hiding place to which he had retired on the installation of the new sheriffs at the end of September 1682.[19] The proximity of the two dates was not coincidental, for, as many of the witnesses emphasized, the new Protestant Plot was an act of desperation undertaken by men who saw their last refuge being wrested from them by the election of Tory sheriffs who would bring *Ignoramus* justice to an end.

The under-plot, to assassinate the king and the duke of York, was originally supposed to take place when the royal brothers were returning to London the previous October from their semiannual visit to Newmarket for the races. As would prove to be the case again and again in a drama that was more often comedy than tragedy, the conspirators assigned the role of assassins, who had been supplied with arms and money by Shaftesbury, missed their cues, and the king and the duke were safely back in London by the time their enemies were ready to act. Foiled for the moment, these secondary conspirators retired to the wings to await the next royal visit to Newmarket in the spring.

At the same time as these plans were being made and abandoned, the attorney general explained, others were busy rehearsing their plot of a general insurrection, "for there was a time that they struggled with themselves, which should be effected first, whether they should first kill the King and the Duke; or whether they should first rise, and so prosecute him in an open Rebellion, and destroy him that way."[20] In this general insurrection Shaftesbury was to be responsible for raising the City of London, while the levying of rebels from the rest of the country was left to the other five principals: Monmouth, Russell, Grey, Armstrong, and Ferguson, described by the attorney general as "the Council of State, as I may call them, to give forth directions for the general Rising that hath appeared was to have been within this Kingdom."[21] This council, he explained to the court, "was the great Consult, and moved all the other Wheels," while the "Underlings," as he called those "who managed the Assassination, did take notice that these Lords and Gentlemen of Quality were to manage and steer the whole business of the Rising."[22] After repeated disappointments and delays, the date of the general insurrection was set for 19 November, but when Shaftesbury sent Colonel Rumsey to his fellow conspirators to learn if all was in readiness, they returned word that the country still was not prepared to rise, and the earl, furious at being disappointed once again, withdrew in disgust to Holland. After Shaftesbury's death in Amsterdam in January 1683, the court was told, the remaining Whig leaders entrusted the direction of the general insurrection to a reorganized Council of Six consisting of Monmouth, Russell, Howard, the earl of Essex, John Hampden, and Algernon Sidney. This cabal, hitting on a new plan for a joint rising in England and Scotland, sent off messengers to propose a treaty to the Scottish Presbyterians, with whom they were still negotiating but making little progress some five months later when Keeling's betrayal of the under-plot led in turn to the exposure of the main plot as well.

The significance of these revelations to the coherence and consistency of the government's successive propaganda campaigns over the previous two years was enormous. What had at first appeared, a month earlier, to be simply a new and unrelated Protestant Plot to add to the sum of crimes with which the Whigs were being charged as each new occasion arose was revealed on closer examination to be a direct confirmation of the campaign against the Association in progress since November 1681, and of the even older offensive against Shaftesbury.

In the first place, the picture of Shaftesbury that emerged at the trials, instigating plans for a general uprising to wage war against the king and impatiently spurring his confederates to greater efforts, accorded exactly with the interpretation of the Association, its contriver, and its secret purpose that Tory propaganda had been presenting all along. Similarly, the "Council of State," as the attorney general dubbed the cabal of Whig magnates, and its successor the Council of Six corresponded closely to the standing committee of "disbanded members" of the last parliament from whom the other members of the Association were supposed to take their orders. The membership of the Council of Six in particular—half of them drawn from the House of Lords, the other half prominent Whig commoners—could have been modeled directly on the paper of Association.[23] Again, that council's negotiations for an alliance with the Scottish Presbyterians to support their rebellion underscored precisely the parallel the Tories had long been drawing between the Association and the Solemn League and Covenant. Less than a week after the conclusion of the trials, therefore, L'Estrange's spokesman was asking in the *Observator*: "And what was this Late Horrid *Conspiracy*, against the Life of his *Sacred Majesty*, and of his *R. H.* but the *Genuine*, and *Naturall* Result of *That Association*? And in fine; take the whole *Series* of that Matter, from *First* to *Last*, and you will find the *Connexion* so *Regular*, as if *Every Respective Part* of it, were only a *severall Link* of the *Same Chain*."[24] Several days earlier the abhorrence from the City of Worcester had already drawn the same connection between the Rye House Plot and the Association, declaring that, thanks to the latest revelations, "we now see a full comment upon the wily Earl's Paper, and yet not written, as design'd, in Characters of Blood."[25]

Yet at the same time, the testimony at the trials seemed to confirm the long-standing arguments of Dryden, the author of *Heraclitus Ridens*, and those other Tory propagandists who claimed that the Whigs had been fatally weakened by the king's decisive action at Oxford, entering a gradual decline that by 1682 rendered them incapable of actualizing their hopes of overthrowing the government. In the case of the latest Protestant Plot, a crucial distinction was drawn between the assassination scheme and the plans for a general rising. The former was indeed dangerous, since, as proved by the example of the king's grandfather, Henri IV, and many another ruler, no public figure, then as now, could hope to be immune from the assault of a determined assassin. As we shall see, the dangers from this side of the conspiracy would be greatly emphasized, in fact, in the last phase of the government's new campaign. But the fluctuating plans for the general insurrection disclosed by the witnesses at the trials were a succession of exaggerated hopes and inevitable disappointments amid mutual recriminations that exactly bore out Dryden's claim in April 1683 that "their Party moulders both in Town and Country." Shaftesbury, the court was told, had boasted to Howard that his support from the town was such that "above *Ten Thousand* brisk Boys are ready to follow me, when ever I hold up my Finger," but his fellow conspirators discounted his claims, Monmouth agreeing with Howard's conclusion that "his Judgment hath deserted him, when he goes about with those strange sanguine Hopes, that I can't see what should Support him in the Ground of them." But the hopes of Monmouth and his confederates that they might still find enough supporters in the country to raise a successful insurrection had proved just as illusory. Monmouth related to Howard the disappointing outcome of a typical interview with one of these country supporters when it came time to put their promises to the test. "Says he, I thought Mr. *Trenchard* had been a brisker fellow; for when I told him of [the rising planned for 19 November], he looked so pale, I thought he would have swooned, when I brought him to the brink of Action."[26]

Finally, the judgment of Dryden and other Tory writers that by 1682 the Whig party had dwindled to an uneasy alliance between libertines and enthusiasts, two groups with widely different social backgounds, religious beliefs, personal morals, and ultimate political aims, was fully buttressed by the repeated testimony that the two plots each had its own cast of characters, "some for the great design of the rising, some for the killing of the King." The gulf between the "Underlings who managed the Assassination" and the "Lords and Gentlemen of Quality" who "were to manage and steer the whole business of the Rising" was not only social but religious and moral.[27] As for the former group, Sir George Jeffreys assured the jury, "the most of these persons, nay, all of them, concerned in this hellish Conspiracy, were Dissenters from the Church of *England*."[28] The "Lords and Gentlemen of Quality" who made up the latter group, on the other hand, were, with the possible exception of Algernon Sidney, nominal members of the Established Church, but some of them, as the attorney general declared of Armstrong and Grey, were men of scandalous personal lives.[29] On the evidence of the latest conspiracy, therefore, L'Estrange was able to reaffirm that "we find *Atheisticall Republicans* and *Schismaticall Dissenters Linkt* in *One Common Interest*, as well as *Principle*, of *Levelling* the *Monarchy*, on the *One* hand, as well as the *Church*, on the *Other*; under *Imaginary Fears* of *Arbitrary Power* & *Popery*."[30]

With such an array of witnesses for the prosecution, it can have come as no surprise that all but one of the prisoners were convicted of treason and sentenced to death, only Blague being acquitted when his jury deemed insufficient the evidence against him of the necessary second witness. An official transcript of the trials, published by authority of the lord mayor, was immediately offered to the public, who did not have to wait long for the sequel. On 20 July, Walcot, Hone, and Rouse were hanged at Tyburn, each of them delivering a dying speech admitting to prior knowledge of the existence of the plot that had made them accessories before the fact, while seeking to mitigate their own part in the conspiracy.[31] If these speeches were not everything the government might have hoped for, they were frank enough to pass for confessions, and since they were spoken in the presence of the crowd attending the executions, they were far more satisfactory than the written confession Fitzharris had delivered to Hawkins at his own execution in 1681, only to have its genuineness disputed by the Whigs as soon as he was dead.

Lord Russell, on the other hand, proved less cooperative. Beheaded in Lincoln's Inn Fields the day after his companions suffered, he died professing that "*I know of no Plot, either against the King's Life or the Government*" and delivering a paper to the sheriffs in which he systematically denied the allegations at his trial.[32] In the face of such publicity, the sheriffs had no choice but to publish the paper under their authority, along with the dying speeches of the other three, and to leave it to L'Estrange to sort them out in the *Observator*, exploiting the penitent speeches of the three hanged men, especially Rouse, who had made "a very *Hopefull End*," while rejecting Russell's protestations of innocence.[33] But Russell's paper certainly weakened the climactic effect anticipated from the executions. He had given advance copies of the paper to his wife, who arranged to have it separately published, and it was being sold on the streets within an hour of her husband's death.[34] The government could not afford to ignore this challenge to the verdict of the court. Two answers to Russell's paper soon appeared, one of them by L'Estrange, a substantial work of over fifty pages.[35] And as had happened at the time of College's execution two years earlier, another Tory pamphleteer produced a bogus account of Russell's behavior on the scaffold where "he at last made a worthy Oration acknowledging his crime, for which he was justly condemned, [and] advising all to be Loyal and True."[36]

The publicizing of the climactic stage of the Protestant Plot in all its dimensions that constituted the second phase of the government's new campaign was to all intents and purposes completed with these trials, dying speeches, and executions, along with the official publications that memorialized them.[37] It was now the turn of lesser Tory propagandists to exploit all the facets of the final Protestant Plot, and they quickly did so, supplying a chorus to accompany L'Estrange's solo on the same refrain in the *Observator* during the months that followed.[38]

Once these trials and their aftermath had taken place in July, the government at Whitehall showed little interest in pursuing the legal aspect of the plot much further, except to prosecute the remaining members of the Council of Six besides Russell and the more fortunate Howard, still eager to repay the king for his pardon. Monmouth remained in hiding, but Essex, Sidney, and Hampden had all been arrested and committed to the Tower before the recent trials began. Essex cut his throat on 13 July, the day of Russell's trial, and the other two remained in confinement for some months before the government tardily acted on their cases. Sidney was at last brought to trial on 21 November.[39] With West, Rumsey, and Howard appearing against him, he was convicted of treason and beheaded on Tower Hill on 7 December, after delivering a paper to the sheriffs on the scaffold in which he defended himself and his contractualist political philosophy with great spirit.[40] Four days after Sidney's conviction Monmouth surrendered himself and confessed to his father and uncle. Still the indulgent David after all, Charles not only pardoned him but granted his plea that he be excused from giving evidence against his confederates.[41] Last of all, Hampden was brought to trial on 6 February 1684. In the absence of a second witness to support Howard's testimony to his treason, he was tried for the misdemeanor of disturbing the peace and spreading sedition, and on conviction was fined £40,000.[42] Unable to pay the fine, he remained in the King's Bench until pardoned by James II shortly after his accession. But neither these two later trials nor the official history of the Rye House Plot published at the beginning of James's reign could add anything of importance to the details of the last Protestant Plot already known to the public in mid-July 1683.[43]

It is quite possible that the government had expected the public confessions and executions of four of the Rye House conspirators in late July to serve as the curtain scene to its latest theatrical performance, a decisive climax demonstrating the guilt of all the traitors beyond any possible cavil and offering the audience an exemplary warning to treasure up against the future. But Russell's death had proved a disappointing anticlimax to that of his companions the previous day, and in more respects than just the publication of his paper and of the Tory answers to it that only prolonged a debate supposed to have ended by now. The first sour note had been struck at Russell's trial when a number of prominent character witnesses appeared on his behalf, including the popular Latitudinarian preachers Gilbert Burnet and John Tillotson, already dean of Canterbury. Burnet had visited Russell daily in the Tower during the week after his sentencing and was known to have assisted him in the composition of his paper for the sheriffs. On the day of Russell's execution, Burnet and Tillotson had accompanied him on the procession from the Tower to the scaffold and, as the official published version of the dying speeches related, had ministered to him before he approached the block. The king and the duke of York were so incensed that they summoned Burnet and Tillotson before them the next day to answer for their behavior.[44]

There were good reasons for the royal anger and disappointment. The spectacle of two prominent clergymen of the Established Church publicly comforting and supporting Russell in his last moments hardly consisted with the Tory line that the remaining Whig membership was confined to

"Atheisticall Republicans and Schismaticall Dissenters." Even worse, it drew public attention to a rift in the supposedly united front of all the Anglican clergy, loyally supporting the government they were committed to uphold by the most fundamental tenets of their religion. Some such considerations as these may have suggested to the government that it had become necessary to introduce a third phase to its new campaign, in which the discovery of the Rye House Plot could be removed from the mundane level of debate in which it threatened to become immersed like the earlier dispute over the Association, and raised to an altogether higher sphere, royal and even divine.

. . . . .

On 28 July, exactly a week after Russell's execution, appeared *His Majesties Declaration to All His Loving Subjects, concerning the Treasonable Conspiracy against His Sacred Person and Government, Lately Discovered.* Like the previous *His Majesties Declaration*, which had led off the first of the government's campaigns twenty-seven months earlier, it was published "By His Majesties Special Command" and "Appointed to be Read in all Churches and Chappels within This Kingdom." But such was the importance the government attached to favorable publicity by this time that the new declaration was also published in the *London Gazette* for good measure, and appointed to be read in the churches not once but on two successive Sundays.[45]

*His Majesties Declaration* professes two ostensible purposes. The first is to give a brief historical review of the political emergency in recent years beginning with the Exclusion Crisis, followed by a more detailed account of the Rye House Plot itself at a time when, these matters safely behind them, Englishmen supposedly awaited a definitive statement of them on the word of their king. As an epitome of the Tory interpretation of events between 1679 and 1682 the review contains nothing that was not already long familiar to the public: the alarming progress of "a Malevolent Party" determined "to Promote Sedition," by which "their Numbers increased" until they threatened to "gain upon the People, so as to perswade them to a total Defection from the Government"; then an abrupt reversal in which their progress was arrested, "the Eyes of Our good Subjects" were finally opened, and "the Factious Party lost Ground daily." But this brief review of earlier events leads to a more comprehensive account of the latest Protestant Plot, hatched when the factious party "became Desperate, and Resolved not to Trust any longer to the slow Methods of Sedition, but to betake themselves to Arms," some "Contriving a General Insurrection in this Kingdom, and likewise in *Scotland*," while "Others were Conspiring to Assassinate Our Royal Person, and

Our Dearest Brother."[46] As a convenient summary of the most pertinent details, this narrative probably ensured a much wider dissemination of information about the recent conspiracy than would have been achieved by the transcripts of the trials alone.

But at the same time that it sealed the second phase of the government's campaign with this authoritative pronouncement, *His Majesties Declaration* inaugurated a third and final phase that was probably the more important of its two announced purposes. This was introduced in the words prefacing the account of the recent conspiracy: "But the Divine Providence, which hath preserved Us through the whole Course of Our life, hath at this time in an Extraordinary manner, shewed it self in the Wonderful and Gracious Deliverance of Us and Our Dearest Brother, and all Our Loyal Subjects from this Horrid and Damnable Conspiracy."[47] When his account reaches the failure of the plans for an ambush at the Rye House, the king produces the explanation: "But it pleased Almighty God, by His wonderful Providence, To Defeat these Councels by the sudden Fire at *Newmarket*, which necessitated Our Return from thence before the time We had Appointed."[48] Finally, *His Majesties Declaration* closes by announcing:

> This We thought fit to make known to Our Loving Subjects, that they being sensible (as We are) of the Mercy of God in this great Deliverance, may Chearfully and Devoutly joyn with Us in Returning Solemn Thanks to Almighty God for the same.
>
> For which end We do hereby Appoint the Ninth day of *September* next, to be observed as a day of Thanksgiving in all Churches and Chappels within this our Kingdom . . . in such manner as shall be by Us Directed, in a Form of Prayer with Thanksgiving, which We have Commanded to be prepared by Our Bishops, and Published for that purpose.[49]

The idea that Providence was responsible for saving the king and his brother from assassination at Newmarket would not have been unfamiliar to many readers of *His Majesties Declaration*. The abhorrences had been making frequent references to the role of Providence in the king's escape ever since they began to appear on 2 July, and for obvious reasons. Expressions of gratitude to Heaven for the king's deliverance were a natural sequel to congratulations on his escape. It was also the highest form of flattery to remind the king, in the fawning language used by the grand jury of Warwickshire, "that as you are the Delight of our Eyes, and the Breath of our Nostrils, so you are the immediate care of Heaven."[50]

But until now the government had not publicly acknowledged the miracle nor taken any steps to turn it to advantage. Sir Leoline Jenkins, when informing the lords-lieutenant of the counties of the king's escape at Newmarket, had innocently referred to "the accident of the fire there" that "hastened his coming for London sooner than the time appointed," and L'Estrange had remained silent on the role of Providence in the king's escape, although the Rye House Plot had been the sole topic of the *Observator* for an entire month before *His Majesties Declaration* was made public.

The appearance of *His Majesties Declaration* in which the king announced that the "miraculous fire" at Newmarket to which he owed his life had been due to a direct intervention of special Providence in English affairs signaled a decision by the government to exploit this rare opportunity to its own advantage, and to solemnize it in the most public manner by a thanksgiving service that would figure as an exceptional event of the greatest importance. Its publication on 28 July was accompanied the same day by the appearance of *Some Seasonable Reflections on the Discovery of the Late Plot*, by William Sherlock, the popular preacher. Although its subtitle vaguely describes this homily as "a Sermon Preacht on That Occasion," the title page omits the information about the date and place of delivery that is regularly supplied when, as in most cases, a printed sermon has earlier been preached to an actual congregation. It is likely, therefore, that Sherlock's homily was written and published by previous arrangement as a model of the kind of sermon expected on the day of solemn thanksgiving, offering those clergymen who needed them the appropriate "heads" of a discourse for this occasion, in the manner of the indispensable Book of Homilies. The paramount importance attached to these thanksgiving sermons by the government would emerge during the weeks following 9 September, in the course of which at least twenty-five of them were separately published: a record unmatched for any other single occasion throughout the reign of Charles II except his restoration.[51]

What made the approaching thanksgiving service such an exceptional event was the infrequency of cases where special Providence was believed to have intervened in the political affairs of the English nation, as distinct from those occasions (also rare) when special Providence interposed to save its creatures from physical danger, as in stopping the Great Fire in the miraculous manner described by Dryden in *Annus Mirabilis*. In his sermon, Sherlock carefully catalogued the four recognized occasions on which Providence had come to the rescue of Charles II during his lifetime: his escape from his enemies in 1651 following his defeat at Worcester; the miraculous Restoration ("a great and wonderful deliverance both to Prince and People; a deliverance immediately wrought by God, without Humane policy, contrivance, or power"); the "discovery" of the Popish Plot; and the defeat of the Rye House Plot ("the fire at *Newmarket* was sent by God for the preservation of our King and his Royal Brother, for the preservation of these Kingdoms, of our Liberties and Religion"). Taking as his text Psalm 18, David's song of thanksgiving for his deliverance from his enemies, Sherlock offered David's behavior as an exemplary lesson teaching the English people to respond with like gratitude on the present occasion, "a case very parallel to *Davids*," since "the deliverances of our Prince are no way inferiour to that mercy God shewed to *David*."[52] The same parallel was officially sanctioned soon afterwards with the publication of the *Form of Prayer* for the approaching thanksgiving service, in which 2 Samuel, chapter 22, a version of the Eighteenth Psalm, was designated the first lesson of the day.[53]

Many of the thanksgiving sermons preached on 9 September, perhaps taking their cue from Sherlock, reiterated the same exhaustive list of four, and only four, cases where special Providence was believed to have intervened to deliver Charles II from his enemies.[54] But his escape at Worcester and the "discovery" of the Popish Plot could be quickly passed over.[55] It was the Restoration that emerged as the closest parallel to the "miraculous fire" at Newmarket, not only in the sermons but in the religious observance at which they were delivered. For in order to find the only exact precedent for this public celebration solemnizing the intervention of special Providence in English national affairs one would have to return to 28 June 1660, the day of solemn thanksgiving at which the nation had offered public thanks for the "miraculous" Restoration, and to the anniversary services commemorating that event every 29 May thereafter.[56]

It was natural that the fire at Newmarket should be paralleled with the miraculous Restoration in the thanksgiving sermons. Preachers who habitually magnified their subject by making it bigger and better than any conceivable competitors—the unparalleled parallel—or than all but a single paragon—"this Plot, the most barbarous and bloody that was ever laid since the *Gun-powder Treason*"—found the manner of the king's deliverance from this latest conspiracy "such an Astonishing, and (almost) Unparallel'd Instance of the Divine Providence" that its only conceivable precedent in their lifetime was "that great *Miracle* of his *Majesty's Restauration*."[57]

This was because the king's restoration and his escape at Newmarket shared a unique relationship in being able to supply preachers with surprising miracles of a kind that invited comparison with some of the more spectacular interventions of Providence recorded in the Old Testament. If Charles's earlier return from exile "without striking a blow, without shedding a drop of Blood" could be described as "no less a Miracle, than dividing the sea to give a safe passsage to the *Israelites*," the fire at Newmarket that snatched the king from the brink of destruction had in a few weeks' time grown into a miracle "like the Angel that hastened *Lot* out of *Sodom*."[58]

The importance of the miracle was that it authenticated Charles's escape as an intervention by special Providence. Supernatural wonders were not essential in such cases—none had accompanied the "discovery" of the Popish Plot certainly—but when vouchsafed they were practically certain to overawe skeptics and forestall argument. "If ever you hear Gods *Providence* call'd in question by our bold *Atheists*," one thanksgiving preacher advised his congregation, "choak them with the *fire at Newmarket*."[59] By the same token, only a hardened religious skeptic could reject the political corollary of such a miracle. For if it were once accepted that special Providence had been moved to make one of its infrequent interventions in English public affairs to preserve the king's life, one could no longer doubt the reality of the assassination plot, the gravity of the danger it had posed both to the king and to his government, or the divine favor exhibited toward Charles through his continued preservation. "And surely," another preacher argued, "he must be an Atheist, or worse (if possible) one that believes there is a God, but is resolved to fight against him and flie in his very face; if after all this he can either plot or speak evil against him whom Heaven it self hath so plainly declared to be its Favourite."[60]

For over two years, from the spring of 1681 until the summer of 1683, government propaganda had been crediting the nation's recovery to the courage, resolution, and political skill with which Charles had outwitted his adversaries and opened the eyes of his deluded subjects to the snares being prepared for them. Nothing proclaimed from the pulpits throughout the land on 9 September was meant to deny the earlier campaign nor to detract from Charles's glory as savior of the nation in one of its darkest hours. But the Rye House Plot had introduced a new factor in which human resourcefulness could no more protect Charles from the treachery of an assassination scheme than his own efforts, or even those of General Monck, it was believed, could have peacefully restored him to his throne in 1660. In making Charles the passive beneficiary of a divine rescue mission, his supporters were far from trying to dismantle the heroic legend they had been diligently embroidering since early 1681. They were simply enlarging it by adding a feature that appears in most such legends at least as early as Homer, and had already appeared, they reminded their audience, on three earlier occasions in the life of their remarkable monarch.

The respects in which religion and loyalty could be seen as supporting each other in the king's providential escape were not limited to Charles personally. As we noticed earlier, the miraculous character of the Restoration had elevated a political settlement into an act of God commanding the assent of all Englishmen. It was the providential nature of the settlement that legitimated the new regime, and the government, by commemorating that fact through the anniversary services, had been republishing its own credentials annually. Now Providence had intervened again, this time to preserve and reinforce its earlier settlement, thereby in a sense renewing the divine charter that legitimized the regime.

Hence the importance of establishing a necessary connection between the miraculous Restoration and the fire at Newmarket as successive publications of the same divine mandate. That thesis had already been propounded by L'Estrange in August, during the interval between the appearance of *His Majesties Declaration* and the day of solemn thanksgiving. Taking his cue from the king's *Declaration*, he had tardily devoted an entire issue of the *Observator* to the wonderful role of Providence in the king's deliverance, in the course of which the government's chief propagandist announced what would be the keynote of the approaching thanksgiving service: "The *Providence* of *This Late Discovery*, is, at least, a *Second Birth*; and a *Second Restauration*: The *King Lives*, and the *King Reigns* again; and the *Same Divine Mercy* that *Restor'd* him to *Us*, out of the very Jaws of *Death*, has set him once again upon his *Throne*."[61]

This is probably the reason why so many preachers at the thanksgiving service chose to expound the same specific instance from David's many providential deliverances, running an extended parallel between Charles's recent escape and David's return to Jerusalem after the defeat of Absalom's rebellion. That, as we noticed earlier, had long been the most popular Old Testament parallel for Charles's restoration, developed so often in anniversary sermons every 29 May (where 2 Samuel, chapter 19, in which it is recorded, was the first lesson of the day) that by this time it must have been indelibly associated with that event. Inevitably its application now to Charles's escape at Newmarket as equally appropriate suggested the close proximity between this latest mercy and his earlier restoration.

The famous story from 2 Samuel was both better and worse as a parallel for Charles's latest deliverance than as an analogue for his restoration. Absalom's rebellion was of course peculiarly appropriate as a parallel for the Rye House Plot, "there being scarce a considerable circumstance in the rise, growth, discovery, or defeating of the one, which hath not a parallel line in the other," according to one thanksgiving preacher.[62] To a far greater extent than was the case with the Puritan Revolution for which it served as an analogue in the anniversary sermons on the Restoration, Absalom's rebellion afforded an uncanny parallel for the Rye House Plot, as it had already done for Whig sedition in 1680 and 1681. Many of the same identifications that had become popular during the Exclusion Crisis, in fact, would be pressed into service again on 9 September. "What befell *David*, in the case of his Son *Absalom*, hath befaln our Sovereign, of a like unnatural Son, both Righteous Kings afflicted with a Rebellious Off-spring," lamented another thanksgiving preacher, adding that the part played in 2 Samuel by the "notable *Achitophel*" was exactly repli-cated in the early stages of the recent conspiracy by "the late Earl of *Shaftsbury*."[63]

But why should David's crossing the Jordan and returning to Jerusa-lem at the invitation of his people, so appropriate an analogue for Char-les's being recalled from foreign exile in 1660 and settled upon his throne, have been enlisted again as a parallel for circumstances so completely dissimilar as Charles's escape at Newmarket? Only because it helped pro-mote the politically useful idea of Charles's recent deliverance as a "*Sec-ond Restoration*" in which Providence had "set him once again upon his *Throne*," thereby placing English affairs on a new footing, just as it had done in 1660 when Charles had returned from exile amidst general accla-mation. In preventing the king's death and extending his reign, Provi-dence had indeed been responsible for a second restoration, and, as the language referring to a second birth makes plain, this restoration, like the first, marked another revolution of the historical cycle, revitalizing a na-tion that had long been sick and establishing its king on a sturdier foun-dation than ever before. "The wonderfull Deliverances He has already receiv'd," declared a preacher on the day of solemn thanksgiving,

> do plainly say, that He is still reserv'd for some extraordinary Work in the world. And from His last miraculous Escape, we may easily Presage what mighty Acts He shall perform for these Kingdoms in Particular. Now shall it be in His Power to subdue that Pestilence of Puritanism, which for above these hundred Years has raged in this Nation, to crush the Seeds, and destroy the very Principles of Schism. To Him it is reserv'd to bring the Church of *England* up to those Glorious Heights, that She shall appear the Envy of *Rome*, and the Terrour of *Geneva*. To settle the Monarchy upon so firm a Basis, that it shall be no more shaken by Republican Rage. His Sacred Person shall be no longer lyable to Violence, nor His Subjects to Oppression. No more shall Majesty be affronted by the Sawcy Votes of a Seditious Senate, nor we made Prisoners by our Representatives. But long and secure shall He Reign in the hearts and Af-fections of His People.[64]

To those in the congregation who had reached middle age, that glowing prospect must have recalled the sanguine prophecies so frequent in press and pulpit at the time of Charles's first restoration. If so, the recollection may have moderated their excitement.

.   .   .   .   .

Just as *The Medall* and *The Duke of Guise* are both part of the campaign of 1682 and early 1683 exploiting the disclosure of the Association at Shaftesbury's inquest, so *The History of the League* and *Albion and Al-*

*banius*, Dryden's last two works of political propaganda during the reign of Charles II, both belong to the new campaign of mid-1683 to 1685 capitalizing on the discovery of the Rye House Plot. But they appeared fairly late in that campaign, and the first of them to do so, *The History of the League*, was not published until a year after *His Majesties Declaration*.

In an exhaustive bibliographical study, Alan Roper has proved conclusively that Dryden made his translation of Louis Maimbourg's *Histoire de la Ligue* from a pirated Dutch edition that probably appeared sometime in March 1684. Since Tonson published the translation in the last week of July, Roper plausibly argues that Dryden must have been occupied almost exclusively with *The History of the League* between March and July of 1684.[65]

Whatever truth there may be to the stories first broached long after Dryden's death that he wrote *Absalom and Achitophel* and *The Medall* at the direction of the king, it is certain that his translation of Maimbourg was undertaken on Charles's orders, since the title page tells us as much, and in dedicating the book to the king Dryden speaks of "having receiv'd the Honour of Your Majesty's Commands to Translate the *History of the League*," adding that the king was "a Master of the Original, . . . having read this piece when it first was publish'd [15 October 1683]."[66] Roper suggests that, once he had read Maimbourg, Charles lost no time in commanding the translation "some time between mid-November 1683 and early January 1684," arguing that "Charles certainly needed great dispatch from Dryden. Above all, there should be no delay. But Dryden delayed," since, as Roper has shown, he only began carrying out the assignment in late March.[67] I think it unlikely, however, that Dryden would have been so dilatory in obeying the king's commands once he received them, and it is unclear why Charles should have been in such haste to issue them under the mistaken impression that he "needed great dispatch." It seems more probable that it was the king who delayed after reading Maimbourg in the autumn of 1683, only deciding as an afterthought to give commands for a translation from Dryden in March 1684, upon which the latter, as he declares in his dedication, "apply'd my self with my utmost diligence to Obey them" (p. 3).[68]

In any case, the public was in no haste to buy and read the translation once it appeared, for as Roper shows, Tonson was still trying without much success to dispose of the edition two years later.[69] This has been attributed to the political mood of a nation no longer in ferment, sated on government propaganda by this time, and particularly on the French Holy League, which had been publicized quite enough already, not least by *The Duke of Guise* and the heated controversy it had provoked in 1682 and early 1683. In Roper's words, "Just then, in the summer of

1684, the constitutional matter seemed settled. There was no more to say. There is, accordingly, an awesome superfluity to the announcement at the end of July 1684 that *The History of the League* was ready for sale."[70]

It seems just as likely, however, that the public was slow to buy the book not because of a sudden distaste for English political propaganda, even in the guise of another parallel between French League and Whig Association, but because it balked at buying the much larger package of which this was only a small component. The English propaganda and its familiar parallel were to be found not in Maimbourg's *History*, after all, but in Dryden's "Postscript of the Translator" appended at the back of the book, a forcefully written essay making an "application" of French history to current English affairs and drawing the parallel between them, just as many anniversary and thanksgiving sermons applied an episode of Old Testament history to contemporary circumstances. But this was buried under a 760-page history addressed to a French audience and describing French affairs from 1574 to 1598 in painstaking detail, to say nothing of another 82 pages of Maimbourg's prolegomena and addenda. Some readers, no doubt, would choose to read the history and judge for themselves its applicability to English affairs, ignoring the "Postscript" as an impertinence. But most, it is safe to guess, preferred taking their history in small doses, as prescribed and administered by the pundits for either party. If "The Postscript of the Translator" had been offered for sale as an independent pamphlet of some fifty pages, in the manner of Dryden's *Vindication of "The Duke of Guise"* the year before, there is no reason to believe it would not have sold as well as the earlier pamphlet, even though it expounded the same parallel in the service of much the same propaganda. Instead, *The History of the League*, replete with Dryden's "Postscript" as well as his "Dedication to the King," tried catering to two audiences: the smaller, with serious historical interests, finding themselves better served in this instance than the larger, whose appetite for political controversy gave no signs of abating as long as the product was clearly labeled and economically packaged.[71]

If there still existed a market for propaganda as well as prudential reasons for the government's supplying that market, this was sufficient justification for rehearsing familiar themes. Even Absalom's rebellion, after all, which had inspired far more parallels than the Holy League and over a much longer period of time, was given a new lease on life by the discovery of the Rye House Plot. There are several good reasons, in fact, why the king might have decided in March 1684 that it would be useful to revive interest in the French exclusion crisis by arranging a translation of Maimbourg's *History of the League*, and why Dryden would not have thought it redundant to publish this along with his "Postscript of the

Translator" only a year after *The Duke of Guise* and its *Vindication* had capitalized on the same subject.[72]

On 28 March 1684 the three-year interval between parliaments permitted by the Triennial Act expired, and thereafter, during the last ten months of his reign, Charles was violating the law under which he was required to summon a new parliament no more than three years after dissolving the last. The matter was obviously a delicate one. Less than a fortnight after dissolving the Oxford Parliament, the king had raised the issue of another parliament himself in *His Majesties Declaration*, denouncing the "restless Malice of ill Men, who are labouring to poyson Our People" by trying to persuade them "that We intend to lay aside the use of Parliaments," and solemnly affirming that "We are Resolved, by the Blessing of God, to have frequent Parliaments."[73] Many Whig pamphleteers had responded by openly disbelieving the king's promise and predicting that he would never summon another parliament. For their part, Tory propagandists had found themselves in an uncomfortable position where they must repeatedly remind the public of the king's promise and confidently assure them of his sincerity in making it. As the months gave place to years and still the king made no sign of ordering new elections, it became increasingly clear that the Whig prophets had been right, and this growing suspicion would have been decisively confirmed for the more observant when the date on which the three-year limit expired was allowed to pass without comment. Yet Tory propagandists could not allude to the subject directly without reminding even the forgetful of a violation of the law they might otherwise have overlooked.

Under the circumstances, it may have occurred to the king that the best oblique defense of his failure to summon another parliament would be to revive the public's flagging interest in the French political crisis of a hundred years earlier, where the Estates General, like Parliament in English affairs more recently, had served as the principal instrument by which the enemies of the government were able to dictate their wishes to the executive with impunity and to threaten its very survival. Some readers of Dryden's translation might be led to reflect by way of analogy that what three English parliaments in succession had done recently another parliament might do again, and that the king was showing commendable caution in hesitating to take an action that could revive the dangers from which he had so recently rescued the nation. Less observant readers could be inspired with the same reflections by the "Postscript of the Translator," where Dryden draws particular attention to specific respects in which the example of the Estates General had supplied the Whigs with "Precedents of undermining the lawful Authority of their Soveraigns" (pp. 409, 413) by parliamentary means.

A second consideration would have suggested to Dryden, and perhaps to the king, the timeliness of a "Postscript of the Translator" that could go well beyond any previous applications of the League to English affairs. The earlier works of Tory propaganda exploiting the French Holy League had likened it to the Whig Association and, in the case of *The Duke of Guise*, had drawn a parallel between the French and English exclusion crises themselves. But the more recent disclosure of the Rye House Plot in all its complexity had uncovered a rich lode of new analogues with the history of the League—events that, unknown to Dryden and Lee, were transpiring at the very time their play made its delayed appearance on the stage in November 1682. Just as *The Duke of Guise* is an updating of *Absalom and Achitophel* in light of the disclosure of the Association a week after the poem appeared, Dryden's "Postscript of the Translator" is an updating of *The Duke of Guise* itself that capitalizes on the discovery of the Rye House Plot some six months after the play was finally performed.

For Dryden, the disclosure that the Rye House Plot consisted of a double plot with separate casts of characters, so that, as he declares in a theatrical figure of his own, "instead of one Conspiracy, the Machines play'd double, and produc'd two, which were carry'd on at the same time" (pp. 412–13), suggested new and previously unsuspected parallels with the French civil disturbances of the 1580s. The plans for a general insurrection, contrived by Whig lords and gentlemen who were prominent veterans of the Exclusion Crisis, could now be found reflected in events already depicted in *The Duke of Guise*, since, as we noticed in the last chapter, matters had reached a more critical stage on the eve of Guise's murder than before the dissolution of the Oxford Parliament. The Whigs' "*Council of Six*," Dryden writes, "was an imitation of the *League*, who set up their famous Council, commonly call'd *Of the Sixteen*: And take notice, that on both sides they pick'd out the most heady and violent men of the whole Party" (p. 411). But the plans to assassinate Charles, instigated by Shaftesbury and entrusted to a group of fanatic Dissenters who had previously attracted no public notice, found their analogue only in events that had occurred well after Guise's death. "For when *Henry* the Third, by the assistance of the King of *Navarre*, had in a manner vanquish'd his Rebels, and was just upon the point of mastring *Paris*, a *Jacobin*, set on by the Preachers of the *League*, most barbarously murther'd him; and by the way take notice, that he pretended *Enthusiasm*, or Inspiration of God's holy Spirit, for the commission of his Parricide," a set of circumstances "much resembling, the intended Murther of our gracious King, at the *Rye*," Dryden observes. " 'Tis true, the *Jacobin* was but one, and there were many joyn'd in our Conspiracy, and more perhaps than *Rumsey* or *West* have ever nam'd; but this, though it takes from the justness of the Comparison, adds incomparably more to the Guilt of it, and makes it fouler on our side of the Water" (pp. 407–8).

But Dryden's "Postscript" updates *The Duke of Guise* in more ways than by simply supplying a sequel to his earlier parallel. By finding a place in that parallel for the events of the Rye House Plot in the manner of someone producing the missing pieces to a puzzle, Dryden attempts to give the aggregate of Whig actions in recent years the kind of consistency and coherence that Maimbourg, with the hindsight of someone writing a century after the events, had given to his *History of the League*. L'Estrange, we noticed earlier, had argued that "this Late Horrid *Conspiracy*" was "the *Genuine*, and *Naturall* Result of [the Whig] *Association*." Dryden shapes his parallel to a similar, but broader, conclusion, "that on both sides they began with a League, and ended with a Conspiracy" (p. 407). For he too wishes to persuade the reader, in L'Estrange's words, to "take the whole *Series* of that Matter, from *First* to *Last*, and you will find the *Connexion* so *Regular*, as if *Every Respective Part* of it, were only a *severall Link* of the *Same Chain*," but he also intends to find counterparts to that chain and to each of its links on the other side of the Channel.[74]

For this reason Dryden's "Postscript" consists of two parts, in which the English and French rebels are considered first in "their Principles," and then in "their Practices." The principles used to justify the Protestant Plot are traced in an unbroken chain from "the *Anabaptists* of *Germany*" through the Scottish Presbyterians to the English Puritans, and this chain is then shown to have its mirror image in the principles of the Jesuits that inspired the Catholic League in France. But this first part of the "Postscript" need not detain us, since, as John Harrington Smith was the first to show, Dryden's entire discussion of the rebels' principles is simply a paraphrase of Sir William Dugdale.[75]

The second, and longer, part that follows, on the practices of the English and French rebels, holds more interest. In setting out to show "that both the last Rebellion," with its Solemn League and Covenant, "and this present Conspiracy," with its Association, "were originally founded on the *French League*" (p. 401), Dryden retraces some of the same ground covered in his earlier *Vindication*, as we noticed in the last chapter. But in comparing the rise and decline of the two plots, Dryden adds some valuable observations on the Exclusion Crisis and its aftermath that bear out the differences we noticed earlier between *Absalom and Achitophel* and *The Medall* as to the gravity of the respective situations depicted in the two poems.

In *The Duke of Guise*, we recall, the Leaguers' power reaches its crest in act 4 on the Day of the Barricades when the king is briefly at their mercy, while the scene in which he manages to escape from Paris and imminent capture at the close of the act marks the turning point of the tragedy. In his "Postscript" Dryden expresses the same view as earlier of the crisis in the French rebels' affairs that he and Lee had dramatized in their play: "The Duke of *Guise* was always ostentatious of his power in the States [General], where he carried all things in opposition to the King: But by relying too much on the power he had there, and not using Arms when he had them in his hand, I mean by not prosecuting his Victory to the uttermost, when he had the King inclos'd in the *Louvre*, he miss'd his opportunity, and Fortune never gave it him again" (p. 414).

With this careful preparation, most readers will have already anticipated Dryden by the time he produces his parallel: not between the rebel leaders themselves, so different in their characters, but, "to pass by their Persons, and consider their Design" (p. 407), between their tactics leading to the fatal mistakes that blasted the hopes of each.

> The late Earl of *Shaftsbury*, who was the undoubted Head and Soul of that Party, went upon the same maximes, being (as we may reasonably conclude) fearful of hazarding his Fortunes, and observing that the late Rebellion under the former King, though successful in War, yet ended in the Restauration of His Present Majesty, his aim was to have excluded His Royal Highness by an Act of Parliament; and to have forc'd such concessions from the King, by pressing the chymerical dangers of a Popish Plot, as wou'd not only have destroy'd the Succession, but have subverted the Monarchy. For he presum'd he ventur'd nothing, if he cou'd have executed his design by form of Law, and in a Parliamentary way. In the mean time, he made notorious mistakes: First, in imagining that his pretensions wou'd have passed in the House of Peers, and afterwards by the King. When the death of Sir *Edmondbury Godfrey* had fermented the people, when the City had taken the alarm of a Popish Plot, and the Government of it was in Fanatique hands; when a Body of white Boys was already appearing in the West, and many other Counties waited but the word to rise, then was the time to have push'd his business (p. 414).

This period of time when Shaftesbury and his confederates were most dangerous and the crown almost within their grasp corresponds exactly to the span of time covered in *Absalom and Achitophel*: the era of popular hysteria over the Popish Plot, of Whig supremacy in the City of London, of Monmouth's triumphant progress in the West, and of repeated efforts to alter the Succession "in a Parliamentary way" which, taken together, describe the Exclusion Crisis in its ascendant, and Shaftesbury at the high tide of his fortunes. "Then was the time to have push'd his business," while the king procrastinated and the friends of the court were disheartened in 1680 and the beginning of 1681. But Shaftesbury too procrastinated, Dryden observes, trusting, like Guise, to his legislative majority to wear down the king eventually instead of "using Arms when he had them in his hand." His last opportunity to do so occurred when he and his confederates "went to the Parliament at *Oxford*," each "attended with his Guard of Janizaries, like *Titus*: So that what with their followers, and the seditious Townsmen of that City, they made the formidable appearance of an Army; at least sufficient to have swallowed up the Guards, and to have seiz'd the Person of the King, in case he had not prevented it by a speedy removal, as soon as he had Dissolv'd that Parliament" (p. 411). But Charles did prevent it, by unexpected and decisive action, and Shaftesbury's opportunity had vanished, "which he himself observ'd too late, and would have redress'd by an Insurrection which was to have begun at *Wapping*, after the King had been murder'd at the *Rye*" (pp. 414–15).

That retrospective view of events, even to the plot to seize the king at Oxford, explicitly supports the rhetoric of *Absalom and Achitophel*, where the grave jeopardy into which the nation has been pushed by Shaftesbury's skillful arts is shown to justify and indeed necessitate the king's severe measures at the end of the poem. But at the same time its emphasis on the missed opportunity supports by implication the rhetoric of *The Medall*, where, their chance of realizing their aims irretrievably lost, the remaining Whigs, weakened in numbers and divided in aims, had become objects of derision rather than alarm.

"There was neither Honour nor Conscience in the Foundation of their *League*," Dryden observes of that later phase of the crisis, "but every man having an eye to his own particular advancement, was no longer a Friend, than while his Interest was carrying on" (p. 404). As he had done two years earlier in depicting Shaftesbury and his supporters in *The Medall*, Dryden dwells on the irreconcilable differences dividing "the Heads of their Faction," among whom "greater looseness of Life, more atheistical Discourse, more open Lewdness" was not to be found, and "the Zealots of their Faction," men "as morose in their Worship, as were those first Sectaries" (pp. 403–4) the Puritans, and again he concludes that no lasting danger was to be feared from such an incongruous combination. "For my own part, when I had once observ'd this fundamental error in their Politiques, I was no longer afraid of their success: No Government was ever ruin'd by the open scandal of its opposers. This was just a *Catiline*'s Conspiracy, of profligate, debauch'd, and bankrupt men" (p. 404).

Yet this is no excuse for complacency, Dryden warns. The religious zealots "are still to be accounted dangerous, because, though they are dispers'd at present, and without an Head, yet time and lenity may furnish them again with a Commander" more compatible with their own beliefs and practices.

What my Author [Maimbourg] says in general of the *Huguenots*, may justly be applyed to all our Sectaries: They are a malicious and bloody Generation, they bespatter honest Men with their Pens when they are not in power; and when they are uppermost, they hang them up like Dogs. To such kind of people all means of reclaiming, but only severity, are useless, while they continue obstinate in their designs against Church and Government: For tho' now their claws are par'd, they may grow again to be more sharp; they are still Lyons in their Nature, and may profit so much by their own errors in their late managements, that they may become more sanctify'd Traytors another time (p. 405).

Paradoxically, this latest setback for the Whigs could provide the grounds for their recovery. The death of Shaftesbury in January 1683 and the arrest or flight the following summer of the other "libertines" and "atheists" who had made up the Whig leadership in recent years may turn out to have been not decapitation but lifesaving surgery. Freed from the divided aims that had proved all but fatal to the party in 1682 and 1683, the religious fanatics may now begin to revive, spawning new leaders who by sharing their objectives will restore their fortunes.

The "severity" Dryden recommends is of course the strict execution of the penal laws against these very Dissenters who now constitute the principal survivors among the "differing Parties" of Whigs whose number and complexity he had been at such pains to emphasize only three years earlier in *Absalom and Achitophel*. As L'Estrange, unveiling the chief remaining cause of all the nation's troubles, declared in the immediate aftermath of the Rye House trials: "Will you have the whole bus'ness in One word? Sum up All the *Apprehensions*; all the *Distempers*; All the *Inconveniencies* that we *Labour* under; and *the Root of them All, is Conventicles*."[76]

By the summer of 1684 when Dryden was writing his "Postscript," L'Estrange was tailoring the *Observator*'s rhetoric to suit its now simplified objective, persistently calling for a more vigorous program of dispersing conventicles and prosecuting their ministers, while brushing aside Trimmer's pleas for toleration by wondering: "Where's the *Hard Usage* of it, to *Execute* the *Law* upon *Those People*, that, by their *Inconformity*, and *Disobedience*, Cast themselves out of the *Protection* of it?"[77] As L'Estrange and Dryden were well aware, the government needed no encouragement from them to enforce that policy. But by warning of the dangerous consequences that could follow from any leniency toward the Dissenters, Dryden seeks to justify the ongoing offensive against conventicles as the only course consistent with the public safety.

.   .   .   .   .

If Dryden's "Postscript of the Translator" calls for "severity" toward the Dissenters by a vigorous enforcement of laws entailing fines or even imprisonment, his "Dedication to the King" appears to advocate such bloodthirsty measures toward the conspirators implicated in the Rye

House Plot that it has embarrassed most of his biographers beginning with Scott, who admitted regretfully that "the dedication to the king contains sentiments which savour strongly of party violence, and even ferocity."[78]

Unlike his discursive "Postscript," Dryden's "Dedication" is a coherent and forceful argument on a single topic: the folly of granting individual pardons or a general amnesty to the Rye House conspirators. Most commentators have assumed that Dryden, relentlessly pursuing a personal vendetta against all those incriminated by the informers, is sternly urging the government to prosecute the remaining plotters for treason, so that they may share the fate already meted out to Russell and his companions. Commenting on one of the most notorious sentences in the "Dedication," "These Sons of Earth are never to be trusted in their Mother Element: They must be hoysted into the Air and Strangled" (p. 4), Scott remarked: "I wish the fervour of Dryden's loyalty had left this exhortation to such writers as the author of 'Justice Triumphant.' "[79] The Tory versifier responsible for that angry broadside, published on 3 November 1683, most certainly did hope to see "the *Whigs* in the *Tower*, / Who thought to make us a prey" speedily brought to justice, predicting that in that event they "to *Tyburn* must trudge amain" in the footsteps of those executed the previous July.[80]

Like many commentators since Scott's time, Charles E. Ward shares his assumption about the purpose of the "Dedication." Pointing out that "some of the lesser figures" implicated in the Rye House Plot "had not been punished, nor were they ever to be," he declares that "this latest example of Charles's clemency irritated Dryden," who "goes as far as he prudently can in reproving the King on this point." In Ward's view, "Dryden not unreasonably could feel that he is being exposed to a danger that might be obviated by sterner actions by the government." Consequently his "Dedication" "seems almost a *cri du coeur*, as strong a remonstrance as an outraged loyal subject can make."[81]

It is true that the four conspirators who were tried, convicted, and executed in July 1683—Russell, Walcot, Hone, and Rouse—represented only a small fraction of those implicated in the Rye House Plot. Even after discounting the sizable number who had escaped prosecution by testifying against their confederates, or who had evaded the government's net and were now safely beyond seas, there still remained several dozen others suspected of involvement in the plot who had been swept up in the mass arrests of June and July and placed in custody.[82] Throughout the summer and autumn of 1683 it was fairly common to hear supporters of the government express vindictive sentiments toward this sizable remnant, even from the pulpit, where a greater spirit of forgiveness might have been wished for, if not expected. One of the thanksgiving preachers

on 9 September, for example, applying to Charles his text, "He shall
Reign over them," declared:

> First in Judgement; in a legal Execution of those Bloudy Conspirators who
> would have murthered Him. They must suffer, or He cannot be safe: Mercy
> would here prove Cruelty, Pardon an affront to Justice, and the highest Ingrat-
> itude to Heaven. They are now under the command of those Laws which they
> would have destroyed, under the hands of those Judges whom they had
> destin'd to Slaughter; and every Judge must remember that He is the Minister
> of God, a Revenger to execute wrath upon him that doth evil.[83]

When even clergymen did not hesitate to express such sentiments, it is not
surprising to find them widely shared by the authors of Tory broadsides,
many of them, like *Justice Triumphant*, published in November 1683.[84]

The timing of these latest Tory calls for the strict enforcement of the
treason statutes can be explained by the approaching deadline under
which a more recent law would have to be obeyed. Under the terms of the
Habeas Corpus Act the Rye House prisoners must be either indicted or
released by the last day of Michaelmas term, 28 November, the same
stipulation under which Shaftesbury and Howard had won their freedom
exactly two years earlier. As we noticed already, however, the government at Whitehall was by this time only seriously interested in prosecuting the two members of the Council of Six who remained in custody. It
made sure therefore that Algernon Sidney was indicted by a grand jury on
7 November, and John Hampden on 27 November, but it took no action
against any of the other prisoners, all of whom were consequently bailed
or discharged by the last day of term.[85] The government's decision was
quietly accepted by its propagandists, the cases of Sidney and Hampden
were disposed of over the next few months as I have related, and the
entire issue had become moot well before Dryden began his translation of
*The History of the League* in March 1684.

If we wish to understand why Dryden's "Dedication," written in late
June or early July 1684, a full year after the discovery of the Rye House
Plot, argues with such vehemence against extending mercy toward those
involved in the conspiracy, we must piece together a now forgotten incident that occurred the previous spring, rousing a furor that was still re-
verberating when Dryden wrote his "Dedication." He had probably intended to dedicate *The History of the League* to the king ever since he
agreed to translate it, and presumably he received Charles's permission
along with his commands. Dryden could not have foreseen in March
1684 the squall that was to develop well before he finished translating the
*History* and writing "The Postscript of the Translator." But by the time
he was ready last of all to write his "Dedication," he was able to make it
the occasion for responding to this recent development.

One of those whom West and Rumsey had implicated in the Rye House Plot was James Holloway, a merchant of Bristol, who was to have been responsible for raising the rebel forces in that city at the time of the general insurrection.[86] Indicted for treason along with his confederates on 12 July 1683, Holloway was one of the fifteen conspirators named in the indictments that day who managed to elude arrest and flee abroad. By absconding instead of appearing to answer the charges in his indictment, Holloway, like his fellow fugitives from justice, incurred outlawry and in consequence stood attainted of high treason without benefit of trial. Seeking refuge in France at first, he eventually made his way to the West Indies with which he had often traded as a merchant. Here he was betrayed by his factor to the authorities on the island of Nevis and arrested in late January 1684.

Like Fitzharris in 1681, Holloway apparently staked his life on making himself useful to both sides—an even more reckless gamble in his case, since the Whigs were no longer able to help their supporters. The pattern of his future behavior was set before he even embarked from Nevis. Among the articles confiscated at the time of his arrest was an extremely damaging paper in his own hand that the governor, Sir William Stapleton, promptly dispatched to Sir Leoline Jenkins with the request that it be shown "to his Royal Highness, he being therein impudently traduced, besides intolerable reflections on his Majesty and government."[87] Yet only a week later Stapleton was writing Jenkins again that on Holloway's "promises to me of doing some considerable service in order to a further discovery I promised him to pray you to intercede for him, as I now earnestly do."[88]

When this news reached London along with the prisoner in early April, it roused much initial excitement among government officials. L'Estrange predicted to Jenkins that the promised information would "produce a great discovery," while Sunderland reported that "the King is very well pleased with the taking of Holloway and hopes it may be of great use towards a further discovery."[89] Apparently the hints Holloway was dropping had led the court to anticipate a previously unsuspected dimension to the Rye House Plot rivaling in importance the assassination scheme and the plans for a general insurrection. Their hopes were quickly dashed. Brought before the Privy Council for questioning on 10 April, Holloway repeated his offer of a confession and was returned to Newgate with orders that he be given "pen and ink in order to a narrative."[90] But when he produced this document before the council the next day it proved to be only another account of the plans and consultations toward a general rising already retailed so many times by earlier informers, along with the names of some citizens of Bristol who had been privy to the scheme. Having emptied the prisons of several dozen such minor conspir-

ators a few months before, the government was not about to launch a
new round of arrests, nor could it repose complete confidence in a confession whose repeated charge that West and Rumsey, Holloway's two accusers, had headed the assassination plot amounted to an obsession.[91]

Although, as Holloway admitted, his confession was "made without
conditions of a pardon," he certainly wrote it, as he was to repeat with
growing alarm, in "hopes of finding mercy" from the king.[92] But when he
was brought before the Court of King's Bench on 21 April he received a
far shorter measure of mercy than he had anticipated, the attorney general announcing that the king was willing to offer the prisoner as "a
Mercy and a Grace" the trial to which he had forfeited any right by incurring outlawry, "if he hath any thing to say that could defend him from
[the indictment]." It was probably a token gesture, offered as a substitute
for the pardon the king was unwilling to grant, and in any case a meaningless concession, for as Holloway explained in declining the favor, "I
cannot undertake to defend my self, for I have Confessed before his Majesty that I am Guilty of many things in that Indictment, and I throw my
self on the Kings Mercy."[93] The lord chief justice thereupon awarded execution upon his attainder and Holloway was returned to Newgate,
whence he sent the king an anguished petition for a pardon on 23 April
that was rejected two days later.[94]

What almost certainly sealed Holloway's fate, however, was not the
disappointing confession he produced before the Privy Council on 11
April but another document from his pen that, unknown to him, had
fallen into Jenkins's hands several days earlier, offering unmistakable evidence of his duplicity. During the ten weeks he had spent crossing the
Atlantic as a prisoner, Holloway had busied himself composing not his
promised confession but a lengthy paper of an altogether different cast,
also addressed to the king. As soon as his ship had anchored in the
Downs, he sent off a messenger to two of his friends with copies of this
paper, accompanied by instructions to arrange for its publication "if I
come to any disaster," presumably execution.[95] But a glance at the contents of the paper was enough to convince Holloway's friends of the jeopardy in which he had placed them should they be found in possession of
such an incriminating document, and they lost no time in turning over
their copies to Jenkins.[96] On Holloway's second examination before the
Privy Council at which his confession was read, he was suddenly questioned about this other paper. Thrown into confusion, he at first denied
its authorship, but when confronted with one of the cover letters he was
forced to own his handwriting.[97]

It was this paper, Holloway came to believe, that would eventually cost
him his life. "If I die," he wrote Jenkins three days later in a frantic effort

to explain away his blunder, "I shall esteem that the cause of my death and that I do not die for the plot."[98] He may have been right, since whatever inclinations the king might otherwise have had toward offering Holloway a pardon would almost certainly have been dispelled on reading his paper and realizing that he had been secretly taking steps to ensure its dissemination among the public.

This other paper addressed to the king boldly challenged the entire thrust of Tory propaganda over the past three years, according to which the Whigs had been losing credibility at such a rate that by the beginning of 1683 their tide of popularity was spent, while a newly enlightened public was eagerly flocking to the king's support. The paper is a fascinating document in which, long before public opinion polls came into existence, Holloway analyzes "the opinion of most of your subjects concerning late proceedings"; carefully distinguishes five persuasions, and then estimates, on the basis of personal observation rather than a canvas, the proportion of the population who subscribed to each of the major opposing views at the time he fled the country in the summer of 1683. Those sharing the first three opinions, "who all agree in the main that there was and is now more than ever a design [by the court] for arbitrary government and Popery," constitute "more than four parts of the nation," i.e., over 80 percent. Those who "pretend to believe as the Court believes, at least will act as those who carry the greatest sway at Court will have them," make up "not near the fifth, I think I may say not the tenth part of the subjects, though they make such a noise with addresses," i.e., less than 10 percent. A third category consists of the remainder, amounting to some 10 percent, who "do not care what is done, who is king, what government they live under nor what religion they are of, provided they can go on quietly with their trades, ploughs, etc.," and who would appear in a modern poll under the heading of "No Opinion."[99]

It is easy to imagine the king's reaction to this document carefully discriminating the views of the first three groups, supposedly constituting 80 percent of his subjects: those who believed that the king was his brother's catspaw, playing the role of Monmouth, as it were, to the duke of York's Shaftesbury; those who believed that the brothers were acting in equal partnership in laying their schemes against English liberties; and those who were convinced that Charles was the prime mover who had been promoting arbitrary government since at least the time of the Second Dutch War and the Fire of London. Holloway's estimates, the product of wishful thinking, greatly exaggerated the proportion of those who still distrusted the king. But had he succeeded in circulating his paper as he had intended, he could have provoked an unwelcome debate over Tory claims about the near unanimity of public support for the government.

Under the circumstances, the king would not have been inspired to go out of his way to save the life of one who had arrived in England already a condemned outlaw.

Holloway was not pardoned, but he did get the last word, and in a most public manner. On 30 April he was drawn to Tyburn, where he was able to play the last of his duplicitous performances before a large and attentive audience. L'Estrange was later to complain in the *Observator* with some bitterness about the strange—though by this time surely not unexpected—discrepancy between the written and oral parts of that production. About the former the government could be fairly confident. The contents of Holloway's confession or "narrative" and of his petition to the king were of course already known to them, and while the officials had no advance knowledge of the contents of a paper he delivered to the sheriffs on the scaffold, this proved to be for the most part innocuous.[100] "I look upon his *Paper* to the *Sheriffs*," Observator declared,

> to be *much at One* with his *Narrative* to his *Majesty*: Which *Narrative*, together with his *Petition*, were written I suppose, in a Prospect of some Possibility of *Pardon*. But his *Discourse* at the Place of *Execution*, falls most *Uncharitably Foul* upon the *Government*, for a man in *his Condition*. . . . For he *Charges* a great deal *more* upon the *Government* at his *Death*, then he takes upon *Himself*. . . .
>
> . . . And Represents the *King* much more *Criminal* toward the *People*, then the *Pris'ner* toward the *Government*.[101]

This "discourse," which occupied eight columns in the published version and, with its speech tags and rapidly alternating dialogue, exactly resembled a printed play, was actually a spontaneous exchange between the condemned man and his three surprised interlocutors, consisting of Sheriffs Daniel and Dashwood and the keeper of Newgate, Captain Richardson. Holloway began by asking liberty "to speak what I desire to speak," which was quickly granted him on the assumption that what he had to say would "be by way of Discovery to the World of what you are brought here to dye for." The officials were soon disabused but they kept their promise, and, although they challenged many of Holloway's accusations and protested at times that "this is not fit" or "this is reflecting upon the Government," they made no attempt to silence him.

Holloway's discourse was in large part a privileged rehearsal of stock Whig charges against the government which by this date could seldom be heard in public. He admitted once again that, besides the assassination plot forwarded by West and Rumsey according to his account, there had been a scheme for a general insurrection in which he had been involved himself, but he blamed the government for driving well-meaning Protestants to such a desperate course. "There was a damnable Popish Plot, and

I look upon the stifling of That to be the only Cause that any man did any thing in This." Finding "that all ways were used against Protestants; several Sham-Plots; but no justice could be had against Papists," men were driven at last to take matters into their own hands. "It was feared that Arbitrary Government and Popery was designed, and truly I think at this present time by what I can understand, that there is little better designed."

While Holloway conceded that Charles was not aware of the extent to which "things have been ill managed in *England*" and to which "many things have been done contrary to Law," he turned the king's refusal of a pardon to his disadvantage and used it to suggest an affinity between the king's unforgiving nature and the arbitrary government that suited his inflexible temperament even if he was not actively engaged in introducing tyranny. "If Truth and Plainness would have merited a Pardon, I might have had it," but obviously such qualities passed for nothing with the one man who could have granted such a boon. More ominously, "I thought that if any good had been designed for *England*, that I had done enough to merit a Pardon, for I had Wrote so much of Truth, and was so fair and plain in it, that I thought it would have merited a Pardon, if any good were designed." The conclusion about the king's real designs for England could be left to the imagination.

Potentially even more damaging was Holloway's parting advice to the king: "That his Majesty would be pleased to call a Parliament, and pass an Act of Oblivion for all Plotters whatsoever." This oblique reminder of the king's violation of the Triennial Act for the past month probably appeared less mischievous to the officials than the other part of his suggestion, repeated later in more menacing terms: "I wish the King would consult his own Safety, and the Safety of the Nation; and that an Act of Oblivion might pass, for I believe there are many Concerned."[102]

Thomas Walcot had begun his own, far more penitential, speech at Tyburn the previous July by referring to similar advice he had offered Charles in person: "I told the King . . . I thought an Act of Indulgence would be very necessary, because he had a great many men to take Judgment of." He had ended his speech by fervently repeating his plea:

And I do most heartily desire, and my earnest Prayer to the Almighty is, That this may be the last Bloud spilt upon this account. I know Acts of Indulgence and Mercy in the King would make him much easier in his Government, and would make his People sit much easier under it; and that the Lord may encline his heart to Mercy, ought to be the Prayer of every good man. . . .

I have not more to say, Mr. Sheriff: but truly you will do an act of a great deal of Charity, if you will prevail with the King for an Act of Indulgence and Liberty to his People; I think so: and so the Lord have mercy upon me.[103]

The suggestion that by nature the king was not prone to mercy was certainly planted by this earlier speech, and would have been confirmed a few months later when the shedding of Sidney's blood proved that the Lord had still not succeeded in inclining Charles's heart to mercy. But Walcot's call for an Act of Indulgence attracted little notice at a time when the Rye House Plot had only recently been discovered, the public was still in a state of shock over its disclosure, and demands for the rigorous prosecution of the perpetrators were still common.

The public's craving for justice is short-lived in every age, however, and by the spring of 1684 the call for an Act of Oblivion might be listened to more readily. A public that in the meantime had grown accustomed to hearing the king's providential escape described as a second restoration might be persuaded that the Act of Oblivion accompanying the first restoration ought to be repeated on the occasion of the second.

An Act of Oblivion, futhermore, carried a very different connotation in the spring of 1684 from what it had implied the previous summer when the prisons were newly filled with dozens of accused persons, most of whom the government itself would see fit to set at liberty before many months had passed. By this time, the only remaining plotters to whom an Act of Oblivion would apply were the dozen or so Rye House conspirators who had fled abroad the previous year, most of them to Holland, and who, like Holloway, had incurred outlawry by which they faced certain death if they were ever to return to England. To many members of the government as well as its supporters this was a fortunate solution to the recurrent threat to its stability posed in recent years by some of the most dangerous and incorrigible of its opponents: men like Ferguson, Grey, and the two Goodenoughs, who were now in voluntary exile, rendered harmless as long as they remained there, yet incapable of ever returning in safety. As a Tory verse broadside in January 1684 showed one such exile lamenting in a letter from Amsterdam,

> Yet do I wish to live, and see once more
> *Britains* chief seat, but dare not venture o're,
> Though I am tyr'd with this detested Shore.[104]

The government and its supporters could not fail to be alarmed at the prospect of a ground swell of public support for an Act of Oblivion that might signal the mass return of this band of exiles, eager to take up their scheming and agitation where they had left off.

Some measure of the court's concern over the possible effects of Holloway's farewell performance and of the inevitable printed version that followed shortly afterwards is provided by the major offensive L'Estrange mounted in the *Observator*, where he began by devoting five consecutive issues to the subject in late May, almost as soon as the printed version appeared.[105] This initial series is about equally divided between attempts to refute Holloway's accusations against the government and efforts to offset the possible attractions of his call for a general amnesty. "If an Act of *Oblivion* would have done the *work*," Observator brusquely declares, "the Safety of the *King* and *Kingdom* had been provided for, over and over, many a Fair Day ago: But the *State* has found, by *Experience*, that *One Execution* works *more*, upon *This* sort of People, then *Twenty Acts of Grace*. Beside, . . . To Grant an *Oblivion*, because the *Offenders* are *Many*; would make it an Act of *Fear*, not of *Mercy*; and Consequently, a Concession, both *Dishonourable*, and *Dangerous*."[106]

But such bluff dismissals of Holloway's appeal for an act of oblivion, coupled with tactless reminders that Walcot's earlier suggestion had also been ignored, were unlikely to dispel any lingering impression of the king's obduracy, and L'Estrange, apparently sensing that he had not laid Holloway's ghost, kept returning to him intermittently over the next two months, bringing his obsessive attack to a close with two successive issues of the *Observator* on 19 and 21 July. The latter also carried Tonson's long-awaited announcement that Dryden's translation of *The History of the League* would be published "at the Latter End of This Week."[107]

.   .   .   .   .

Although Dryden had written nearly a score of dedications by 1684, *The History of the League* was the only one of his works to be dedicated to the king. It offered him a unique opportunity, therefore, of publicly addressing Charles in prose, and he made full use of it.

Holloway, a condemned traitor, had petitioned the king for a pardon and urged him to extend an amnesty to the other Rye House conspirators as well. Dryden, while never so much as mentioning Holloway's case, petitions the king to discontinue the general policy of indulgence toward the Rye House conspirators he had adopted upon the first discovery of the plot, now that "Pardons are grown dangerous to Your Safety, and consequently to the Welfare of Your Loyal Subjects," for whom Dryden claims to be acting as spokesman.

> This, Sir, is the general voice of all true *Englishmen*; I might call it the Loyal Address of three Nations infinitely solicitous of Your Safety, which includes their own Prosperity. 'Tis indeed an high presumption for a man so inconsiderable as I am to present it, but Zeal, and dutifull Affection in an Affair of this Importance, will make every good Subject a Counsellor: 'Tis (in my Opinion) the Test of Loyalty, and to be either a Friend or Foe to the Government, needs no other distinction than to declare at this time, either for Remisness, or Justice (p. 4).

The present situation whereby only a foe to the government could wish to see the continuation of a policy that all loyal Englishmen have come to deplore is due to the unforeseen effects of indulgence. Whereas forgiveness is meant to recognize repentance and encourage reformation, the royal policy, now a year old, of granting pardons to the Rye House conspirators in return for their confessions, under which Holloway came to expect a pardon in his own case, has had just the opposite effect on their confederates. "But frequent forgiveness is their Encouragement, they have the Sanctuary in their Eye before they attempt the Crime, and take all measures of Security, either not to need a Pardon, if they strike the Blow, or to have it granted if they fail: Upon the whole matter Your Majesty is not upon equal Terms with them, You are still forgiving, and they still designing against Your Sacred Life; Your principle is Mercy, theirs inveterate Malice" (p. 3). While the policy of offering a general amnesty to the Rye House conspirators has not yet been tried, the likelihood, amounting to a near certainty, that this would lead to the same dangerous consequences as the granting of individual pardons is suggested by the results of this policy "at Your Majesty's happy Restauration," when "the Amnesty you gave, produc'd not all the desir'd Effects" (p. 5). For as Dryden explains a little earlier,

If the Experiment of Clemency were new, if it had not been often try'd without Effect, or rather with Effects quite contrary to the intentions of Your Goodness, your Loyal Subjects are generous enough to pity their Countrey-men, though Offenders: But when that pity has been always found to draw into example of greater Mischiefs; . . . Ingratitude so far from being Converted by gentle means, that it is turn'd at last into the nature of the damn'd, desirous of Revenge, and harden'd in Impenitence; 'Tis time at length, for self preservation to cry out for Justice, and to lay by Mildness when it ceases to be a Vertue (p. 4).

By attributing exclusive responsibility for the pardons to the king, whom he portrays as motivated solely by "Your natural Clemency," "Your Fatherly Indulgence," and "that Treasury of Mercy which is within Your Royal Breast," Dryden greatly simplifies both the governmental authority with which the pardons originated and the considerations that led to their being granted. These were far more complex and less altruistic than he intimates.

Holloway was by no means the first Rye House conspirator to confess his part in the plot without receiving a pardon. Russell and Sidney, who died protesting their innocence, and Blague, who won acquittal at his trial, did not, of course, at any time admit to prior knowledge of the plot. But Walcot, Hone, and Rouse all confessed their guilt to government officials fully and at length as soon as they were captured and examined, only to find themselves put on trial, convicted, and executed.[108] With such an array of witnesses appearing against them, it mattered little that the government magnanimously declined to introduce their confessions as evidence before the court.

At no time following the first discovery of the Rye House Plot were pardons offered as a matter of course to all voluntary informers, as had been the case with the Popish Plot, when the king routinely granted such pardons under pressure from Parliament and the public.[109] Josiah Keeling, it is true, who first revealed the existence of the plot to startled government officials, was treated in the traditional fashion and given not only a pardon but a reward of £500 and a pension.[110] But thereafter the government grew more circumspect. West and Rumsey, whose testimony at the trials of their fellow conspirators was to carry so much weight, both began by approaching government officials with an offer to confess in return for the promise of a pardon. Each was firmly rebuffed and told that the government was not prepared to make terms with the conspirators, but that the king would deal with their individual cases thereafter as they deserved.[111] The same policy was adopted toward the others who came in voluntarily or were captured in late June and July 1683 and who, like West and Rumsey, agreed in the end to confess without conditions and to throw themselves on the king's mercy.

Under these circumstances, those who acknowledged their guilt found themselves on an equal footing at first, all of them ignorant of their fates, which had not yet been decided. For over a week before the trials of July 1683 began, the Privy Council, with the king in attendance, met daily. Depositions were read and discussed, their authors produced for diligent examination, and confrontations arranged in which pairs of deponents would be brought face to face before the council in hopes of uncovering discrepancies in their accounts.[112] With their lives hanging in the balance, the culprits must compete with each other to win the trust of the king and council. These were eager to learn as much as possible about the nature and extent of the plot and to ensure that it had been effectively disabled; but they were also bent on choosing witnesses whose testimony at the trials would both convict the defendants and persuade the public beyond any doubt that the Rye House Plot was a genuine conspiracy. As late as 10 July, two days before the trials were to begin, West was still protesting his veracity in an agony of doubt as to whether his role would be that of witness or defendant, while the council debated his fate.[113] On the other hand, Rouse went on clinging to hope that his life might be spared until 9 July, when the Council finally decided to cast him as one of the "examples" who must stand trial for treason.[114] Even after the conclusion of the trials when the usefulness of the witnesses was at an end, only Shepherd and Lord Howard were actually issued pardons, while the others, only some of whom were ever called to testify, were bailed or discharged by the end of term along with the other remaining culprits, or, in the case of West and Rumsey, paroled in the custody of messengers who were still acting as their warders the following year.[115]

By ignoring the role of the Privy Council in these decisions as well as the prudential considerations that influenced them, Dryden creates the impression that the "pardons" originated solely with the tenderhearted king, acting on his own responsibility and against the better judgment of his advisers. The recent denial of a pardon to Holloway, the reader is left to infer, must have been at the more successful suit of these same advisers, and as an exception to the king's continuing policy of indulgence toward the conspirators. In this way Dryden deflects accusations of rigor from the mild-natured king, heedless of his own safety, to his more prudent "Counsellors," among whom he willingly numbers himself, loyal subjects who must persuade their monarch to set aside his natural feelings and replace mildness with justice for the sake of self preservation.

This tactic is similar to the one Dryden had used in *Absalom and Achitophel*, of course, where we are told that David's advisers, "a small but faithful Band / Of Worthies,"

> shew'd the King the danger of the Wound:
> That no Concessions from the Throne woud please,
> But Lenitives fomented the Disease.
>
> (924–26)

In his "Dedication," Dryden returns to this earlier occasion on which the king had heeded the advice of his counselors to the benefit of himself and his subjects, reminding Charles of "Your Declaration, after the Dissolution of the last Parliament, which put an end to the Arbitrary Encroachments of a Popular Faction" that had threatened the very survival of his government.

> Since which time it has pleas'd Almighty God so to prosper Your Affairs, that without searching into the secrets of Divine Providence, 'tis evident Your Magnanimity and Resolution, next under him, have been the immediate Cause of Your Safety and our present Happiness: By weathering of which Storm, may I presume to say it without Flattery, You have perform'd a Greater and more Glorious work than all the Conquests of Your Neighbours. . . . To Govern a Kingdom which was either possess'd, or turn'd into a *Bedlam*, and yet in the midst of ruine to stand firm, undaunted, and resolv'd, and at last to break through all these difficulties, and dispell them, this is indeed an Action which is worthy the Grandson of *Henry* the Great (p. 6).

But the firmness and resolution Charles had adopted three years earlier have proved to be no more than a temporary measure, succeeded since the discovery of the Rye House Plot by a return of the king's inherent mildness. Dryden's language, in fact, draws an explicit contrast between Charles's earlier behavior, in which he "contended with Your natural Clemency to make some Examples of Your Justice" (p. 6), this proving to be "the immediate Cause of Your Safety and our present Happiness," and the "unseasonable" renewal of "Your Royal Clemency" in recent months, whereby "Pardons are grown dangerous to Your Safety, and consequently to the Welfare of Your Loyal Subjects" (p. 3). Indeed, the king's present policy threatens to undo the heroic achievements that had led Dryden and the government's other supporters in recent years to celebrate Charles as the nation's savior: "But by how much the more You have been willing to spare them, by so much has their Impudence increas'd, and if by this Mildness they recover from the Great Frost, which has almost blasted them to the roots, if these venemous plants shoot out again, it will be a sad Comfort to say they have been ungratefull, when 'tis Evident to Mankind that Ingratitude is their Nature" (pp. 6–7).

The earlier situation had been one in which, under the ordinary operations of common Providence, the king's own efforts were "the immediate Cause" of the nation's recovery. But since the miraculous intervention of special Providence at the time of the Rye House Plot, Dryden implies, the king has resumed a less active role, in which "Fatherly Indulgence" has replaced the vigorous exercise of exemplary justice.

> Almighty God has hitherto Miraculously preserv'd You; but who knows how long the Miracle will continue? His Ordinary Operations are by second Causes, and then Reason will conclude that to be preserv'd, we ought to use the lawfull means of preservation. If on the other side it be thus Argu'd, that of many Attempts one may possibly take place, if preventing Justice be not employ'd against Offenders; What remains but that we implore the Divine Assistance to Avert that Judgment: which is no more than to desire of God to work another, and another, and in Conclusion a whole *Series* of Miracles? (p. 4)

Dryden argues that we have no right to depend on special Providence to remedy our own lack of prudence, and that such occasional miracles must not be made the excuse for relaxing human exertion. Far from reflecting a skeptical attitude toward the doctrine of Providence, his argument expresses a long familiar warning against permitting providential interventions to encourage presumption. Archbishop Sancroft, preaching before the House of Lords on the preceding occasion when Providence had come to the rescue of Charles II, the "discovery" of the Popish Plot, pointed out that

> in the Age of Miracles indeed, . . . well might the watch-word be, *Stand still and see the Salvation of God; The Lord shall fight for you, and ye shall do*

*nothing.* But the season is chang'd, and 'tis now, *Come forth, and help the Lord against the Mighty.* . . .

We must not presume to use our Lord, as *Herod* did; call for him, when we please, to Work us a fine Miracle; neglect our Affairs, and leave them embroyl'd, and ruffled on purpose, that he may come down *apo mēkhanēs* [ex machina], to disentangle them. . . .

. . . They trust not in God, they presume, and tempt him, who work not together with him, but receive his Aids in vain, and look, that He should bring about in extraordinary manner, what they take no care of themselves; but lie flat upon their Backs looking upward, and will stir neither Hand, nor Foot, to help themselves.[116]

At the time of the thanksgiving service for the king's miraculous escape from assassination at the Rye House, preachers had likewise cautioned the government against relaxing its vigilance. John Cave, for example, assured his congregation that "*God* by this *Deliverance*, hath told our *King*, and his *Magistrates*, as by a Voice from Heaven, how much it concerns them to keep a watchful Eye, and a strict Hand, upon Men of such lewd, loose, and dangerous Principles; to mark their Motions, observe their Tendencies, and by prudent and timely Restraints, to curb the first stirrings of *Rebellion.*" But he also assumed that the king and his magistrates were harking to that voice, and that loyal subjects need fear no further dangers, since

from the miscarriage of this Attempt, we may conceive some good reason to hope, that *the Workers of Iniquity are* already *fallen,* and *are so cast down, that they shall not be able to rise.* . . .

We have reason to hope, that *God who hath* graciously *delivered the Soul of our King* from this *Death,* also hath now *delivered his feet from falling*; that he hath not only *stilled the Raging of the Sea, the Noise of the Waves,* the *Tumults of the People*; but thereby brought our *Soveraign* into his Haven: And that the Winds and Storms which so lately shook and threatned our *Royal Oak,* have only setled it, and given it a surer and firmer rooting; and that our Government stands upon a more stable and durable Basis than heretofore, if God so please.[117]

That feeling of euphoria at the nation's providential delivery had been nearly universal at the time of the Rye House Plot's discovery, but Dryden, writing a year later, encourages a very different mood.

To measure the distance that Dryden's rhetoric had moved in the space of the two or three years that separate *The Medall* and *The Duke of Guise* from *The History of the League,* we need only recall that earlier time. In 1682 and early 1683, at a time when some Tory spokesmen were raising alarms over the projected Association that had never actually materialized, Dryden, along with the author of *Heraclitus Ridens*, sought to calm those fears and to assure the public that the danger was past. In the special prologue to *Venice Preserv'd* he wrote for the performance of Otway's play on 31 May 1682, at which the duchess of York made her first public appearance since returning from Scotland, Dryden predicted to the audience at Dorset Garden that

> Distemper'd Zeal, Sedition, canker'd Hate,
> No more shall vex the Church, and tear the State;
> No more shall Faction civil Discords move,
> Or onely discords of too tender love.[118]

And as late as April 1683 he was affirming in his *Vindication of "The Duke of Guise"* that in putting the Whigs to flight at Oxford two years earlier the king had "not only preserv'd our present quiet, but secur'd the Peace of our Posterity" (p. 35).

But that was two months before the discovery of the Rye House Plot. Now in June or July 1684, in his "Dedication," Dryden changes his tack completely, warning the king:

> I look not on the Storm as Overblown. 'Tis still a gusty kind of Weather: there is a kind of Sickness in the Air; it seems indeed to be clear'd up for some few hours; but the Wind still blowing from the same Corner; and when new matter is gather'd into a body, it will not fail to bring it round and pour upon us a second Tempest. I shall be glad to be found a false Prophet; but he was certainly Inspir'd, who when he saw a little Cloud arising from the Sea, and that no bigger than a hand, gave immediate notice to the King, that he might mount the Chariot, before he was overtaken by the Storm (pp. 4–5).

The immediate purpose of this alarmist rhetoric is of course to persuade the public that in such perilous times it would be folly for the king, who already "stands expos'd by his too much Mercy to the unwearied and endless Conspiacies of Parricides" (p. 5), to grant a general amnesty, inviting the most dangerous of the Rye House conspirators to return from exile. But Dryden's ominous tone here serves a wider purpose as well. His admonition in the "Dedication to the King" to "lay by Mildness" and administer "preventing Justice" to the conspirators who stand ready to "pour upon us a second Tempest" accords exactly with his call in the "Postscript of the Translator" for "severity" toward the Sectaries, who, "tho' now their claws are par'd," may "grow again to be more sharp" (p. 405). It is a note that L'Estrange had never stopped sounding in the *Observator*, but which Dryden would only come to adopt in the aftermath of the Rye House Plot.

It is characteristic of such rhetoric to hint at grounds for alarm that are never specified. The very absence of civil commotion, oddly enough, becomes a portent of approaching peril. In the "Postscript," as we noticed earlier, Dryden intimates that the Whigs' quiescence may prove to be a time of convalescence and reorganization from which they will emerge stronger than ever. L'Estrange, writing in the *Observator* during this same period at the end of June 1684, suggests through his spokesman that the suppression of overt sedition has simply made way for more insidious threats to the kingdom: "The *King*, and the *Church* have *several sorts* of *Enemies*; . . . and those *Enemies*, are either *Open*, or *Secret*: Thereafter as they find Themselves, *Stronger*, or *Weaker*. When they see they cannot Carry it by *Battery*, or *Assault*; they fall to *Mining*; And while *One Part* of them is at work *Under-Ground*, there's *Another Part* is Employ'd to *Spy* upon us; *Creeps* into the *Town*, and makes an *Interest* within the *Walls*."[119] In any case, and from whatever quarter, the enemies of the state are already regrouping and preparing for a new assault in which they may well prove stronger than before, cleverly learning from their earlier mistakes.

This new rhetoric of suspicion and fear is obviously designed to support the government's escalating consolidation of power, which a continuation of the earlier propaganda could only discredit. The king's policy of dissolving four parliaments in twenty-six months had been justified in 1681 as a response to a grave emergency, a pro tempore measure whose wisdom was proved by the result: the king had thereby saved the nation from anarchy, and, as the loyal addresses testified, his subjects had awakened at last to the snares from which he had rescued them. But three years had now passed since that time and, if the emergency had ceased, the justification for these or any other extraordinary measures on the part of the government no longer existed. Yet borough corporations went on forfeiting their charters through quo warranto proceedings, conventicles up and down the land were being dispersed week after week, and the king gave no sign of intending to summon another parliament in spite of the fair words in *His Majesties Declaration* at the time of the Oxford dissolution. Clearly the government's defenders needed to change their tack. Henceforth the nation would be pictured as existing in a continuing state of crisis whose end could not be predicted and therefore ought not to be expected. Consequently the saving of the nation through emergency measures must no longer be presented as a finite action, confined to a particular place and time—Oxford in March 1681—and producing a permanent settlement that would shortly allow a return to normal conditions as they existed before the Exclusion Crisis. Instead, the saving of the nation became an ongoing activity by a government that, in the face of an indefinite state of emergency, must constantly adopt sterner measures to meet fresh threats from its tireless enemies and to safeguard its endlessly beleaguered people.

The note of urgency in Dryden's "Dedication to the King" enhances the impression of continuing crisis, as does the fervor of his plea for less mercy and greater severity toward the nation's enemies. But it is hardly the cri de coeur that Ward hears from a Dryden "irritated" by Charles's clemency. The "pardons" Dryden professes to deplore were, as he surely realized, motivated by reasons of state and granted with the advice and consent of those very counselors he portrays as dismayed by the king's imprudent exercise of forgiveness.

Furthermore, those "pardons" were hardly evidence of an ongoing policy of indulgence toward the Rye House conspirators, since they were now a year old and had been followed by no sequels, either in Holloway's case or in that of another culprit whose fate was being decided even as Dryden worked on his "Postscript" and "Dedication" for The History of the League.

In May 1684 Sir Thomas Armstrong, one of the fugitive members of the "Council of State" originally responsible for planning the Rye House Plot, was arrested in Leiden and, with the acquiescence of the Dutch authorities, brought back to England. Like Holloway, he had been indicted for treason on 12 July 1683, and, by fleeing abroad instead of appearing to answer the charges in his indictment, had incurred outlawry, with the result that he stood attainted of high treason without benefit of trial. Brought before the Court of King's Bench on 14 June, Armstrong demanded a trial, arguing that under a statute of Edward VI he had reversed his outlawry by yielding himself within a year's time, and protesting that Holloway had been offered a trial under similar circumstances. His plea was brusquely denied on the grounds that he had not yielded himself voluntarily, and that Holloway had been offered a trial not as a right but as a grace and mercy of the king, who did not choose to extend Armstrong the same favor. The lord chief justice thereupon awarded execution upon his attainder and on 20 June Armstrong was drawn to Tyburn, where he delivered a paper to the sheriffs in which he protested his innocence and denied any knowledge of the plot, bitterly complaining at his treatment before the bench, where he had been "denied the Laws of the Land."[120] The paper was published along with the proceedings early in July and attracted widespread attention.[121]

The issues raised by Armstrong's case were entirely different from Holloway's, of course. Since he denied his guilt, he was in no position to seek a pardon, and he never raised the subject of a general amnesty. But many of the public were shocked at the handling of Armstrong's case and believed that he had been treated with unprecedented rigor in being denied due process. So widespread was the indignation that the government, reluctant to prolong public discussion of the matter, took the unusual step of quietly forbidding its propagandists to publish any of the usual "reflections" on the paper Armstrong had delivered to the sheriffs, and L'Estrange, with rare self-denial, refrained from any comment on the subject in the *Observator*.[122]

If Dryden's vigorous protest in his "Dedication to the King" against continued indulgence toward the Rye House conspirators creates a fiction that glosses over the facts, his argument that rigor is essential to the survival of king and country becomes an oblique vindication of the government's actual policy. By ostensibly advising the king to adopt a course he is already embarked upon and can be expected to continue to pursue in the future, Dryden implicitly justifies Charles's behavior to the reading public who make up the actual audience he is seeking to persuade.[123]

.  .  .  .  .

Just as Dryden's translation of *The History of the League* with its "Postscript of the Translator" and "Dedication to the King" harks back to the second phase of the campaign of 1683—the public disclosure of the plot against the government through the trials, confessions, and executions of the conspirators in July of that year—*Albion and Albanius* draws its inspiration from the third phase of that campaign—the celebration of the king's providential deliverance solemnized in the day of public thanksgiving on 9 September 1683. Thus Dryden's last two works of propaganda in Charles's service complement each other by dealing with the Rye House Plot in two separate dimensions: one natural, the other supernatural.

The fact that *Albion and Albanius*, no less than *The History of the League*, is part of the propaganda offensive first launched in the summer of 1683 has been obscured by the circumstances of its composition. Begun and in large part written before *The History of the League*, Dryden's opera did not reach the stage or appear in print until almost a year after his translation of Maimbourg was published, by which time the campaign for which it was written had already come to an end.

In the preface to *Albion and Albanius*, first published in June 1685, Dryden traces the genesis of his opera: "It was Originally intended only for a Prologue to a Play. . . . But some intervening accidents having hitherto deferr'd the performance of the main design, I propos'd to the Actors, to turn the intended Prologue into an Entertainment by it self, as you now see it, by adding two acts more to what I had already Written."[124] He would later identify the "play" as his semiopera *King Arthur* (whose performance continued to be deferred until 1691), indicating the year of this twin birth as 1684.[125] Presumably Dryden had been at work writing *King Arthur* and turning its "intended Prologue into an Entertainment by it self" in the early months of that year before the king interposed his commands to translate Maimbourg. For in a letter to Tonson in the late summer of 1684, shortly after his translation of *The History of the League* was published, Dryden reveals that only one act of *King Arthur* still remains to be written, while he has finished *Albion and Albanius* and is anxious to know "whether the Dukes house [Dorset Garden] are makeing cloaths & putting things in a readiness" so that it can "be playd immediately after Michaelmasse."[126]

But *Albion and Albanius* was not ready to be performed after Michaelmas, and although Charles was "pleas'd twice or thrice to command, that it shou'd be practis'd, before him, especially the first and third Acts," in rehearsal, its public performance continued to be delayed, perhaps because of the elaborate scenery and machines required for such a production. At last, Dryden relates, "it was all compos'd [arranged], and was just ready to have been perform'd when he, in Honor of whom it was principally made, was taken from us."[127] With Charles's death on 6 February 1685 the theaters were immediately closed, and they remained shut until 27 April.[128] As a result of this series of misfortunes, it was not until 3 June, some four months after James II had succeeded his brother, that the opera was finally seen at Dorset Garden. "It might reasonably have been expected," Dryden observed, "that [the king's] Death must have chang'd the whole Fabrick of the *Opera*; or at least a great part of it. But the design of it Originally, was so happy, that it needed no alteration, properly so call'd: for the addition of twenty or thirty lines, in the Apotheosis of *Albion*, has made it entirely of a Piece. This was the only way which cou'd have been invented, to save it from a botch'd ending; and it fell luckily into my imagination."[129]

But if the design of the opera remained unaltered, the same could not be said of the political climate in which it had been written or the government policies it had been designed to support. By the time *Albion and Albanius* finally opened at Dorset Garden, the new king's coronation had taken place, elections to the House of Commons had been held for the first time in four years, and a new parliament had been sitting for six weeks. In yet another week Monmouth would land at Lyme Regis to begin the last and briefest of his ventures for the crown, quickly supplanting in importance the earlier conspiracies in which he had been involved. In the light of these new circumstances accompanying its appearance, Dryden's opera would later come to be seen in a very different light, as a retrospective tribute to the dead king where, in Scott's words, "the leading incidents of the busy and intriguing reign of Charles II are successively introduced."[130]

In order to understand what Dryden's opera is all about, however, we must return to the period in which it originated: the weeks immediately following the thanksgiving service of 9 September 1683. It was in this same month that Thomas Betterton, dispatched to France on an operatic mission by the king, persuaded Louis Grabu, who would write the music for Dryden's opera, to return with him to England, and it was probably during the autumn of 1683 that Dryden began work on the earliest version of *Albion and Albanius*, the one-act prologue to *King Arthur*.[131]

It is invariably assumed in discussions of *Albion and Albanius* that when Dryden speaks of "adding two acts more to what I had already Written" he means that he appended them seriatim to the intended prologue, which must have corresponded therefore to the first act of the present opera, referring to Charles's restoration in 1660. On the same assumption, the two acts written later are identified with the second and third acts of the present opera, referring to the Protestant Plot and its collapse when the assassination of the king was averted. But it is distinctly improbable that in the immediate wake of the excitement over the Rye House Plot Dryden would have reached back to the king's restoration in 1660 to find a subject for his prologue. It is far more likely that the prologue would have concerned the one topic of consuming interest in the autumn of 1683 (and for many months afterwards), the king's providential deliverance at Newmarket. In that case, when Dryden speaks of "adding two acts more" he means that he expanded what he "had already Written" (the present third act) by writing two additional acts to precede it, one representing the miraculous Restoration, the other providing a transition between the two providential deliverances, thus producing "an Entertainment by it self" that, he points out, "plainly represents the double restoration of his Sacred Majesty" (p. 11), the very keynote, as we have seen, of the solemn thanksgiving service on 9 September 1683.

It is a mistake, therefore, to think of *Albion and Albanius* as representing any "incidents" of Charles's reign, much less all the leading ones, if this term is taken, as it usually is, to mean historical events in their natural dimension. Dryden's opera translates several widely separated incidents into their supernatural dimension and presents them from an unfamiliar perspective. This is why he considers the twenty or thirty lines he later added to the third act such a lucky stroke of invention. To have represented Charles's death or any other natural event would have created a jarring shift of perspective bringing the spectacle down to a lower plane, and producing the "botch'd ending" he was striving to avoid. Only by transforming the king's death into an apotheosis, in which Charles is visibly translated to a higher sphere through divine agency, could Dryden maintain a supernatural perspective consistent with the rest of the opera and make it "entirely of a Piece."

As several critics have suggested in recent years, *Albion and Albanius* is a hybrid form that owes at least as much to the early Stuart court masque as to opera itself.[132] In fact, Dryden found in both genres those

elements that served his purpose of bringing upon the stage visible embodiments of things unseen. Opera suited his needs because, as he pointed
out in his Preface, "the suppos'd Persons of this musical Drama, are generally supernatural," and because its subject, "being extended beyond the
Limits of Humane Nature, admits of . . . marvellous and surprizing conduct" (p. 3). The same, he might have added, was true of the court
masque, but in a form more specifically adapted to his needs, its supernatural persons being allegorized divinities and personifications precisely
suited to *Albion and Albanius*, since, as Dryden observed, "the Subject of
it is wholly Allegorical" (p. 11). The theatrical components of his opera
were also to be found just as readily in the court masque, "consisting
largely of music, dancing, pageantry, and spectacular scenic effects," as
Stephen Orgel describes the latter genre. Finally, the subject of Dryden's
opera, representing "the double restoration of his Sacred Majesty," has
obvious affinities with that of the court masque, which, Orgel observes,
"is always about the resolution of discord; antitheses, paradoxes, and the
movement from disorder to order are central to its nature."[133]

But if, like the court masque, *Albion and Albanius* is in a general sense
about the resolution of discord, the means by which that resolution is
brought about in Dryden's opera are entirely different and reflect an altogether distinct purpose: the portrayal of the role of Providence in the
king's double restoration. To disregard the role of Providence in *Albion
and Albanius* and to assume that it was written for the same purpose as
the early Stuart court masques is to misunderstand Dryden's opera completely. One recent critic, for example, observing that in the early Stuart
period "masques are celebrations of political order," that "the politics of
the masque are heroic," and that the hero celebrated in a masque is the
king (who is "the power by which miracles are performed"), reads Dryden's text in the light of this heroic tradition and finds in his opera "the
theme of the rescue and revival of Augusta, or London, by Albion and
Albanius [Charles and his brother James]."[134] Another, who sees the
opera as "Dryden's deployment of traditional iconography in the cause of
the restored Stuart monarchy, meeting the uncertainty of a new reign with
a slightly strident assertion of kingly power," severely criticizes *Albion
and Albanius* as "an unsatisfactory work" because that assertion is never
realized dramatically as it is in the early Stuart court masques. "Charles
as Albion moves through a play in which he is essentially passive in the
face of the personified hostility of the London opposition. He does not
act, either as a politician or as a monarch with kingly power and sacred
aura, and there is little encompassing imagery to supplement the meaning
of his role."[135]

But since *Albion and Albanius*, written not in the uncertainty of a new
reign but in the apparent certainties of an old one, was never intended as

an assertion of kingly power, such criticism is beside the point. If we want to find Dryden celebrating Charles's exercise of kingly power to save the nation, we can read *Absalom and Achitophel*. *Albion and Albanius* on the other hand is, for once, a dramatic work centrally concerned with Divine Providence, a subject much rarer in Restoration drama than some recent critics would have us believe, but which, once adopted, excludes all claims for kingly power or any other human agency. In such a case, Dryden writes in his Preface, "Humane Impossibilities, are to be receiv'd, as they are in Faith; because where Gods are introduc'd, a Supreme Power is to be understood; and second Causes are out of doors" (p. 3). The Christian doctrine of Providence undergirds Dryden's entire opera, in which "a Supreme Power is to be understood," although it never appears, and could not easily be made to appear without irreverence. Instead, the allegorized pagan divinities Dryden borrowed from the court masque are put to new uses as dramatic agents, messengers, manifestations, and infernal adversaries of the Christian God who, under the name of Jove, invisibly orders, permits, or nullifies the actions observed on stage. In such a scenario, these allegorized divinities are the only conceivable agents of change, while the terrestrial characters and personifications about whom all this celestial and infernal traffic revolves—Albion and Albanius as well as Augusta and Thamesis—are by design represented as completely passive creatures, unable to move or act without external prompting from above or below.

.   .   .   .   .

The intervention of special Providence in human affairs is an inherently dramatic subject and naturally invites the use of dramaturgic imagery. Anglican clergymen delivering sermons on special Providence found it natural to resort to the imagery of the playhouse, and in dramatizing Charles's two providential deliverances Dryden was adopting the form most congenial to his materials. But the interventions of special Providence were as varied as the crises that provoked them, and Charles's two deliverances were no exception. By examining the somewhat different theatrical imagery applied in the pulpit to the Restoration and to the kind of deliverance exemplified by the fire at Newmarket we can better appreciate Dryden's distinct ways of dramatizing each of these miraculous occurrences in *Albion and Albanius*, bringing out differences between them as well as similarities.

In a sermon marking the anniversary of the Restoration, preached on 29 May 1684, George Hickes chose as his subject special Providence and the seven marks or characters "whereby we may know, when any Event is the Lords special doing, or an Effect of his Special Providence." The fifth indication of God's special Providence in any event is the harmony of its parts, which is particularly exemplified by the miraculous Restoration. That

> so many different Interests should combine, and so many accidents at several times, and divers places, should all concurr, as it were by design, to work the deliverance of this day, cannot without manifest Violence to common Reason, but be ascribed to his particular Contrivance, who was able to range so many Causes in Order, and judge of the Seasons, and Junctures of Affairs. As Nature is nothing but Divine Art; so such admirable revolutions [as the Restoration] can be nothing but Divine Artifice, and Contrivance; unless it can be imagined, that a thing wherein there is so much of Plot, and which was so curiously contrived, that no Human Wisdom could wish it, or contrive it better, may reasonably be imputed to Chance. . . . Wherefore is it not most reasonable to conclude, that it was the Consult of a special Providence, since it was contrived in a manner so apparently worthy of the Divine Wisdom, and since the united Reason of Men and Angels, could not have contrived it in a better way, than it really fell out. Certainly the seasonable contrivance of so many wonderful Scenes into every Act, and of so many curious Acts into one harmonious Play, must needs have been the study and invention of a very skilful Author, even of the All-wise, and Almighty Dramatist; who hath the World for his Theatre, and seldom less than a Kingdom for his Stage.[136]

The divine dramatist and the *theatrum mundi* were long-familiar images for Providence and its domain. But their normal use was to express the creation, conservation, and governance of the world by general or common Providence through a portrayal of human life as a vast ongoing play written, cast, staged, and kept in production by the divine dramatist who will finally close the performance on Judgment Day.[137] Hickes's use of these images, however, is very different from this. He employs them here to express the particular interventions of special Providence, as in the case of the Restoration, as individual well-made plays specially written and produced for the occasion by the divine dramatist, their plots so skillfully designed that they benefit not only the dramatis personae themselves but also the audience, awed and edified by a spectacle in which they perceive the handiwork of divine wisdom. The key words are "contrive" and "contrivance," used more than half a dozen times in this brief passage, and suggesting an artifice in which characters and events are at every moment completely responsive to the mysterious designs of their heavenly creator.

Dryden need not have been indebted to any particular source for his conception of the Restoration in the first act of *Albion and Albanius*, which in any case probably antedates Hickes's sermon by a few months. The habitual manner in which the miraculous Restoration had been represented in the pulpit ever since 1660 would have suggested Hickes's sermon as well as Dryden's opera, which opens on a scene not of disorder but of the exhaustion that succeeds disorder. In front of the Royal Exchange, Thamesis, personifying London's river, and Augusta, its population, are found lying in "*dejected postures*," sunk beneath calamities they are incapable of repairing by their own efforts. Mercury appears and, after listening to Augusta's complaints that Albion, her "Plighted Lord," is gone, prompts her to confess her culpability for his loss, admitting that she has broken her nuptial vow. The moment she has confessed her sin, Mercury announces that he has been sent from Heaven "Thy *Albion* to restore" (1.1.62) if she will meet certain conditions. That is to say, Albion's restoration is made dependent on divine forgiveness of his subjects' guilt. The conditions of forgiveness are confession, repentance, and amendment. Mercury's first question, therefore, once Augusta has made confession of her sin, is "Can'st thou repent?" When she answers "My falshood I deplore," Mercury next requires of her "some loyal Deed" whereby she may "regain / Thy long lost Reputation," that is to say, an outward sign of her conversion from sin. Democracy and Zeal, by whom she was formerly seduced, now put in their appearance to make fresh demands of her.[138] But Augusta, urged by Mercury to "Resist, and do not fear" (1.1.80), remains firm in spite of their angry threats, thus giving proof of her amendment.

Oblivious of the god's presence, Archon (General Monck) now approaches Augusta independently, offering, like Mercury before him, "thy *Albion* to restore" (1.1.129), but by force of arms. Mercury orders him to "Cease your Alarmes," since it is Heaven that will bring about Albion's restoration, and by peaceful means at that. But when Archon, his well-meant efforts rebuffed, asks "What then remaines for me," Mercury assigns him an instrumental role as his assistant, inviting him to "Take my *Caduceus*" with which to touch Democracy and Zeal, thereby plunging them into a deep slumber.

Mercury's "aweful Wand" may evoke pagan magic more readily than Christian Providence, but it is actually an effective way of externalizing the invisible means by which the Restoration was supposed to have been produced. The miraculous nature of that event consisted of a change of heart among Charles's enemies whereby they came to acquiesce in a bloodless Restoration: a reversal so unexpected and improbable that it must be credited to a divine influence softening the hearts of his once implacable foes. Hickes, using the Restoration to illustrate his first mark of special Providence in any event, "*when it is brought about by Invisible Means*," declares:

> That so many different Elements should jumble into such an happy mixture, and Causes so contrary conspire to one Effect, that all the Enemies of the Gov-

ernment should be, as it were Planet-struck, and all the Interests against it invisibly subdued, that scarce one Party, or one Man among them should appear to oppose this Revolution, nor one Dog among them move his Tongue, but that it should be brought about without Mutiny, without Murmur, or without a drop of Blood, was an admirable Scene of Affairs, worthy the contrivance of infinite Wisdom, and ought to be esteemed, as his doing alone, who can work by repugnant Causes, bring Order out of Confusion, and *take from men their Hearts of Stone, and give them Hearts of Flesh.*[139]

Democracy and Zeal, personifying the political and religious ideologies responsible for Albion's exile, are literally "Planet-struck" and visibly subdued by Mercury's wand, murmuring "Let *Albion*! let him take the Crown!" (1.1.151) before they fall asleep, leaving the way open for his return.

Juno, "Great Queen of Nuptial Rites," now appears, announcing that the gods have agreed to the reunion of Albion with his contrite spouse, Augusta. Iris relates how Albion, conducted safely across the seas by Venus, has been welcomed at Dover by the unanimous acclaim of his subjects. Then, their mission accomplished, the gods return to heaven, making way for a mute Albion, accompanied by Albanius, to appear at last, sent by the gods, Augusta declares, "to pardon and to pity me, / And to forgive a guilty Nation!" (1.1.252–53).

Every detail of this act has been calculated to minimize the human factors involved in the Restoration in the interest of focusing attention on divine intervention. Archon's share in the event is acknowledged, but only in the modest role of an instrument of Providence. Albion's share is even less; he is simply an automaton who responds on cue to Heaven's bidding. The entire scenario dramatizes the providential version of events we earlier saw expressed by Gilbert Sheldon, preaching before the king on the solemn day of thanksgiving for the Restoration, 28 June 1660, when he reminded his congregation of the infinite gulf between human instruments and divine power, warning them that "whoever were the Instruments of our *deliverance*, we must still remember to raise up our thoughts to him by whose power they wrought it, and give him the glory of all; since nothing is more certain that none did it, none could do it but he."[140]

Reading the first act of *Albion and Albanius*, it is easy to understand why the terms "contrivance" and "artifice" are so appropriate to dramaturgic portrayals of the miraculous Restoration. For from this perspective it appears as an episode in which the human characters, whether wittingly or not, are enacting parts assigned them by the divine dramatist, their speeches and actions following a carefully prepared script. When all is in readiness, the heavenly emissaries descend in their machines, not in order to interfere in the action or interrupt impending events but to hasten the ordained outcome toward which every incident has been moving from the outset.

The fire at Newmarket, on the other hand, suggested very different dramaturgic imagery by which to express the action of special Providence. For the miraculous fire was seen as a last-minute intervention by Providence to frustrate the evil designs laid by others without its contrivance and to rescue its people from harm. In dramatic terms, this is the kind of celestial interference with which the phrase "deus ex machina" has come exclusively to be associated. Its paradigm in seventeenth-century sermons was the discovery of the Gunpowder Plot, an exhibition of divine brinkmanship that supplied the closest analogue to the fire at Newmarket. For as Edward Pelling reminded his congregation in his 5 November sermon in 1683, only two months after the day of solemn thanksgiving for Charles's happy deliverance, "the difference is not great, whether a *Powder-Treason* be Acted at the *Parliament*-House, or at *Rumbolds*: the *Principle* upon which both Parties Act, is the same."[141] And so, he might have added, was the theatrical manner in which Providence itself had acted, choosing in both cases to allow matters to proceed to the verge of disaster before at last intervening. No wonder, then, that both events suggested the same imagery drawn from the playhouse.

In the 5 November sermon he preached in 1673, Isaac Barrow had chosen as his subject special Providence and the seven marks or characters "upon which may be grounded Rules declarative of special Providence," unknowingly providing Hickes with the quarry from which, a decade later, he would appropriate most of the same rules along with much of Barrow's language. The second "character of special Providence," according to Barrow, is "the Seasonableness, and Suddenness of Events. When that which in it self is not ordinary, nor could well be expected, doth fall out happily, in the nick of an exigency, for the relief of innocence" or such another cause. In view of the occasion for his sermon, the example that a providential intervention "in the nick of an exigency" is meant to recall is the discovery of the Gunpowder Plot; but the fire at Newmarket would fit just as well. Warming to his subject, Barrow envisions the scenario preceding such a dramatic intervention by special Providence:

> God ever doth see those deceitful workers of iniquity, laying their mischief in the dark; he is always present at their Cabals, and clandestine meetings, wherein they brood upon it. He often doth suffer it to grow on to a pitch of maturity, till it be thoroughly formed, till it be ready to be hatched, and break forth in its mischievous effects; then in a trice he snappeth and crusheth it to nothing. God beholdeth violent men setting out in their unjust attempts, he letteth them proceed on in a full career, until they reach the edge of their design;

then instantly he checketh, putteth in a spoak, he stoppeth, he tumbleth them down, or turneth them backward.[142]

In such cases as these, God is conceived of as playing a complex theatrical role, first as spectator, observing with distaste a play contrived by other hands, and then as deus ex machina, suddenly intervening in the action on stage, circumventing the expected outcome, and giving the plot a surprising denouement. As Barrow explains, "God could prevent the beginnings of wicked designs; he could supplant them in their first onsets; he could any-where sufflaminate and subvert them: but he rather winketh for a time, and suffereth the designers to go on, till they are mounted to the top of confidence, and good people are cast on the brink of ruine; then *apo mēkhanēs* [ex machina], surprisingly, unexpectedly he striketh in with effectual succour."[143] Barrow reinforces this dramaturgic image of the deus ex machina, which we earlier noticed Archbishop Sancroft using in a sermon on the providential discovery of the Popish Plot, by quoting in the margin Horace's advice to the aspiring dramatist: "*Nec Deus intersit, nisi dignus vindice nodus inciderit* [And let no god intervene, unless a knot come worthy of such a deliverer]."[144]

To dramatize this kind of providential intervention adequately in *Albion and Albanius*, Dryden needed two acts, the earlier to represent the contrivance of the evil designs that the later will show being turned to nought. In the tradition of the early Stuart court masque that lies behind *Albion and Albanius*, the second act is an antimasque whose infernal dramatis personae, committed to destroying order, are the direct antitheses of those celestial agents responsible for the resolution of disorder in the first and last acts. More specifically, as the table shows, Dryden has designed act 2 as an antithetical parallel to the previous act, recalling and inverting each of its four principal episodes in their exact order.

Antithetical Parallelism in *Albion and Albanius*

| *Act 1* | *Act 2* |
| --- | --- |
| Thamesis and Augusta plead with Mercury to restore Albion. | Democracy and Zeal implore Pluto to undermine Albion's authority. |
| Mercury's caduceus lulls Democracy and Zeal to sleep, restoring peace to Augusta and Thamesis. | Alecto's serpent stings Augusta to madness and jealousy, destroying her former peace. |
| Juno renews the marriage bonds between Augusta and Albion. | Democracy and Zeal seduce Augusta into breaking her marriage vows. |
| Albion and Albanius, returning by water from exile, are restored to their native land. | Albanius, torn from Albion's side, departs by water to undergo a second exile. |

The events represented by these allegorical episodes of act 2 are relevant not to the Rye House Plot immediately but to the alleged Popish Plot and the Exclusion Crisis, the earlier stages of what Dryden portrays in his opera as being a seamless Protestant Plot culminating in the assassination scheme. The act begins with Pluto and his cohorts contriving, with the assistance of "a Rogue" (Titus Oates), "To forge a Plot / In seeming Care of *Albion*'s Life" and to "Inspire the Crowd / With Clamours loud / T' involve his Brother and his Wife" (2.1.85–89). It ends with their plan succeeding so far that Albion is forced to send Albanius into exile in order to calm public excitement over "imaginary Dangers" (2.2.48), alluding to James's enforced absences abroad during the height of the Exclusion Crisis.

Act 3 opens at Dover, where Albion, "Betray'd, forsaken, and of hope bereft," stands deploring his lot, despondent and defenseless in the face of "Rebellion arm'd with zeal" (3.1.20). Democracy and Zeal appear in the company of their allies, Tyranny and Asebia (atheism), with whom they soon come to blows over their differing goals: an overt allusion to the divided aims of those who contrived the Association. Yet in spite of Proteus's assurance to Albion that "Thou shalt be restor'd agen" (3.1.145), his life hangs in the balance as Democracy and Zeal, having subdued their rivals, "*return with their Faction*," announcing "'tis by us that *Albion* must be Slain" (3.1.161). But just as the "*one-Ey'd Archer*" (Rumbold) advances to do their bidding, "*a fire arises betwixt them and* Albion," the surprised conspirators "*all sink together*," and Albion calls for a public thanksgiving in acknowledgement of Heaven's intervention:

> Let our tuneful accents upwards move,
> Till they reach the vaulted Arch of those above;
> Let us adore 'em;
> Let us fall before 'em.

(3.1.179–82)

Venus now emerges from the sea escorting the exiled Albanius, whom she restores to the grateful Albion, and the opera, as originally written before Charles's death, closes with a brief scene, set at Windsor, where Fame decrees everlasting renown for "Great *Albion*'s Name" (3.2.3).

Albanius's role in Dryden's opera is always subordinate to Albion's, and never more so than in the climactic scenes of his exile and restoration in the second and third acts.[145] By agreeing to accept banishment in order to protect Albion from the same fate—"Oh *Albion*! hear the Gods and me! / Well am I lost in saving Thee" (2.2.98–99)—Albanius endures a vicarious exile in his brother's place, and Dryden is able to dramatize "the double restoration of his Sacred Majesty" through the recurrent images of Albion or his proxy Albanius departing and returning by water.

The incident to which Albanius's reunion with his brother refers, James's return to London from exile, had taken place not after the failure of the Rye House Plot, of course, which was meant to destroy the two brothers at a single stroke, but a year before that event, on 8 April 1682. It was celebrated by bonfires, bell ringing, and a series of public appearances over the next fortnight culminating in a public dinner at Merchant Taylors' Hall on 20 April, and a special performance of *Venice Preserv'd* the following night to which Dryden contributed a new prologue. This public fanfare over the duke's return had been carefully orchestrated as a Tory response to the bonfires that had accompanied Shaftesbury's acquittal, and to the public dinner the Whig leader had been given at Skinners' Hall following his release from the Tower some five months earlier.[146] It was designed as a victory celebration signaling the decisive end of the Exclusion Crisis that had made James's exile necessary, but it was also reminiscent in some respects of the excited welcome given Charles on his entry into London on 29 May 1660. In the interest of enhancing the parallelism of the double restoration, Dryden reverses the order of events and makes this episode, rather than the miraculous fire at Newmarket, the climax of the third act, and rightly so. Albanius's return from exile here mirrors closely his appearance in the company of Albion at the end of the first act, whereas the miraculous fire has no counterpart elsewhere in the opera. Furthermore, Dryden intensifies the similarity by having both returns from exile take place at Dover under the mantle of Venus, the mother and protector of Aeneas, whom he had used as an analogue for the exiled Charles in his poems celebrating the king's restoration in 1660 as well as his coronation the following year.[147]

Although Dryden and the other Tory propagandists had long been crediting the resolution of the Exclusion Crisis to the king, extolling him as the savior of the nation, Albion is assigned as passive a role in the second act of Dryden's opera, referring to that crisis, as in the third, which leads without interruption to the Rye House Plot. Albion's speeches in both acts express a wide range of descending and ascending emotions, successively registering disillusionment, anguish, despair, gratitude toward the gods, and joy at being reunited with his brother. But none of his speeches ever initiates an action or influences an event. In act 2 Albion declares, in words recalling *Absalom and Achitophel*, "The fumes of madness that possest / The Peoples giddy Brain, / Once more disturb the Nations rest" (2.2.57–59), and he goes on to draw for himself the same lesson that David had to learn from his "faithful Band of Worthies":

I thought their love by mildness might be gain'd,
By Peace I was restor'd, in Peace I Reign'd:
But Tumults, Seditions,
And haughty Petitions,
Are all the effects of a merciful Nature;
Forgiving and granting,
E're Mortals are wanting,
But leads to Rebelling against their Creator.

(2.2.67–74)

Yet Albion never acts on his newly acquired wisdom as David had done in *Absalom and Achitophel*, and of course it would violate dramatic decorum if he did. For in an opera solely concerned with the role of special Providence in the king's double restoration there is no room whatever for human agency. From that perspective, "second Causes are out of doors," and Albion's part in the latter two acts is simply to react emotionally to events initiated by others, sinking ever deeper into helplessness and despair, like Barrow's good people "cast on the brink of ruine," until he is suddenly delivered from all his troubles by a single divine action.

In one respect, *Albion and Albanius* is unique among Dryden's historical parallels, or at least those we have been considering. Unlike *Absalom and Achitophel*, *The Duke of Guise*, and *The History of the League*, which only imply a parallel with their subject either by alluding to another series of events or, in the case of the *History*, by relying on its timeliness, *Albion and Albanius* overtly dramatizes both poles of the parallel by representing in allegory "the double restoration of his Sacred Majesty."[148] But as was the case with Dryden's earlier political parallels, disparities are as important as similarities here, as Proteus makes explicit in a song to Albion epitomizing the subject of the opera just before the appearance of the miraculous fire:

Still thou art the care of Heav'n,
In thy Youth to Exile driv'n:
Heav'n thy ruin then prevented,
Till the guilty Land repented:
In thy Age, when none could aid Thee,
Foes conspir'd, and Friends betray'd Thee;
To the brink of danger driv'n,
Still thou art the Care of Heav'n.

(3.1.147–54)

The similarity of the two restorations, both of them divine interventions on Albion's behalf, conveys the same political lesson here—"still thou art the Care of Heav'n"—as on the day of solemn thanksgiving for the king's escape from assassination, when preachers proclaimed Charles "him whom Heaven it self hath so plainly declared to be its Favourite."[149] The disparities in the parallel, between a first restoration brought about when "the guilty Land repented," imploring the gods for Albion's return, and a second where "Foes conspir'd, and Friends betray'd Thee" until their designs were unexpectedly frustrated by the gods, are intrinsic to the dissimilar theatrical imagery associated, as we have noticed, with different providential interventions. The first, traditionally associated with the Restoration, had emphasized a reconciliation of political differences among English Protestants that, for the moment at least, had restored national harmony. The second, traditionally associated with the Gunpowder Plot but also applied in recent years to the Popish Plot, turned on the presence of an internal enemy—stubbornly refusing allegiance to a heretical prince, implacable in its hostility to the Church of England, and impervious to overtures of forgiveness—who could only be curbed by external restraints. In adopting this familiar image for Catholic intrigues and applying it to the Protestant Plot in *Albion and Albanius*, Dryden was drawing the same political lesson from the Rye House Plot as other propagandists for the government had already done the year before.

On the day of solemn thanksgiving for the king's escape from assassination, one of the preachers described Charles's second restoration in terms that implicitly emphasized the differences setting it apart from his first.

> *God* hath made it a new Settlement to his *Throne*; an addition of Strength and Security to his Empire, by washing off the Paints, the Colourings, and Counterfeits, both of *Religion* and *Loyalty*; shewing him who are *True Protestants*, and who are *False Brethren*; who are good *Subjects*, and who are Movers of *Sedition*, and inordinate *Seekers* of *Preheminence*. In a word, who are the Friends, and who are the Enemies, not only of the *Succession*, but of the *Monarchy*.[150]

That view of events offers, in place of the perfect harmony between king and people celebrated on the occasion of the first restoration nearly a quarter of a century earlier, the prospect of a nation permanently divided between friends and enemies of the Crown. It is the same view that inspires Dryden's allegorical dramatization of Charles's second restoration in *Albion and Albanius*, as well as his "Dedication to the King" of *The History of the League*, both written within a few months of each other. It envisions a future in which a permanently disaffected minority of Protestant Dissenters will linger in the nation's midst, unreconciled to the monarchy and the Established Church and relentlessly plotting their destruction by any available means. It involves relinquishing once and for all the sanguine expectations accompanying Charles's first restoration that had produced a degree of euphoria never quite recaptured in the celebrations of his deliverance from the Rye House Plot. But the change is not all loss, as the thanksgiving preacher appreciates. With greater insight into the real state of the nation and a clearer recognition of his enemies, the king has gained the greater "Strength and Security" he will need to maintain order in a society where false brethren will always be found alongside true Protestants, and movers of sedition amidst good subjects. Or so the propagandists of press and pulpit would now have the public believe.

# EPILOGUE

W E MUST NOT exaggerate the importance of Tory propaganda. It was not directly responsible for the government's success or for the collapse of the Whig party. But while such measures as dispensing with parliaments, suppressing newspapers, seizing charters, and dispersing conventicles were responsible for the government's actual victory, it was propaganda that must win public tolerance for these debatable actions.[1] By late summer of 1683 those policies had to all appearance gained the widespread, though not of course the universal, compliance of a public for whom the Rye House Plot as skillfully exploited by the government figured as the final episode laying to rest any lingering doubts about the existence of a Protestant Plot.[2] Gilbert Burnet, whose views were certainly not biased in favor of the government, believed that if Charles had summoned a parliament at any time thereafter, "both the king and the duke might have expected every thing that they could desire: for the body of the nation was yet so possessed with the belief of the [Rye House] Plot, that probably all elections would have gone as the court directed, and scarce any of the other party would have had the courage to have stood for an election any where."[3]

To establish and maintain general credit in this, the last and most convincing of a series of Protestant Plots it had publicized in recent years with growing success, the government had been able to draw freely on the whole range of propaganda resources it had been developing since early 1681 and tailoring constantly to fit changing political conditions and successive crises: addressing movements, the politicized theaters of Drury Lane and Dorset Garden, along with the political theater of trials, executions, and anniversary or thanksgiving services, and the inexhaustible stream of contributions from the press: printed sermons, dying speeches, newspapers, pamphlets, and anonymous broadsides, quite as much as the political poems, prose works, dedications, prologues, epilogues, and productions for the stage that came to monopolize Dryden's energies during the last four years of Charles's reign.

The evidence presented above shows Dryden to have been far more widely acquainted with contemporary Tory propaganda than has previously been realized, and also much more deeply committed to every one of the government's successive campaigns aimed at winning public acquiescence in its policies. In his "Epistle to the Whigs" prefixed to *The Medall*, Dryden established his credentials as a political polemicist by assuring the writers for the opposition that "I have perus'd many of your

Papers" (p. 40). He could have made an even stronger claim of this kind to fellow Tory writers, with many of whose newspapers, pamphlets, and broadsides he demonstrates the close familiarity of a colleague engaged with them in a common cause, and wishing to ensure that his goals accord with theirs.

That engagement on Dryden's part was slow in coming, and only took place once the government's supporters, having abandoned a defensive and apparently deteriorating position, were already mounting an offensive in support of the more resolute and effective policy adopted by the king and his advisers in the spring of 1681. But from the time that Dryden joined the first of these Tory campaigns later that year he entered into a firm commitment to the cause of persuading the public to accept the king's policies, and he never deviated from that resolution as long as Charles lived. Thereafter Dryden would lead the way in shaping a variety of literary genres into new and effective instruments of political propaganda appealing to a reading public whose own interests had been increasingly concentrated and politicized by a long succession of public crises and partisan debates.

Varied as were the journalistic, literary, and subliterary media in which Tory propaganda was conveyed to the public, there was remarkable agreement among the authors themselves in the objectives that they pursued in each of the government's three campaigns between early 1681 and the end of Charles's reign. Yet it would be a mistake to think of the Tory propaganda machine as an organization in any modern sense. There is no evidence that at any time officials were orchestrating the efforts of this sprawling mass of writers in the way that L'Estrange and other courtiers directed and regulated the successive addressing movements. L'Estrange's intimacy with other government officials, as well as the privileged status granted the *Observator*, undoubtedly encouraged many Tory writers to take their cues from that newspaper in particular, and, as was certainly true in Dryden's case, the government's more effective publicists were probably loyal readers of each other's publications. But the principal guideposts for both publicists and public alike in each new propaganda campaign, and in each new phase of those campaigns, were undoubtedly that remarkable series of official publications provided by the government itself at every stage along the way: *His Majesties Declaration*, Fitzharris's *Confession*, the proceedings at Shaftesbury's grand inquest, the royal proclamations against the Rye House conspirators, the printed trials of five of them, and finally the second of these publications to bear the title of *His Majesties Declaration*.

It was these documents, most of them published by order in council, that set the course to be followed by the official bodies involved in the addressing movements as well as by the government's unofficial journalists and pamphleteers. With these clear guidelines for publicizing and making palatable the government's policies, the propagandists could be left to themselves to develop their own individual means of achieving the common goal, in this way supplying the variety and vitality that are such noticeable characteristics of every one of the successive Tory campaigns.

As is well known, Dryden's commitment to writing propaganda in support of the Crown, once made, did not end with Charles's death. During the brief reign of James II that followed, he was to write three substantial poems in favor of the king whose succession he had worked so long to ensure. But in certain important respects his later activity on behalf of James was less a continuation of his earlier career as a government publicist than a new and very different kind of loyal effort. For Dryden's political poems written between 1685 and 1688—*Threnodia Augustalis*, mourning the death of Charles II and welcoming his brother's accession, *The Hind and the Panther*, supporting James's policy of religious toleration, and *Britannia Rediviva*, celebrating the birth of the Prince of Wales—are addressed to distinct occasions and issues, consistent with each other and with the policies of the Crown, certainly, but displaying none of that singleness of purpose, month after month and year after year, that distinguishes Dryden's literary activities in response to the paramount political crisis of Charles's last years. More important, Dryden's poems on behalf of James were in most respects autonomous. For even though the death of Charles and the birth of the Prince of Wales were marked by the usual outpouring of loyal tributes, these were not produced to advance a particular political goal. The great Tory propaganda campaigns of Charles's last years in which Dryden took part were a unique phenomenon. They were invigorated by a sense of common purpose among a wide variety of writers with different backgrounds and unequal talents. Dryden would never share that kind of exhilarating experience again.

## Appendix 1

## POLITICAL ALLUSIONS IN DRYDEN'S PROLOGUES
## AND EPILOGUES, 1678–1684

WHERE A PROLOGUE or epilogue was written for the first performance of a play, I have in most cases taken the date of the latter from the *London Stage*. In the case of three plays, however, I have followed the modified dates of first performance suggested by Judith Milhous and Robert D. Hume in "Dating Play Premières from Publication Data, 1660–1700" (*Harvard Library Bulletin* 22 [1974]: 374–405). They suggest that Dryden's *Troilus and Cressida* may have been performed slightly earlier than the *London Stage* date of April 1679 (p. 389), that "Lee's *The Princess of Cleve* is a real puzzle," with the *London Stage* date of September 1680 no better than a *terminus a quo* for the first performance (p. 393), and that Saunders's *Tamerlane the Great* was probably first performed at Drury Lane before the *London Stage* date of March 1681 (p. 393).

In the case of prologues and epilogues written for revivals or special performances of plays, I have generally followed volumes 1 and 2 of Dryden's *Works*. In three cases, however, the California editors seem to me to be clearly wrong, and I have therefore revised their conclusions for the following reasons.

John Harold Wilson has shown from internal evidence in Dryden's epilogue to Banks's *The Unhappy Favourite* that the play almost certainly received its first performance in the late spring of 1681—perhaps May. (See his "Six Restoration Play-Dates," *Notes and Queries* 9 [1962]: 221–23.) This date has been accepted by the editors of the *London Stage* and of Dryden's *Works*. The latter comment, however: "The first edition of the play (1682) contains another prologue, preceding Dryden's, with the heading 'Spoken by Major Mohun, the First Four Dayes'. Whether Dryden's pieces were spoken on the fifth day or later we do not know. . . . The full title of Dryden's prologue makes clear that his pieces were written for a very special occasion, but we do not know when the King and Queen attended a performance of *The Unhappy Favourite* . . . [that] was acted at the Theatre Royal, and it is probable that the company called upon Dryden for the special prologue and epilogue, even though he knew nothing of Banks" (2:388–89). There are no grounds, however, for linking the prologue and epilogue together as having both been written at the same time for the special performance. In fact, their titles draw a clear distinction between the two in the edition of Banks's play: "Prologue, Spoken to the King and Queen on their coming to the House, and Written on purpose by Mr. Dryden," and, at the end of the play, "Epilogue, By Mr. Dryden." Furthermore, the first edition of the play contains not two but three prologues: the one spoken by Major Mohun the first four days, Dryden's written for the command performance, and a third "Prologue, Intended to be spoken, Written by the Author." It seems most likely that, after the first four nights, Banks's prologue was spoken for the remainder of the play's first run. There is no reason to believe that the special performance before the King and Queen, for which Dryden wrote his prologue, necessarily took place during the initial run. It may just as easily have taken place later in the spring, or sometime in the following autumn, since the play, with its three prologues, was not published until the beginning of 1682. On the other hand, the only epilogue published with the play is Dryden's, which was presumably written, therefore, for the first performance. This is of course the assumption underlying Wilson's argument that the first performance of *The Unhappy Favourite* took place in the spring, since Dryden's epilogue alludes to various events that occurred at that time. Clearly, then, Dryden's prologue was written later than his epilogue, and for a different occasion, although we do not know how long an interval separates the two.

There are two versions of Dryden's "Prologue at Oxford, 1680," the first of which was included in the second edition of Lee's *Sophonisba* in the spring of 1681, while the second, which differs from the first in a number of respects, was published in Dryden's *Miscellany Poems* in 1684 (see *Works*, 1:160–61). On the gratuitous assumption that the two versions were written for two different plays, the editors of Dryden's *Works* speculate that the 1684 version was written first, for a performance of a play at Oxford in July 1679, while the 1681 version, suitably revised, was used for the performance of a different play at Oxford in the summer of 1680. "The allusion to 'us Cardinals' and 'Pope Joan' in line 22 [of the 1684 version] identifies the play for which it must have been spoken as Settle's *The Female Prelate: Being the History of the Life and Death of Pope Joan*. Settle's play was first introduced to the London audience about September 1679. . . . [It presumably] was tried at Oxford in July of 1679, before its London première, the prologue in the version [of 1684] being used on that occasion; and . . . when the company returned the following summer it used the prologue again, for *Sophonisba*, but in so doing had to refurbish it" (1:362–63). It is now known for certain, however, that *The Female Prelate* had its first performance on 31 May 1680 (see the *London Stage*, p. 286; Milhous and Hume, "Dating Play Premières," p. 376). There are therefore no grounds for believing that

Dryden's prologue was written in 1679, and scarcely more for believing that it was first written, at any date, for *The Female Prelate*. The mention of "us Cardinals" and "Pope Joan" can just as easily be explained as allusions to Settle's new play in July 1680 when Dryden's prologue was spoken at the revival of Lee's play, judging from its publication with *Sophonisba* the following spring. In any case, whatever the play for which it was written, there is no reason to question the accuracy of the title in *Miscellany Poems*, "The Prologue at Oxford, 1680." The text of the prologue in that collection certainly differs from the one found in the second edition of *Sophonisba*, but there is no solid evidence for believing that Dryden's revision, whichever text is the later, was due to his refurbishing the prologue for another play.

Finally, it is probable that the "Prologue to the University of Oxford" (not to be confused with the preceding) was written for a performance there in the summer of 1679 rather than, as the editors of Dryden's *Works* have suggested, the summer of 1680. In this prologue (see *Works*, 1:164–65), Dryden draws a humorous comparison between the rebellion in Scotland and another that had taken place in the King's Company, some of whose principal members had deserted it to form a theatrical company in Scotland.

> Discord, and Plots which have undone our Age
> With the same ruine, have o'erwhelm'd the Stage.
> Our House has suffer'd in the common Woe,
> We have been troubled with *Scotch* Rebels too;
> Our Brethren, are from *Thames* to *Tweed* departed,
> And of our Sisters, all the kinder hearted,
> To *Edenborough* gone, or Coacht, or Carted.
> With bonny Blewcap there they act all night
> For *Scotch* half Crown, in *English* Three-pence hight.

As he regularly does in his prologues and epilogues, Dryden alludes here to events of current interest. The Scottish rebels had been crushed by Monmouth's army at Bothwell Bridge the previous month, on 22 June 1679, and the news of this victory was still causing great excitement in July. It was during the theatrical season of 1678–79 that some of the King's Company's members deserted it and went to Edinburgh: another event of recent interest in the summer of 1679. By February 1680 the rebels had returned to the King's Company. (See the *London Stage*, pp. 271, 279.) In choosing to date Dryden's prologue in July 1680, the editors of Dryden's *Works* must argue that in Scotland "trouble was still going on in the summer of 1680," as evidenced by an entry in Luttrell's *Diary* in July, although they admit that "whether this latest affray would have come to Dryden's attention early enough to have inspired the comparison in l.4 it is impossible to say" (1:367–68). Similarly, they argue that some rebels from the King's Company still remained in Scotland after their leaders' return in February. In both cases, they are appealing for support to the mere vestiges in 1680 of two rebellions that commanded greatest attention in 1679, when they would have been far more likely to invite allusions.

Under "First Publication" below I have indicated when and in what form the prologue or epilogue was first published: in the first edition of the play for which it was written, or independently, either as a single half sheet soon after it was spoken in the theater, or in Dryden's *Miscellany Poems* or *Examen Poeticum* some years later. I have also indicated in the same column whether or not Dryden's authorship of these verses was made known at the time of first publication.

Dryden's Prologues and Epilogues, 1678–1684

| Piece | Play | First Performance | First Publication | Allusions |
|-------|------|-------------------|-------------------|-----------|
| Prologue | *Oedipus* (Dryden and Lee) | Early autumn of 1678 Dorset Garden | March 1679 with play Identified as Dryden's | None |
| Epilogue | *Oedipus* (Dryden and Lee) | Early autumn of 1678 Dorset Garden | March 1679 with play Identified as Dryden's | None |
| Prologue | *Troilus and Cressida* (Dryden) | Early 1679 Dorset Garden | Autumn 1679 with play Identified as Dryden's | None |
| Epilogue | *Troilus and Cressida* (Dryden) | Early 1679 Dorset Garden | Autumn 1679 with play Identified as Dryden's | Anti-Catholic |
| Prologue | *Caesar Borgia* (Lee) | May 1679 Dorset Garden | November 1679 with play Identified as Dryden's | Anti-Catholic |
| "Prologue to the University of Oxford" | Play unknown | July 1679 Oxford | 1684 (*Miscellany Poems*) Identified as Dryden's | Playful hit at Scottish rebels |
| Prologue | *The Loyal General* (Tate) | December 1679 Dorset Garden | February 1680 with play Identified as Dryden's | Complaints about current turmoil |
| "Prologue at Oxford, 1680" | *Sophonisba* (Lee) | July 1680 Oxford (Revival) | Spring of 1681 with play Identified as Dryden's | Anti-Dissenter |
| Prologue | *The Princess of Cleve* (Lee) | Late 1680–end 1682 Dorset Garden | 1684 (*Miscellany Poems*) Identified as Dryden's | None |
| Epilogue | *The Princess of Cleve* (Lee) | Late 1680–end 1682 Dorset Garden | 1684 (*Miscellany Poems*) Identified as Dryden's | None |

Dryden's Prologues and Epilogues, 1678–1684 (*cont.*)

| Piece | Play | First Performance | First Publication | Allusions |
|---|---|---|---|---|
| Prologue | *The Spanish Fryar* (Dryden) | November 1680 Dorset Garden | March 1681 with play Identified as Dryden's | Anti-Catholic |
| Epilogue | *Tamerlane the Great* (Saunders) | Early 1681 Drury Lane | Spring of 1681 with play Identified as Dryden's | None |
| "Epilogue Spoken to the King at Oxford" | *Tamerlane the Great* (Saunders) | 19 March 1681 Oxford (Special performance) | (1) March 1681 (Oxford) Separate publ. (anon.) (2) Early 1681 (London) Separate publ. (Dryden) | Impartial |
| Epilogue | *The Unhappy Favourite* (Banks) | April or May 1681 Drury Lane | Early 1682 with play Identified as Dryden's | Anti-Whig banter |
| "Prologue to the University of Oxford, 1681" | Play unknown | July 1681 Oxford | 1693 (*Examen Poeticum*) Identified as Dryden's | Seriously loyalist |
| Prologue | *The Unhappy Favourite* (Banks) | Late spring or autumn of 1681 Drury Lane (Special performance) | Early 1682 with play Identified as Dryden's | Seriously loyalist |
| Prologue | *Mithridates* (Lee) | October 1681 Drury Lane (Revival) | (1) 28 October 1681 in part (*Impartial Protestant Mercury*) (anon.) (2) End of 1681 Separate publ. (anon.) | Anti-Popish Plot witnesses |
| Epilogue | *Mithridates* (Lee) | October 1681 Drury Lane (Revival) | (1) 29 October 1681 in part (*Loyal Protestant*) (anon.) (2) End of 1681 Separate publ. (anon.) | Anti-Popish Plot witnesses |
| Prologue | *The Loyal Brother* (Southerne) | February 1682 Drury Lane | 7 February 1682 Separate publ. (Dryden) | Seriously anti-Whig |
| Epilogue | *The Loyal Brother* (Southerne) | February 1682 Drury Lane | 7 February 1682 Separate publ. (Dryden) | Anti-Whig banter |
| "Prologue to His Royal Highness" | *Venice Preserv'd* (Otway) | 21 April 1682 Dorset Garden (Special performance) | 21 April 1682 Separate publ. (Dryden) | Seriously anti-Whig |
| "Prologue to the Dutchess" | *Venice Preserv'd* (Otway) | 31 May 1682 Dorset Garden (Special performance) | 1 June 1682 Separate publ. (Dryden) | Seriously anti-Whig |
| "Prologue to the King and Queen" | Play unknown | November 1682 Drury Lane United Co. | 16 November 1682 Separate publ. (Dryden) | Anti-Whig banter |

Dryden's Prologues and Epilogues, 1678–1684 (*cont.*)

| Piece | Play | First Performance | First Publication | Allusions |
|---|---|---|---|---|
| "Epilogue to the King and Queen" | Play unknown | November 1682 Drury Lane United Co. | 16 November 1682 Separate publ. (Dryden) | None |
| Prologue | *The Duke of Guise* (Dryden and Lee) | 28 November 1682 Drury Lane United Co. | 30 November 1682 Separate publ. (Dryden) | Seriously anti-Whig |
| Epilogue | *The Duke of Guise* (Dryden and Lee) | 28 November 1682 Drury Lane United Co. | 30 November 1682 Separate publ. (Dryden) | Anti-Whig and anti-Trimmer |
| Another Epilogue | *The Duke of Guise* (Dryden and Lee) | 28 November 1682 Drury Lane United Co. | 30 November 1682 Separate publ. (Dryden) | Anti-Whig banter |
| Epilogue | *Constantine the Great* (Lee) | November 1683 Drury Lane United Co. | 14 November 1683 Separate publ. (Dryden) | Anti-Trimmer |
| Prologue | *The Disappointment* (Southerne) | April 1684 Drury Lane United Co. | 5 April 1684 Separate publ. (anon.) | None |

# Appendix 2

## THE MISPLACED LINES IN

## *ABSALOM AND ACHITOPHEL*

SOME EIGHTY-FIVE LINES into *Absalom and Achitophel*, Dryden turns from relating the earlier part of the king's reign, when "*David*'s mildness manag'd it so well, / The Bad found no occasion to Rebell" (77–78), to describe the abrupt reappearance of civil unrest occasioned by public excitement over the Popish Plot, explaining that "The Good old Cause reviv'd, a Plot requires" (82). He begins his account of this plot by tracing its origins to the civil disabilities of the Catholic minority.

     Th' inhabitants of old *Jerusalem*  
Were *Jebusites*: the Town so call'd from them;  
And their's the Native right————  
But when the chosen people grew more strong,  
The rightfull cause at length became the wrong:  
90  And every loss the men of *Jebus* bore,  
They still were thought God's enemies the more.  
Thus, worn and weaken'd, well or ill content,  
Submit they must to *David*'s Government:  
Impoverisht, and depriv'd of all Command,  
Their Taxes doubled as they lost their Land,  
And, what was harder yet to flesh and blood,  
Their Gods disgrac'd, and burnt like common wood.  
This set the Heathen Priesthood in a flame;  
For Priests of all Religions are the same:  
100 Of whatsoe'r descent their Godhead be,  
Stock, Stone, or other homely pedigree,  
In his defence his Servants are as bold  
As if he had been born of beaten gold.  
The *Jewish Rabbins* thô their Enemies,  
In this conclude them honest men and wise:  
For 'twas their duty, all the Learned think,  
T' espouse his Cause by whom they eat and drink.  
From hence began that Plot, the Nation's Curse,  
Bad in it self, but represented worse:  

110    Rais'd in extremes, and in extremes decry'd;
       With Oaths affirm'd, with dying Vows deny'd:
       Not weigh'd, or winnow'd by the Multitude;
       But swallow'd in the Mass, unchew'd and Crude.
       Some Truth there was, but dash'd and brew'd with Lyes;
       To please the Fools, and puzzle all the Wise.
       Succeeding times did equal folly call,
       Believing nothing, or believing all.
       Th' *Egyptian* Rites the *Jebusites* imbrac'd;
       Where Gods were recommended by their Tast.
120    Such savory Deities must needs be good,
       As serv'd at once for Worship and for Food.
       By force they could not Introduce these Gods;
       For Ten to One, in former days was odds.
       So Fraud was us'd, (the Sacrificers trade,)
       Fools are more hard to Conquer than Perswade.
       Their busie Teachers mingled with the *Jews*;
       And rak'd, for Converts, even the Court and Stews:
       Which *Hebrew* Priests the more unkindly took,
       Because the Fleece accompanies the Flock.
130    Some thought they God's Anointed meant to Slay
       By Guns, invented since full many a day:
       Our Authour swears it not; but who can know
       How far the Devil and *Jebusites* may go?
       This Plot, which fail'd for want of common Sense,
       Had yet a deep and dangerous Consequence:
       For, as when raging Fevers boyl the Blood,
       The standing Lake soon floats into a Flood;
       And every hostile Humour, which before
       Slept quiet in its Channels, bubbles o'r:
140    So, several Factions from this first Ferment,
       Work up to Foam, and threat the Government.

The entire passage is clearly designed to show, first, how the depressed condition of the English Catholics led some of them to concoct a genuine plot against the lawful government, and, secondly, how this embryonic conspiracy was then exaggerated and exploited by Protestant adherents of the Good Old Cause to create public "Jealosies and Fears" that were readily believed because of the contempt and distrust in which the Catholics were held by their countrymen. But while no one seems to have raised the subject before, there are a number of serious problems with the arrangement and continuity of these lines as they appear in all editions of *Absalom and Achitophel* starting with the first, and continuing down to the California edition from which I quote here.

First of all, where we would expect Dryden's account to follow a straightforward course showing how the peculiar situation of the Catholics led to the Popish Plot, we find that in reality it wanders back and forth between the two topics in a puzzling manner. The passage begins, as we might expect, by introducing the Catholic minority (85), and after twenty-three lines turns to the second topic: "From hence began that Plot, the Nation's Curse" (108). But ten lines later the account digresses unexpectedly to describe certain Catholic beliefs and practices not immediately related to the Plot ("Th' *Egyptian* Rites the *Jebusites* imbrac'd" [118]), while after another twelve lines it returns abruptly to the subject of the Plot ("Some thought they God's Anointed meant to Slay" [130]).

Secondly, there is a noticeable absence of transitions to prepare the reader for any of these sudden changes of subject. In the first of these, the words "From hence began that Plot" (108) directly follow four lines explaining that "the *Jewish Rabbins*" (the Anglican priesthood) agreed with the "Heathen Priesthood" (the Catholic clergy) that it was their duty "T' espouse his Cause by whom they eat and drink." But how does this explain the beginnings of the Plot or the readiness with which it was believed? Again, there is no discernible reason why a digression on the rites and practices of the English Catholics (118) should be occasioned by the previous lines assessing the credibility of the Plot, a subject resumed just as inexplicably at the end of the digression (130).

The only satisfactory way of accounting for this confusion, I believe, is to hypothesize that for some unexplained reason the twelve lines beginning "Th' *Egyptian* Rites the *Jebusites* imbrac'd" (118–29) were in the first edition set in type (or imposed on the stone) ten lines beyond their proper position, and were never restored in subsequent editions to their correct location between the present lines 107 and 108. My reasons for entertaining this hypothesis should become clear when these twelve lines (printed in italics below for easier identification) are restored to what I believe was their original place in Dryden's holograph. Once this is done, the confusion disappears entirely.

> Th' inhabitants of old *Jerusalem*
> Were *Jebusites*: the Town so call'd from them;
> And their's the Native right———
> But when the chosen people grew more strong,
> The rightfull cause at length became the wrong:
> 90    And every loss the men of *Jebus* bore,
> They still were thought God's enemies the more.
> Thus, worn and weaken'd, well or ill content,
> Submit they must to *David*'s Government:
> Impoverisht, and depriv'd of all Command,
> Their Taxes doubled as they lost their Land,

And, what was harder yet to flesh and blood,
Their Gods disgrac'd, and burnt like common wood.
This set the Heathen Priesthood in a flame;
For Priests of all Religions are the same:
100 Of whatsoe'r descent their Godhead be,
Stock, Stone, or other homely pedigree,
In his defence his Servants are as bold
As if he had been born of beaten gold.
The *Jewish Rabbins* thô their Enemies,
In this conclude them honest men and wise:
For 'twas their duty, all the Learned think,
T' espouse his Cause by whom they eat and drink.
*Th' Egyptian Rites the Jebusites imbrac'd;*
*Where Gods were recommended by their Tast.*
110 *Such savory Deities must needs be good,*
*As serv'd at once for Worship and for Food.*
*By force they could not Introduce these Gods;*
*For Ten to One, in former days was odds.*
*So Fraud was us'd, (the Sacrificers trade,)*
*Fools are more hard to Conquer than Perswade.*
*Their busie Teachers mingled with the* Jews;
*And rak'd, for Converts, even the Court and Stews:*
*Which* Hebrew *Priests the more unkindly took,*
*Because the Fleece accompanies the Flock.*
120 From hence began that Plot, the Nation's Curse,
Bad in it self, but represented worse:
Rais'd in extremes, and in extremes decry'd;
With Oaths affirm'd, with dying Vows deny'd:
Not weigh'd, or winnow'd by the Multitude;
But swallow'd in the Mass, unchew'd and Crude.
Some Truth there was, but dash'd and brew'd with Lyes;
To please the Fools, and puzzle all the Wise.
Succeeding times did equal folly call,
Believing nothing, or believing all.
130 Some thought they God's Anointed meant to Slay
By Guns, invented since full many a day:
Our Authour swears it not; but who can know
How far the Devil and *Jebusites* may go?
This Plot, which fail'd for want of common Sense,
Had yet a deep and dangerous Consequence:
For, as when raging Fevers boyl the Blood,
The standing Lake soon floats into a Flood;
And every hostile Humour, which before

Slept quiet in its Channels, bubbles o'r:
140   So, several Factions from this first Ferment,
Work up to Foam, and threat the Government.

As soon as this single transposition is made, the Jebusites become the exclusive subject of the first thirty-five lines (85–119), after which, with the words "From hence began that Plot," Dryden takes up this second subject, pursuing it without interruption throughout the remainder of the passage (120–41). Similarly, the awkward breaks we noticed earlier in Dryden's account disappear, to be replaced by smooth transitions. The first and most striking of these occurs at the point, following line 107, where I have inserted the twelve italicized lines. The preceding couplet, referring to the Catholic priesthood, declares: "For 'twas their duty, all the Learned think, / T' espouse his Cause by whom they eat and drink" (106–7). The italicized lines then go on to develop this imagery of eating and drinking for another four lines in order to ridicule the Catholic doctrine of Transubstantiation:

Th' *Egyptian* Rites the *Jebusites* imbrac'd;
Where Gods were recommended by their Tast.
Such savory Deities must needs be good,
As serv'd at once for Worship and for Food.

With these twelve italicized lines (108–19), the account of the English Catholics comes to an end, providing a logical transition to the subject of the Plot and its credibility, which is now prepared for not by a topic on which the Anglican clergy consider the Catholic priesthood "honest men and wise," as before, but by the Catholic practice of proselytizing among the members of the Church of England, whereby they incur the hatred and distrust of an Anglican clergy eager to believe, and to encourage the faithful to believe, the most damaging accusations against their enemies. Finally, the subsequent account of the avidity with which the multitude credited every allegation concerning the Popish Plot, however extravagant, now logically includes the succeeding (but formerly separated) lines, "Some thought they God's Anointed meant to Slay / By Guns, invented since full many a day: / Our Authour swears it not" (130–32).

This is not the place to speculate on how these twelve lines came to be misplaced or, even more curiously, why they were never restored to their original position in subsequent editions. But those who wish to pursue the matter further might begin by noting that in the first edition (Macdonald 12a, a folio) the point at which the twelve lines were apparently omitted occurs four lines from the bottom of B2v (i.e., toward the end of the gathering), while the point at which they do appear, out of their proper order, occurs six lines from the top of C1r. Now as is well known,

C1 is a cancel leaf, and another, more famous, set of twelve lines—those expanding the verse character of Achitophel (180–91) first printed in the third London edition (Macdonald 12e, a quarto)—would have followed immediately after what is now the last line of C1v if indeed, as is widely believed, they existed from the start in Dryden's holograph, but were deleted from the first edition—perhaps to make room for other lines—when the original C1 was replaced by the cancel leaf after the poem (but not the preliminary matter) had been printed. Speculation until now has focused understandably on the contents of C1v before the original leaf was canceled (see Vinton A. Dearing's textual notes in the California edition [*Works*, 2:411–12] and Edward L. Saslow, "Shaftesbury Cursed: Dryden's Revision of the *Achitophel* Lines," *Studies in Bibliography* 28 [1975]: 276–83). But of course C1r also had to be reset in making up the cancel leaf, and the appearance there of the twelve misplaced lines discussed above should encourage attention to the obverse of C1 just as much as to its reverse side.

## ABBREVIATIONS

| | |
|---|---|
| CJ | *Journals of the House of Commons.* |
| CSPD | *Calendar of State Papers, Domestic Series, of the Reign of Charles II, 1660–1685.* 28 vols. London: H. M. Stationery Office, 1860–1938. |
| Dryden, Works | *The Works of John Dryden.* To be completed in 20 vols. Berkeley: University of California Press, 1956–. |
| Grey | *Debates of the House of Commons, From the Year 1667 to the Year 1694.* Collected by the Hon. Anchitell Grey, Esq. 10 vols. London, 1763. |
| HMC Ormonde | Historical Manuscripts Commission. *Calendar of the Manuscripts of the Marquess of Ormonde, K. P., Preserved in Kilkenny Castle.* New Series, vol. 6. London: H. M. Stationery Office, 1911. |
| LJ | *Journals of the House of Lords.* |
| London Stage | *The London Stage, 1660–1800; Part I: 1660–1700.* Ed. William Van Lennep, Emmett L. Avery, and Arthur H. Scouten. Carbondale: Southern Illinois University Press, 1965. |

## NOTE ON DOCUMENTATION

For all printed works earlier than 1900, the place of publication is London unless otherwise indicated. Where exact dates of publication (day, month, and year) for Restoration works are supplied, the source is in every case Narcissus Luttrell, unless some other authority is specified. Where dates by month and year are given, these are based on firm internal evidence, unless some other source, such as Anthony Wood, is identified.

# NOTES

## CHAPTER 1
## THE PULPIT

1. The most thorough recent study of popular attitudes to the Restoration can be found in Tim Harris, *London Crowds in the Reign of Charles II: Propaganda and Politics from the Restoration until the Exclusion Crisis* (Cambridge: Cambridge University Press, 1987), chap. 3. He concludes that in spite of doubts expressed by some recent historians, "most Londoners did support a restoration of monarchy by the spring of 1660," although it would be "wrong to assume from this that there was a political consensus amongst Londoners at this time" (pp. 60–61).

2. *The Diary of John Evelyn*, ed. E. S. de Beer, 6 vols. (Oxford: Clarendon Press, 1955), 3:246.

3. *The Speech of Sir Harbottle Grimston, Baronet, Speaker of the Honorable House of Commons, to the Kings Most Excellent Majesty, Delivered in the Banquetting House at Whitehal, 29 May 1660, the Members of That House Being There Present* (1660), pp. 3–4.

4. Gilbert Sheldon, *Davids Deliverance and Thanksgiving: A Sermon Preached before the King at Whitehall upon June 28, 1660, Being the Day of Solemn Thanksgiving for the Happy Return of His Majesty* (1660), pp. 17–18.

5. Ibid., p. 17.

6. Andrew Browning, ed., *English Historical Documents, 1660–1714* (London: Eyre and Spottiswoode, 1953), p. 61.

7. Richard L. Greaves, *Deliver Us from Evil: The Radical Underground in Britain, 1660–1663* (Oxford: Oxford University Press, 1986), p. 6. For the government's exaggerated fears that such incidents as White's Plot and Venner's Rising represented "only a corner of a nation-wide conspiracy," see pp. 38–40, 53–57, 70–72; and Ronald Hutton, *The Restoration: A Political and Religious History of England and Wales, 1658–1667* (Oxford: Clarendon Press, 1985), pp. 136, 151, 178–79, 231.

8. Quoted by Gerald Straka in "The Final Phase of Divine Right Theory in England, 1688–1702," *English Historical Review* 77 (1962): 638–58, an excellent account of the use of "providential theory" to justify the revolution of 1688–89. (The citation appears on pp. 653–54.) See also J. P. Kenyon, *Revolution Principles: The Politics of Party, 1689–1720* (Cambridge: Cambridge University Press, 1977), pp. 24–29.

9. Dryden, "Postscript" to *The History of the League*, *Works*, 18:399.

10. For general accounts of these sermons, see Helen W. Randall, "The Rise and Fall of a Martyrology: Sermons on Charles I," *Huntington Library Quarterly* 10 (1947): 135–67; Carolyn A. Edie, "Right Rejoicing: Sermons on the Occasion of the Stuart Restoration, 1660," *Bulletin of the John Rylands University Library of Manchester* 62 (1979): 61–86. A recent article by John Spurr, " 'Virtue, Religion and Government': The Anglican Uses of Providence," in *The Politics of Reli-*

*gion in Restoration England*, ed. Tim Harris, Paul Seaward, and Mark Goldie (Oxford: Basil Blackwell, 1990), pp. 29–47, brings a different perspective to these and numerous other Restoration sermons on both general and particular Providence, considering their role in a "campaign for the reformation of national manners" that laid the foundation for "the 'moral revolution' of the 1690s."

11. Thomas Sprat, *The History of the Royal-Society of London for the Improving of Natural Knowledge* (1667), p. 357.

12. Sheldon, *Davids Deliverance*, p. 16. (Placement of parentheses as in original.)

13. Robert South, *Ecclesiasticall Policy the Best Policy; or, Religion the Best Reason of State: In a Sermon Delivered before the Honourable Society of Lincolnes Inn* (Oxford, 1660), pp. 6–7.

14. John Tillotson, *Sermons Preach'd upon Several Occasions* (1671), pp. 136–37.

15. *Certain Sermons or Homilies Appointed to Be Read in Churches, in the Time of Queen Elizabeth of Famous Memory, and Now Thought Fit to Be Reprinted by Authority from the Kings Most Excellent Majesty* (1673), pp. 343–44, 346, 359–60. (Roman substituted for black letter.)

16. See the useful list of such sermons in the index to Evelyn's *Diary*, 6:135.

17. Robert Twisse, *England's Breath Stopp'd: Being the Counter-part of Judah's Miseries, Lamented Publickly in the New-Church at Westminster, on January 30, Being the Anniversary of the Martyrdom of King Charles the First of Blessed Memory* (1665), p. 4.

18. Isaac Barrow, *A Sermon Preached on the Fifth of November, 1673* (1679), pp. 26–27.

19. Sprat, *History of the Royal-Society*, p. 360.

20. William Whitaker, *A Disputation on Holy Scripture* [1588], trans. William Fitzgerald (Cambridge, 1849), p. 407.

21. *Certain Sermons or Homilies*, pp. 366–67. (Roman substituted for black letter.)

22. Sheldon, *Davids Deliverance* (n. 4 above) discusses David's sufferings from Absalom on p. 8; he speaks of Moses' troubles related in Numbers, chapter 16 (Corah's rebellion), on pp. 10–11.

23. George Stradling, *A Sermon Preach'd before the King at White-Hall, Jan. 30, 1675, at the Anniversary Commemoration of the Martyrdom of King Charles I. Printed by His Majesties Special Command* (1675), p. 13.

24. John Spencer, *The Righteous Ruler: A Sermon Preached at St. Maries in Cambridge, June 28, 1660, Being Appointed a Day of Publick Thanksgiving to God for the Happy Restauration of His Majesty to his Kingdomes* (Cambridge, 1660), p. 5.

25. William Haywood, *A Sermon Disswading from Obloquie against Governours, Preached on Sunday, Decemb. 7, 1662, in a Solemne Audience* (1663), p. 14.

26. Richard Meggott, *A Sermon Preached before the Right Honourable the Lord Mayor and Aldermen, &c. at Guild-Hall Chappel, January the 30th, 1673/4* [1674], p. 19.

27. William Sancroft, *A Sermon Preach'd to the House of Peers, Novemb.*

*13th, 1678, Being the Fast-Day Appointed by the King to Implore the Mercies of Almighty God in the Protection of His Majesties Sacred Person, and His Kingdoms* (1678), pp. 25–26.

28. For examples of sermons drawing detailed parallels between Charles and Christ, see Thomas Lambert, *Sad Memorials of the Royal Martyr; or, A Parallel betwixt the Jewes Murder of Christ, and the English Murder of King Charls the First* (1670); Stradling, *Sermon Preach'd before the King.*

29. For examples of such elaborate parallels, see Henry Glover, *Cain and Abel Parallel'd with King Charles and His Murderers* (1664); David Jenner, *Cain's Mark and Murder, K. Charls the I His Martyrdom: Delivered in a Sermon on January the Thirtieth* (1681); Twisse, *England's Breath Stopp'd* (n. 17 above) (Charles and Zedekiah); Samuel Crossman, *Two Sermons Preached in the Cathedral-Church of Bristol, January the 30th, 1679/80, and January the 31th, 1680/1, Being Days of Humiliation for the Execrable Murder of Our Late Soveraign, King Charles I* (1681) (Charles and Zedekiah in both); John Allington, *The Regal Protomartyr; or, The Memorial of the Martyrdom of Charles the First. In a Sermon Preached upon the First Fast of Publick Appointment for It* (1672) (Charles and Stephen); James Duport, *Three Sermons Preached in St. Maries Church in Cambridg, upon the Three Anniversaries of the Martyrdom of Charles I, Jan. 30; Birth and Return of Charles II, May 29; Gun-powder Treason, Novemb. 5* (1676), the first of which is a martyrdom sermon drawing a parallel between Charles and Stephen.

30. "The Comparison of Tiberius and Caius Gracchus with Agis and Cleomenes" is unique in considering four rather than the usual two lives.

31. *Plutarchs Lives. Translated from the Greek by Several Hands. To which is prefixt the Life of Plutarch* [by Dryden]. *The First Volume* (1683), p. 260.

32. For a thoughtful recent essay on the use of parallels in this period, see Alan Roper, "Drawing Parallels and Making Applications in Restoration Literature," in Richard Ashcraft and Alan Roper, *Politics as Reflected in Literature* (Los Angeles: William Andrews Clark Memorial Library, 1989), pp. 29–65. As his title indicates, Roper is concerned with literary rather than homiletic uses of the parallel, but his observations are applicable to both. I believe Roper is mistaken, however, in the case of two of the "four reasonably constant features" he predicates of Restoration parallels: "Secondly, parallels concentrated upon similarity to the exclusion of difference, thus diverging from the practice of Plutarch," and "Thirdly, parallels aimed to blacken by association and only incidentally celebrated by association" (pp. 40–41). As the present and succeeding chapters will show, I find the exact opposite to be true of both homiletic and literary parallels of the Restoration period.

33. Glover, *Cain and Abel Parallel'd*, p. 1. He compares and contrasts Charles I with Conradin, king of Naples, on p. 2. Twisse, *England's Breath Stopp'd*, compares and contrasts Charles I with Edward II and Richard II on p. 4.

34. Peter Heylyn, *A Sermon Preached in the Collegiate Church of St. Peter in Westminster, on Wednesday, May 29th, 1661, Being the Anniversary of His Majesties Most Joyful Restitution to the Crown of England* (1661), p. 25. Heylyn's text is Ps. 31:21.

35. Ibid., pp. 26, 29.

36. See *A Form of Common Prayer, to Be Used upon the Thirtieth of January, Being the Anniversary Day Appointed by Act of Parliament for Fasting and Humiliation. Published by His Majestie's Command* (1661).

37. Simon Ford, *Parallēla dusparallēla; or, The Loyal Subjects Indignation for His Royal Sovereign's Decollation, Expressed in an Unparallel'd Parallel between the Professed Murtherer of K. Saul, and the Horrid Actual Murtherers of King Charles I* (1661), pp. 36, 44.

38. Gilbert Burnet, *The Royal Martyr Lamented, in a Sermon Preached at the Savoy, on King Charles the Martyr's Day, 1674/5* (1675), p. 15. For other martyrdom sermons using 2 Samuel to draw an extended parallel between the deaths of Saul and Charles I, see Arthur Bury, *The Bow; or, The Lamentation of David over Saul and Jonathan, Applyed to the Royal and Blessed Martyr, King Charles the I* (1662); Henry Hesketh, *A Sermon Preached before the Right Honorable Lord Mayor and Aldermen of the City of London at Guild-Hall Chappel, on January 30th, 1677/8* (1678).

39. See *A Form of Prayer, with Thanksgiving, to Be Used of All the Kings Majesties Loving Subjects the 29th of May Yearly, for His Majestie's Happy Return to His Kingdoms; It Being also the Day of His Birth. Set Forth by His Majesties Authority* (1661).

40. Simon Ford, *Parallēla; or, The Loyall Subjects Exultation for the Royall Exiles Restauration, in the Parallel of K. David and Mephibosheth on the One Side; and Our Gracious Sovereign, K. Charls, and His Loving Subjects, on the Other. Set Forth in a Sermon Preached at All-Saints Church in Northampton, Jun. 28, 1660, Being the Day Appointed for Solemn Thanksgiving for His Royal Majesties Happy Restitution* (1660), pp. 1–2.

41. Ibid., pp. 3–4.

42. See John Parker, *A Sermon Preached at Christ-Church, Dublin, before Both Houses of Parliament, May the 29th, 1661, Being the Anniversary of His Majesty King Charles the Second, His Most Memorable and Happy Restauration* (Dublin, 1661).

43. See *The Diary of Samuel Pepys*, ed. Robert Latham and William Matthews, 11 vols. (Berkeley: University of California Press, 1970–83): 2:109.

44. Parker, *Sermon Preached at Christ-Church*, pp. 34–35.


CHAPTER 2
PARLIAMENT AND THE PRESS

1. Andrew Browning, *Thomas Osborne, Earl of Danby and Duke of Leeds, 1632–1712*, vol. 2: *Letters* (Glasgow: Jackson, Son and Co., 1944), p. 70.

2. See John Kenyon, *The Popish Plot* (London: William Heinemann, 1972), pp. 157–65, 178–80.

3. See ibid., pp. 168–76.

4. Grey, 8:60.

5. *CJ*, 9:530.

6. Grey, 6:365.

7. Ibid., p. 362.

8. Ibid., p. 363.

9. Ibid., p. 306.

10. See J. R. Jones, *The First Whigs: The Politics of the Exclusion Crisis, 1678–1683* (London: Oxford University Press, 1961), pp. 35–40.

11. Grey, 7:4.

12. *CJ*, 9:575.

13. Grey, 7:67.

14. Ibid., p. 72.

15. Ibid., p. 125.

16. See ibid., p. 116.

17. Ibid., p. 179.

18. *CJ*, 9:605.

19. Ibid., p. 607.

20. Ibid., p. 620.

21. Grey, 7:266.

22. Ibid., p. 325.

23. See Kenyon, *Popish Plot*, p. 183.

24. Grey, 8:111.

25. Ibid., p. 159.

26. For the royal declaration, see *London Gazette*, 10 June 1680.

27. See the Whig account of this progress in *A True Narrative of the Duke of Monmouth's Late Journey into the West, in a Letter from an Eye-witness Thereof, to His Correspondent in London* (3 Nov. 1680).

28. See *The Humble Address and Advice of Several of the Peeres of This Realm, for the Sitting of the Parliament, Presented to His Majesty at White-Hall, the 7th of December, 1679* (1679).

29. For the royal proclamation against tumultuous petitions, see *London Gazette*, 15 Dec. 1679.

30. *True Domestick Intelligence*, 6 Jan. 1680.

31. *The Diary of John Evelyn*, ed. E. S. de Beer, 6 vols. (Oxford: Clarendon Press, 1955), 4:172.

32. Timothy Crist, "Government Control of the Press after the Expiration of the Printing Act in 1679," *Publishing History* 5 (1979): 49–77. (The citation appears on p. 53.) I am indebted here to Crist's excellent account of the subject.

33. See ibid., pp. 56–57.

34. For the royal proclamation against unlicensed newspapers, see *London Gazette*, 20 May 1680.

35. See *A Letter from Legorn, Decem. 1, 1679* (12 Jan. 1680).

36. See *A Second Letter from Legorn, with a Farther Account, as Incredible and Unparalell'd as the First, from aboard the Van-herring, December 10, 1679* (14–17 Jan. 1680); *An Answer Returned to the Letter from Legorn, by a Merchant concerned in the Ship* (19 Jan. 1680); *An Answer to the Second Letter from Legorn: Being an Account of Some Further Discovery of a Continued Plot aboard the Ship Van Herring* (23 Jan. 1680).

37. See *An Answer to the Merchants Letter, Directed to Ralph Mean-well, Now on Board the Van-Herring, with a Pursuit of the Former Legorn Letter, 19 January 1679* (22 Jan. 1680). There was one further sham *Legorn Letter* from the Tories, mentioned in the next chapter, but it was published in the late summer of

1681, long after the second Whig series of *Legorn Letters*, listed below, had ceased.

38. See *Another Letter from Legorn, to an Eminent Merchant in Lond., Sept. 23, 1680* (25 Oct. 1680); *An Answer to Another Letter from Legorn, to an Eminent Merchant in Lond., Octob. 29, 1680* (2 Nov. 1680); *The Answer to the Letter from Legorn Answered, in a Third Letter to a Merchant in London* (November 1680); *From aboard the Van-Herring: Being a Full Relation of the Present State and Sad Condition of That Ship, in a New Letter from Legorn, to a Merchant in London* (January 1681).

39. Valuable information on the legal technicalities involved in the selection of juries can be found in Roger North's *Examen* (1740), pp. 89–117 and 582–624.

40. See Crist, "Government Control of the Press," pp. 63–67. *Ignoramus* juries were less common before Bethel and Cornish took office, but not entirely unknown. Crist seems to overlook the fact that not Bethel and Cornish, installed on 28 September, but their immediate predecessors would have been responsible for the recalcitrant juries of September 1680 that he discusses.

41. *The Car-man's Poem; or, Advice to a Nest of Scriblers* (2 Feb. 1680).

42. *The Good Old Cause Revived* (2 Feb. 1680); *New Advice to a Painter* (23 Feb. 1680), p. 4.

43. The notation appears on the title page of Wood's copy of the poem, now in the Bodleian Library.

44. Wood identifies Malchus and Python with Oates and Tonge in his copy of the poem, but does not identify Arod with any individual.

45. [John Caryll], *Naboth's Vinyard; or, The Innocent Traytor: Copied from the Original of Holy Scripture, in Heroick Verse* (October 1679), p. 12.

46. *Absalom's Conspiracy; or, The Tragedy of Treason* (1 July 1680), p. 1. There is another Tory parallel between Absalom and Monmouth written in 1680, which I have not discussed above because it was apparently never published. This is "A Dialogue between Nathan and Absolome," a poem discovered in manuscript and subsequently published by Howard H. Schless. (See his "Dryden's *Absalom and Achitophel* and *A Dialogue between Nathan and Absolome*," *Philological Quarterly* 40 [1961]: 139–43.) The poem is a dramatic scene in which the prophet Nathan reproves Absalom for his disobedience, Absalom stubbornly defies him, and a voice warns of Absalom's impending death upon the tree. The scene, though invented, is faithful to the biblical story, like the episodes in *Naboth's Vinyard*. It contains no allusions to the present, however, and the implicit parallel with Monmouth depends entirely on its timeliness.

47. In some anniversary sermons as well the preacher omits the application, inviting the congregation to develop the implicit parallel themselves. Thus in a 5 November sermon one preacher finishes the exposition of his text by announcing, "I shall leave it to your memories to run the parallel between *David*'s Conspirators and these Traytors [Guy Fawkes and his associates]" (Henry Dove, *A Sermon Preached before the Honourable House of Commons, at St. Margarets Westminster, November 5, 1680* [1680], p. 12).

48. See Arthur Jackson, *Annotations upon the Remaining Historicall Part of the Old Testament* (Cambridge, 1646), pp. 343, 385; John Mayer, *Many Com-*

mentaries in One (1647), p. 367; *Annotations upon All the Books of the Old and New Testament*, 2nd ed. (1651), comments on 2 Sam. 3:2, 3:3, and 3:5. For the customary denial of "any right of inheritance" to the children of concubines, see *Annotations upon All the Books*, comment on 1 Kings 11:3.

49. See Jackson, *Annotations*, pp. 389, 391; Mayer, *Many Commentaries in One*, pp. 410, 424; *Annotations upon All the Books*, comments on 2 Sam. 14:1 and 15:1; John Diodati [Giovanni Diodate], *Pious and Learned Annotations upon the Holy Bible*, 4th ed. (1664), comments on 2 Sam. 14:14 and 15:1.

50. The commentators based their inference that Maachah was David's wife and consequently Absalom his heir not on anything found in 2 Samuel but on a passage in a later book of the Old Testament, where a list of David's nineteen sons, including Absalom, constructed from the inventories in 2 Sam. 3:2–5 and 5:13–16, ends with a new verse: "These were all the sons of David, besides the sons of the concubines, and Tamar their sister" (1 Chron. 3:9), implying that all those named were the offspring of David's wives.

51. Matthew Poole, *Annotations upon the Holy Bible*, vol. 1 (1683), comment on 2 Sam. 15:12. This is an English redaction of the five volumes of Poole's *Synopsis Criticorum* (1669–76).

52. *A Letter to His Grace the D. of Monmouth, This 15th of July, 1680. By a True Lover of His Person, and the Peace of the Kingdom* (15 July 1680), p. 3. (Italics reversed.)

53. *A Ballad: The Third Part* (1679).

54. [Thomas Durfey], *The Progress of Honesty; or, A View of a Court and City* (11 Oct. 1680), pp. 11–12.

55. *A Seasonable Address to Both Houses of Parliament concerning the Succession, the Fears of Popery, and Arbitrary Government* (1681), p. 13.

56. *A Ballad upon the Popish Plot* (1679). See also *A Ballad: The Third Part*, which characterizes Shaftesbury as the "politique head" who "first framed this [Popish] Plot." For a Tory broadside of 1680 that singles out Shaftesbury as the chief among "the Makers of the [Popish] Plot," see *The Loyal Tories Delight; or, A Pill for Fanaticks* [1680].

57. *LJ*, 13:610.

58. Grey, 7:441.

59. Ibid., 8:262.

60. *CJ*, 9:665–67.

61. Ibid., p. 655.

62. Grey, 8:150.

63. Ibid., p. 266.

64. *CJ*, 9:679.

65. Ibid., p. 685.

66. *A Speech Lately Made by a Noble Peer of the Realm* (31 Dec. 1680), pp. 1–2.

67. See *William Late Viscount of Stafford, His Last Speech upon the Scaffold on Tower-hill, Decemb. 29, 1680, as It Was Given by His Own Hand to a Spectator There* [1680].

68. See K. H. D. Haley, *The First Earl of Shaftesbury* (Oxford: Clarendon Press, 1968), pp. 571–72, 575.

69. *LJ*, 13:733.

70. *CJ*, 9:701.

71. Grey, 8:254.

72. Ibid., p. 261.

73. *CJ*, 9:702.

74. See *A Coppy of the Journal-Book of the House of Commons for the Sessions of Parliament Begun at Westminster the 21 Day of October, 1678, and Continued until the 30 Day of December Next Following, Being Then Prorogued* (1680).

75. See *A True Copy of the Journal-Book of the Last Parliament, Begun at Westminster the Sixth Day of March 1678/79, Containing the Transactions from the First Day of Their Sitting, to the Day of Their Prorogation and Dissolution* (1680).

76. *CJ*, 9:643.

77. See *Votes of the House of Commons, Perused and Signed, to Be Printed According to the Order of the House of Commons, by Me, William Williams, Speaker*. Fifty-eight continuously numbered and separately published half-sheets (1 Nov. 1680–10 Jan. 1681), plus an unnumbered preliminary issue of 16 pp. covering the business of the Commons from 21 to 30 October 1680, four additional issues of 8 to 15 pp. with numbers duplicating some of those in the regular series, and seven unnumbered issues dealing with the appearance of witnesses concerning the Popish Plot.

78. See *An Exact Collection of the Most Considerable Debates in the Honourable House of Commons, at the Parliament Held at Westminster the One and Twentieth of October, 1680, Which Was Prorogued the Tenth, and Dissolved the Eighteenth of January Following* (1681).

79. *England's Mournful Elegy for the Dissolving the Parliament* (21 Jan. 1681), p. 1.

80. *Protestant (Domestick) Intelligence*, 25 Feb. 1681. (Italics reversed.)

81. Ibid., 15 Mar. 1681. (Italics omitted.)

82. [Elkanah Settle], *The Character of a Popish Successour, and What England May Expect from Such a One: Humbly Offered to the Consideration of Both Houses of Parliament, Appointed to Meet at Oxford, on the One and Twentieth of March, 1680/1* (1681), p. 15.

83. *Vox Populi; or, The Peoples Claim to Their Parliaments Sitting, to Redress Grievances, and Provide for the Common Safety, by the Known Laws and Constitutions of the Nation: Humbly Recommended to the King and Parliament at Their Meeting at Oxford, the 21th of March* (March 1681), pp. 5, 13.

84. Thomas Long, *A Sermon against Murmuring: Preached in the Cathedral Church of St. Peter Exon, on the 29th of May, 1680* (13 July 1680), sig. A3. (Italics omitted.)

85. Samuel Crossman, *Two Sermons Preached in the Cathedral-Church of Bristol, January the 30th, 1679/80, and January the 31th, 1680/1, Being the Days of Humiliation for the Execrable Murder of Our Late Soveraign, King Charles I* (1681), pp. 34, 36–37.

86. Francis Turner, *A Sermon Preached before the King on the 30/1 of January 1680/1, Being the Fast for the Martyrdom of King Charles I of Blessed Memory* (1681), p. 8.

87. *A Letter from a Citizen of Oxford to a Citizen of London, concerning the Dissolution of the Parliament* (January 1681), pp. 1–2.

88. *A Letter from Scotland, Written Occasionally upon the Speech made by a Noble Peer of This Realm* (1681), pp. 1–2.

89. *Oedipus*, which Dryden wrote with Nathaniel Lee, was apparently finished no later than September 1678 and first performed early in the autumn. Oates and Tonge did not make their first appearance before the Privy Council until 28 September. For the dates of Dryden's plays, prologues, and epilogues written between 1678 and 1684, see Appendix 1.

90. See, for example, Bruce King's discussion of *The Spanish Fryar* in *Dryden's Major Plays* (New York: Barnes and Noble, 1966), pp. 148–64.

91. Irvin Ehrenpreis, "Dryden the Playwright," in *Acts of Implication: Suggestion and Covert Meaning in the Works of Dryden, Swift, Pope, and Austen* (Berkeley: University of California Press, 1980), p. 34.

92. [Robert Gould], *The Laureat* (24 Oct. 1687), p. 3.

93. See Edmund Malone, *The Critical and Miscellaneous Prose Works of John Dryden*, 4 vols. (1800), 1:119; Sir Walter Scott, *The Works of John Dryden*, 18 vols. (1808), 1:233–37, 6:368–69, 9:443; Robert Bell, *Poetical Works of John Dryden* (1854), pp. 48–52; W. D. Christie, *The Poetical Works of John Dryden* (1870), pp. xlvi–xlvii; Louis I. Bredvold, "Political Aspects of Dryden's *Amboyna* and *The Spanish Fryar*," *University of Michigan Publications in Language and Literature* 8 (1932): 119–32.

94. Judith Milhous and Robert D. Hume, *Producible Interpretation: Eight English Plays, 1675–1707* (Carbondale: Southern Illinois University Press, 1985), pp. 146–49. Their discussion of the play (pp. 141–71) is in many respects invaluable.

95. Susan Staves, *Players' Scepters: Fictions of Authority in the Restoration* (Lincoln: University of Nebraska Press, 1979), p. 77.

96. My remarks about an assumed system of values in a play apply equally to *Troilus and Cressida*. Recently, the California editors (Dryden, *Works* 13:518) have argued that in this play "Dryden appears to be drawing specific parallels between the contemporary political situation and the time of the Trojan War." As their example, however, they cite the popular hostility at this time to the king's mistress, the duchess of Portsmouth, and comment: "When Troilus is made to defend the virtue of Cressida in a violent quarrel with his brother Hector, the audience could not help but be reminded of another pair of royal brothers and the way a mistress was helping to destroy everyone's peace of mind." The parallel, if there is one, is extremely farfetched: Portsmouth was the elder, not the younger, brother's mistress, the royal brothers did not quarrel over her, and no one (least of all Charles) would have attempted to defend her chastity. It is even harder to imagine why Dryden would have drawn a parallel so offensive to the court. I have discussed other recent attempts to find political parallels in Dryden's plays of this period in "Dryden in 1678–1681: The Literary and Historical Perspectives," in *The Golden and the Brazen World: Papers in Literature and History, 1650–1800*, ed. John M. Wallace (Berkeley: University of California Press, 1985), pp. 55–77.

97. Dryden, "Second Prologue to *Secret Love*" [1667], *Works* 9:120. (Italics omitted.)

98. Dryden, "Prologue at Oxford, 1680," ibid. 1:160–61, 401. (Italics reversed in last couplet quoted.)

99. Dryden, "Prologue to *The Spanish Fryar; or, The Double Discovery*" (1681), sig. a1. (Italics reversed.) The date of first performance is November 1680.

100. Dryden, "Prologue to *Caesar Borgia*" [May 1679], *Works* 1:162.

101. Dryden, "Epistle Dedicatory," *Troilus and Cressida*, ibid., pp. 221–22. The prologue to Nahum Tate's *The Loyal General*, first performed in December 1679, offers a similar case where Dryden is content to deplore the present confusions without adopting a partisan stance (see ibid. 1:163–64). Here his chief complaint is that the nation's turmoil has corrupted its literary taste to the disadvantage of both players and serious playwrights like Tate:

> The Plays that take on our Corrupted Stage,
> Methinks resemble the distracted Age;
> Noise, Madness, all unreasonable Things,
> That strike at Sense, as Rebels do at Kings!
> The stile of Forty One our Poets write,
> And you [the audience] are grown to judge like Forty Eight.
> Such Censures our mistaking Audience make,
> That 'tis almost grown Scandalous to Take!

This is comic raillery at the expense of both audiences and the playwrights who cater to their corrupted taste by writing farces instead of tragedies. But in another year or two these jocular similes of rebels and regicides for bad poets and censorious audiences respectively would become too highly charged for any use except a political (and therefore divisive) one.

102. Dryden, "Epistle Dedicatory," *The Spanish Fryar*, sig. A4. (Italics reversed.)

103. See Haley, *First Earl of Shaftesbury* (n. 68 above), pp. 357, 360.

104. See *True Domestick Intelligence*, 9 Dec. 1679.

105. *The Cabal* (18 Feb. 1680).

106. See J. R. Jones, "Shaftesbury's 'Worthy Men': A Whig View of the Parliament of 1679," *Bulletin of the Institute of Historical Research* 30 (1957): 232–41.

107. See Andrew Browning and Doreen J. Milne, "An Exclusion Bill Division List," ibid., 23 (1950): 205–25.

108. See *The Humble Address and Advice of Several of the Peeres of This Realm* (n. 28 above).

109. See *Reasons for the Indictment of the D. of York, Presented to the Grand-Jury of Middlesex, Saturday, June 26, 80, by the Persons here undernam'd* [1680]. This broadside also describes the renewal of the attempt on 30 June in which Lord Clare was involved.

110. See E. S. de Beer, "The House of Lords in the Parliament of 1680," *Bulletin of the Institute of Historical Research* 20 (1943–45): 22–37; *LJ*, 13:666.

111. *The Earl of Essex His Speech at the Delivery of the Petition* (27 Jan. 1681), p. 2.

112. At about the same time as his dedication of *Troilus and Cressida* to Sunderland (the autumn of 1679), Dryden dedicated *The Kind Keeper* to Lord

Vaughan. But this latter dedication makes only the most perfunctory allusion to contemporary affairs.

CHAPTER 3
THE NATION'S SAVIOR

1. See the chapter on "Revenue and Taxation" in David Ogg, *England in the Reign of Charles II*, 2 vols. (Oxford: Clarendon Press, 1934), 2:421–49, still one of the best discussions of the subject.

2. *The Country-mans Complaint, and Advice to the King* (9 Feb. 1681), pp. 1–2.

3. *His Majesties Most Gracious Speech to Both Houses of Parliament, at the Opening of the Parliament at Oxford, Monday, the 21th day of March 1681* (Oxford, 1681), pp. 5–6, 3–4, 4–6, 7.

4. *CJ*, 9:708.

5. See *Votes of the House of Commons, at Oxford*. Five continuously numbered and separately published half-sheets (23–28 Mar. 1681). The first issue covers the initial three days of the session before the passage of the resolution.

6. *CJ*, 9:711.

7. *LJ*, 13:757.

8. On the subject of Charles's negotiations with the French over a subsidy and of his deliberately laid strategy against the Whigs at Oxford, my assessment agrees with that of J. R. Jones (*Charles II: Royal Politician* [London: Allen & Unwin, 1987], pp. 166–70) and most other recent historians. For a contrary interpretation, which represents Charles as indifferent to Barillon's proposals until the last moment, and sees his dissolution of Parliament as a decision reluctantly reached only after the session was already in progress, see Ronald Hutton, *Charles the Second: King of England, Scotland, and Ireland* (Oxford: Clarendon Press, 1989), pp. 398–403. He appears to confuse Charles's seeming indifference to Barillon's overtures, for the sake of driving the best financial bargain, with genuine nonchalance at the prospect of a subsidy. Hutton's idiosyncratic judgment on Charles's dissolution of the Oxford Parliament is that this action did not represent "the end of the 'Exclusion Crisis', with Charles's 'triumph' over the Whigs," but "a moment of profound failure" in which "before the eyes of Europe the English sovereign had admitted his inability to work with his national assembly" (pp. 401–2). He does not explain why this spectacle would have dismayed or disappointed observers in contemporary Europe, or why it did not just as easily show "the world," as Charles and his advisers hoped, the unwillingness of his national assembly, or at least the majority of its lower house, to work with their king.

9. *His Majesties Declaration to All His Loving Subjects, Touching the Causes and Reasons That Moved Him to Dissolve the Two Last Parliaments* (1681), passim. (Printed by order in council of 8 April 1681.)

10. *The Good Old Cause Revived* (2 Feb. 1680).

11. *The Disloyal Forty and Forty One, and the Loyal Eighty, Presented to Publick View in a Prospect and Scheme; Shewing the Difference of the Years Forty, and Forty One, from the Year Eighty* (1680), p. 1.

12. *A Letter to the Earl of Shaftsbury This 9th of July, 1680, from Tom Tell-Troth, a Downright Englishman* (9 July 1680), pp. 3–4.

13. *The Presentment and Humble Petition of the Grand Jury for the County of Middlesex* (23 May 1681), p. 2.

14. *A Letter from a Person of Quality to His Friend concerning His Majesties Late Declaration Touching the Reasons Which Moved Him to Dissolve the Two Last Parliaments at Westminster and Oxford* (April 1681), p. 1.

15. *A Just and Modest Vindication of the Proceedings of the Two Last Parliaments* [1681], p. 46.

16. *The Genius of True English-men* (18 Apr. 1681).

17. *Oxfords Lamentation in a Dialogue between Oxford and London, concerning the Dissolution of the Parliament* (30 Mar. 1681), p. 2. (Italics reversed.)

18. See *Vox Patriae; or, The Resentments and Indignation of the Free-born Subjects of England, against Popery, Arbitrary Government, the Duke of York, or Any Popish Successor: Being a True Collection of the Petitions and Addresses Lately Made from Divers Counties, Cities, and Boroughs of This Realm, to Their Respective Representatives, Chosen to Serve in the Parliament Held at Oxford, March 21, 1680* (13 Apr. 1681).

19. See *The Debates in the House of Commons Assembled at Oxford the Twenty First of March, 1680[/81]* (28 Apr. 1681).

20. *The Country-mans Complaint* (n. 2 above), p. 2.

21. *The Answers Commanded by His Majesty to Be Given . . . upon Several Addresses Presented to His Majesty in Council at Hampton-Court* (24 May 1681), pp. 2, 4.

22. *The E. of Shaftsbury's Expedient for Setling the Nation, Discoursed with His Majesty in the House of Peers, at Oxford, Mar. 24th, 1680/1* (1681), passim. A full account of Shaftesbury's proposal for "settling the Crown upon the Duke of *Monmouth*" was also published in the *Loyal Protestant*, 9 Apr. 1681.

23. *The Deliquium; or, The Grievances of the Nation Discovered in a Dream* (8 Apr. 1681), p. 2. Almanzor, the name used for the duke of York here, was of course the hero of *The Conquest of Granada*. Dryden had already drawn a flattering comparison between the two in dedicating his play to the duke in 1672. See *Works*, 11:6–7.

24. *Poor Robins Dream; or, The Visions of Hell, with a Dialogue between the Two Ghosts of Dr. Tonge and Capt. Bedlow* (30 Apr. 1681), p. 3.

25. *The Waking Vision; or, Reality in a Fancy* (April 1681). There were at least two editions of this broadside, both published by Thompson. The date is supplied by Anthony Wood on his copy of the poem, now in the Bodleian. The fact that this poem ends with advice to the king that, along the lines of *The Country-mans Complaint* two months earlier, urges him to exert himself, indicates that it appeared in early April, perhaps before the publication of *His Majesties Declaration*, and certainly before the new Tory propaganda campaign was launched later in the month.

26. *Grimalkin; or, The Rebel-Cat: A Novell Representing the Unwearied Attempts of the Beasts of His Faction against Sovereignty and Succession since the Death of the Lyons in the Tower* (4 May 1681), p. 3.

27. *A Seasonable Invitation for Monmouth to Return to Court* (23 June 1681), p. 2.

28. *Observator*, 13 Apr. 1681.

29. Ibid., 16 Apr. 1681.

30. *Loyal Protestant*, 9 Mar. 1681. (Italics reversed.)

31. *Memoirs of Sir John Reresby*, ed. Andrew Browning (Glasgow: Jackson, Son and Co., 1936), p. 247.

32. *Domestick Intelligence*, 18 July and 8 Aug. 1681.

33. *Religion and Loyalty Supporting Each Other; or, A Rational Account How the Loyal Addressors Maintaining the Lineal Descent of the Crown Is Very Consistent with Their Affection to the Established Protestant Religion* (1681), p. 2.

34. *Loyal Protestant*, 10 May 1681. (Italics reversed.)

35. *Domestick Intelligence*, 13 May and 14 July 1681.

36. *A Vindication of Addresses in General, and of the Middle-Temple Address and Proceedings in Particular, in Answer to the Impartial Account of Addresses, Wherein the Popular Pretences of Some Men Are Exposed* (19 Aug. 1681), p. 1.

37. *Vox Angliae; or, The Voice of the Kingdom: Being a Compleat Collection of All Those Numerous Addresses Lately Presented to His Majesty, from the Greatest Part of the Counties, Cities, Boroughs, and Other Corporations and Societies in England and Wales, &c. Expressing Their Thanks for His Late Gracious Declaration* (1682), vols. 1/1, pp. 3, 6, 1/2, p. 14. (Advertised in the *Loyal Protestant*, 28 Feb. 1682.)

38. Ibid., 1:7 (italics omitted), 25.

39. Ibid., p. 3.

40. See, for example, the loyal address from the borough of Haslemere, ibid., p. 5.

41. *Heraclitus Ridens*, 12 April 1681. (Italics reversed.)

42. Edward Sclater, *A Sermon Preached in the Church of Putney in the County of Surrey, upon the 24th of April, 1681, His Majesty's Declaration Being Read That Day* (1681), pp. 3, 4, 31.

43. Henry Anderson, *A Sermon Preached in the Cathedral Church at Winchester, the 29 of May 1681* (1681), pp. 26–27.

44. *Domestick Intelligence*, 21 July 1681.

45. *A New Letter from Leghorn, from aboard the Van-Herring to a Merchant in London, Fully Discovering the Present State of That Ship* (1681), pp. 1, 3–4. This was published between 14 July and 17 August (internal evidence).

46. The libel was subsequently published as *Treason in Graine: That Most Traiterous [sic], or Libel of Fitzharris, . . . Falsly and Malitiously Called by Him, The True English-man Speaking Plain English, in a Letter from a Friend to a Friend* [1681]. In spite of the scandalized tone of the title, the pamphlet appeared without an imprint and was probably a Whig publication whose purpose was anything but loyal.

47. See *The Arraignment and Plea of Edw. Fitz-Harris, Esq; with All the Arguments in Law, and Proceedings of the Court of Kings-Bench Thereupon, in Easter Term 1681* (1681).

48. *Loyal Protestant*, 10 May 1681. (Italics reversed.)

49. See *The Tryal and Condemnation of Edw. Fitz-Harris, Esq; for High-Treason, at the Barr of the Court of King's Bench, at Westminster, on Thursday,*

*the 9th of June, in Trinity Term, 1681* (1681). The story spread by the Tory journalists was that the Whig jurors had planned to acquit Fitzharris, but that one of their number (William Cleave) proved to be a Tory and threatened to produce a hung jury until he secured a conviction. See *Heraclitus Ridens*, 21 June 1681, and *Observator*, 16 July 1681.

50. *Impartial Protestant Mercury*, 14 June 1681.

51. Ibid., 17 June 1681.

52. *Notes of the Evidence Given against the Lord Howard of Escrick* (1681), p. 2 (italics reversed); *Impartial Protestant Mercury*, 24 June 1681 (italics reversed).

53. See *Impartial Protestant Mercury*, 1 July 1681, for Janeway's account of these arrests.

54. See *The Last Speech of Edward Fitz-harris, at the Time of His Execution at Tyburn, the First of July, 1681* (1681).

55. *The Confession of Edward Fitz-harys, Esquire, Written with His Own Hand, and Delivered to Doctor Hawkins, Minister of the Tower, the First of July, 1681, Being the Day of His Execution. Together with His Last Speech* (1681), pp. 3–4. (Printed by order in council of 2 July 1681.) There is another edition of this confession in a two-column format.

56. *A Narrative: Being a True Relation of What Discourse Passed between Dr. Hawkins and Edward Fitz-Harys, Esq; Late Prisoner in the Tower; with the Manner of Taking His Confession. Published by Authority* (1681), p. 4. (Printed by order in council of 2 July 1681.)

57. See *Fitz-Harys's Last Sham Detected; or, A Vindication of His Sacred Majesty from Those Foul Aspersions Cast upon Him by That Impudent Libel Called, Fitz-Harys's Last Confession, Left under His Own Hand, and Published by Dr. Hawkins* (1681); *Truth Vindicated; or, A Detection of the Aspersions and Scandals . . . in a Paper Published in the Name of Dr. Francis Hawkins, Minister of the Tower, Intituled, The Confession of Edward Fitz-Harris, Esq.* (1681); *Some Short but Necessary Animadversions on the Paper Delivered to Dr. Hawkins, together with a Copy of the Paper It Self Entituled, The Confession of Edward Fitz-Harris, Esq; Written with His Own Hand, and Delivered, &c.* (1681); *A Vindication of the Honourable the Sheriffs and Recorder of London, from Those Impudent Reflections Cast upon Them in Fitzharris's Libel, Entituled, His Confession, &c.* [1681]. See also Howard's own denial of Fitzharris's charges against him in *A Letter from My Lord Howard of Escrick, to His Friend* (1681).

58. See *The Ghosts of Edward Fits Harris and Oliver Plunket, Who Was Lately Executed at Tyburn for High-Treason, with Their Sentiments about the Times* (7 July 1681).

59. *The Tryal and Condemnation of Several Notorious Malefactors, at a Sessions of Oyer and Terminer Holden for the City of London, County of Middlesex, and Goal Delivery of Newgate, Beginning July 6, 1681, Ending the 9 of the same Month, at the Sessions House in the Old-Bayly* (1681), p. 3.

60. For early examples, see *A Congratulation on the Happy Discovery of the Hellish Fanatick Plot* (26 July 1681); *A Song of the New Plot* (5 Aug. 1681); *The Mad-men's Hospital; or, A Present Remedy to Cure the Presbyterian Itch. A Poem* (5 Aug. 1681).

61. *CSPD 1680–81*, p. 372.

62. Ibid., p. 399.

63. *The Arraignment, Tryal, and Condemnation of Stephen Colledge for High-Treason, in Conspiring the Death of the King, the Levying of War, and the Subversion of the Government* (1681), pp. 2–3, 19, 28–30, 34. (Italics reversed for pp. 2–3; two sequences of pp. 27–30.) Besides the statute of 25 Edward III to which North referred in his instruction, College was also convicted under the Act for the Preservation of the King (1661), which explicitly made it a capital offense to devise or intend the imprisonment or restraint of the king's person. See Andrew Browning, ed., *English Historical Documents, 1660–1714* (London: Eyre & Spottiswoode, 1953), pp. 63–65.

64. *The Speech and Carriage of Stephen Colledge at Oxford, before the Castle, on Wednesday, August 31, 1681: Taken Exactly from His Own Mouth at the Place of Execution* (1681), pp. 4, 2.

65. See *The Last Speech and Confession of Mr. Stephen Colledge, Who Was Executed at Oxford on Wednesday, August 31, 1681* (1681).

66. See *A Ra-ree Show* (1681). College insisted at his trial that "I know nothing of the Original, the Printer, nor the Author" (*Arraignment, Tryal, and Condemnation of Stephen Colledge*, p. 75).

67. See, for example, *A Song of the New Plot*, where Fitzharris, Howard, College, and Shaftesbury are specifically linked as the four principal culprits in the new plot.

68. *Vox Angliae* (n. 37 above), 1:42 (grand jury of the County of Wilts, 18 July). See also the addresses from the grand juries of the counties of Essex (12 July), Hereford (12 July), and Durham (13 July), ibid., pp. 31–33.

69. *The Ignoramus Ballad* (27 Aug. 1681); *The Riddle of the Roundhead* (9 Sept. 1681).

70. *Some Modest Reflections upon the Commitment of the Earl of Shaftsbury, Arising from the Late Indictment against Mr. Stephen Colledge* (12 July 1681), p. 3. (Exact date from imprint.)

71. *Truth Vindicated* (n. 57 above), p. 8.

72. *Some Modest Reflections*, p. 4.

73. *A Civil Correction of a Sawcy Impudent Pamphlet, Lately Published, Entituled, A Brief Account of the Designs Which the Papists Have Had against the Earl of Shaftsbury, &c.* (1681), pp. 1, 4. (Italics reversed.)

74. *A Dialogue between Mrs. Celier and the L. S        y* (5 Aug. 1681). (Printed on the same broadsheet with *A Song of the New Plot*.)

75. *An Excellent New Ballad of the Plotting Head* (26 Sept. 1681).

76. See *A Congratulation on the Happy Discovery of the Hellish Fanatick Plot* and *A Song of the New Plot* (n. 60 above); *The Riddle of the Roundhead*; *Stephen Colledge's Ghost to the Fanatical Cabal* (15 Sept. 1681); *An Excellent New Ballad of the Plotting Head*; *Have You Any Work for a Cooper? or, A Comparison betwixt a Cooper's, and a Joyner's Trade* (26 Sept. 1681); and *Treason Unmasqued; or, Truth Brought to Light* (1681; another version of *The Riddle of the Roundhead*).

77. *A Dialogue between the E. of Sh[aftesbury] and L. Bell[asyse] in the Tower, concerning the Plot* (13 July 1681), p. 1.

78. *Arraignment, Tryal, and Condemnation of Stephen Colledge* (n. 63 above), p. 30.

79. *The Riddle of the Roundhead.*

80. A rare exception seems to be *A New Ballad Of Jocky's Journey into England, in the Year 1681, with His Remarkes upon the Times* (29 Sept. 1681). The author of these wretched verses describes the conspirators as agreeing to Shaftesbury's "Traiterous Design" and deciding "'twas fit that Young J[emm]y su'd Joyn. / Who Guld with the glittering Hopes of a Crown; / And with Fatal Applause, was to side with 'em, led." The purpose of the conspiracy is "Their *Monarch* to Seiz."

81. See the letter of Richard Mulys dated 11 July in *HMC Ormonde*, p. 97. See also *Impartial Protestant Mercury*, 29 July 1681, and *Loyal Protestant*, 15 Oct. 1681. The possibility of obtaining an indictment in either Westminster or Southwark was also being considered.

82. *An Excellent New Ballad of the Plotting Head.* For other hopeful predictions of Shaftesbury's execution, see *A New Ballad of Londons Loyalty* (July 1681) and *A Congratulation on the Happy Discovery of the Hellish Fanatick Plot.*

83. See *Memoirs of Sir John Reresby* (n. 31 above), p. 233 (entry for 13 Oct.).

84. Letter dated 18 October, *HMC Ormonde*, p. 198.

85. See *A Particular Account of the Proceedings at the Old Bayly, the 17 and 18 of this Instant October, with Relation to the Earl of Shaftsbury, and Others, Prisoners in the Tower; and Mr. Rouse, Who Was Indicted of High Treason, &c.* (1681).

86. See the letter from Longford to Ormond dated 25 October, *HMC Ormonde*, p. 208.

87. See the letter of Peter Rich to Jenkins dated 11 October, *CSPD 1680–81*, p. 504, and the information of Laurence Mowbray dated 28 October, ibid., p. 538.

88. *Memoirs of Sir John Reresby*, p. 236 (entry for 6 Nov.).

89. Letter to Ormond dated 15 November, *HMC Ormonde*, p. 229.

90. *The Whiggs Lamentation for the Death of Their Dear Brother Colledge, the Protestant Joyner* (4 Nov. 1681).

91. *Heraclitus Ridens*, 15 Nov. 1681. (Italics reversed.)

92. [Robert Ferguson], *No Protestant-Plot; or, The Present Pretended Conspiracy of Protestants against the King and Government Discovered to Be a Conspiracy of the Papists against the King and His Protestant-Subjects* (October 1681), p. 32. In the *Loyal Protestant* of 15 October 1681, Thompson denounced the recent publication of this "scurrilous, false Seditious Libel."

93. *The Information of Capt. Hen. Wilkinson, of What Hath Passed betwixt Him and Some Other Persons, Who Have Attempted to Prevail with Him to Swear High Treason against the Earl of Shaftsbury* (1681), p. 2. There are two editions of this publication, differing in pagination.

94. [Robert Ferguson], *The Second Part of No Protestant Plot. By the Same Hand* (November 1681), p. 12. This appeared after *The Information of Capt. Hen. Wilkinson*, but before Shaftesbury's inquest (internal evidence).

95. See Ferguson, *No Protestant-Plot*, pp. 19–20, 28–32.

96. Roger L'Estrange, *Notes upon Stephen College: Grounded Principally upon His Own Declarations and Confessions, and Freely Submitted to Publique Censure* (1681). p. 35. (Roman substituted for black letter.) (Advertised in the *Observator*, 2 Nov. 1681.)

97. Ferguson, *The Second Part of No Protestant Plot*, p. 4.

98. *His Majesties Gracious Speech to Both Houses of Parliament, on Thursday, the 21st of October, 1680* (22 Oct. 1680), pp. 6–7.

99. Dryden, "Epilogue Spoken to the King at Oxford," *Works*, 2:180–81. Dustin Griffin interprets this epilogue as evidence of Dryden's open enlistment in the Tory cause as early as March 1681 (see "Dryden's Charles: The Ending of *Absalom and Achitophel*," *Philological Quarterly* 57 [1978]: 359–82 [especially 373–74]). By misinterpreting Dryden's words about the "Genius" of "This Place the seat of Peace" (genius loci) as referring to Charles rather than to the peaceful spirit of Oxford, he finds a partisan tone in the epilogue that is not justified by Dryden's lines.

100. Dryden, "Epilogue to *The Unhappy Favourite*," *Works*, 2:182.

101. Dryden, "Prologue to the University of Oxford, 1681," ibid., p. 184.

102. See my discussion of the date of this prologue in Appendix 1.

103. Dryden, "Prologue, Spoken to the King and Queen at their coming to the House, and Written on purpose by Mr. Dryden," *Works*, 2:181.

104. Dryden, "Prologue to *Mithridates*," ibid., p. 186.

105. *Impartial Protestant Mercury*, 28 Oct. 1681. To "admire at" is of course to feel surprise or astonishment, often accompanied by indignation.

106. *Loyal Protestant*, 29 Oct. 1681. Janeway's and Thompson's extracts were presumably taken from shorthand transcriptions made in the theater. For a summary by the California editors of the vexed textual problems connected with these two pieces, see *Works*, 2:459–60.

107. The prologue and epilogue to *Mithridates* were published anonymously at the end of 1681 or the beginning of 1682. Those to *The Unhappy Favourite* were published at the beginning of 1682 and attributed to Dryden. The epilogue at the time of the Oxford Parliament was published twice in the spring of 1681, and on one of these occasions under Dryden's name, but this theater piece was, as we have seen, impartial.

108. An anonymous prose pamphlet, *His Majesties Declaration Defended, in a Letter to a Friend: Being an Answer to a Seditious Pamphlet, Called, A Letter from a Person of Quality to His Friend*, was attributed to Dryden by Roswell G. Ham ("Dryden as Historiographer-Royal: The Authorship of *His Majesties Declaration Defended*, 1681," *Review of English Studies* 11 [1935]: 284–98) and subsequently included by the California editors in the appropriate volume of Dryden's *Works* (17:195–225). The attribution has been challenged, persuasively I believe, by Edward L. Saslow ("Dryden as Historiographer Royal, and the Authorship of *His Majesties Declaration Defended*," *Modern Philology* 75 [1978]: 261–72), who argues very cogently that the supposedly parallel ideas Ham detected in this pamphlet and in Dryden's acknowledged political writings beginning with *Absalom and Achitophel*, when they do not prove on closer examination to be actually dissimilar, are simply commonplaces shared by numerous Tory pamphlets, while the alleged stylistic similarities, traditionally regarded as the

weakest kind of internal evidence in arguments for attribution, are particularly unconvincing in this case. James Anderson Winn continues to accept Dryden's authorship of the pamphlet, citing further verbal parallels that I do not find persuasive (*John Dryden and His World* [New Haven, Conn.: Yale University Press, 1987], pp. 343–48, 596). In any case, acceptance of the attribution does not affect my argument that Dryden maintained the nonpartisan stance he had been adopting throughout the Exclusion Crisis until sometime in the spring of 1681, for *His Majesties Declaration Defended* was not published until 15 June 1681.

109.  There are no grounds for the assertion, repeated by several of Dryden's biographers in recent years, that "the actual beginning of *Absalom and Achitophel*" took place in the summer and autumn of 1680, over a year before its publication. See Charles E. Ward, *The Life of John Dryden* (Chapel Hill: University of North Carolina Press, 1961), p. 156; George McFadden, *Dryden: The Public Writer, 1660–1685* (Princeton: Princeton University Press, 1978), p. 208.

110.  My view that the poem was written to celebrate and justify remedial actions on the king's part that had already taken place is in some respects the exact opposite of McFadden's, who sees the poem as deliberative rhetoric by means of which Dryden "wished to bring the nation to its senses and stiffen the backbone of his royal master" (*Dryden: The Public Writer*, p. 236). This certainly describes the wishes of many Tory propagandists a year earlier, but would have been an anachronism long before November 1681. It may explain, however, McFadden's belief, indicated above, that Dryden began work on *Absalom and Achitophel* in the summer of 1680 when the Tories were close to despair.

111.  Dryden, "To the Reader," *Absalom and Achitophel. A Poem, Works,* 2:4 (italics reversed).

112.  Luttrell's copy of the poem is now in the Huntington Library.

113.  Dryden, "The Life of Plutarch" [1683], *Works*, 17:281. As the California editors point out, Dryden is here paraphrasing Montaigne's *Defence de Seneque et de Plutarque.*

114.  See Steven N. Zwicker, *Dryden's Political Poetry: The Typology of King and Nation* (Providence, R.I.: Brown University Press, 1972).

115.  *Annotations upon All the Books of the Old and New Testament*, 2nd ed. (1651), sig. XXX1. (Italics reversed.) This popular commentary was the combined labor of eight English scripturists.

116.  Several revisionist studies of *Absalom and Achitophel* in recent years have emphasized the fallible David of 2 Samuel and the commentaries, refuting the popular view that Dryden's biblical parallel excuses and justifies Charles's promiscuity, and offering a valuable corrective to the exclusively mystical view of David (see Zwicker, *Dryden's Political Poetry*) drawn uncritically from Puritan sermons and typological manuals of the Elizabethan and early Stuart periods. See K. E. Robinson, "A Reading of *Absalom and Achitophel*," *Yearbook of English Studies* 6 (1976): 53–62; Jerome Donnelly, "Fathers and Sons: The Normative Basis of Dryden's *Absalom and Achitophel*," *Papers in English Language and Literature* 17 (1981): 363–80; Howard D. Weinbrot, "'Nature's Holy Bands' in *Absalom and Achitophel*: Fathers and Sons, Satire and Change," *Modern Philology* 85 (1988): 373–92. But by emphasizing to different degrees the adulterous David of 2 Samuel, chapters 11 and 12, and arguing that Dryden likens Charles to this David in order to blame the king's sexual promiscuity for his recent trou-

bles, these studies argue the presence of a primarily moral theme in *Absalom and Achitophel* that I am unable to find there.

117. John Trapp, *Annotations upon the Old and New Testament*, 5 vols. (1662), vol. 1/2, p. 276; *Annotations upon All the Books*, comment on 2 Sam. 18:4.

118. Ibid., comment on 2 Sam. 15:1. See also Arthur Jackson, *Annotations upon the Remaining Historicall Part of the Old Testament* (Cambridge, 1646), p. 395; Matthew Poole, *Annotations upon the Holy Bible*, 2 vols. (1683), vol. 1, comment on 2 Sam. 14:22.

119. Trapp, *Annotations*, vol. 1/2, p. 278.

120. Ibid., p. 279.

121. *Annotations upon All the Books*, comment on 2 Sam. 18:32; see also Trapp, *Annotations*, vol. 1/2, p. 273.

122. John Mayer, *Many Commentaries in One* (1647), p. 441; see also Trapp, *Annotations*, vol. 1/2, pp. 293–94.

123. For Dryden to call the biblical David "godlike" for this reason is no more serious than his applying the epithet to Charles at this point in the poem. As one biblical commentator pointed out, "Polygamy (howsoever it was tolerated, in those times, yet it) was not allowed, as his ordinance, to make a fruitful Progeny" (*Annotations upon All the Books*, comment on 2 Sam. 3:2). That is to say, polygamy was allowed in biblical times not because of the divine command to "be fruitful, and multiply," but as a temporary concession to human weakness.

124. Trapp, *Annotations*, vol. 1/2, p. 279.

125. Dryden, "Threnodia Augustalis" [1685], *Works*, 3:99.

126. See Steven N. Zwicker, *Politics and Language in Dryden's Poetry: The Arts of Disguise* (Princeton, N.J.: Princeton University Press, 1984), pp. 97–98. In Zwicker's view, "the harsh remedy that this poem prescribes is the block for Whig leaders" (p. 93) in place of the misguided policy adopted toward the king's former enemies at the time of the Restoration.

127. All peers of the rank of earl or higher are styled "cousins" of the sovereign in royal writs and commissions.

128. Dryden, "Astraea Redux" [1660], *Works*, 1:29.

129. Dryden, "To My Lord Chancellor" [1662], ibid., p. 39.

130. By disregarding this change of circumstances and assuming that the couplet "And *David*'s mildness manag'd it so well, / The Bad found no occasion to Rebell" applies to the period of the Exclusion Crisis as well, Griffin concludes that Dryden is celebrating Charles's successful resolution of the crisis through an unchanging policy of mildness and mercy. "His mild, indulgent nature and his exceptional political skills enabled him to defuse the opposition" ("Dryden's Charles" [n. 99 above], p. 373).

131. For recent examples that had appeared since Shaftesbury's arrest, see *The Badger in the Fox-Trap; or, A Satyr upon Satyrs* (9 July 1681); *A Vision in the Tower, to the L. H      d in His Contemplation* (22 July 1681); *A Dialogue, between Toney, and the Ghost of the Late Lord Viscount Stafford* (24 July 1681); *An Elegy on the Death of the Plot* (19 Sept. 1681).

132. The anonymous author of *A Seasonable Invitation for Monmouth to Return to Court* (n. 27 above), published the previous 23 June, had in fact combined 2 Samuel and Genesis (not *Paradise Lost*) to create a fitting image of Mon-

mouth, who, "like Sinful *Adam*, shrouds himself in craggy and obscure Places, fearing to appear before that *Majesty* who gave him Being," after he has succumbed to the temptations of Shaftesbury. "Who is it, that hath Exiled you from your *Father*'s Love? Who is it that hath turned you out of a Paradise of Delights, to wander in strange and unknown Paths. . . . where you meet with no other Company than *Caballing Devils*; who, like cursed *Achitophel*, are ever pouring Poison in the Ears of poor Young *Absolom?*" (p. 1). In the context of a pamphlet concerned with Monmouth's loss of royal favor and his banishment from court, the biblical account of Adam's fall from grace and his expulsion from Paradise affords an appropriate analogy. But it would have been completely irrelevant to Dryden's subject: Shaftesbury's tempting Monmouth with the prospect of his father's throne.

133. Most of the above allusions to *Paradise Regained* have been noted previously by A. B. Chambers, "*Absalom and Achitophel*: Christ and Satan," *Modern Language Notes* 74 (1959): 592–96, or W. K. Thomas, *The Crafting of "Absalom and Achitophel"* (Waterloo, Ont.: Wilfrid Laurier University Press, 1978), p. 77. For the text of my quotations from *Paradise Regained* I have used *The Poetical Works of John Milton*, ed. Helen Darbishire (London: Oxford University Press, 1958).

134. *A Seasonable Address to Both Houses of Parliament concerning the Succession, the Fears of Popery, and Arbitrary Government* (1681), p. 5.

135. *The Country-mans Complaint* (n. 2 above), p. 2.

136. *The Ghost of the Late House of Commons, to the New One Appointed to Meet at Oxford* (18 Feb. 1681); *The Deliquium* (n. 23 above), p. 1.

137. *The Good Old Cause Revived* (n. 10 above).

138. *The Country-mans Complaint*, p. 2.

139. *The Waking Vision* (n. 25 above) (italics reversed); *New Advice to a Painter* (23 Feb. 1680), p. 4.

140. *The True Englishman: Being a Vindication of Those Many Loyal Addresses Presented to His Majesty for His Late Gracious Declaration* (1681), p. 8. (Advertised in the *Loyal Protestant*, 15 Oct. 1681.)

141. As commentators have frequently observed, the details of Absalom's "Progress" here are drawn from Monmouth's journey through the west of England in the late summer of 1680. But Dryden rearranges the order of events so that the journey follows the second Exclusion Parliament instead of preceding it, in order to make Monmouth's progress a final canvass of popular support for altering the Succession by force "before they came to blows."

142. For a recent example of this popular assumption, see Michael McKeon, "Historicizing *Absalom and Achitophel*," in *The New Eighteenth Century: Theory, Politics, English Literature*, ed. Felicity Nussbaum and Laura Brown (London: Methuen, 1987), pp. 23–40 (especially p. 32).

143. [Roger L'Estrange], *An Answer to the Appeal from the Country to the City* (1679), p. 24.

144. *A Seasonable Address* (n. 134 above), pp. 1, 18.

145. *An Answer to a Late Pamphlet, Entituled, A Character of a Popish Successor, and What England May Expect from Such a One* (1681), p. 13. (Advertised in the *Loyal Protestant*, 15 Mar. 1681.)

146. *A Seasonable Address*, pp. 14–15.

147. *Englands Concern in the Case of His R. H.* (1680), pp. 10, 14.

148. *An Answer to a Late Pamphlet*, p. 15.

149. See Grey, 7:243, 246–48, 257. The same argument was offered during the debate on the second reading of the bill on 21 May 1679. See ibid., p. 313. In a recent article on "Otway's *Caius Marius* and the Exclusion Crisis" (*Modern Philology* 85 [1988]: 363–72), John M. Wallace discusses the use of this argument in the debate on 11 May 1679 (p. 368).

150. See Grey, 7:402–3, 407–9. The same argument was offered during the debate on the third reading of the bill on 11 November 1680. See ibid., pp. 450–51.

151. See ibid., 8:318.

152. *His Majesties Declaration* (n. 9 above), p. 7.

153. For a convenient summary of these exaggerated conceptions of "godlike" as applied to Dryden's David, see Griffin, "Dryden's Charles" (n. 99 above), pp. 360–61. Adopting an opposite extreme to these views, Griffin denies any seriousness to the epithet here, arguing that "the ending of the poem brings not cosmic affirmation from divine thunder but comic recognition of the king's political adeptness at *appearing* godlike" (pp. 361–62).

154. *Certain Sermons or Homilies Appointed to Be Read in Churches, in the Time of Queen Elizabeth of Famous Memory, and Now Thought Fit to Be Reprinted by Authority from the Kings Most Excellent Majesty* (1673), pp. 344–45. (Roman substituted for black letter.)

155. *The Country-mans Complaint* (n. 2 above), p. 2.

156. See Zwicker, *Politics and Language* (n. 126 above), p. 99.

157. See Godfrey Davies, "The Conclusion of Dryden's *Absalom and Achitophel*," *Huntington Library Quarterly* 10 (1946): 69–82.

158. See *His Majesties Declaration*, pp. 9, 5, 4.

159. *The True Englishman* (n. 140 above), p. 9.

160. Ibid., p. 18.

CHAPTER 4
THE ASSOCIATION

1. *The Proceedings at the Sessions House in the Old-Baily, London, on Thursday, the 24th Day of November, 1681, before His Majesties Commissioners of Oyer and Terminer, upon the Bill of Indictment for High-Treason against Anthony Earl of Shaftsbury* (25 Nov. 1681), p. 6.

2. See ibid., pp. 19–22.

3. The testimony of the witnesses at College's trial implicated Shaftesbury as a central figure in the conspiracy, but because the Whig leader had not yet been indicted the printed account of the trial substituted for his name such circumlocutions as "a great Man," "a Person of Honour," and "a Person of Quality."

4. [Robert Ferguson], *No Protestant-Plot; or, The Present Pretended Conspiracy of Protestants against the King and Government Discovered to Be a Conspiracy of the Papists against the King and His Protestant-Subjects* (October 1681), pp. 30–32. Richard Baldwin was charged on 14 October for its publication.

5. See *The Narrative of Mr. John Smith of Walworth, in the County-Palatine of Durham, Gent.: Containing a Further Discovery of the Late Horrid and Popish-Plot* (1679).

6. See John Kenyon, *The Popish Plot* (London: Heinemann, 1972), pp. 138–41, 148, 159, 162, 191–92, 243.

7. *The Tryal of William Viscount Stafford for High Treason* (1681), p. 60.

8. *The Arraignment, Tryal, and Condemnation of Stephen Colledge for High-Treason, in Conspiring the Death of the King, the Levying of War, and the Subversion of the Government* (1681), p. 88.

9. Ibid., pp. 92–94.

10. *CSPD* 1682, pp. 162–63 (12 Apr.).

11. *Proceedings at the Sessions House*, p. 23. Rouse's "trial" was his inquest on 18 October at which a London grand jury returned the bill endorsed *Ignoramus*.

12. *Advice to the Painter, from a Satyrical Night-Muse, for Limning to the Life the Witnesses against the Right Honourable Anthony Earl of Shaftsbury* (3 Dec. 1681).

13. *Proceedings at the Sessions House*, pp. 15–18. (Italics and black letter omitted.)

14. See, for example, *Ignoramus: An Excellent New Song* (15 Dec. 1681), and *An Excellent New Song of the Unfortunate Whigs* (1682).

15. *Observator*, 17 Dec. 1681. L'Estrange returned to this criticism of the grand jury in the issues of 2 and 4 March 1682. The argument was developed most fully in an anonymous Tory pamphlet that appeared in February, *Billa Vera; or, The Arraignment of Ignoramus, Put Forth Out of Charity, for the Use of Grand Inquests and Other Jurys, the Sworn Assertors of Truth and Justice: In a Letter to a Friend* (1682).

16. *Observator*, 3 Dec. 1681. See also *Billa Vera*, p. 26.

17. *Observator*, 5 Nov. 1681.

18. *Remarques upon the New Project of Association: In a Letter to a Friend* (1682 [but published before 21 Dec. 1681, when L'Estrange referred to it in the *Observator* as already in print]), pp. 4–6. (Italics omitted.)

19. See *The Two Associations: One Subscribed by 156 Members of the House of Commons in the Year 1643, the Other Seized in the Closet of the Earl of Shaftsbury* (1681). (Advertised in the *London Gazette*, 19 Dec. 1681.)

20. [John Northleigh], *The Parallel; or, The New Specious Association an Old Rebellious Covenant. Closing with a Disparity between a True Patriot, and a Factious Associator* (6 Feb. 1682), p. 13.

21. Ibid., p. 18.

22. *Remarques*, p. 5. (Italics omitted.)

23. Northleigh, *The Parallel*, p. 19.

24. *Proceedings at the Sessions House* (n. 1 above), p. 34.

25. *CJ*, 9:680.

26. Ibid., p. 685.

27. For the debate of 15 December in the House, sitting as a committee of the whole, see Grey, 8:153–71.

28. *Remarques*, pp. 6–8. (Italics omitted.) For other catalogues listing the antitheses between the Elizabethan and Whig Associations, see Northleigh, *The Parallel*, pp. 25–26, and *Observator*, 4 Mar. 1682.

29. *Remarques*, p. 6. (Italics omitted.)

30. Northleigh, *The Parallel*, p. 19.

31. Ibid., pp. 24–25. See also pp. 16 and 19.

32. *The Addresses Importing an Abhorrence of an Association, Pretended to Have Been Seized in the E. of Shaftsbury's Closet, Laid Open and Detected: In a Letter to a Friend* (1682), p. 1.

33. *Memoirs of Sir John Reresby*, ed. Andrew Browning (Glasgow: Jackson, 1936), p. 246.

34. *The Addresses Importing an Abhorrence*, p. 3.

35. *London Gazette*, 6 Feb. 1682. (Italics reversed.)

36. Ibid., 20 Feb. 1682. (Italics reversed.)

37. Ibid., 6 Mar., and 16, 13, and 27 Feb. 1682. (Italics reversed.) For a Whig rejoinder to the abhorrences that draws a parallel between the Whig and Elizabethan Associations, see *A Discourse Touching the Addresses or Presentments to the King against the Association, with an Account of the Association Made and Confirmed in the Reign of Queen Elizabeth* (1682). (Advertised in the *Impartial Protestant Mercury*, 3 Mar. 1682.)

38. Northleigh, *The Parallel* (n. 20 above), p. 1.

39. Ibid.

40. *London Gazette*, 20 Feb. 1682. (Italics reversed.) See also the Whig reply to this abhorrence, *The Earl of Shaftsbury's Grand-Jury Vindicated from the Aspersions Cast on Them in the Late Address from Some of the Middle Temple, London* (1682), which ignores the Association and takes the easier, but irrelevant, course of impugning the credibility of the witnesses.

41. See *The Two Associations* (n. 19 above), pp. 7–8.

42. Northleigh, *The Parallel*, p. 33. (Italics omitted.)

43. Ibid., p. 2.

44. Ibid., pp. 6, 8, 9.

45. *Observator*, 10 Dec. 1681.

46. Ibid., 11 Feb. 1682.

47. *London Gazette*, 9 and 6 Mar. 1682. (Italics reversed.)

48. See, for example, ibid., 16 and 19 Jan., and 9 Feb. 1682.

49. *The Stuart Constitution, 1603–1688: Documents and Commentary*, ed. J. P. Kenyon, 2nd ed. (Cambridge: Cambridge University Press, 1986), p. 240.

50. *Observator*, 10 Dec. 1681, and 28 Jan., 25 Feb., and 10 Mar. 1682.

51. *Billa Vera* (n. 15 above), pp. 1–2.

52. Northleigh, *The Parallel* (n. 20 above), p. 2.

53. In a valuable recent study, Gary S. De Krey argues that it "should occasion little surprise" that Tory propaganda regularly linked the City of London with religious dissent and political radicalism, since "the London Whig leadership was tightly interlocked with a London dissenting leadership of noteworthy social calibre," while the "London Whigs were imbued with radical ideas [that] probably reflected the dissenting and puritan heritage of so many of their leaders"

("The London Whigs and the Exclusion Crisis Reconsidered," in *The First Modern Society: Essays in English History in Honour of Lawrence Stone*, ed. A. L. Beier, David Cannadine and James M. Rosenheim [Cambridge: Cambridge University Press, 1989], pp. 457–82).

54. *Observator*, 28 Jan. 1682.

55. [Robert Ferguson], *The Third Part of No Protestant Plot, with Observations on the Proceedings upon the Bill of Indictment against the E. of Shaftsbury* (1682), pp. 18–37 passim. (Described as "newly come out" in the *Observator* of 20 February 1682.) Ferguson identifies "the Three late Adventures and Essays which [the Papists] made towards the proof of a Protestant Conspiracy" as "the *Meal-Tub Sham*, in the year 1679," the allegation "in the year 1681 . . . of a Design to seize the King at *Oxford*," and the Association (pp. 36–37).

56. *Observator*, 22 Feb. 1682.

57. See *A Protestant Plot No Paradox; or, Phanaticks under That Name Plotting against the King and Government: Proved First, from Their Principles, Secondly, from Their Practices* (1682), pp. 8–34. (Advertised in the *Loyal Protestant*, 4 Mar. 1682.)

58. George Hickes, *A Sermon Preached before the Lord Mayor, Aldermen, and Citizens of London, at Bow Church, on the 30th of January, 1681/2* (1682), pp. 17, 28–31. See also Thomas Wilson, *A Sermon on the Martyrdom of King Charles I, Preached January 30, 1681 [i.e., 1681/2]: With a Relation of Some Rebellious Practices and Principles of Fanaticks* (1682). This sermon argues the seamless continuity between past Puritans and present Dissenters by following an account of the Royal Martyr's troubles with a history of "the Rebellious Practices of some of our Fanaticks since the Restauration of our present King," from Venner's Plot in 1661 down to the Scots Rebellion of 1679 (pp. 21–30). (Italics omitted.) Like Hickes, Wilson quotes and condemns a formidable list of antiepiscopal writers (pp. 30–37), but in this case without paralleling them with contemporary Whigs.

59. Edward Pelling, *A Sermon Preached on the Anniversary of That Most Execrable Murder of K. Charles the First, Royal Martyr* (1682), p. 11.

60. Ibid., pp. 32–33.

61. Dustin Griffin, "Dryden's Charles: The Ending of *Absalom and Achitophel*," *Philological Quarterly* 57 (1978): 375; Thomas H. Fujimura, "Dryden's Changing Political Views," *Restoration* 10 (1986): 96.

62. Sanford Budick, *Poetry of Civilization: Mythopoeic Displacement in the Verse of Milton, Dryden, Pope, and Johnson* (New Haven: Yale University Press, 1974), pp. 105–6.

63. Dryden, "Epistle to the Whigs," *The Medall. A Satyre against Sedition*, *Works* 2:38–39.

64. See *A Letter from a Person of Quality to His Friend, about Abhorrers and Addressors, &c.* (24 Feb. 1682). Its date of publication is supplied by L'Estrange in his answer to it in the *Observator* of 1 March 1682. It was followed almost immediately by *A Second Letter from a Person of Quality to His Friend, about Abhorrers and Addressors, &c.* (1682).

65. See *A Letter from a Friend, to a Person of Quality, in Answer to A Letter from a Person of Quality, to His Friend, about Abhorrers and Addressers* (1682).

66. See *The Addresses Importing an Abhorrence of an Association ... Detected: In a Letter to a Friend* (n. 32 above).

67. See *A Second Return to the Letter of a Noble Peer, concerning the Addresses* (1682). There is another issue of this pamphlet with a different title page that omits "Second."

68. See *A Reply to the Second Return* (1682). Another edition was published in the spring as *A Modest Account of the Present Posture of Affairs in England, with Particular Reference to the Earl of Shaftsbury's Case, and a Vindication of Him from Two Pretended Letters of a Noble Peer. By a Person of Quality* (1682). In a lame attempt to turn the hoax to the advantage of the Whigs, the author professes to believe that the Tory letters are themselves written by "a Noble Peer," the earl of Halifax (as he was until created a marquess the following August). He borrows his enemies' device of identifying him by unmistakable allusions, and attacks him as an apostate from the Whig party.

69. See [Christopher Nesse], *A Key (with the Whip) to Open the Mystery of Iniquity of the Poem Called, Absalom and Achitophel: Shewing Its Scurrilous Reflections upon Both King and Kingdom* (13 Jan. 1682). The whip, without the key, had already appeared as *A Whip for the Fools Back, Who Styles Honorable Marriage a Curs'd Confinement, in His Profane Poem of Absalom and Achitophel* (24 Dec. 1681).

70. Ferguson was one of those Whigs who had recourse to both "evasions." See *The Third Part of No Protestant Plot* (n. 55 above), pp. 132–38.

71. William Myers, *Dryden* (London: Hutchinson, 1973), p. 98.

72. *The Recovery* [1681]. The date on Anthony Wood's copy of the poem, now in the Bodleian, is December 1681 or January 1682.

73. Cf., for example, *Dagon's Fall; or, The Charm Broke* (15 Aug. 1681), in which the Exclusion Crisis is described as a magician's charm, and we are told that "the King by his own hand lately remov'd the Evil of the Charm, by certain Printed Characters called a *Declaration*, or Counter-charm" (p. 2).

74. See *Observator*, 22 Feb. 1682; Northleigh, *The Parallel*, p. 13; Hickes, *A Sermon Preached before the Lord Mayor*, p. 31.

75. See, for example, the following Whig verse broadsides: *Advice to the Painter* (n. 12 above); *The Popes Evidence to a Cardinal, One of His Privados, about the Deliverance of the Earl of Shaftsbury Out of the Tower* (6 Dec. 1681); *A New Ignoramus: Being the Second New Song* (16 Dec. 1681; an answer to the Tories' *Ignoramus: An Excellent New Song* [n. 14 above]); and *Jemmy and Anthony* (1682).

76. *Heraclitus Ridens*, 6 Dec. 1681.

77. Ibid., 10 Jan. 1682.

78. Ibid., 6 Dec. 1681. (Italics reversed.)

79. Ibid., 13 Dec. 1681. The Polish joke at Shaftesbury's expense had of course been making the rounds in Tory circles for some time. See, for example, their pamphlet of the preceding autumn, *A Modest Vindication of the Earl of S——y: In a Letter to a Friend concerning His Being Elected King of Poland* (5 Sept. 1681).

80. *Heraclitus Ridens*, 27 Dec. 1681. (Italics reversed in last phrase.)

81. See ibid., 20 Dec. 1681 and 24 Jan. 1682.

82. See ibid., 20 Dec. 1681 and 10 Jan. 1682.

83. Ibid., 31 Jan. 1682.

84. See ibid., 17 and 31 Jan. 1682.

85. The California editors (Dryden, *Works* 2:286) report that "the earliest reference to the medal seems to be in a newsletter from London dated 16 March 1682: 'A medal has been lately engraved for the Earl of Shaftesbury. The author of *Absalom and Achitophel* made a very severe satire on it'" (*CSPD* 1682, p. 128). But of course the author of the newsletter may have learned of the event from reading Dryden's poem, published that day, to which he ties it. James Anderson Winn has recently drawn attention to a probable allusion to the medal by Christopher Nesse in *A Key (with the Whip)*, published on 13 January 1682 (see *John Dryden and His World* [New Haven, Conn.: Yale University Press, 1987], p. 601, n. 66)

86. On the basis of the newsletter above, Charles E. Ward states categorically that the medal was struck "in February or early March," and that "Dryden went to work at once, and in a very short time wrote *The Medal*" (*The Life of John Dryden* [Chapel Hill, N.C.: University of North Carolina Press, 1961], p. 179). Myers elaborates: "In late February a medal was struck to celebrate the acquittal and within three weeks Dryden replied" (*Dryden* [n. 71 above], p. 97). But the term "lately" in the newsletter is too vague to support any definite conjecture, least of all this improbable feat on Dryden's part.

87. See A. E. Wallace Maurer, "The Design of Dryden's *The Medall*," *Papers on Language and Literature* 2 (1966): 293–304.

88. An accurate and legible reproduction of Bower's medal is supplied by the California editors in Dryden, *Works*, 2:43.

89. The etching, entitled "A True and Exact Prospect of the Famous Citty of London from S. Marie Overs Steeple in Southwarke in Its Flourishing Condition before the Fire," is one of a pair published soon after the Fire. The other is entitled "Another Prospect of the Sayd Citty Taken from the Same Place as It Appeareth Now after the Sad Calamitie and Destruction by Fire, in the Yeare M.DC.LXVI." They are reproduced and discussed by Arthur M. Hind, *Wenceslaus Hollar and His Views of London and Windsor in the Seventeenth Century* (London: John Lane, 1922). The vantage point and relevant details of the first etching are so similar to those of Bower's medal as to leave little doubt of their relationship. (In both, for example, the north end of London Bridge, directly opposite St. Mary Overie, is exactly midpoint between St. Paul's and the Tower.)

90. Such anachronisms were not unusual in late seventeenth-century panoramas of London. Hollar's earlier "Long Bird's-Eye View of London from Bankside," published in 1647, continued to be issued long after the Fire. Hind (*Wenceslaus Hollar*, p. 45) records a later state of this etching in which the Monument has been added near London Bridge, while Wren's dome, completed in 1697, has replaced the square tower on what is otherwise old St. Paul's.

91. The scale of Hollar's etching is suggested by its length, which is twenty-seven inches.

92. Hollar's "Long Bird's-Eye View of London," for example, extends from beyond Whitehall on the west to beyond St. Katherine's on the east. His panorama for James Howell's *Londinopolis* (1657) covers approximately the same area.

93. Bower has omitted many intermediate details found in Hollar's panorama, of course, but he has retained the most prominent topographical features of the City within the walls, including (from left to right) St. Lawrence Poultney, the Royal Exchange, St. Michael Cornhill, St. Dunstan-in-the-East, and All Hallows Barking.

94. Neither of Jonson's poems to Shakespeare at the beginning of the First Folio was included in his collected *Works* (1640–41). Dryden shows a long-standing familiarity with the First Folio, however, and had the use of a copy if he did not own one. He alludes to the second of the two Jonson poems, "To the Memory of . . . Mr. William Shakespeare," in *An Essay of Dramatick Poesie* [1668] and in the "Preface" to *All for Love* [1678] (*Works* 17:55, 13:18). In the "Preface" to *Troilus and Cressida* [1679], he writes of the play: "so lamely is it left to us, that it is not divided into Acts: which fault I ascribe to the Actors, who Printed it after *Shakespear*'s death; and that too, so carelessly, that a more uncorrect Copy I never saw" (*Works* 13:226; italics reversed).

95. *Absolon's IX Worthies* appeared less than a week before *The Medall*, on 10 March. *Absalom Senior; or, Achitophel Transpos'd* was not published until 6 April.

96. The allegation was repeated frequently in Tory accounts of Shaftesbury's career. In touching on his service under the Protectorate, *An Excellent New Ballad* (18 Feb. 1681) describes him as "the Mouth of all Presbyter Peers," while *A Modest Vindication of the Earl of S      y* (n. 79 above) speaks ironically of "his steady adherence to every Religion that had but hopes to be established" (p. 1).

97. The rumors of Shaftesbury's lechery were particularly current at the time *The Medall* appeared because of the "Nicky-Nacky" scenes in Otway's *Venice Preserv'd*, first produced the previous month on 9 February.

98. For a discussion of this passage from *The Medall* that explains the difference between the "private spirit" used by the Dissenters to interpret Scripture and the "private judgment" or "private reason" upheld by the Church of England, see my *Contexts of Dryden's Thought* (Chicago: University of Chicago Press, 1968), pp. 232–34.

99. Northleigh, *The Parallel* (n. 20 above), p. 4.

100. Pelling, *A Sermon Preached on the Anniversary* (n. 59 above), "Epistle Dedicatory," sigs. A2v–A3. (Italics reversed.)

101. Northleigh, *The Parallel*, p. 22.

102. Cf. the similar jeer in *Heraclitus Ridens* (20 Dec. 1681), quoted earlier, doubting "whether he were ever of any Religion." This had long been a charge against Shaftesbury in Tory propaganda. The author of *The Character of a Disbanded Courtier* (18 July 1681), for example, declares: "Being a Gentleman of little or no *Religion* himself, he seems for all that to espouse every Division and Sub-division of it, every Faction and Person who are bold enough to stand stiff in opposition against the well setled Government" (p. 2).

103. Dryden, "The Life of Plutarch" [1683], *Works*, 17:270–71.

104. See the *London Stage*, p. 310, which quotes a letter of Sunday, 26 July 1682, from John Drummond, stating that *The Duke of Guise* was supposed "to be acted sometime nixt weik."

105. Dryden, *The Vindication; or, The Parallel of the French Holy-League, and the English League and Covenant, Turn'd into a Seditious Libell against the*

*King and His Royal Highness, by Thomas Hunt and the Authors of the Reflections upon the Pretended Parallel in the Play Called The Duke of Guise* (1683), p. 3. All quotations are taken from this first edition.

106. Winn, *John Dryden and His World* (n. 85 above), p. 365.

107. In the printed quarto, act 1 consists of only one scene. If Dryden had written the whole of act 1, however, presumably he would have said so, as he did in the case of act 4. I assume that by "the first scene" he means the meeting of the Council of Sixteen, soon joined by the Curate of St. Eustace and a little later by Guise in the company of the Cardinal and Aumale. This meeting ends on p. 5, where the entrance of Malicorne, shortly joined by a devil, begins what is actually a new scene, in spite of the quarto. Dryden's estimate of his share of act 5 suggests to me that it ends with Melanax carrying Malicorne off to hell on p. 68, where the entrance of Guise, the Cardinal, and Aumale introduces what is effectively a new scene, although it is not called such in the quarto. This is the earliest point "somewhat more" than halfway through the last act where Lee could have replaced Dryden without a noticeable break. I am grateful to Judith Milhous and Robert D. Hume for valuable advice on this subject.

108. Evidence of how widespread the rumor had become by this date can be found in the *London Stage*, p. 310, which quotes a private letter and two newsletters repeating this allegation, all written during the last week of July.

109. Thomas Hunt, *A Defence of the Charter, and Municipal Rights of the City of London* [1683], p. 25. See also [Thomas Shadwell], *Some Reflections upon the Pretended Parallel in the Play Called The Duke of Guise* (1683), pp. 9, 13. Dryden believed that Shadwell had a collaborator in his pamphlet, which may have been the case.

110. See Hunt, *A Defence of the Charter*, pp. 26–27; Shadwell, *Some Reflections*, pp. 21–23.

111. An English translation of Enrico Davila's work, entitled *The History of the Civil Wars of France*, had been published in 1647, a second edition appearing in 1678.

112. See Charles H. Hinnant, "The Background of the Early Version of Dryden's *The Duke of Guise*," *English Language Notes* 6 (1968): 102–10.

113. See [Sir William Dugdale], *A Short View of the Late Troubles in England: Briefly Setting Forth Their Rise, Growth, and Tragical Conclusion, as also, Some Parallel Thereof with the Barons-Wars in the Time of King Henry III, but Chiefly with That in France, Called the Holy League, in the Reign of Henry III and Henry IV, Late Kings of That Realm* (Oxford, 1681).

114. Laurence L. Bachorik, "*The Duke of Guise* and Dryden's *Vindication*: A New Consideration," *English Language Notes* 10 (1973): 208–12 (quotation on p. 211).

115. *London Gazette*, 16 and 27 Feb. 1682. (Italics reversed.) For examples of other abhorrences that parallel the Association with the Holy League, see ibid., 1 and 12 June 1682.

116. Northleigh, *The Parallel* (n. 20 above), pp. 26–27.

117. Dryden and Lee, *The Duke of Guise. A Tragedy* (London, 1683), sig. A2. (Advertised in the *Observator*, 13 Feb. 1683.) All quotations are taken from this first edition.

118. Italics omitted. This epilogue was written for the delayed premiere of the play on 28 November 1682, and is the only one included in the printed quarto. It replaced the original epilogue "Intended to have been Spoken to the Play, before it was forbidden, last Summer," and was clearly a last-minute effort to answer the rumors responsible for the play's postponement. Both epilogues were included in the separately printed *Prologue to The Duke of Guise* (1683), actually published, according to Luttrell, on 30 November 1682.

119. *A Gentle Reflection on the Modest Account, and a Vindication of the Loyal Abhorrers, from the Calumnies of a Factious Pen* (30 May 1682), p. 7.

120. See Dryden, *Vindication*, pp. 12, 16, 32. The king of Navarre does not appear in the play, but he is often mentioned by the dramatis personae.

121. Winn, *John Dryden and His World*, pp. 383–84. This scene, as I indicated earlier, is probably by Lee. I see no reason, however, why Lee should not have exploited echoes of his friend's popular poem as readily as Dryden himself was doing.

122. Dryden, "The Life of Plutarch" [1683], *Works*, 17:281.

123. Dryden, "Epistle Dedicatory" to *All for Love*, ibid., 13:5–6. (Italics omitted.)

124. Dryden, "Prologue to His Royal Highness, upon His first appearance at the Duke's Theatre since his Return from Scotland," ibid., 2:194.

125. Dryden, "Preface" to *Religio Laici*, ibid., p. 107. (Italics reversed in Dryden's quotation from Hooker.) Although much of this preface deals with the political corollaries of recusancy and dissent, Dryden is for the most part rehearsing attitudes he had already expressed elsewhere. Thus he reiterates here (p. 103) the view of the Popish Plot as genuine but greatly exaggerated that he had put forward in *Absalom and Achitophel* (lines 108–17). Likewise he repeats here (p. 108) the association of Dissenters with "the Doctrines of King-killing and Deposing" that he had made in the "Epistle to the Whigs" prefixed to *The Medall* (p. 40).

CHAPTER 5
A SECOND RESTORATION

1. *Vive le Roy; or, London's Joy: A New Song on the Instalment of the Present Lord Mayor of London* (2 Nov. 1681). (Italics reversed.)

2. *Iter Boreale; or, Tyburn in Mourning for the Loss of a Saint* (11 Aug. 1682). See also *The Loyal Sherifs of London and Middlesex, upon Their Election* (1682); *A New Song: Being the Tories Imploration for Protection against the Whiggs* (1682); *Loyalty Triumphant, on the Confirmation of Mr. North and Mr. Rich, Sheriffs of London and Middlesex* (7 Oct. 1682).

3. Thompson briefly revived the *Loyal Protestant* on 20 February 1683, but abandoned the effort after a month. Four more recent newspapers that had first appeared in the spring and summer of 1682—*The London Mercury*, *The Loyal Impartial Mercury*, *The Moderate Intelligencer*, and *The Loyal London Mercury*—all vanished in October or November 1682 when the government was making a clean sweep of the survivors. Henry Care, the indomitable Whig whose *Weekly Pacquet of Advice from Rome*, a serial book rather than a newspaper, had

survived the proclamation against newspapers in May 1680, managed to carry on his publication until 13 July 1683, by which time he had become an informer for the government. I am indebted for information about the suppression of the newspapers in 1682 to the excellent account by James Sutherland, *The Restoration Newspaper and Its Development* (Cambridge: Cambridge University Press, 1986), pp. 19–20, 201–4.

4. The divided aims of the remaining Whigs had become a favorite topic of Dryden's by this time. A month later, in May 1683, dedicating the translation of *Plutarchs Lives* to the duke of Ormond, he declared the "two sorts [of which] they are principally compos'd" to be "zealous Sectaries" and "prophane Republicans," who, "if ever this ill contriv'd and equivocal association shou'd get uppermost, . . wou'd infallibly contend for the supream right" (*Works*, 17:231–32).

5. *Observator*, 15 Nov. 1682. Starting with the issue of 8 September 1682, Observator had replaced Tory as L'Estrange's spokesman; but the replacement of Whig by Trimmer did not begin until the issue of 13 November.

6. Italics reversed.

7. *London Gazette*, 14 June 1683. See *Londons Lamentation; or, An Excellent New Song on the Loss of London's Charter* (14 June 1683), signaling what would have been, no doubt, the start of a series of Tory broadsides celebrating the event, had not more exciting developments soon monopolized public attention.

8. *London Gazette*, 25 June 1683. (Italics reversed.) The only one of the nine whose name would have been recognized by many of the public was Richard Goodenough, the under sheriff during the term of Slingsby Bethel and Henry Cornish who had been responsible for the *Ignoramus* juries in the Middlesex sessions.

9. *CSPD*, Jan.–June 1683, pp. 339–40 (Jenkins to the lords-lieutenant, 23 June).

10. Ibid., p. 337 (William Jordan to Jenkins, 23 June).

11. *Observator*, 3 July 1683.

12. See, for example, *The Last and Truest Discovery of the Popish-Plot* (30 June 1683); *No Protestant Plot; or, The Whigs Loyalty, with the Doctor's New Discovery* (30 June 1683); *Murder Out at Last, in a Ballad on the New Plot* (30 June 1683); *The Old New True Blew Protestant Plot; or, Five Years Sham-Plots Discovered in One True One* (7 July 1683); *The Conspiracy; or, The Discovery of the Fanatick Plot* (11 July 1683).

13. L'Estrange marked the appearance of the "*Fourth Fit of Addressing*" in as many years by reviewing the history of all four addressing movements in the *Observator* of 18 July 1683.

14. See, for example, the *London Gazette* of 19 July 1683, "Great Sir, We cannot but be Joy'd even to a Ravishment, when we fall upon the consideration of Your Majesty's Gracious and Princely Regards towards us" (Barbados); and that of 5 November 1683, "*Great Sir*, Our obscure and private Condition makes us Strangers to the Majesty of Kings, and the Sacredness of their Persons, possesseth us with an awful Fear, to offend their Greatness; but like the Dumb Son of Croesus, when our Soveraign hath been in Danger of Assassination, we must cry out against the Horridness of the Attempt" (Kingston upon Hull).

15. See ibid., 2 July 1683.

16. For the exact chronology of the successive informers (some fifteen in all) and the texts of their individual depositions to Jenkins and the other officials, see *Copies of the Informations and Original Papers Relating to the Proof of the Horrid Conspiracy against the Late King, His Present Majesty, and the Government, as They Were Order'd to Be Published by His Late Majesty* (1685). This was published in late May 1685, according to Anthony Wood's notation on his copy, now in the Bodleian.

17. One of the few public allusions to the new developments at this early date is *The Last and Truest Discovery of the Popish-Plot, by Rumsey, West, and Other Great Patriots of Their Countrey*, which attacks Shaftesbury as the principal culprit responsible for the new plot.

18. For a list of the names contained in the four indictments returned on 12 July, see Narcissus Luttrell, *A Brief Historical Relation of State Affairs from September 1678 to April 1714*, 6 vols. (Oxford, 1857), 1:267.

19. *The Tryals of Thomas Walcot, William Hone, William Lord Russell, John Rous, and William Blagg for High-Treason, for Conspiring the Death of the King, and Raising a Rebellion in This Kingdom, at the Sessions-House in the Old-Baily, London . . . on Thursday, Friday, and Saturday, July 12, 13, and 14, 1683* (1683), pp. 2–3.

20. Ibid., p. 3.

21. Ibid., p. 37 (misnumbered 35).

22. Ibid., p. 38.

23. Both Russell and Hampden were prominent Whig members of the Commons in all three Exclusion Parliaments. Algernon Sidney was elected to the second and third Exclusion Parliaments, but his election was voided in both cases.

24. *Observator*, 18 July 1683.

25. *London Gazette*, 16 July 1683. (Italics omitted.)

26. *Tryals*, pp. 43–45 (testimony of Howard at Russell's trial).

27. A recent "biographical survey" of many of the Rye House conspirators confirms the differences in social and economic status between the two groups involved. See Gary S. De Krey, "London Radicals and Revolutionary Politics, 1675–1683," in *The Politics of Religion in Restoration England*, ed. Tim Harris, Paul Seaward, and Mark Goldie (Oxford: Basil Blackwell, 1990), pp. 133–62, especially pp. 149–55.

28. *Tryals*, p. 4.

29. See ibid., p. 38. Ferguson was of course a Dissenter, but he was a social misfit among the "Lords and Gentlemen of Quality." Two months earlier, in his dedication of *Plutarchs Lives* to the duke of Ormond, Dryden had described the "prophane Republicans" who were the political bedfellows of the "zealous Sectaries" as "Men of Atheistick principles, nominal Christians, who are beholding to the Font, only that they are so call'd," adding that "Lewdness, Rioting, Cheating and Debauchery, are their work-a-day practise" (*Works*, 17:232).

30. *Observator*, 14 Aug. 1683.

31. See *The Last Speech and Behaviour of William Late Lord Russel, upon the Scaffold in Lincolns-Inne-Fields, a Little before His Execution, on Saturday, July 21, 1683. . . . Also the Last Speeches, Behaviour, and Prayers of Capt.*

*Thomas Walcot, John Rouse, Gent., and William Hone, Joyner, a Little before Their Execution at Tyburn, on Friday, the 20th of July, 1683* (1683).

32. Ibid., p. 1.

33. L'Estrange exploited the Tyburn confessions in the issues of the *Observator* of 25 and 28 July, and of 1 and 27 August 1683. He answered Russell's paper in the issues of 11 and 23 August 1683.

34. See *The Speech of the Late Lord Russel, to the Sheriffs, Together with the Paper Deliver'd by Him to Them, at the Place of Execution, on July 21, 1683* (21 July 1683).

35. See [Roger L'Estrange], *Considerations upon a Printed Sheet Entituled, The Speech of the Late Lord Russel to the Sheriffs, Together with the Paper Delivered by Him to Them, at the Place of Execution, on July 21, 1683* (1683); *An Antidote against Poison, Composed of Some Remarks upon the Paper Printed by the Direction of the Lady Russel, and Mentioned to Have Been Delivered by the Lord Russel to the Sheriffs at the Place of His Execution* (1683).

36. *The Speech and Confession of William Lord Russel, Who Was Executed for High-Treason against His Majesty, and Conspiring the Death of His Royal Highness, James Duke of York* (1683), p. 3.

37. Besides the official transcripts of the trials and the dying speeches of those convicted, a particularly effective means of publicizing the plot on a more popular level was *A History of the New Plot; or, A Prospect of Conspirators, Their Designs Damnable, Ends Miserable, Deaths Exemplary* (1683). This broadside consists of a series of woodcuts portraying the principal stages of the plot from Shaftesbury's machinations to the traitors' executions, accompanied by a prose summary of the plot.

38. See, for example, the following verse broadsides that appeared during the weeks immediately following the trials: *Whig upon Whig; or, A Pleasant Dismal Ballad on the Old Plotters Newly Found Out* (20 July 1683); *The Loyal Conquest; or, Destruction of Treason: A Song* (20 July 1683); *Inimicus Patriae; or, A New Satyr against the Horrid Plot* (26 July 1683); *A Satyr, by Way of Dialogue between Lucifer, and the Ghosts of Shaftsbury and Russell* (6 Aug. 1683); *A Lash to Disloyalty* (13 Aug. 1683); *A New Narrative of the Old Plot* (26 Aug. 1683); *A New Way to Play an Old Game* (20 Sept. 1683).

39. See *The Arraignment, Tryal, and Condemnation of Algernon Sidney, Esq., for High-Treason, for Conspiring the Death of the King, and Intending to Raise a Rebellion in This Kingdom* (1684).

40. See *The Very Copy of a Paper Delivered to the Sheriffs, upon the Scaffold on Tower-hill, on Friday, Decemb. 7, 1683, by Algernoon Sidney, Esq., before His Execution There* (1683). For examples of the gleeful Tory broadsides occasioned by this event, see *Algernoon Sidneys Farewel* (8 Dec. 1683); *Pluto, the Prince of Darkness, His Entertainment of Coll. Algernoon Sidney, upon His Arrival at the Infernal Palace, with the Congratulations of the Fanatick Cabal for His Arrival There* (10 Dec. 1683).

41. The reconciliation of father and son was celebrated by a Tory verse broadside that notes the Old Testament parallel, *Good News in Bad Times; or, Absaloms Return to David's Bosome* (30 Nov. 1683). See also *Monmouth's Return; or, The Mistaken Whiggs* (6 Dec. 1683).

42. See *The Tryal and Conviction of John Hambden, Esq., upon an Indictment of High-Misdemeanour, for Contriving and Practising to Disturb the Peace of Our Soveraign Lord the King, and Stirring up Sedition in This Kingdom* (1684).

43. See [Thomas Sprat], *A True Account and Declaration of the Horrid Conspiracy against the Late King, His Present Majesty, and the Government, as It Was Order'd to Be Published by His Late Majesty* (1685). This was published in late May 1685, according to Anthony Wood's notation on his copy, now in the Bodleian.

44. See Burnet's detailed account of the friendly offices he and Tillotson performed for Russell, beginning with his trial, and of their interview with the king and the duke of York in *Burnet's History of My Own Time*, ed. Osmund Airy, 2 vols. (Oxford: Clarendon Press, 1897–1900), 2:372–86. Burnet acknowledges here having given Russell "a scheme of the heads fit to be spoken to, and of the order in which they should be laid" in his paper (p. 379). He also provides the information (pp. 379, 384) about Lady Russell's arranging the publication and sale of the paper, within an hour of her husband's death, as *The Speech of the Late Lord Russel* (n. 34 above).

45. See the *London Gazette*, 6 Aug. 1683.

46. *His Majesties Declaration to All His Loving Subjects, concerning the Treasonable Conspiracy against His Sacred Person and Government, Lately Discovered: Appointed to be Read in All Churches and Chappels within This Kingdom. By His Majesties Special Command* (1683), pp. 1–6. (Printed by order in council of 27 July 1683.)

47. Ibid., p. 7.

48. Ibid., pp. 12–13.

49. Ibid., p. 19.

50. *London Gazette*, 20 Aug. 1683.

51. Besides those sermons cited in subsequent notes, there were separately published thanksgiving sermons for 9 September by Jonathan Clapham, John Fitz-William, E. Foreness, Henry Hesketh, Luke Milbourne, William Payne, Thomas Pomfret, John Price, William Smith, John Turner, and Thomas Wagstaffe, as well as the anonymous *A Sermon of Thanksgiving for the Happy Delivery of Charles the Second . . . from the Conspiracy of 1683* (Dublin, [1683]).

52. William Sherlock, *Some Seasonable Reflections on the Discovery of the Late Plot: Being a Sermon Preacht on That Occasion* (1683), pp. 4–8. (Advertised in the *Observator*, 28 July 1683.)

53. See *A Form of Prayer with Thanksgiving, to Be Used on Sunday, September the 9th, Being the Day of Thanksgiving Appointed by the Kings Declaration* (1683).

54. See William Hughes, *Two Sermons Preach'd on the Ninth of September 1683 (Being the Thanksgiving-Day)* (1684), pp. 20–30; Benjamin Calamy, *A Sermon Preached at St. Lawrence-Jury, London, upon the 9th of September, Being the Day of Thanksgiving* (1683), pp. 16–17; John Cave, *King David's Deliverance, and Thanksgiving, Applied to the Case of Our King and Nation in Two Sermons, the One Preached on the Second, the Other on the Ninth of September, 1683* (1683), pp. 28–31.

55. During the height of the excitement over the Popish Plot, its "discovery," like that of the Gunpowder Plot, had commonly been described as providential, and since the king had found it expedient at the time to profess belief in the plot, it was now too late to disown the role of Providence in bringing it to light. "For is not the *Royal Word*, and often repeated, pass'd upon it?" one preacher reminded his congregation at the thanksgiving service on 9 September. "Is not the *Publick Justice of the Nation*, in several Tryals, Sentences, and Executions, a voucher for it? . . . Who, on the disbelief of such a Plot, shall atone for so much innocent blood-shed in the case?" (Hughes, *Two Sermons*, p. 24).

56. The role of Providence in the discovery of the Popish Plot had never been acknowledged by a day of solemn thanksgiving, in part because the king would have been reticent to order such an observance, but also because those who exploited the Popish Plot were never willing to concede that it had been fully discovered and was now ready to be considered a completed event. The actual religious observance connected with the Popish Plot, ordered by the king on three occasions in response to joint addresses from the Lords and Commons, was not a public thanksgiving but a "Solemn Day of Fasting and Humiliation" (13 November 1678, 11 April 1679, and 22 December 1680) in which the nation might "Implore the Mercy and Protection of Almighty God" in the face of new and constantly emerging information about the plot. For the texts of the royal proclamations, see the *London Gazette*, 31 Oct. 1678, 31 Mar. 1679, and 6 Dec. 1680.

57. Cave, *King David's Deliverance*, pp. 28, 30; Richard Pearson, *Providence Bringing Good Out of Evil, in a Sermon Preached on the Ninth of September, Being the Day of Thanksgiving for the Discovery of the Late Treasonable Conspiracy* (1684), p. 27.

58. Sherlock, *Some Seasonable Reflections*, p. 5; William Bolton, *Core Redivivus, in a Sermon Preached at Christ-Church Tabernacle in London, upon Sunday, September 9, 1683, Being a Day of Publick Thanksgiving for the Deliverance of His Sacred Majesties Person and Government from the Late Treasonable Rebellion and Fanatick Conspiracy* (1684), p. 27. (Italics reversed.)

59. Francis Turner, *A Sermon Preach'd before the King in the Cathedral Church of Winchester, upon Sunday, Septemb. 9, 1683, Being the Day of Publick Thanksgiving for the Deliverance of His Sacred Majesties Person and Government from the Late Treasonable Conspiracy* (1683), p. 22.

60. Samuel Scattergood, *A Sermon Preached at Blockley in Worcestershire upon the Thanksgiving-day, Sept. 9th, 1683* (1683), pp. 17–18.

61. *Observator*, 14 Aug. 1683.

62. Thomas Long, *King David's Danger and Deliverance; or, The Conspiracy of Absolon and Achitophel Defeated, in a Sermon Preached in the Cathedral Church of Exon, on the Ninth of September, 1683, Being the Day of Thanksgiving Appointed for the Discovery of the Late Fanatical Plot* (1683), p. 1. This sermon deserves the attention of anyone interested in Restoration parallelism. David's and Charles's experiences are related simultaneously and assimilated so closely that they are practically indistinguishable from each other.

63. John Harrison, *A Thanksgiving Sermon for Discovery of the Late Phanatick Plot, September 9, 1683* (1683), pp. 2, 4. For other sermons besides those of Long and Harrison that run a parallel between Absalom's rebellion and the Rye

House Conspiracy, see John Chapman, *A Sermon Preached September 9th, 1683, Being the Day of Thanksgiving for God's Wonderful Providence and Mercy in Discovering and Defeating the Late Treasonable Conspiracy against His Sacred Majesty's Person and Government* (1684, but advertised in the *Observator*, 12 Dec. 1683), and the anonymous *Ahitophel's Policy Defeated: A Sermon Preached on the 9th of September, Being the Day Appointed by His Majesty for a Publick Thanksgiving for His and the Kingdoms Great Deliverance from the Late Treasonable Conspiracy against His Sacred Person and Government* (1683). Ever since the witnesses at the trials in July had assigned central importance in the conspiracy to Shaftesbury and Monmouth, the abhorrences had been alluding to Absalom and Achitophel with increasing frequency. See, for example, the *London Gazette*, 2, 9, and 30 Aug., and 20 Sept. 1683.

64. Miles Barne, *A Sermon Preach'd before the University of Cambridge on the Ninth of September, Being the Day of Publick Thanksgiving for the Deliverance of His Majesties Sacred Person* (Cambridge, 1683), pp. 30–31.

65. See Alan Roper, "Dryden's *The History of the League* and the Early Editions of Maimbourg's *Histoire de la Ligue*," *Papers of the Bibliographical Society of America* 66 (1972): 245–75.

66. Dryden, "Dedication to the King," *The History of the League. Written in French by Monsieur Maimbourg. Translated into English According to His Majesty's Command*, *Works*, 18:3.

67. Alan Roper, Headnote to *The History of the League*, pp. 463–64.

68. Edward L. Saslow also argues that Dryden did not receive the royal commands until March 1684, but on different grounds. Accepting Roper's premise that Charles issued his commands as soon as he had finished reading the original, Saslow interprets Dryden's statement that the king had read the *Histoire de la Ligue* "when it first was publish'd" as referring to its publication in the pirated Dutch edition, in which case Charles could not have read Maimbourg before March 1684. I find it hard to reconcile this interpretation with Dryden's words. See "Dryden in 1684," *Modern Philology* 72 (1975): 248–55.

69. See Roper, Headnote to *The History of the League*, pp. 423–24.

70. Ibid., p. 426.

71. My views on this subject differ considerably from those expressed by Roper, who argues that "litigious history" (to which Dryden's "Postscript" belongs) had discredited itself by this time through its partiality; hence the king's need for "prudential history" (which Charles mistakenly believed Maimbourg's *Histoire de la Ligue* to be) "in order to make his propaganda appear impartial." See ibid., pp. 428–39, 456.

72. My hypothesis concerning the king's motives rests on totally different assumptions from those of George McFadden, who believes that Charles commanded Dryden's translation at the instigation of the duke of York, intent on strengthening his own position at court. See *Dryden: The Public Writer, 1660–1685* (Princeton, N.J.: Princeton University Press, 1978), pp. 266–68.

73. *His Majesties Declaration to All His Loving Subjects, Touching the Causes and Reasons That Moved Him to Dissolve the Two Last Parliaments* (1681), p. 9.

74. *Observator*, 18 July 1683.

75. See John Harrington Smith, "Some Sources of Dryden's Toryism, 1682–1684," *Huntington Library Quarterly* 20 (1956–57): 233–43. Roper, who documents Dryden's debt even more precisely in his valuable notes to *The History of the League*, points out that in this part of the "Postscript" "every historical detail and political maxim and many of the words are copied from the first nineteen pages of Dugdale's *A Short View of the Late Troubles*" (p. 529).

76. *Observator*, 19 July 1683.

77. Ibid., 11 June 1684.

78. Sir Walter Scott, "Life of John Dryden," *The Works of John Dryden* (1808), 1:290–91.

79. Ibid., 17:82.

80. *Justice Triumphant: An Excellent New Song in Commendation of Sir George Jeffreys, Lord-Chief-Justice of England* (3 Nov. 1683).

81. Charles E. Ward, *The Life of John Dryden* (Chapel Hill: University of North Carolina Press, 1961), p. 204.

82. See *A List of All the Conspirators That Have Been Seiz'd, (and Where Committed) since the Discovery of the Horrid and Bloody Plot, Contriv'd by the Phanaticks against the Lives of His Majesty and His Royal Highness. To Which Is Annexed, the Names of the Late Most Famous Ignoramus Juries* [1683].

83. Barne, *A Sermon Preach'd before the University of Cambridge* (n. 64 above), pp. 28–29.

84. See, for example, *The Plot and Plotters Confounded; or, The Down-fall of Whiggism* (24 Nov. 1683) and *The Whigs Elevation, for His Grace the Duke of Monmouth's Happy Return to Court* (29 Nov. 1683), both of which express hopes that the remaining conspirators will be "brought to Death and Shame" at Tyburn.

85. Luttrell records the various appearances of Rye House prisoners before the Court of King's Bench between 23 October and 28 November in order to be bailed or discharged, as well as the indictments of Sidney and Hampden, in his *Brief Historical Relation* (n. 18 above), pp. 286–88, 292–93.

86. For the allegations against Holloway made to government officials in June and July 1683 by West, Rumsey, and a third informer, Zachary Bourne, see *Copies of the Informations* (n. 16 above), pp. 13, 18, 35, 38, and 51.

87. *CSPD*, Oct. 1683–Apr. 1684, p. 238 (Stapleton to Jenkins, 25 Jan. 1684). A summary of this paper on pp. 239–40 fully justifies Stapleton's description of it.

88. Ibid., p. 255 (Stapleton to Jenkins, 1 Feb. 1684). Holloway's letter to Stapleton offering to confess and implicate others is printed on pp. 240–41.

89. Ibid., pp. 364 (L'Estrange to Jenkins, 7 Apr. 1684), 373 (Sunderland to Jenkins, 9 Apr. 1684).

90. Ibid., p. 376 (Jenkins to Sunderland, 10 Apr. 1684).

91. For the text of Holloway's confession or "narrative," see *The Free and Voluntary Confession and Narrative of James Holloway (Addressed to His Majesty) Written with His Own hand, and Delivered by Himself to Mr. Secretary Jenkins, as also the Proceedings against the Said James Holloway in His Majesties Kings-Bench Court, Westminster, and His Petition to His Majesty, Together with*

*a Particular Account of the Discourse as Passed between the Sheriffs of London and the Said James Holloway at the Time of His Execution for High-Treason at Tyburn, April 30, 1684. With His Prayer Immediately Before, and the True Copy of the Paper Delivered Them at the Same Time and Place* (1684), pp. 1–8.

92. *CSPD*, Oct. 1683–Apr. 1684, pp. 395–96 (Holloway to Sidney Godolphin, 25 Apr. 1684).

93. *Free and Voluntary Confession and Narrative*, pp. 9–10 (text of the court proceedings).

94. For the text of the petition, see *Free and Voluntary Confession and Narrative*, p. 11. For the dates, see *CSPD*, Oct. 1683–Apr. 1684, pp. 393, 395.

95. See ibid., pp. 366 (Holloway to William Clarke, 7 Apr. 1684), 370 (Holloway to Samuel Tucker, 7 Apr. 1684).

96. See ibid., pp. 379–80. Tucker's copy was already in Jenkins's possession by the time of Holloway's first examination before the Privy Council on 10 April, although the prisoner was kept in ignorance of this fact until the next day (see p. 376). Clarke's copy reached Jenkins on the eleventh.

97. See ibid., p. 379.

98. Ibid., pp. 380–81 (Holloway to Jenkins, 14 Apr. 1684).

99. For the text of this document, see ibid., pp. 366–70.

100. For the text of the paper to the sheriffs, see *Free and Voluntary Confession and Narrative*, pp. 14–16.

101. *Observator*, 21 May 1684.

102. *Free and Voluntary Confession and Narrative*, pp. 11–14.

103. *The Last Speech and Behaviour* (n. 31 above), pp. 1, 3 (separate pagination for "The Speeches of Captain Walcot, Jo. Rouse, and Will. Hone").

104. *The Recanting Whigg; or, John Thumb's Confession: Being His Sentiments on the Present Times, in a Letter from Amsterdam, to the Fragment of That Hypocritical, Diabolical, Fanatical Association* (7 Jan. 1684).

105. See the issues of the *Observator* of 17–24 May 1684.

106. Ibid., 22 May 1684.

107. See ibid., 7 and 9 June, and 19 and 21 July 1684. For another Tory response to Holloway, see *Some Reflections on the Paper Delivered unto the Sheriffs of London, by James Holloway at the Time of His Execution* (1684).

108. The minutes of Walcot's oral confession before the king on 8 July 1683 are printed in *Copies of the Informations* (n. 16 above), p. 87. For Hone's deposition before a justice of the peace on 4 July, see *Copies of the Informations*, pp. 63–64. For Rouse's deposition on 5 July, see *CSPD*, July–Sept. 1683, pp. 47–48.

109. The most liberal applications of this policy were two royal proclamations of 31 October 1679 and 30 October 1680 "Promising and Assuring Our Free and Gracious Pardon to all and every Person and Persons, who . . . shall come in and give further Information and Evidence concerning the said Popish Plot" within the next four months in the first case, and two in the second. (Italics omitted.) The proclamations are printed in the issues of the *London Gazette* of 3 November 1679 and 1 November 1680.

110. See *CSPD*, July–Sept. 1683, pp. 182 and 208.

111. See Roger North, *Examen* (1740), p. 380.

112. See the minutes of the council meetings for 4–12 July 1683 in *CSPD*, July–Sept. 1683, pp. 32–33, 38–41, 52–57, 63–64, 70–72, 78–81, 89–92, 98–101, and 106–7; also the memorandum in North's *Examen*, pp. 378–91, written by his brother Francis, who, as lord keeper, was a member of the Privy Council during this time, and an active participant in its meetings during the week before the trials.

113. See *CSPD*, July–Sept. 1683, pp. 26, 34–35, 85–86 (West's letters of 4, 5 and 10 July 1683 to Jenkins) and 91 (the council's decision on 10 July to use West as a witness). According to Lord Keeper North, some members of the council wished to put West on trial, but the king declared "that if the Lords were satisfied that *West* had told all he knew, there was no Reason to hang him, because he knew no more" (North, *Examen*, p. 381 [italics reversed]).

114. See *CSPD*, July–Sept. 1683, p. 79 (the council's decision on 9 July 1683 to try Rouse).

115. See ibid., pp. 224, 331; ibid., Oct. 1683–Apr. 1684, pp. 256, 267.

116. William Sancroft, *A Sermon Preach'd to the House of Peers, Novemb. 13th, 1678, Being the Fast-Day Appointed by the King to Implore the Mercies of Almighty God in the Protection of His Majesties Sacred Person, and His Kingdoms* (1678), pp. 25–28.

117. Cave, *King David's Deliverance* (n. 54 above), pp. 32–33.

118. Dryden, "Prologue to the Dutchess, on Her Return from Scotland," *Works*, 2:196.

119. *Observator*, 26 June 1684.

120. *The Proceedings against Sir Thomas Armstrong, in His Majesties Court of Kings-Bench, at Westminster, upon an Outlawry for High-Treason, &c., as also an Account of What Passed at His Execution at Tyburn, the 20th of June, 1684, Together with the Paper He Delivered to the Sheriffs of London at the Same Time and Place* (1684), p. 4.

121. It was advertised in the *Observator* of 3 July 1684.

122. See *Burnet's History of My Own Time* (n. 44 above), 2:414–15.

123. My interpretation of the "Dedication to the King" differs completely from that of McFadden in *Dryden: The Public Writer* (n. 72 above), who argues that Dryden designed it as an answer to Halifax's *The Character of a Trimmer*, which was written and circulated in manuscript in June 1684, he suggests, and occasioned, in his view, by the Armstrong case (see pp. 268–76). But the issues of individual pardons and a general amnesty that Dryden considers in his "Dedication" were never raised in the Armstrong case, and in his recent edition of Halifax, Mark N. Brown infers the date of composition of *The Character of a Trimmer*, from internal evidence, to be December 1684 (see *The Works of George Savile Marquis of Halifax*, 3 vols. [Oxford: Clarendon Press, 1989], 1:46). Brown thus confirms the date assigned to this work by Halifax's earlier editors, H. C. Foxcroft and J. P. Kenyon. Finally, I do not find convincing the similarities in language McFadden detects between Dryden's "Dedication" and Halifax's *Character of a Trimmer*.

124. Dryden, "The Preface," *Albion and Albanius: An Opera*, *Works*, 15:10–11.

125. See Dryden, "The Epistle Dedicatory," *King Arthur: or, The British*

*Worthy. A Dramatick Opera* (1691), sigs. A1, A3. *King Arthur* was very likely another of Dryden's works of propaganda for Charles, since he was working on it at about the same time as *Albion and Albanius* and his translation of *The History of the League*. But he revised it extensively after the Revolution for its production in 1691, and the original version has not survived.

126. *The Letters of John Dryden*, ed. Charles E. Ward (Durham, N.C.: Duke University Press, 1942), p. 23. Saslow, in "Dryden in 1684" (n. 68 above), was the first to identify correctly Dryden's references to his two operas in this letter and to draw the proper inferences about their dates of composition, which are now widely accepted.

127. Dryden, Postscript to "The Preface," *Albion and Albanius*, p. 12. (Italics omitted.)

128. See the *London Stage*, pp. 335–36.

129. Dryden, Postscript to "The Preface," pp. 12–13. (Italics reversed.)

130. Scott, Headnote to *Albion and Albanius, The Works of John Dryden* (n. 78 above), 7:211. For more recent expressions of this view, see John Loftis, *The Politics of Drama in Augustan England* (Oxford: Clarendon Press, 1963), p. 7; Robert D. Hume, *The Development of English Drama in the Late Seventeenth Century* (Oxford: Clarendon Press, 1976), p. 363.

131. For a convenient and up-to-date summary of the evidence, see James Anderson Winn, *John Dryden and His World* (New Haven, Conn.: Yale University Press, 1987), pp. 393–94.

132. See Eugene M. Waith, "Spectacles of State," *Studies in English Literature* 13 (1973): 317–30; and, in greater detail, Paul Hammond, "Dryden's *Albion and Albanius*: The Apotheosis of Charles II," in *The Court Masque*, ed. David Lindley (Manchester: Manchester University Press, 1984), pp. 169–83.

133. Stephen Orgel, "Introduction" to *Ben Jonson: The Complete Masques* (New Haven: Yale University Press, 1969), pp. 1, 3.

134. Waith, "Spectacles of State," pp. 324, 326, 328–29.

135. Hammond, "Dryden's *Albion and Albanius*," pp. 178, 180–81.

136. George Hickes, *A Sermon Preached at the Cathedral Church of Worcester, on the 29th of May, 1684, Being the Anniversary Day of His Majesty's Birth, and Happy Restauration* (1684), pp. 17, 29–30. My attention was drawn to this sermon in reading Aubrey L. Williams, *An Approach to Congreve* (New Haven, Conn.: Yale University Press, 1979), pp. 22–32, where it is cited frequently, and the last sentence above is quoted.

137. See ibid., pp. 22–24, for a discussion of this older tradition. But as my argument above indicates, I disagree with Williams's view that Hickes's imagery belongs to this tradition, since the chief purpose of Hickes's sermon is to show the ways of distinguishing special Providence from "common Providence, or Chance" (p. 29).

138. The names "Zeal" and "Zelota" are used interchangeably throughout the play for the same character, identified in the Dramatis Personae as "Zelota. Feign'd Zeal."

139. Hickes, *A Sermon Preached at the Cathedral Church of Worcester*, pp. 17, 20–21.

140. Gilbert Sheldon, *Davids Deliverance and Thanksgiving: A Sermon*

*Preached before the King at Whitehall upon June 28, 1660, Being the Day of Solemn Thanksgiving for the Happy Return of His Majesty* (1660), p. 18.

141. Edward Pelling, *A Sermon Preached before the Lord Mayor and Court of Aldermen at St. Mary le Bow, on Nov. 5, 1683, Being the Commemoration-Day of Our Deliverance from a Popish Conspiracy* (1683), p. 16.

142. Isaac Barrow, *A Sermon Preached on the Fifth of November, 1673* (1679), pp. 11, 15, 16–17. My attention was drawn to this sermon in reading Williams, *An Approach to Congreve*, pp. 27–29, where it is discussed, and several of the above sentences are quoted.

143. Barrow, *A Sermon Preached on the Fifth of November*, pp. 17–18. For Archbishop Sancroft's use of the same dramaturgic phrase, *apo mēkhanēs* (*ex machina*), for a similar purpose, see *A Sermon Preach'd to the House of Peers* (n. 116 above), p. 25.

144. Horace, *De Arte Poetica*, lines 191–92. I quote the Loeb translation above. My attention was drawn to Barrow's use of dramaturgic imagery here, and to the source of his quotation, in reading Derek Hughes, "Providential Justice and English Comedy, 1660–1700: A Review of the External Evidence," *Modern Language Review* 81 (1986): 273–92 (especially pp. 278–79), a perceptive criticism of Williams's *An Approach to Congreve*. Hughes argues convincingly that since the infrequent interventions of special Providence were reserved for occasions of great public moment, they would scarcely have been introduced by Congreve and other Restoration dramatists into their domestic comedies, or, for that matter, into tragedies or tragicomedies representing private life.

145. For a very different view, which sees *Albion and Albanius* as designed by Dryden to promote the interests of the duke of York with the king, see McFadden, *Dryden: the Public Writer* (n. 72 above), pp. 280–84.

146. For an account of the ceremony on 20 April, see the *London Gazette*, 24 Apr. 1682. For a sampling of the massive press campaign in support of all this fanfare, see *His Royal Highness the Duke of York's Welcom to London: A Congratulatory Poem* (8 Apr. 1682); *A Congratulatory Poem upon the Happy Arrival of His Royal Highness James, Duke of York, at London, April 8, 1682* (8 Apr. 1682); *A Panegyrick on Their Royal Highnesses, and Congratulating His Return from Scotland* (13 Apr. 1682); *A Congratulatory Poem, on His Royal Highness James, Duke of York* (14 Apr. 1682); *A Welcom to His Royal Highness into the City, April the Twentieth, 1682* (20 Apr. 1682); *Prologue to His Royal Highness, upon His First Appearance at the Duke's Theatre since His Return from Scotland. Written by Mr. Dryden* (21 Apr. 1682); *The Epilogue, Written by Mr. Otway to His Play Call'd Venice Preserv'd, or A Plot Discover'd: Spoken upon His Royal Highness the Duke of York's Coming to the Theatre, Friday, April 21, 1682* (21 Apr. 1682).

147. See Dryden, "Astraea Redux," *Works*, 1:23, describing Charles as "toss'd by Fate," the phrase (*fato profugus*) Virgil applies to Aeneas at the beginning of his epic; Dryden, "To My Lord Chancellor," ibid., p. 38.

148. As we noticed in the last chapter, *The Medall* also contains an internal parallel between the Roundheads of Shaftesbury's youth and the Whigs of his old age, but of course the poem as a whole is not a parallel.

149. Scattergood, *A Sermon Preached at Blockley* (n. 60 above), p. 18.

150. Cave, *King David's Deliverance* (n. 54 above), p. 32.

EPILOGUE

1.   For a valuable recent study of Whig and Tory propaganda during the Exclusion Crisis with a different emphasis from mine, see Tim Harris, *London Crowds in the Reign of Charles II: Propaganda and Politics from the Restoration until the Exclusion Crisis* (Cambridge: Cambridge University Press, 1987), chaps. 5, 6, and 7. Harris focuses principally, though not exclusively, on the manipulation of crowd psychology by both parties through the "theatre of the street" such as pope-burning processions and lord mayor's shows, "forms of visual symbolism" such as graphic prints, illustrated tracts, playing cards, and almanacs, and other kinds of propaganda designed to appeal directly to a mass audience.

2.   For a careful assessment of the actual state of public opinion at this time, see Tim Harris, "Was the Tory Reaction Popular? Attitudes of Londoners towards the Persecution of Dissent, 1681–6," *London Journal* 13 (1988): 106–20. He finds "a large degree of popular acquiescence in the tory reaction, and perhaps even popular support for it" (p. 114). For evidence of surviving Whig dissent, based on indictments by assizes for seditious words, see Buchanan Sharp, "Popular Political Opinion in England 1660–1685," *History of European Ideas* 10 (1989): 13–29 (especially pp. 19–24).

3.   *Burnet's History of My Own Time*, ed. Osmund Airy, 2 vols. (Oxford: Clarendon Press, 1897–1900), 2:388.

# INDEX